D1155597

THE CIVICALLY ENGAGED READER

THE CIVICALLY ENGAGED READER

A Diverse Collection of Short Provocative Readings on Civic Activity

Edited by Adam Davis and Elizabeth Lynn

Published by

THE GREAT BOOKS FOUNDATION

Published and distributed by

 THE GREAT BOOKS FOUNDATION
A nonprofit educational organization

35 E. Wacker Drive, Suite 2300
Chicago, IL 60601-2205
www.greatbooks.org

Copyright © 2006 by the Great Books Foundation
Chicago, Illinois
All rights reserved.

ISBN 0-945159-49-8

First printing
9 8 7 6 5 4 3 2 1

Library of Congress Cataloging-in-Publication Data

The civically engaged reader: a diverse collection of short provocative readings on civic
   activity / edited by Adam Davis and Elizabeth Lynn. —1st ed.
      p. cm.

   ISBN 0-945159-49-8 (alk. paper)
      1. Civics. 2. Political participation. I. Davis, Adam, 1970– II. Lynn, Elizabeth, 1958–

JF801.C5765 2006
320.4—dc22

                                                                    2006043739

Shared Inquiry™ is a trademark of the Great Books Foundation. The contents of this publication
include proprietary trademarks and copyrighted materials, and may be used or quoted only with
permission and appropriate credit to the Foundation.

Book cover and interior design:
Judy Sickle, Forward Design
Chicago, Illinois

Books are to be call'd for, and supplied, on the assumption that the process of reading is not a half sleep, but, in the highest sense, an exercise, a gymnast's struggle; that the reader is to do something for himself, must be on the alert, must himself or herself construct indeed the poem, argument, history, metaphysical essay—the text furnishing the hints, the clue, the start or framework. Not the book needs so much to be the complete thing, but the reader of the book does. That were to make a nation of supple and athletic minds, well-train'd, intuitive, used to depend on themselves, and not on a few coteries of writers.

—*Walt Whitman, "Democratic Vistas"*

CONTENTS

PREFACE

Preface

The readings brought together in this book—drawn from literature, philosophy, and religion—invite reflection about civically engaged activity. Such activity takes many forms: volunteer work, service learning, philanthropy, trusteeship, membership in civic associations, social or military service, and political participation, to name just a few. Yet whatever form our civic engagement may take, it demands that we join with others not only as friends, family, or colleagues but as fellow citizens, people who share a common world and seek in some way to improve it.

The rationale for assembling a collection of readings about civic activity rests on three premises. First, we have observed that civically engaged people want to think more deeply and to talk more comfortably with colleagues about the beliefs and opinions that inform their activity. Second, we believe this kind of thinking and deliberative discussion is good for the civic activity in question; efforts to improve our communities and the world are strengthened when we reflect on what we are doing and why we are doing it. Third, we have found that texts, or certain kinds of texts, enable people to think about and discuss their underlying beliefs and opinions in a more focused, congenial, and fruitful way than they might otherwise be inclined to do. Reading deepens reflection; reflection deepens action.

THE CONTENTS OF THE CIVICALLY ENGAGED READER

The readings collected in this volume are short and provocative, and all raise deep questions about civic activity. They include short stories, philosophy, poetry, and essays. The authors are young, old, male, female, ancient, modern, black, white, western, and eastern. The perspectives they offer are alternately uplifting and dismaying, enigmatic and clear. Always they are probing.

The readings, organized thematically, illuminate the four principal activities of civically engaged life: *associating, serving, giving,* and *leading.* These four activities are not necessarily the *highest forms* of civic engagement (arguably, political participation would qualify for that honor); but they are the *most basic forms* of civic engagement. They define what we do when we engage as citizens, and therefore they merit careful consideration. We also think that such consideration should itself be shared, at least some of the time, and hope that these selections will not only be read in solitude but also discussed in groups.

The section introductions are meant to offer preliminary thoughts about the activity in question and some general remarks about the readings that follow. Each reading selection is prefaced with a very brief biographical account, or headnote, about its author.

There are two appendixes at the end of the *Reader.* Appendix A offers a brief guide to planning and leading discussions with service organizations, service-learning programs, and other civically engaged groups. Appendix B consists of discussion questions for each selection in the *Reader.* These questions start with the meaning of the selection itself and then broaden in scope to consider the reader's own opinions, experience, and involvement in civically engaged activity.

We have designed the anthology with multiple approaches in mind. You can read it from start to finish. You can jump in and read any selection at random. You can take in one thematic section at a time, or begin with the questions in Appendix B and follow them back to a reading that interests you. In short, you are free to use this book in the way that works best for your own purposes.

THE AUDIENCE OF THE CIVICALLY ENGAGED READER

The *Civically Engaged Reader* is intended for several groups of readers. The first group is relatively small but growing, composed of the approximately 75,000 mostly younger people who choose annually to devote one year of their lives to full-time service in programs such as AmeriCorps. This anthology has been designed to serve as a core text for reflective discussion among volunteers and staff within these national service programs, in fulfillment of AmeriCorps' "civic engagement" component. In fact, many of the selections have been used in precisely this way as part of "Justice Talking," an Illinois Humanities Council program that has served Chicago-area AmeriCorps organizations since 2001 and, with support from the National Endowment for the Humanities, has become a model for similar programs throughout Illinois and in many other states.

The second group of readers is composed of high school, college, and university students involved in service-learning programs. Many secondary and undergraduate institutions now build service learning into their curricula, while national service-learning organizations such as Campus Compact share resources and know-how to help implement these programs. This anthology offers service-learning programs and organizations a needed resource to help students reflect more deeply on their experiences. With the aid of this reader, students (along with their teachers and community partners) may explore the ways their assumptions relate to their actions. They may also discover in the words and stories of others a way to articulate and examine their own chosen forms of civic engagement.

The third group of readers is much larger and more diffuse than either of the first two: it is composed of the many millions of Americans who volunteer through nonprofit organizations to serve their communities. This anthology is ideal for use in orientation and debriefing sessions for volunteers. They, too, will find that reading and discussing these complex but lively short selections will help them articulate and explore the meaning of their activity with other civic-minded people.

It also happens that the questions implicit in occasional volunteer service activities underlie more structured or systematic forms of civic engagement, such as political service, military service, and social service. This takes us to our fourth group of intended readers, the largest of all, which is composed of anyone involved with some kind of civic activity and searching for help in reflecting upon it. For this fourth potential reader, the civically engaged individual interested in thinking about the nature of our obligations to ourselves and others, this anthology serves the functions named above and also provides fodder for considering differences among various kinds of civic activity. Readers in this fourth and final group might come from a city council, veterans' group, social service organization, or book club, just to name a few possibilities.

With these numerous audiences in mind, *The Civically Engaged Reader* makes available a collection of readings that will stimulate a range of responses—evoking pleasure, challenging our opinions, maybe even troubling our conscience. All of the selections will aid civically engaged people in reflecting, in solitude and in conversation with colleagues, on the foundations, means, and ends of their actions. The selected readings have this potential not so much because of what they *prescribe* or *proscribe* but because of what they *provoke*. In a word, they provoke reflection.

We believe that these texts, read with a lively and open mind—and, even better, energetically discussed with peers—can help us explore questions that we know at some deep level call for shared consideration. We hope you agree.

Adam Davis
Elizabeth Lynn

About the Great Books Foundation

The Great Books Foundation, an independent, nonprofit educational organization whose mission is to help people learn how to think and share ideas, was established in 1947 by two University of Chicago educators, Robert Maynard Hutchins and Mortimer Adler. The Foundation promotes the reading and discussion of classic and contemporary texts across the disciplines and publishes books and anthologies for readers of all ages. It also conducts hundreds of professional development courses each year in Shared Inquiry,™ a text-based Socratic method of learning that helps participants read actively, pose evocative questions, and listen and respond to others effectively in dialogue.

ABOUT SHARED INQUIRY

For more than fifty years, the Great Books Foundation has developed guidelines that distill the experience of many successful discussion groups. We have found that these guidelines are helpful in keeping conversation focused on the text and allowing all of the participants a voice.

1. **Read the selection carefully before participating in the discussion.** This ensures that all participants are equally prepared to talk about the ideas in the work and helps prevent talk that would distract the group from its purpose.

2. **Discuss the ideas in the selection and try to understand them fully before exploring issues that go beyond the selection.** Reflecting on the ideas in the text and the evidence to support them makes the exploration of related issues more productive.

3. **Support your ideas with evidence from the text.** This keeps the discussion focused on understanding the selection and enables the group to weigh textual support for different answers and to choose intelligently among them.

4. **Listen to other participants and respond to them directly.** Shared Inquiry is about the give-and-take of ideas and the willingness to listen to others and talk with them respectfully. Directing your comments and questions to other group members, not always to the leader, will make the discussion livelier and more dynamic.

5. **Expect the leader to only ask questions.** Effective leaders help participants develop their own ideas, with everyone gaining a new understanding in the process. When participants hang back and wait for the leader to suggest answers, discussion tends to falter.

About the Project on Civic Reflection

The Project on Civic Reflection encourages the practice of *civic reflection*—reading and conversation on fundamental questions of civic activity. Established in 1998 with support from the Lilly Endowment, the Project on Civic Reflection develops and disseminates resources to help civic groups and organizations engage in reading and discussion about giving, serving, leading, and associating. These resources include anthologies like *The Civically Engaged Reader,* small grants to support civic reflection programs, facilitation workshops, and the Web site civicreflection.org, which features an electronic library of suggested readings and a facilitators' forum.

The Project on Civic Reflection can be reached at
1401 Linwood Avenue
Valparaiso University
Valparaiso, IN 46383
Phone: (219) 464-6767
E-mail: civic.reflection@valpo.edu
Web site: civicreflection.org

Project on Civic Reflection

PART I

Associating

Voyaging across the open sea, a man suddenly finds himself struggling in the water after his ship goes down. The sole survivor, he washes up on the beach of an uninhabited island and lives there for more than twenty years. He has no human company during this time. When he talks, he provides his own audience. He labors to train a bird to speak his name. He diligently organizes his daily routine—not only to survive but also to prevent his mind from slipping into madness. Isolation can kill you, the story seems to say, and perhaps that is one reason that Daniel Defoe's seventeenth-century novel continues to spin off retellings, new versions (set in locales that range from tropical islands to the reaches of intergalactic space), cartoons, movies, and sequels. Robinson Crusoe is the archetypal castaway. He has become our most famous solitary, a prisoner of one, looking for the human companionship that can restore and save him.

This matter of associating, which to most of us in our casual waking hours seems more a matter of routine appointments than of survival and dignity, is brought into sharp focus by Defoe's story. Isolation turns Crusoe desperate. In *Cast Away*, a recent film version of the tale starring Tom Hanks, the main character goes so far as to paint a face on a volleyball, name the thing Wilson, and converse with it.

This is fiction, but it speaks to the truth of human experience. To be human is to live among and with others. We are born out of—and into—association, and we learn and grow by living in relation with others. A few of us may survive, briefly, as solitaries. But our natural habitat is society.

And if associating is where being human begins, it is also where the civic begins. There must be some gathering of people, some joining together, for us to have any kind of community or society. Associating is thus the underlying *condition* of civically engaged activity, and it is also the most general *form* of

3

civically engaged activity. Giving and serving and leading—other forms of civically engaged activity—are ways of associating. But only if we join together, or associate, with others does it make sense to consider how we act toward and with them.

We associate with family members, with groups of friends or colleagues, with people who live nearby, with people who speak our language, with people who share our politics, our faith, our tastes. We ally ourselves with certain others and set ourselves, implicitly or explicitly, against other others. We become White Sox fans rather than Red Sox fans, Mothers Against Drunk Driving rather than Americans for Peace in the Middle East, Rotarians rather than Lions rather than Shriners rather than Elks. And many of these associations can come to feel inevitable, the reasons for them invisible or forgotten.

It is against this tendency to take our group involvements for granted that we present the following readings, all of which help us think and talk about how, why, and with whom we associate.

The section opens with a selection from **Aristotle**, who declares, in the *Politics*, that every human association, or community, serves some good, while the political community—the most complete form of association—serves the highest good of all: the good life. *But what constitutes the political community and gives it unity? And what is the good life?*

Constantine Cavafy's call-and-response poem, "Waiting for the Barbarians," portrays the darker side of Aristotle's civic association, as the inhabitants of a city wait for the arrival of barbarian invaders. *What problems are solved and created for a community—or any group—when it looks outside itself to explain and justify its internal bonds?*

In his 1868 speech to the Georgia State Legislature, **Henry MacNeal Turner** argues that anyone who gives to the community—whether the community considers that person an insider or an outsider—ought to receive certain things from it, rights above all. *But what is a right? Who has the responsibility for deciding which rights exist?*

"The Boy Without a Flag," a short story by **Abraham Rodriguez Jr.**, depicts a child's attempts to form allegiances in a world of uncertain loyalties. *How do children develop a sense of belonging to a larger community? How do they decide what to salute?*

Imtiaz Dharker's poem, "They'll Say, 'She Must Be from Another Country,'" explores instances in which people raise barriers between themselves and others by what they say. *How do the words people use create and reinforce these barriers?*

Franz Kafka's parable, "Fellowship," invites us to ask what it is that makes individuals into something with a collective identity. *What sustains and limits* the bonds that people form among themselves? How do these bonds determine who can be excluded from a group?

In a much less ominous tone, **Jane Addams** opens her memoir, *Twenty Years at Hull-House*, by recounting in "Earliest Impressions" how her father drew her into "the moral concerns" of life. *Who teaches us concern for others, and how do they teach us?*

Alden Nowlan's poem "He Sits Down on the Floor of a School for the Retarded" considers this sense of concern for others through the disconcerting effect on the writer of a stranger's plea for physical closeness. *What basic human connections do we all share with each other? What kinds of barriers make it difficult for us to recognize these connections?*

In an excerpt from *The Theory of Moral Sentiments*, **Adam Smith** precisely analyzes our care for others. *What does imagination have to do with the capacity to feel sympathy and compassion?*

Alexis de Tocqueville celebrates the American passion for forming associations of all kinds in a chapter from *Democracy in America*, "On the Use Which the Americans Make of Associations in Civil Life." *Why do Americans associate with one another in civic groups and associations? Are there uniquely American modes of association?*

The final readings in this section address the challenges of connecting with others in the face of various kinds of difference. In an excerpt from *The Souls of Black Folk*, **W. E. B. Du Bois** suggests that something more than charity will be needed to bridge the distance between races in the United States. *But what is that something more, and can it be created through deliberate social change?*

In **Langston Hughes**'s poem "Theme for English B," a student mulls over the differences and striking similarities between himself and his teacher. *What sorts of differences—and similarities—matter most in the classroom, or any learning environment?*

Toni Morrison's short story "Recitatif" traces the relationship between two girls of different races through the years. *What connects people across race, and what limits such connection?*

Finally, **Robert Frost**'s poem "Mending Wall" invites us to consider that a wall between neighbors may not, after all, be the thing that keeps them apart. *How do boundaries between neighbors both separate and connect us?*

Aristotle

Aristotle (384–322 BCE), the most famous student of the ancient Greek philosopher Plato, lived and taught in Athens. He wrote on a remarkable range of subjects, including politics, biology, rhetoric, logic, and the nature of knowledge itself. The philosophical and scientific system Aristotle devised greatly influenced medieval Christian and Islamic scholastic thought, and his concepts remain embedded in the Western intellectual tradition. This selection is drawn from the beginning of his *Politics*.

Selection from *Politics*

1.

Every state is a community of some kind, and every community is established with a view to some good; for everyone always acts in order to obtain that which they think good. But, if all communities aim at some good, the state or political community, which is the highest of all, and which embraces all the rest, aims at good in a greater degree than any other, and at the highest good.

Some people think that the qualifications of a statesman, king, householder, and master are the same, and that they differ not in kind but only in the number of their subjects. For example, the ruler over a few is called a master; over more, the manager of a household; over a still larger number, a statesman or king, as if there were no difference between a great household and a small state. The distinction that is made between the king and the statesman is as follows: when the government is personal, the ruler is a king; when, according to the rules of the political science, the citizens rule and are ruled in turn, then he is called a statesman.

But all this is a mistake, as will be evident to anyone who considers the matter according to the method that has hitherto guided us. As in other departments of science, so in politics, the compound should always be resolved into the simple elements or least parts of the whole. We must therefore look at the elements of which the state is composed, in order that we may see in what the different kinds of rule differ from one another and whether any scientific result can be attained about each one of them.

2.

He who thus considers things in their first growth and origin, whether a state or anything else, will obtain the clearest view of them. In the first place, there must be a union of those who cannot exist without each other; namely, of male and female, that the race may continue (and this is a union that is formed not of choice but because, in common with other animals and with plants, mankind have a natural desire to leave behind them an image of themselves), and of natural ruler and subject, that both may be preserved. For that which can foresee by the exercise of mind is by nature lord and master, and that which can with its body give effect to such foresight is a subject, and by nature a slave; hence, master and slave have the same interest. Now nature has distinguished between the female and slave. For she is not niggardly, like the smith who fashions the Delphian knife for many uses; she makes each thing for a single use, and every instrument is best made when intended for one and not for many uses. But among barbarians, no distinction is made between women and slaves, because there is no natural ruler among them: they are a community of slaves, male and female. That is why the poets say,

It is meet that Hellenes should rule over barbarians,

as if they thought that the barbarian and the slave were by nature one.

Out of these two relationships, the first thing to arise is the family, and Hesiod is right when he says,

First house and wife and an ox for the plough,

for the ox is the poor man's slave. The family is the association established by nature for the supply of men's everyday wants, and the members of it are called by Charondas, "companions of the cupboard," and by Epimenides the Cretan, "companions of the manger." But when several families are united, and the association aims at something more than the supply of daily needs, the first society to be formed is the village. And the most natural form of the village appears to be that of a colony from the family, composed of the children and grandchildren, who are said to be "suckled with the same milk." And this is the reason why Hellenic states were originally governed by kings: because the Hellenes were under royal rule before they came together, as the barbarians still are. Every family is ruled by the eldest, and therefore in the colonies of the family, the kingly form of government prevailed because they were of the same blood. As Homer says:

Each one gives law to his children and to his wives

for they lived dispersedly, as was the manner in ancient times. That is why men say that the gods have a king, because they themselves either are or were in ancient times under the rule of a king. For they imagine not only the forms of the gods but their ways of life to be like their own.

When several villages are united in a single complete community, large enough to be nearly or quite self-sufficing, the state comes into existence, originating in the bare needs of life and continuing in existence for the sake of a good life. And, therefore, if the earlier forms of society are natural, so is the state, for it is the end of them, and the nature of a thing is its end. For what each thing is when fully developed, we call its nature, whether we are speaking of a man, a horse, or a family. Besides, the final cause and end of a thing is the best, and to be self-sufficing is the end and the best.

Hence, it is evident that the state is a creation of nature, and that man is by nature a political animal. And he who by nature and not by mere accident is without a state is either a bad man or above humanity; he is like the

Tribeless, lawless, heartless one,

whom Homer denounces—the natural outcast is forthwith a lover of war; he may be compared to an isolated piece at draughts.

Now, that man is more of a political animal than bees or any other gregarious animals is evident. Nature, as we often say, makes nothing in vain, and man is the only animal who has the gift of speech. And whereas mere voice is but an indication of pleasure or pain, and is therefore found in other animals (for their nature attains to the perception of pleasure and pain and the intimation of them to one another, and no further), the power of speech is intended to set forth the expedient and inexpedient, and therefore likewise the just and the unjust. And it is a characteristic of man that he alone has any sense of good and evil, of just and unjust, and the like, and the association of living beings who have this sense makes a family and a state.

Further, the state is by nature clearly prior to the family and to the individual, since the whole is of necessity prior to the part; for example, if the whole body be destroyed, there will be no foot or hand, except homonymously, as we might speak of a stone hand; for when destroyed, the hand will be no better than that. But things are defined by their function and power; and we ought not to say that they are the same when they no longer have their proper quality, but only that they are homonymous. The proof that the state is a creation of nature and prior to the individual is that the individual, when isolated, is not self-sufficing; and therefore he is like a part in relation to the whole. But he who is unable to live in society, or who has no need because he is sufficient for himself, must be either a beast or a god: he is no part of a state. A social instinct is implanted in all men by nature, and yet he who first founded the state was the greatest of benefactors. For man, when perfected, is the best of animals, but, when separated from law and justice, he is the worst of all, since armed injustice is the more dangerous, and he is equipped at birth with arms, meant to be used by intelligence and excellence, which he may use for the worst ends. That is why, if he has not excellence, he is the most unholy and the most savage of animals, and the most full of lust and gluttony. But justice is the bond of men in states; for the administration of justice, which is the determination of what is just, is the principle of order in political society.

Constantine Cavafy

Constantine Cavafy (1863–1933) was born to Greek-speaking parents in Alexandria, Egypt. Between the ages of nine and sixteen he lived in England, where his father worked in the family's import-export firm; upon returning to Alexandria in 1879, he received some formal education and began writing. Between 1882 and 1885, Cavafy lived in Constantinople, and there he started to write poetry. He settled permanently in Alexandria in 1885, finding employment first as a newspaper correspondent and then in the Egyptian Stock Exchange. For thirty years he held an appointment in the Egyptian Irrigation Service of the Ministry of Public Works. Although Cavafy has been recognized posthumously as a preeminent Greek poet of the twentieth century, his poems were published only after his death.

Waiting for the Barbarians

What are we waiting for, assembled in the forum?

> The barbarians are due here today.

Why isn't anything going on in the senate?
Why are the senators sitting there without legislating?

> Because the barbarians are coming today.
> What's the point of senators making laws now?
> Once the barbarians are here, they'll do the legislating.

Why did our emperor get up so early,
and why is he sitting enthroned at the city's main gate,
in state, wearing the crown?

Because the barbarians are coming today
and the emperor's waiting to receive their leader.
He's even got a scroll to give him,
loaded with titles, with imposing names.

Why have our two consuls and praetors come out today
wearing their embroidered, their scarlet togas?
Why have they put on bracelets with so many amethysts,
rings sparkling with magnificent emeralds?
Why are they carrying elegant canes
beautifully worked in silver and gold?

Because the barbarians are coming today
and things like that dazzle the barbarians.

Why don't our distinguished orators turn up as usual
to make their speeches, say what they have to say?

Because the barbarians are coming today
and they're bored by rhetoric and public speaking.

Why this sudden bewilderment, this confusion?
(How serious people's faces have become.)
Why are the streets and squares emptying so rapidly,
everyone going home lost in thought?

Because night has fallen and the barbarians haven't come.
And some of our men just in from the border say
there are no barbarians any longer.

Now what's going to happen to us without barbarians?
They were, those people, a kind of solution.

Henry MacNeal Turner

Although born free, near Abbeville, South Carolina, Henry MacNeal Turner (1834–1915) was nevertheless bound to a planter under whom he lived in conditions resembling slavery until, at the age of fifteen, he ran away. Turner taught himself to read and write, and worked as a messenger in a lawyer's office and then as a handyman in a Baltimore medical school. Choosing the vocation of a minister in the African Methodist Episcopal Church, he was the first African American to be commissioned as an army chaplain during the American Civil War. After the war, he served in the first reconstruction legislature in Georgia until 1868, when the white majority expelled all black legislators. Turner delivered the speech from which this selection is taken on September 3, 1868.

I Shall Not Beg for My Rights

Before proceeding to argue this question upon its intrinsic merits, I wish the members of this house to understand the position that I take. I hold that I am a member of this body. Therefore, sir, I shall neither fawn or cringe before any party, nor stoop to beg them for my rights. Some of my colored fellow members, in the course of their remarks, took occasion to appeal to the sympathies of members on the opposite side, and to eulogize their character for magnanimity. It reminds me very much, sir, of slaves begging under the lash. I am here to demand my rights. . . .

The scene presented in this house, today, is one unparalleled in the history of the world. . . . Never has a man been arraigned before a body clothed with legislative, judicial, or executive functions, charged with the offense of being of a darker hue than his fellow men . . . charged with an offense committed by the God of heaven himself. Cases may be found where men have been deprived of their rights for crimes and misdemeanors; but it has remained for the State of Georgia, in the very heart of the nineteenth century, to call a man before the bar, and there charge him with an act for which he is no more responsible than for the head that he carries upon his shoulders. . . .

Whose legislature is this? Is it a white man's legislature, or is it a black man's legislature? Who voted for a constitutional convention, in obedience to the mandate of the Congress of the United States? Who first rallied around the standard of Reconstruction? Who set the ball of loyalty rolling in the State of Georgia? And whose voice was heard on the hills and in the valleys of his state? It was the voice of the brawny-armed Negro, with the few humanitarian-hearted white men who came to our assistance. I claim the honor, sir, of having been the instrument of convincing hundreds—yea, thousands—of white men, that to reconstruct under the measures of the United States Congress was the safest and the best course for the interest of the state.

Let us look at some facts in connection with this matter. Did half the white men of Georgia vote for this legislature? Did not the great bulk of them fight, with all their strength, the Constitution under which we are acting? And did they not fight against the organization of this legislature? And further, sir, did they not vote against it? Yes, sir! And there are persons in this legislature today who are ready to spit their poison in my face, while they themselves opposed, with all their power, the ratification of this Constitution. They question my right to a seat in this body, to represent the people whose legal votes elected me. . . . We are told that if black men want to speak, they must speak through white trumpets; if black men want their sentiments expressed, they must be adulterated and sent through white messengers, who will quibble, and equivocate, and evade, as rapidly as the pendulum of a clock. If this be not done, then the black men have committed an outrage, and their representatives must be denied the right to represent their constituents.

The great question, sir, is this: am I a man? If I am such, I claim the rights of a man. Am I not a man because I happen to be of a darker hue than honorable gentlemen around me?

We have pioneered civilization here; we have built up your country; we have worked in your fields, and garnered your harvests, for two hundred and fifty years! And what do we ask of you in return? Do we ask you for compensation for the sweat our fathers bore for you—for the tears you have caused, and the hearts you have broken, and the lives you have curtailed, and the blood you have spilled? Do we ask retaliation? We ask it not. We are willing to let the dead past bury its dead; but we ask you now for our rights.

You have all the elements of superiority upon your side; you have our money and your own; you have our education and your own; and you have your land and our own, too. We, who number hundreds of thousands in Georgia, including our wives and families, with not a foot of land to call our own—strangers in the land of our birth; without money, without education, without aid, without a roof to cover us while we live, nor sufficient clay to cover us when we die! . . .

You may expel us, gentlemen, but I firmly believe that you will someday repent it. The black man cannot protect a country, if the country doesn't protect him; and if, tomorrow, a war should arise, I would not raise a musket to defend a country where my manhood is denied. The fashionable way in Georgia when hard work is to be done is for the white man to sit at his ease while the black man does the work; but, sir, I will say this much to the colored men of Georgia, as if I should be killed in this campaign, I may have no opportunity of telling them at any other time: never lift a finger nor raise a hand in defense of Georgia, unless Georgia acknowledges that you are men and invests you with the rights pertaining to manhood. . . .

Abraham Rodriguez Jr.

Abraham Rodriguez Jr. (b. 1961) was born in New York City and grew up in the South Bronx. He began writing at age ten and dropped out of high school at sixteen. He later earned a high school equivalency degree and attended the City College of New York. Rodriguez's first collection of stories, *The Boy Without a Flag: Tales of the South Bronx*, was published in 1992 and was named a *New York Times* Notable Book in 1993. His first novel, *Spidertown*, received a 1995 American Book Award. The following short story, "The Boy Without a Flag," appeared in Rodriguez's story collection of 1992 and gave that collection its memorable name.

The Boy Without a Flag

—To Ms. Linda Falcón, wherever she is

Swirls of dust danced in the beams of sunlight that came through the tall windows, the buzz of voices resounding in the stuffy auditorium. Mr. Rios stood by our Miss Colon, hovering as if waiting to catch her if she fell. His pale mouse features looked solemnly dutiful. He was a versatile man, doubling as English teacher and gym coach. He was only there because of Miss Colon's legs. She was wearing her neon pink nylons. Our favorite.

We tossed suspicious looks at the two of them. Miss Colon would smirk at Edwin and me, saying, "Hey, face front," but Mr. Rios would glare. I think he knew that we knew what he was after. We knew, because on Fridays, during our free period when we'd get to play records and eat stale pretzel sticks, we would see her way in the back by the tall windows, sitting up on a radiator like a schoolgirl. There would be a strange pinkness on her high cheekbones, and there was Mr. Rios, sitting beside her, playing with her hand. Her face, so thin and girlish, would blush. From then on, her eyes, very close together like a cartoon rendition of a beaver's, would avoid us.

Miss Colon was hardly discreet about her affairs. Edwin had first tipped me off about her love life after one of his lunchtime jaunts through the empty hallways. He would chase girls and toss wet bathroom napkins into classrooms where kids in the lower grades sat, trapped. He claimed to have seen Miss Colon slip into a steward's closet with Mr. Rios and to have heard all manner of sounds through the thick wooden door, which was locked (he tried it). He had told half the class before the day was out, the boys sniggering behind grimy hands, the girls shocked because Miss Colon was married, so married that she even brought the poor unfortunate in one morning as a kind of show-and-tell guest. He was an untidy dark-skinned Puerto Rican type in a colorful dashiki. He carried a paper bag that smelled like glue. His eyes seemed sleepy, his Afro an uncombed Brillo pad. He talked about protest marches, the sixties, the importance of an education. Then he embarrassed Miss Colon greatly by disappearing into the coat closet and falling asleep there. The girls, remembering him, softened their attitude toward her indiscretions, defending her violently. "Face it," one of them blurted out when Edwin began a new series of Miss Colon tales, "she married a bum and needs to find true love."

"She's a slut, and I'm gonna draw a comic book about her," Edwin said, hushing when she walked in through the door. That afternoon, he showed me the first sketches of what would later become a very popular comic book entitled *Slut at the Head of the Class.* Edwin could draw really well, but his stories were terrible, so I volunteered to do the writing. In no time at all, we had three issues circulating under desks and hidden in notebooks all over the school. Edwin secretly ran off close to a hundred copies on a copy machine in the main office after school. It always amazed me how copies of our comic kept popping up in the unlikeliest places. I saw them on radiators in the auditorium, on benches in the gym, tacked up on bulletin boards. There were even some in the teachers' lounge, which I spotted one day while running an errand for Miss Colon. Seeing it, however, in the hands of Miss Marti, the pig-faced assistant principal, nearly made me puke up my lunch. Good thing our names weren't on it.

It was a miracle no one snitched on us during the ensuing investigation, since only a blind fool couldn't see our involvement in the thing. No bloody purge followed, but there was enough fear in both of us to kill the desire to continue our publishing venture. Miss Marti, a woman with a battlefield face and constant odor of Chiclets, made a forceful threat about finding the culprits while holding up the second issue, the one with the hand-colored cover. No one moved. The auditorium grew silent. We meditated on the sound of a small plane flying by, its engines rattling the windows. I think we wished we were on it.

It was in the auditorium that the trouble first began. We had all settled into our seats, fidgeting like tiny burrowing animals, when there was a general call for quiet. Miss Marti, up on stage, had a stare that could make any squirming fool sweat. She was a gruff, nasty woman who never smiled without seeming sadistic.

Mr. Rios was at his spot beside Miss Colon, his hands clasped behind his back as if he needed to restrain them. He seemed to whisper to her. Soft, mushy things. Edwin would watch them from his seat beside me, giving me the details, his shiny face looking worried. He always seemed sweaty, his fingers kind of damp.

"I toldju, I saw um holdin hands," he said. "An now lookit him, he's whispering sweet shits inta huh ear."

He quieted down when he noticed Miss Marti's evil eye sweeping over us like a prison-camp searchlight. There was silence. In her best military bark, Miss Marti ordered everyone to stand. Two lone, pathetic kids, dragooned by some unseen force, slowly came down the center aisle, each bearing a huge flag on a thick wooden pole. All I could make out was that great star-spangled, unfurling, twitching thing that looked like it would fall as it approached over all those bored young heads. The Puerto Rican flag walked beside it, looking smaller and less confident. It clung to its pole.

"The Pledge," Miss Marti roared, putting her hand over the spot where her heart was rumored to be.

That's when I heard my father talking.

He was sitting on his bed, yelling about Chile, about what the CIA had done there. I was standing opposite him in my dingy ProKeds. I knew about politics. I was eleven when I read William Shirer's book on Hitler. I was ready.

"All this country does is abuse Hispanic nations," my father said, turning a page of his *Post*, "tie them down, make them dependent. It says democracy with one hand while it protects and feeds fascist dictatorships with the other." His eyes blazed with a strange fire. I sat on the bed, on part of his *Post*, transfixed by his oratorical mastery. He had mentioned political things before, but not like this, not with such fiery conviction. I thought maybe it had to do with my reading Shirer. Maybe he had seen me reading that fat book and figured I was ready for real politics.

Using the knowledge I gained from the book, I defended the Americans. What fascism was he talking about, anyway? I knew we had stopped Hitler. That was a big deal, something to be proud of.

"Come out of fairy-tale land," he said scornfully. "Do you know what imperialism is?"

I didn't really, no.

"Well, why don't you read about that? Why don't you read about Juan Bosch and Allende, men who died fighting imperialism? They stood up against American big business. You should read about that instead of this crap about Hitler."

"But I like reading about Hitler," I said, feeling a little spurned. I didn't even mention that my fascination with Adolf led to my writing a biography of him, a book report one hundred and fifty pages long. It got an A-plus. Miss

Colon stapled it to the bulletin board right outside the classroom, where it was promptly stolen.

"So, what makes you want to be a writer?" Miss Colon asked me quietly one day, when Edwin and I, always the helpful ones, volunteered to assist her in getting the classroom spiffed up for a Halloween party.

"I don't know. I guess my father," I replied, fiddling with plastic pumpkins self-consciously while images of my father began parading through my mind.

When I think back to my earliest image of my father, it is one of him sitting behind a huge rented typewriter, his fingers clacking away. He was a frustrated poet, radio announcer, and even stage actor. He had sent for diplomas from fly-by-night companies. He took acting lessons, went into broadcasting, even ended up on the ground floor of what is now Spanish radio, but his family talked him out of all of it. "You should find yourself real work, something substantial," they said, so he did. He dropped all those dreams that were never encouraged by anyone else and got a job at a Nedick's on Third Avenue. My pop the counterman.

Despite that, he kept writing. He recited his poetry into a huge reel-to-reel tape deck that he had, then he'd play it back and sit like a critic, brow furrowed, fingers stroking his lips. He would record strange sounds and play them back to me at outrageous speeds, until I believed that there were tiny people living inside the machine. I used to stand by him and watch him type, his black pompadour spilling over his forehead. There was energy pulsating all around him, and I wanted a part of it.

I was five years old when I first sat in his chair at the kitchen table and began pushing down keys, watching the letters magically appear on the page. I was entranced. My fascination with the typewriter began at that point. By the time I was ten, I was writing war stories, tales of pain and pathos culled from the piles of comic books I devoured. I wrote unreadable novels. With illustrations. My father wasn't impressed. I guess he was hard to impress. My terrific grades did not faze him, nor the fact that I was reading books as fat as milk crates. My unreadable novels piled up. I brought them to him at night to see if he would read them, but after a week of waiting I found them thrown in the bedroom closet, unread. I felt hurt and rejected, despite my mother's kind words. "He's just too busy to read them," she said to me one night when I mentioned it to her. He never brought them up, even when I quietly took them out of the closet one day or when he'd see me furiously hammering on one of his rented machines. I would tell him I wanted to be a writer, and he would smile sadly and pat my head, without a word.

"You have to find something serious to do with your life," he told me one night, after I had shown him my first play, eighty pages long. What was it I had read that got me into writing a play? Was it Arthur Miller? Oscar Wilde? I don't remember, but I recall my determination to write a truly marvelous play about combat because there didn't seem to be any around.

"This is fun as a hobby," my father said, "but you can't get serious about this." His demeanor spoke volumes, but I couldn't stop writing. Novels, I called them, starting a new one every three days. The world was a blank page waiting for my words to re-create it, while the real world remained cold and lonely. My schoolmates didn't understand any of it, and because of the fat books I carried around, I was held in some fear. After all, what kid in his right mind would read a book if it wasn't assigned? I was sick of kids coming up to me and saying, "Gaw, lookit tha fat book. Ya teacha make ya read tha?" (No, I'm just reading it.) The kids would look at me as if I had just crawled out of a sewer. "Ya crazy, man." My father seemed to share that opinion. Only my teachers understood and encouraged my reading, but my father seemed to want something else from me.

Now, he treated me like an idiot for not knowing what imperialism was. He berated my books and one night handed me a copy of a book about Albizu Campos, the Puerto Rican revolutionary. I read it through in two sittings.

"Some of it seems true," I said.

"Some of it?" my father asked incredulously. "After what they did to him, you can sit there and act like a Yankee flag-waver?"

I watched that Yankee flag making its way up to the stage over indifferent heads, my father's scowling face haunting me, his words resounding in my head.

"Let me tell you something," my father sneered. "In school, all they do is talk about George Washington, right? The first president? The father of democracy? Well, he had slaves. We had our own Washington, and ours had real teeth."

As Old Glory reached the stage, a general clatter ensued.

"We had our own revolution," my father said, "and the United States crushed it with the flick of a pinkie."

Miss Marti barked her royal command. Everyone rose up to salute the flag.

Except me. I didn't get up. I sat in my creaking seat, hands on my knees. A girl behind me tapped me on the back. "Come on, stupid, get up." There was a trace of concern in her voice. I didn't move.

Miss Colon appeared. She leaned over, shaking me gently. "Are you sick? Are you okay?" Her soft hair fell over my neck like a blanket.

"No," I replied.

"What's wrong?" she asked, her face growing stern. I was beginning to feel claustrophobic, what with everyone standing all around me, bodies like walls. My friend Edwin, hand on his heart, watched from the corner of his eye. He almost looked envious, as if he wished he had thought of it. Murmuring voices around me began reciting the Pledge while Mr. Rios appeared, commandingly grabbing me by the shoulder and pulling me out of my seat into the aisle. Miss Colon was beside him, looking a little apprehensive.

"What is wrong with you?" he asked angrily. "You know you're supposed to stand up for the Pledge! Are you religious?"

"No," I said.

"Then what?"

"I'm not saluting that flag," I said.

"What?"

"I said, I'm not saluting that flag."

"Why the . . . ?" He calmed himself; a look of concern flashed over Miss Colon's face. "Why not?"

"Because I'm Puerto Rican. I ain't no American. And I'm not no Yankee flag-waver."

"You're supposed to salute the flag," he said angrily, shoving one of his fat fingers in my face. "You're not supposed to make up your own mind about it. You're supposed to do as you are told."

"I thought I was free," I said, looking at him and at Miss Colon.

"You are," Miss Colon said feebly. "That's why you should salute the flag."

"But shouldn't I do what I feel is right?"

"You should do what you are told!" Mr. Rios yelled into my face. "I'm not playing no games with you, mister. You hear that music? That's the anthem. Now you go stand over there and put your hand over your heart." He made as if to grab my hand, but I pulled away.

"No!" I said sharply. "I'm not saluting that crummy flag! And you can't make me, either. There's nothing you can do about it."

"Oh yeah?" Mr. Rios roared. "We'll see about that!"

"Have you gone crazy?" Miss Colon asked as he led me away by the arm, down the hallway, where I could still hear the strains of the anthem. He walked me briskly into the principal's office and stuck me in a corner.

"You stand there for the rest of the day and see how you feel about it," he said viciously. "Don't you even think of moving from that spot!"

I stood there for close to two hours or so. The principal came and went, not even saying hi or hey or anything, as if finding kids in the corners of his office was a common occurrence. I could hear him talking on the phone, scribbling on pads, talking to his secretary. At one point I heard Mr. Rios outside in the main office.

"Some smart-ass. I stuck him in the corner. Thinks he can pull that shit. The kid's got no respect, man. I should get the chance to teach him some."

"Children today have no respect," I heard Miss Marti's reptile voice say as she approached, heels clacking like gunshots. "It has to be forced upon them."

She was in the room. She didn't say a word to the principal, who was on the phone. She walked right over to me. I could hear my heart beating in my ears as her shadow fell over me. Godzilla over Tokyo.

"Well, have you learned your lesson yet?" she asked, turning me from the wall with a finger on my shoulder. I stared at her without replying. My face burned, red hot. I hated it.

"You think you're pretty important, don't you? Well, let me tell you, you're nothing. You're not worth a damn. You're just a snotty-nosed little kid with a lot of stupid ideas." Her eyes bored holes through me, searing my flesh. I felt as if I were going to cry. I fought the urge. Tears rolled down my face anyway. They made her smile, her chapped lips twisting upward like the mouth of a lizard.

"See? You're a little baby. You don't know anything, but you'd better learn your place." She pointed a finger in my face. "You do as you're told if you don't want big trouble. Now go back to class."

Her eyes continued to stab at me. I looked past her and saw Edwin waiting by the office door for me. I walked past her, wiping at my face. I could feel her eyes on me still, even as we walked up the stairs to the classroom. It was close to three already, and the skies outside the grated windows were cloudy.

"Man," Edwin said to me as we reached our floor, "I think you're crazy."

The classroom was abuzz with activity when I got there. Kids were chattering, getting their windbreakers from the closet, slamming their chairs up on their desks, filled with the euphoria of soon-home. I walked quietly over to my desk and took out my books. The other kids looked at me as if I were a ghost.

I went through the motions like a robot. When we got downstairs to the door, Miss Colon, dismissing the class, pulled me aside, her face compassionate and warm. She squeezed my hand.

"Are you okay?"

I nodded.

"That was a really crazy stunt there. Where did you get such an idea?"

I stared at her black flats. She was wearing tan panty hose and a black miniskirt. I saw Mr. Rios approaching with his class.

"I have to go," I said, and split, running into the frigid breezes and the silver sunshine.

At home, I lay on the floor of our living room, tapping my open notebook with the tip of my pen while the Beatles blared from my father's stereo. I felt humiliated and alone. Miss Marti's reptile face kept appearing in my notebook, her voice intoning, "Let me tell you, you're nothing." Yeah, right. Just what horrible hole did she crawl out of? Were those people really Puerto Ricans? Why should a Puerto Rican salute an American flag?

I put the question to my father, strolling into his bedroom, a tiny M-1 rifle that belonged to my GI Joe strapped to my thumb.

"Why?" he asked, loosening the reading glasses that were perched on his nose, his newspaper sprawled open on the bed before him, his cigarette streaming blue smoke. "Because we are owned, like cattle. And because nobody has any pride in their culture to stand up for it."

I pondered those words, feeling as if I were being encouraged, but I didn't dare tell him. I wanted to believe what I had done was a brave and noble thing, but somehow I feared his reaction. I never could impress him with my grades, or my writing. This flag thing would probably upset him. Maybe he, too, would think I was crazy, disrespectful, a "smart-ass" who didn't know his place. I feared that, feared my father saying to me, in a reptile voice, "Let me tell you, you're nothing."

I suited up my GI Joe for combat, slipping on his helmet, strapping on his field pack. I fixed the bayonet to his rifle, sticking it in his clutching hands so he seemed ready to fire. "A man's gotta do what a man's gotta do." Was that John Wayne? I don't know who it was, but I did what I had to do, still not telling my father. The following week, in the auditorium, I did it again. This time, everyone noticed. The whole place fell into a weird hush as Mr. Rios screamed at me.

I ended up in my corner again, this time getting a prolonged, pensive stare from the principal before I was made to stare at the wall for two more hours. My mind zoomed past my surroundings. In one strange vision, I saw my crony Edwin climbing up Miss Colon's curvy legs, giving me every detail of what he saw.

"Why?" Miss Colon asked frantically. "This time you don't leave until you tell me why." She was holding me by the arm, masses of kids flying by, happy blurs that faded into the sunlight outside the door.

"Because I'm Puerto Rican, not American," I blurted out in a weary torrent. "That makes sense, don't it?"

"So am I," she said, "but we're in America!" She smiled. "Don't you think you could make some kind of compromise?" She tilted her head to one side and said, "Aw, c'mon," in a little-girl whisper.

"What about standing up for what you believe in? Doesn't that matter? You used to talk to us about Kent State and protesting. You said those kids died because they believed in freedom, right? Well, I feel like them now. I wanna make a stand."

She sighed with evident aggravation. She caressed my hair. For a moment, I thought she was going to kiss me. She was going to say something, but just as her pretty lips parted, I caught Mr. Rios approaching.

"I don't wanna see him," I said, pulling away.

"No, wait," she said gently.

"He's gonna deck me," I said to her.

"No, he's not," Miss Colon said, as if challenging him, her eyes taking him in as he stood beside her.

"No, I'm not," he said. "Listen here. Miss Colon was talking to me about you, and I agree with her." He looked like a nervous little boy in front of the class, making his report. "You have a lot of guts. Still, there are rules here. I'm willing to make a deal with you. You go home and think about this. Tomorrow

I'll come see you." I looked at him skeptically, and he added, "To talk."

"I'm not changing my mind," I said. Miss Colon exhaled painfully.

"If you don't, it's out of my hands." He frowned and looked at her. She shook her head, as if she were upset with him.

I reread the book about Albizu. I didn't sleep a wink that night. I didn't tell my father a word, even though I almost burst from the effort. At night, alone in my bed, images attacked me. I saw Miss Marti and Mr. Rios debating Albizu Campos. I saw him in a wheelchair with a flag draped over his body like a holy robe. They would not do that to me. They were bound to break me the way Albizu was broken, not by young smiling American troops bearing chocolate bars, but by conniving, double-dealing, self-serving Puerto Rican landowners and their ilk, who dared say they were the future. They spoke of dignity and democracy while teaching Puerto Ricans how to cling to the great coat of that powerful northern neighbor. Puerto Rico, the shining star, the great lap dog of the Caribbean. I saw my father, the nationalist hero, screaming from his podium, his great oration stirring everyone around him to acts of bravery. There was a shining arrogance in his eyes as he stared out over the sea of faces mouthing his name, a sparkling audacity that invited and incited. There didn't seem to be fear anywhere in him, only the urge to rush to the attack, with his armband and revolutionary tunic. I stared up at him, transfixed. I stood by the podium, his personal adjutant, while his voice rang through the stadium. "We are not, nor will we ever be, Yankee flag-wavers!" The roar that followed drowned out the whole world.

The following day, I sat in my seat, ignoring Miss Colon as she neatly drew triangles on the board with the help of plastic stencils. She was using colored chalk, her favorite. Edwin, sitting beside me, was beaning girls with spitballs that he fired through his hollowed-out Bic pen. They didn't cry out. They simply enlisted the help of a girl named Gloria who sat a few desks behind him. She very skillfully nailed him with a thick wad of gum. It stayed in his hair until Edwin finally went running to Miss Colon. She used her huge teacher's scissors. I couldn't stand it. They all seemed trapped in a world of trivial things, while I swam in a mire of oppression. I walked through lunch as if in a trance, a prisoner on death row waiting for the heavy steps of his executioners. I watched Edwin lick at his regulation cafeteria ice cream, sandwiched between two sheets of paper. I was once like him, laughing and joking, lining up for a stickball game in the yard without a care. Now it all seemed lost to me, as if my youth had been burned out of me by a book.

Shortly after lunch, Mr. Rios appeared. He talked to Miss Colon for a while by the door as the room filled with a bubbling murmur. Then, he motioned for me. I walked through the sudden silence as if in slow motion.

"Well," he said to me as I stood in the cool hallway, "have you thought about this?"

"Yeah," I said, once again seeing my father on the podium, his voice thundering.

"And?"

"I'm not saluting that flag."

Miss Colon fell against the doorjamb as if exhausted. Exasperation passed over Mr. Rios's rodent features.

"I thought you said you'd think about it," he thundered.

"I did. I decided I was right."

"*You* were right?" Mr. Rios was losing his patience. I stood calmly by the wall.

"I told you," Miss Colon whispered to him.

"Listen," he said, ignoring her, "have you heard of the story of the man who had no country?"

I stared at him.

"Well? Have you?"

"No," I answered sharply; his mouse eyes almost crossed with anger at my insolence. "Some stupid fairy tale ain't gonna change my mind anyway. You're treating me like I'm stupid, and I'm not."

"Stop acting like you're some mature adult! You're not. You're just a puny kid."

"Well, this puny kid still ain't gonna salute that flag."

"You were born here," Miss Colon interjected patiently, trying to calm us both down. "Don't you think you at least owe this country some respect? At least?"

"I had no choice about where I was born. And I was born poor."

"So what?" Mr. Rios screamed. "There are plenty of poor people who respect the flag. Look around you, dammit! You see any rich people here? I'm not rich either!" He tugged on my arm. "This country takes care of Puerto Rico, don't you see that? Don't you know anything about politics?"

"Do you know what imperialism is?"

The two of them stared at each other.

"I don't believe you," Mr. Rios murmured.

"Puerto Rico is a colony," I said, a direct quote of Albizu's. "Why I gotta respect that?"

Miss Colon stared at me with her black saucer eyes, a slight trace of a grin on her features. It encouraged me. In that one moment, I felt strong, suddenly aware of my territory and my knowledge of it. I no longer felt like a boy but some kind of soldier, my bayonet stained with the blood of my enemy. There was no doubt about it. Mr. Rios was the enemy, and I was beating him. The more he tried to treat me like a child, the more defiant I became, his arguments falling like twisted armor. He shut his eyes and pressed the bridge of his nose.

"You're out of my hands," he said.

Miss Colon ·gave me a sympathetic look before she vanished into the classroom again. Mr. Rios led me downstairs without another word. His face was completely red. I expected to be put in my corner again, but this time Mr. Rios sat me down in the leather chair facing the principal's desk. He stepped outside, and I could hear the familiar clack-clack that could only belong to Miss Marti's reptile legs. They were talking in whispers. I expected her to come in at any moment, but the principal walked in instead. He came in quietly, holding a folder in his hand. His soft brown eyes and beard made him look compassionate, rounded cheeks making him seem friendly. His desk plate solemnly stated: Mr. Sepulveda, PRINCIPAL. He fell into his seat rather unceremoniously, opened the folder, and crossed his hands over it.

"Well, well, well," he said softly, with a tight-lipped grin. "You've created quite a stir, young man." It sounded to me like movie dialogue.

"First of all, let me say I know about you. I have your record right here, and everything in it is very impressive. Good grades, good attitude, your teachers all have adored you. But I wonder if maybe this hasn't gone to your head? Because everything is going for you here, and you're throwing it all away."

He leaned back in his chair, "We have rules, all of us. There are rules even I must live by. People who don't obey them get disciplined. This will all go on your record, and a pretty good one you've had so far. Why ruin it? This'll follow you for life. You don't want to end up losing a good job opportunity in government or in the armed forces because as a child you indulged your imagination and refused to salute the flag? I know you can't see how childish it all is now, but you must see it, and because you're smarter than most, I'll put it to you in terms you can understand.

"To me, this is a simple case of rules and regulations. Someday, when you're older," he paused here, obviously amused by the sound of his own voice, "you can go to rallies and protest marches and express your rebellious tendencies. But right now, you are a minor, under this school's jurisdiction. That means you follow the rules, no matter what you think of them. You can join the Young Lords later."

I stared at him, overwhelmed by his huge desk, his pompous mannerisms and status. I would agree with everything, I felt, and then, the following week, I would refuse once again. I would fight him then, even though he hadn't tried to humiliate me or insult my intelligence. I would continue to fight, until I . . .

"I spoke with your father," he said.

I started. "My father?" Vague images and hopes flared through my mind briefly.

"Yes. I talked to him at length. He agrees with me that you've gotten a little out of hand."

My blood reversed direction in my veins. I felt as if I were going to collapse. I gripped the armrests of my chair. There was no way this could be true, no way at all! My father was supposed to ride in like the cavalry, not abandon me to the enemy! I pressed my wet eyes with my fingers. It must be a lie.

"He blames himself for your behavior," the principal said. "He's already here," Mr. Rios said from the door, motioning my father inside. Seeing him wearing his black weather-beaten trench coat almost asphyxiated me. His eyes, red with concern, pulled at me painfully. He came over to me first while the principal rose slightly, as if greeting a head of state. There was a look of dread on my father's face as he looked at me. He seemed utterly lost.

"Mr. Sepulveda," he said, "I never thought a thing like this could happen. My wife and I try to bring him up right. We encourage him to read and write and everything. But you know, this is a shock."

"It's not that terrible, Mr. Rodriguez. You've done very well with him, he's an intelligent boy. He just needs to learn how important obedience is."

"Yes," my father said, turning to me, "yes, you have to obey the rules. You can't do this. It's wrong." He looked at me grimly, as if working on a math problem. One of his hands caressed my head.

There were more words, in Spanish now, but I didn't hear them. I felt like I was falling down a hole. My father, my creator, renouncing his creation, repentant. Not an ounce of him seemed prepared to stand up for me, to shield me from attack. My tears made all the faces around me melt.

"So you see," the principal said to me as I rose, my father clutching me to him, "if you ever do this again, you will be hurting your father as well as yourself."

I hated myself. I wiped at my face desperately, trying not to make a spectacle of myself. I was just a kid, a tiny kid. Who in the hell did I think I was? I'd have to wait until I was older, like my father, in order to have "convictions."

"I don't want to see you in here again, okay?" the principal said sternly. I nodded dumbly, my father's arm around me as he escorted me through the front office to the door that led to the hallway, where a multitude of children's voices echoed up and down its length like tolling bells.

"Are you crazy?" my father half-whispered to me in Spanish as we stood there. "Do you know how embarrassing this all is? I didn't think you were this stupid. Don't you know anything about dignity, about respect? How could you make a spectacle of yourself? Now you make us all look stupid."

He quieted down as Mr. Rios came over to take me back to class. My father gave me a squeeze and told me he'd see me at home. Then, I walked with a somber Mr. Rios, who oddly wrapped an arm around me all the way back to the classroom.

"Here you go," he said softly as I entered the classroom, and everything fell quiet. I stepped in and walked to my seat without looking at anyone. My cheeks were still damp, my eyes red. I looked like I had been tortured. Edwin stared at me, then he pressed my hand under the table.

"I thought you were dead," he whispered.

Miss Colon threw me worried glances all through the remainder of the class. I wasn't paying attention. I took out my notebook, but my strength ebbed away. I just put my head on the desk and shut my eyes, reliving my father's betrayal. If what I did was so bad, why did I feel more ashamed of him than I did of myself? His words, once so rich and vibrant, now fell to the floor, leaves from a dead tree.

At the end of the class, Miss Colon ordered me to stay after school. She got Mr. Rios to take the class down along with his, and she stayed with me in the darkened room. She shut the door on all the exuberant hallway noise and sat down on Edwin's desk, beside me, her black pumps on his seat.

"Are you okay?" she asked softly, grasping my arm. I told her everything, especially about my father's betrayal. I thought he would be the cavalry, but he was just a coward.

"Tss. Don't be so hard on your father," she said. "He's only trying to do what's best for you."

"And how's this the best for me?" I asked, my voice growing hoarse with hurt.

"I know it's hard for you to understand, but he really was trying to take care of you."

I stared at the blackboard.

"He doesn't understand me," I said, wiping my eyes.

"You'll forget," she whispered.

"No, I won't. I'll remember every time I see that flag. I'll see it and think, 'My father doesn't understand me.'"

Miss Colon sighed deeply. Her fingers were warm on my head, stroking my hair. She gave me a kiss on the cheek. She walked me downstairs, pausing by the doorway. Scores of screaming, laughing kids brushed past us.

"If it's any consolation, I'm on your side," she said, squeezing my arm. I smiled at her, warmth spreading through me. "Go home and listen to the Beatles," she added with a grin.

I stepped out into the sunshine, came down the white stone steps, and stood on the sidewalk. I stared at the towering school building, white and perfect in the sun, indomitable. Across the street, the dingy row of tattered uneven tenements where I lived. I thought of my father. Her words made me feel sorry for him, but I felt sorrier for myself. I couldn't understand back then about a father's love and what a father might give to ensure his son safe transit. He had already navigated treacherous waters and now couldn't have me rock the boat. I still had to learn that he had made peace with the Enemy, that the Enemy was already in us. Like the flag I must salute, we were inseparable, yet his compromise made me feel ashamed and defeated. Then I knew I had to find my own peace, away from the bondage of obedience. I had to accept that flag, and my father, someone I would love forever, even if at times to my young, feeble mind he seemed a little imperfect.

Imtiaz Dharker

Imtiaz Dharker (b. 1954) was born in Lahore, Pakistan, grew up in Glasgow, Scotland, and has lived in London and Mumbai (Bombay). She is an award-winning documentary filmmaker and has written three books of poetry, *Purdah*, *Postcards from God*, and *I Speak for the Devil*, in which this selection appears.

They'll Say, "She Must Be from Another Country"

When I can't comprehend
why they're burning books
or slashing paintings,
when they can't bear to look
at god's own nakedness,
when they ban the film
and gut the seats to stop the play
and I ask why
they just smile and say,
"She must be
from another country."

When I speak on the phone
and the vowel sounds are off
when the consonants are hard
and they should be soft,
they'll catch on at once
they'll pin it down
they'll explain it right away

to their own satisfaction,
they'll cluck their tongues
and say,
"She must be
from another country."

When my mouth goes up
instead of down,
when I wear a tablecloth
to go to town,
when they suspect I'm black
or hear I'm gay
they won't be surprised,
they'll purse their lips
and say,
"She must be
from another country."

When I eat up the olives
and spit out the pits
when I yawn at the opera
in the tragic bits
when I pee in the vineyard
as if it were Bombay,
flaunting my bare ass
covering my face
laughing through my hands
they'll turn away,
shake their heads quite sadly,
"She doesn't know any better,"
they'll say,
"She must be
from another country."

Maybe there is a country
where all of us live,
all of us freaks
who aren't able to give
our loyalty to fat old fools,
the crooks and thugs
who wear the uniform
that gives them the right
to wave a flag,
puff out their chests,
put their feet on our necks,
and break their own rules.

But from where we are
it doesn't look like a country,
it's more like the cracks
that grow between borders
behind their backs.
That's where I live.
And I'll be happy to say,
"I never learned your customs.
I don't remember your language
or know your ways.
I must be
from another country."

Franz Kafka

Born in the Jewish ghetto of Prague, Franz Kafka (1883–1924) earned a law degree and became a clerk for an accident insurance company. Though he wrote a number of enigmatic and compelling stories and novels, he published little during his lifetime. As he was dying of tuberculosis, Kafka requested that his unpublished manuscripts be burned. However, his good friend Max Brod preserved them, including "A Hunger Artist," *The Castle*, and *The Trial*. This selection, translated by Tania and James Stern, was written between 1917 and 1923.

Fellowship

We are five friends; one day we came out of a house one after the other; first one came and placed himself beside the gate, then the second came, or rather he glided through the gate like a little ball of quicksilver, and placed himself near the first one, then came the third, then the fourth, then the fifth. Finally we all stood in a row. People began to notice us; they pointed at us and said: those five just came out of that house. Since then we have been living together; it would be a peaceful life if it weren't for a sixth one continually trying to interfere. He doesn't do us any harm, but he annoys us, and that is harm enough; why does he intrude where he is not wanted? We don't know him and don't want him to join us. There was a time, of course, when the five of us did not know one another, either; and it could be said that we still don't know one another, but what is possible and can be tolerated by the five of us is not possible and cannot be tolerated with this sixth one. In any case, we are five and don't want to be six. And what is the point of this continual being together anyhow? It is also pointless for the five of us, but here we are together and will remain together; a new combination, however, we do not want, just because of our experiences. But how is one to make all this clear to the sixth one? Long explanations would almost amount to accepting him in our circle, so we prefer not to explain and not to accept him. No matter how he pouts his lips we push him away with our elbows, but however much we push him away, back he comes.

Jane Addams

A native of Cedarville, Illinois, Jane Addams (1860–1935) moved to Chicago as a young woman and founded Hull-House, a residential community that offered a wide range of help and hospitality to immigrants on the city's west side. It would become the most famous "settlement house" in America. Addams lived and worked at Hull-House for the rest of her life, while also writing and speaking on an ever-widening stage. Her efforts on behalf of international peace earned her the Nobel Peace Prize in 1931. The following selection, "Earliest Impressions," opens *Twenty Years at Hull-House*.

Earliest Impressions

On the theory that our genuine impulses may be connected with our childish experiences, that one's bent may be tracked back to that "no man's land" where character is formless but nevertheless settling into definite lines of future development, I begin this record with some impressions of my childhood.

All of these are directly connected with my father, although of course I recall many experiences apart from him. I was one of the younger members of a large family and an eager participant in the village life, but because my father was so distinctly the dominant influence and because it is quite impossible to set forth all of one's early impressions, it has seemed simpler to string these first memories on that single cord. Moreover, it was this cord that not only held fast my supreme affection but also first drew me into the moral concerns of life, and later afforded a clue there to which I somewhat wistfully clung in the intricacy of its mazes.

It must have been from a very early period that I recall "horrid nights" when I tossed about in my bed because I had told a lie. I was held in the grip of a miserable dread of death, a double fear: first, that I myself should die in my sins and go straight to that fiery hell that was never mentioned at home but that I had heard all about from other children, and, second, that my father—representing the entire adult world that I had basely deceived—should himself die before I had time to tell him. My only method of obtaining relief was to go downstairs to my father's room and make full confession. The high resolve to do this would push me out of bed and carry me down the stairs without a touch of fear. But at the foot of the stairs I would be faced by the awful necessity of passing the front door—which my father, because of his Quaker tendencies, did not lock—and of crossing the wide and black expanse of the living room in order to reach his door. I would invariably cling to the newel post while I contemplated the perils of the situation, complicated by the fact that the literal first step meant putting my bare foot upon a piece of oilcloth in front of the door, only a few inches wide, but lying straight in my path. I would finally reach my father's bedside perfectly breathless and, having panted out the history of my sin, invariably received the same assurance that if he "had a little girl who told lies," he was very glad that she "felt too bad to go to sleep afterward." No absolution was asked for or received, but apparently the sense that the knowledge of my wickedness was shared, or an obscure understanding of the affection that underlay the grave statement, was sufficient, for I always went back to bed as bold as a lion, and slept, if not the sleep of the just, at least that of the comforted.

I recall an incident that must have occurred before I was seven years old, for the mill in which my father transacted his business that day was closed in 1867. The mill stood in the neighboring town, adjacent to its poorest quarter. Before then I had always seen the little city of ten thousand people with the admiring eyes of a country child, and it had never occurred to me that all its streets were not as bewilderingly attractive as the one that contained the glittering toy shop and the confectioner. On that day I had my first sight of the poverty that implies squalor and felt the curious distinction between the ruddy poverty of the country and that which even a small city presents in its shabbiest streets. I remember launching at my father the pertinent inquiry why people lived in such horrid little houses so close together, and that after receiving his explanation I declared with much firmness when I grew up I should, of course, have a large house, but it would not be built among the other large houses, but right in the midst of horrid little houses like these.

That curious sense of responsibility for carrying on the world's affairs that little children often exhibit because "the old man clogs our earliest years" I remember in myself in a very absurd manifestation. I dreamed night after night that everyone in the world was dead excepting myself and that upon me rested the responsibility of making a wagon wheel. The village street remained as usual, the village blacksmith shop was "all there," even a glowing fire upon the forge and the anvil in its customary place near the door, but no human being was within sight. They had all gone around the edge of the hill to the village cemetery, and I alone remained alive in the deserted world. I always stood in the same spot in the blacksmith shop, darkly pondering as to how to begin, and never once did I know how, although I fully realized that the affairs of the world could not be resumed until at least one wheel should be made and something started. Every victim of nightmare is, I imagine, overwhelmed by an excessive sense of responsibility and the consciousness of a fearful handicap in the effort to perform what is required; but perhaps never were the odds more heavily against "a warder of the world" than in these reiterated dreams of mine, doubtless compounded in equal parts of a childish version of Robinson Crusoe and of the end-of-the-world predictions of the Second Adventists, a few of whom were found in the village. The next morning would often find me, a delicate little girl of six, with the further disability of a curved spine, standing in the doorway of the village blacksmith shop, anxiously watching the burly, red-shirted figure at work. I would store my mind with such details of the process of making wheels as I could observe, and sometimes I plucked up courage to ask for more. "Do you always have to sizzle the iron in water?" I would ask, thinking how horrid it would be to do. "Sure!" the good-natured blacksmith would reply, "that makes the iron hard." I would sigh heavily and walk away, bearing my responsibility as best I could, and this, of course, I confided to no one, for there is something too mysterious in the burden of "the winds that come from the fields of sleep" to be communicated, although it is at the same time too heavy a burden to be borne alone.

My great veneration and pride in my father manifested itself in curious ways. On several Sundays, doubtless occurring in two or three different years, the Union Sunday School of the village was visited by strangers, some of those "strange people" who live outside a child's realm, yet constantly thrill it by their close approach. My father taught the large Bible class in the left-hand corner of the church next to the pulpit, and, to my eyes at least, was a most imposing figure in his Sunday frock coat, his fine head rising high above all the others. I imagined that the strangers were filled with admiration for this dignified person, and I prayed with all my heart that the ugly, pigeon-toed little girl, whose crooked back obliged her to walk with her head held very much upon one side, would never be pointed out to these visitors as the daughter of this fine man. In order to lessen the possibility of a connection being made, on these particular Sundays I did not walk beside my father, although this walk was the great event of the week, but attached myself firmly to the side of my uncle James Addams, in the hope that I should be mistaken for his child, or at least that I should not remain so conspicuously unattached that troublesome questions might identify an ugly duckling with her imposing parent. My uncle, who had many children of his own, must have been mildly surprised at this unwonted attention, but he would look down kindly at me, and say, "So you are going to walk with me today?" "Yes, please, Uncle James," would be my meek reply. He fortunately never explored my motives, nor do I remember that my father ever did, so that in all probability my machinations have been safe from public knowledge until this hour.

It is hard to account for the manifestations of a child's adoring affection, so emotional, so irrational, so tangled with the affairs of the imagination. I simply could not endure the thought that "strange people" should know that my handsome father owned this homely little girl. But even in my chivalric desire to protect him from his fate, I was not quite easy in the sacrifice of my uncle, although I quieted my scruples with the reflection that the contrast was less marked and that, anyway, his own little girl "was not so very pretty." I do not know that I commonly dwelt much upon my personal appearance, save as it thrust itself as an incongruity into my father's life, and in spite of unending evidence to the contrary, there were even black moments when I allowed myself to speculate as to whether he might not share the feeling. Happily, however, this specter was laid before it had time to grow into a morbid familiar by a very trifling incident. One day I met my father coming out of his bank on the main street of the neighboring city, which seemed to me a veritable whirlpool of society and commerce. With a playful touch of exaggeration, he lifted his high and shining silk hat and made me an imposing bow. This distinguished public recognition, this totally unnecessary identification among a mass of "strange people" who couldn't possibly know unless he himself made the sign, suddenly filled me with a sense of the absurdity of the entire feeling. It may not even then have seemed as absurd as it really was, but at least it seemed enough so to collapse or to pass into the limbo of forgotten specters.

I made still other almost equally grotesque attempts to express this doglike affection. The house at the end of the village in which I was born, and that was my home until I moved to Hull-House, in my earliest childhood had opposite to it—only across the road and then across a little stretch of greensward—two mills belonging to my father; one flour mill, to which the various grains were brought by the neighboring farmers, and one sawmill, in which the logs of the native timber were sawed into lumber. The latter offered the great excitement of sitting on a log while it slowly approached the buzzing saw that was cutting it into slabs, and of getting off just in time to escape a sudden and gory death. But the flouring mill was much more beloved. It was full of dusky, floury places that we adored, of empty bins in which we might play house; it had a basement with piles of bran and shorts that were almost as good as sand to play in, whenever the miller let us wet the edges of the pile with water brought in his sprinkling pot from the millrace.

In addition to these fascinations was the association of the mill with my father's activities, for doubtless at that time I centered upon him all that careful imitation that a little girl ordinarily gives to her mother's ways and habits. My mother had died when I was a baby, and my father's second marriage did not occur until my eighth year.

I had a consuming ambition to possess a miller's thumb and would sit contentedly for a long time rubbing between my thumb and fingers the ground wheat as it fell from between the millstones, before it was taken up on an endless chain of mysterious little buckets to be bolted into flour. I believe I have never since wanted anything more desperately than I wanted my right thumb to be flattened, as my father's had become, during his earlier years of a miller's life. Somewhat discouraged by the slow process of structural modification, I also took measures to secure on the backs of my hands the tiny purple and red spots that are always found on the hands of the miller who dresses millstones. The marks on my father's hands had grown faint, but were quite visible when looked for, and seemed to me so desirable that they must be procured at all costs. Even when playing in our house or yard, I could always tell when the millstones were being dressed, because the rumbling of the mill then stopped, and there were few pleasures I would not instantly forgo, rushing at once to the mill that I might spread out my hands near the millstones in the hope that the little hard flints flying from the miller's chisel would light upon their backs and make the longed-for marks. I used hotly to accuse the German miller, my dear friend Ferdinand, "of trying not to hit my hands," but he scornfully replied that he could not hit them if he did try, and that they were too little to be of use in a mill anyway. Although I hated his teasing, I never had the courage to confess my real purpose.

This sincere tribute of imitation, which affection offers its adored object, had later, I hope, subtler manifestations, but certainly these first ones were altogether genuine. In this case, too, I doubtless contributed my share to that stream of admiration that our generation so generously poured forth for the self-made man. I was consumed by a wistful desire to apprehend the hardships of my father's earlier life in that faraway time when he had been a miller's apprentice. I knew that he still woke up punctually at three o'clock because for so many years he had taken his turn at the mill in the early morning, and if by chance I awoke at the same hour, as curiously enough I often did, I imagined him in the early dawn in my uncle's old mill reading through the entire village library, book after book, beginning with the lives of the signers of the Declaration of Independence. Copies of the same books, mostly bound in calfskin, were to be found in the library below, and I courageously resolved that I, too, would read them all and try to understand life as he did. I did in fact later begin a course of reading in the early morning hours, but I was caught by some fantastic notion of chronological order and early legendary form. Pope's translation of the *Iliad*, even followed by Dryden's *Virgil*, did not leave behind the residuum of wisdom for which I longed, and I finally gave them up for a thick book entitled *The History of the World* as affording a shorter and an easier path.

Although I constantly confided my sins and perplexities to my father, there are only a few occasions on which I remember having received direct advice or admonition; it may easily be true, however, that I have forgotten the latter, in the manner of many seekers after advice who enjoyably set forth their situation but do not really listen to the advice itself. I can remember an admonition on one occasion, however, when, as a little girl of eight years, arrayed in a new cloak, gorgeous beyond anything I had ever worn before, I stood before my father for his approval. I was much chagrined by his remark that it was a very pretty cloak—in fact so much prettier than any cloak the other little girls in the Sunday school had that he would advise me to wear my old cloak, which would keep me quite as warm, with the added advantage of not making the other little girls feel bad. I complied with the request but I fear without inner consent, and I certainly was quite without the joy of self-sacrifice as I walked soberly through the village street by the side of my counselor. My mind was busy, however, with the old question eternally suggested by the inequalities of the human lot. Only as we neared the church door did I venture to ask what could be done about it, receiving the reply that it might never be righted so far as clothes went, but that people might be equal in things that mattered much more than clothes, the affairs of education and religion, for instance, which we attended to when we went to school and church, and that it was very stupid to wear the sort of clothes that made it harder to have equality even there.

It must have been a little later when I held a conversation with my father upon the doctrine of foreordination, which at one time very much perplexed my childish mind. After setting the difficulty before him and complaining that I could not make it out, although my best friend "understood it perfectly," I settled down to hear his argument, having no doubt that he could make it quite clear. To my delighted surprise, for any intimation that our minds were on an equality lifted me high indeed, he said that he feared that he and I did not have the kind of mind that would ever understand foreordination very well and advised me not to give too much time to it; but he then proceeded to say other things of which the final impression left upon my mind was that it did not matter much whether one understood foreordination or not, but that it was very important not to pretend to understand what you didn't understand and that you must always be honest with yourself inside, whatever happened. Perhaps on the whole as valuable a lesson as the shorter catechism itself contains.

My memory merges this early conversation on religious doctrine into one that took place years later when I put before my father the situation in which I found myself at boarding school when under great evangelical pressure, and once again I heard his testimony in favor of "mental integrity above everything else."

At the time we were driving through a piece of timber in which the wood-choppers had been at work during the winter, and so earnestly were we talking that he suddenly drew up the horses to find that he did not know where he was. We were both entertained by the incident, I that my father had been "lost in his own timber" so that various cords of wood must have escaped his practiced eye, and he on his side that he should have become so absorbed in this maze of youthful speculation. We were in high spirits as we emerged from the tender green of the spring woods into the clear light of day, and as we came back into the main road I categorically asked him:

"What are you? What do you say when people ask you?"

His eyes twinkled a little as he soberly replied:

"I am a Quaker."

"But that isn't enough to say," I urged.

"Very well," he added, "to people who insist upon details, as someone is doing now, I add that I am a Hicksite Quaker"; and not another word on the weighty subject could I induce him to utter.

These early recollections are set in a scene of rural beauty, unusual at least for Illinois. The prairie around the village was broken into hills, one of them crowned by pine woods, grown up from a bagful of Norway pine seeds sown by my father in 1844, the very year he came to Illinois, a testimony perhaps that the most vigorous pioneers gave at least an occasional thought to beauty. The banks of the millstream rose into high bluffs too perpendicular to be climbed without skill, and containing caves of which one at least was so black that it could not be explored without the aid of a candle; and there was a deserted limekiln that became associated in my mind with the unpardonable sin of Hawthorne's "Lime-Burner." My stepbrother and I carried on games and crusades that lasted week after week, and even summer after summer, as only free-ranging country children can do. It may be in contrast to this that one of the most piteous aspects in the life of city children, as I have seen it in the neighborhood of Hull-House, is the constant interruption to their play that is inevitable on the streets, so that it can never have any continuity—the most elaborate "plan or chart" or "fragment from their dream of human life" is sure to be rudely destroyed by the passing traffic. Although they start over and over again, even the most vivacious become worn out at last and take to that passive "standing 'round" varied by rude horseplay, which in time becomes so characteristic of city children.

We had, of course, our favorite places and trees and birds and flowers. It is hard to reproduce the companionship that children establish with nature, but certainly it is much too unconscious and intimate to come under the head of aesthetic appreciation or anything of the sort. When we said that the purple windflowers—the anemone patens—"looked as if the winds had made them," we thought much more of the fact that they were wind-born than that they were beautiful: we clapped our hands in sudden joy over the soft radiance of the rainbow, but its enchantment lay in our half-belief that a pot of gold was to be found at its farther end; we yielded to a soft melancholy when we heard the whippoorwill in the early twilight, but while he aroused in us vague longings of which we spoke solemnly, we felt no beauty in his call.

We erected an altar beside the stream, to which for several years we brought all the snakes we killed during our excursions, no matter how long the toilsome journey that we had to make with a limp snake dangling between two sticks. I remember rather vaguely the ceremonial performed upon this altar one autumn day, when we brought as further tribute one out of every hundred of the black walnuts that we had gathered, and then poured over the whole a pitcher full of cider, fresh from the cider mill on the barn floor. I think we had also burned a favorite book or two upon this pyre of stones. The entire affair carried on with such solemnity was probably the result of one of those imperative impulses under whose compulsion children seek a ceremonial that shall express their sense of identification with man's primitive life and their familiar kinship with the remotest past.

Long before we had begun the study of Latin at the village school, my brother and I had learned the Lord's Prayer in Latin out of an old copy of the Vulgate and gravely repeated it every night in an execrable pronunciation because it seemed to us more religious than "plain English."

When, however, I really prayed, what I saw before my eyes was a most outrageous picture that adorned a songbook used in Sunday school, portraying the Lord upon his throne surrounded by tiers and tiers of saints and angels all in a blur of yellow. I am ashamed to tell how old I was when that picture ceased to appear before my eyes, especially when moments of terror compelled me to ask protection from the heavenly powers.

I recall with great distinctness my first direct contact with death when I was fifteen years old: Polly was an old nurse who had taken care of my mother and had followed her to frontier Illinois to help rear a second generation of children. She had always lived in our house but made annual visits to her cousins on a farm a few miles north of the village. During one of these visits, word came to us one Sunday evening that Polly was dying, and for a number of reasons I was the only person able to go to her. I left the lamp-lit, warm house to be driven four miles through a blinding storm that every minute added more snow to the already high drifts, with a sense of starting upon a fateful errand. An hour after my arrival all of the cousin's family went downstairs to supper, and I was left alone to watch with Polly. The square, old-fashioned chamber in the lonely farmhouse was very cold and still, with nothing to be heard but the storm outside. Suddenly the great change came. I heard a feeble call of "Sarah," my mother's name, as the dying eyes were turned upon me, followed by a curious breathing and in place of the face familiar from my earliest childhood and associated with homely household cares, there lay upon the pillow strange, august features, stern and withdrawn from all the small affairs of life. That sense of solitude, of being unsheltered in a wide world of relentless and elemental forces that is at the basis of childhood's timidity and that is far outgrown at fifteen, seized me irresistibly before I could reach the narrow stairs and summon the family from below.

As I was driven home in the winter storm, the wind through the trees seemed laden with a passing soul and the riddle of life and death pressed hard; once to be young, to grow old and to die, everything came to that, and then a mysterious journey out into the unknown. Did she mind faring forth alone? Would the journey perhaps end in something as familiar and natural to the aged and dying as life is to the young and living? Through all the drive and indeed throughout the night these thoughts were pierced by sharp worry, a sense of faithlessness because I had forgotten the text Polly had confided to me long before as the one from which she wished her funeral sermon to be preached. My comfort as usual finally came from my father, who pointed out what was essential and what was of little avail even in such a moment as this, and while he was much too wise to grow dogmatic upon the great theme of death, I felt a new fellowship with him because we had discussed it together.

Perhaps I may record here my protest against the efforts, so often made, to shield children and young people from all that has to do with death and sorrow, to give them a good time at all hazards on the assumption that the ills of life will come soon enough. Young people themselves often resent this attitude on the part of their elders; they feel set aside and belittled as if they were denied the common human experiences. They, too, wish to climb steep stairs and to eat their bread with tears, and they imagine that the problems of existence that so press upon them in pensive moments would be less insoluble in the light of these great happenings.

An incident that stands out clearly in my mind as an exciting suggestion of the great world of moral enterprise and serious undertakings must have occurred earlier than this, for in 1872, when I was not yet twelve years old, I came into my father's room one morning to find him sitting beside the fire with a newspaper in his hand, looking very solemn; and upon my eager inquiry what had happened, he told me that Joseph Mazzini was dead. I had never even heard Mazzini's name, and after being told about him I was inclined to grow argumentative, asserting that my father did not know him, that he was not an American, and that I could not understand why we should be expected to feel badly about him. It is impossible to recall the conversation with the complete breakdown of my cheap arguments, but in the end I obtained that which I have ever regarded as a valuable possession, a sense of the genuine relationship that may exist between men who share large hopes and like desires, even though they differ in nationality, language, and creed; that those things count for absolutely nothing between groups of men who are trying to abolish slavery in America or to throw off Hapsburg oppression in Italy. At any rate, I was heartily ashamed of my meager notion of patriotism, and I came out of the room exhilarated with the consciousness that impersonal and international relations are actual facts and not mere phrases. I was filled with pride that I knew a man who held converse with great minds and who really sorrowed and rejoiced over happenings across the sea. I never recall those early conversations with my father, nor a score of others like them, but there comes into my mind a line from Mrs. [Elizabeth Barrett] Browning in which a daughter describes her relations with her father:

> He wrapt me in his large
> Man's doublet, careless did it fit or no.

Alden Nowlan

Born in Nova Scotia, Alden Nowlan (1933–1983) passed most of his career in Canada's maritime provinces. Early in his life, he worked as a logger and a night watchman, and at a number of other physically demanding jobs, educating himself along the way. Nowlan went on to newspaper work and wrote poetry, drama, short stories, and novels. In 1967, he won the Governor General's award in Canada for his poetry collection *Bread, Wine, and Salt.*

He Sits Down on the Floor of a School for the Retarded

I sit down on the floor of a school for the retarded,
a writer of magazine articles accompanying a band
that was met at the door by a child in a man's body
who asked them, "Are you the surprise they promised us?"

It's Ryan's Fancy, Dermot on guitar,
Fergus on banjo, Denis on pennywhistle.
In the eyes of this audience, they're everybody
who has ever appeared on TV. I've been telling lies
to a boy who cried because his favorite detective
hadn't come with us; I said he had sent his love
and, no, I didn't think he'd mind if I signed his name
to a scrap of paper: when the boy took it, he said,
"Nobody will ever get this away from me,"
in the voice, more hopeless than defiant,
of one accustomed to finding that his hiding places
have been discovered, used to having objects snatched

out of his hands. Weeks from now I'll send him
another autograph, this one genuine
in the sense of having been signed by somebody
on the same payroll as the star.
Then I'll feel less ashamed. Now everyone is singing,
"Old MacDonald had a farm," and I don't know what to do

about the young woman (I call her a woman
because she's twenty-five at least, but think of her
as a little girl, she plays that part so well,
having known no other), about the young woman who
sits down beside me and, as if it were the most natural
thing in the world, rests her head on my shoulder.

It's nine o'clock in the morning, not an hour for music.
And, at the best of times, I'm uncomfortable
in situations where I'm ignorant
of the accepted etiquette: it's one thing
to jump a fence, quite another to blunder
into one in the dark. I look around me
for a teacher to whom to smile out my distress.
They're all busy elsewhere. "Hold me," she whispers. "Hold me."
I put my arm round her. "Hold me tighter."
I do, and she snuggles closer. I half-expect
someone in authority to grab her
or me; I can imagine this being remembered
for ever as the time the sex-crazed writer
publicly fondled the poor retarded girl.
"Hold me," she says again. What does it matter
what anybody thinks? I put my other arm around her,
rest my chin in her hair, thinking of children
real children, and of how they say it, "Hold me,"
and of a patient in a geriatric ward
I once heard crying out to his mother, dead
for half a century, "I'm frightened! Hold me!"

and of a boy-soldier screaming it on the beach
at Dieppe, of Nelson in Hardy's arms,
of Frieda gripping Lawrence's ankle
until he sailed off in his Ship of Death.

It's what we all want, in the end,
to be held, merely to be held,
to be kissed (not necessarily with the lips,
for every touching is a kind of kiss).

She hugs me now, this retarded woman, and I hug her.
We are brother and sister, father and daughter,
mother and son, husband and wife.
We are lovers. We are two human beings
huddled together for a little while by the fire
in the Ice Age, two hundred thousand years ago.

Adam Smith

Celebrated today as one of the founders of modern political economy, Adam Smith (1723–1790) was by profession a philosopher. At the age of fourteen, he entered the University of Glasgow, the center of what came to be known as the Scottish Enlightenment, and he continued his education at Balliol College, Oxford. In his late twenties, Smith became the chair of logic and then the chair of moral philosophy at Glasgow. In 1759, he published *The Theory of Moral Sentiments*, from which this selection is taken. Smith left the university in 1764 to tutor the Duke of Buccleuch, after which he was able to retire to his birthplace, Kirkcaldy, Scotland, where he wrote the book for which he is most famous, *The Wealth of Nations*.

Selection from
The Theory of Moral Sentiments

Chapter 1: Of Sympathy

1.

How selfish soever man may be supposed, there are evidently some principles in his nature, which interest him in the fortune of others and render their happiness necessary to him, though he derives nothing from it except the pleasure of seeing it. Of this kind is pity or compassion, the emotion that we feel for the misery of others, when we either see it or are made to conceive it in a very lively manner. That we often derive sorrow from the sorrow of others is a matter of fact too obvious to require any instances to prove it; for this sentiment, like all the other original passions of human nature, is by no means confined to the virtuous and humane, though they perhaps may feel it with the most exquisite sensibility. The greatest ruffian, the most hardened violator of the laws of society, is not altogether without it.

***

2.

As we have no immediate experience of what other men feel, we can form no idea of the manner in which they are affected but by conceiving what we ourselves should feel in the like situation. Though our brother is upon the rack, as long as we ourselves are at our ease, our senses will never inform us of what he suffers. They never did, and never can, carry us beyond our own person, and it is by the imagination only that we can form any conception of what are his sensations. Neither can that faculty help us to this any other way than by representing to us what would be our own, if we were in his case. It is the impressions of our own senses only, not those of his, that our imaginations copy. By the imagination we place ourselves in his situation, we conceive ourselves enduring all the same torments, we enter as it were into his body, and become in some measure the same person with him, and thence form some idea of his sensations, and even feel something that, though weaker in degree, is not altogether unlike them. His agonies, when they are thus brought home to ourselves, when we have thus adopted and made them our own, begin at last to affect us, and we then tremble and shudder at the thought of what he feels. For as to be in pain or distress of any kind excites the most excessive sorrow, so to conceive or to imagine that we are in it excites some degree of the same emotion, in proportion to the vivacity or dullness of the conception.

3.

That this is the source of our fellow feeling for the misery of others, that it is by changing places in fancy with the sufferer, that we come either to conceive or to be affected by what he feels may be demonstrated by many obvious observations, if it should not be thought sufficiently evident of itself. When we see a stroke aimed and just ready to fall upon the leg or arm of another person, we naturally shrink and draw back our own leg or our own arm; and when it does fall, we feel it in some measure and are hurt by it as well as the sufferer. The mob, when they are gazing at a dancer on the slack rope, naturally writhe and twist and balance their own bodies, as they see him do, and as they feel that they themselves must do if in his situation. Persons of delicate fibers and a weak constitution of body complain that in looking on the sores and ulcers that are exposed by beggars in the streets they are apt to feel an itching or uneasy sensation in the correspondent part of their own bodies. The horror that they conceive at the misery of those wretches affects that particular part in themselves more than any other; because that horror arises from conceiving what they themselves would suffer, if they really were the wretches whom they are looking upon, and if that particular part in themselves was actually affected in the same miserable manner. The very force of this conception is sufficient, in their feeble frames, to produce that itching or uneasy sensation complained of. Men of the most robust make observe that in looking upon sore eyes they often feel a very sensible soreness in their own, which proceeds from the same reason; that organ being in the strongest man more delicate than any other part of the body is in the weakest.

4.

Neither is it those circumstances only, which create pain or sorrow, that call forth our fellow feeling. Whatever is the passion that arises from any object in the person principally concerned, an analogous emotion springs up, at the thought of his situation, in the breast of every attentive spectator. Our joy for the deliverance of those heroes of tragedy or romance who interest us is as sincere as our grief for their distress, and our fellow feeling with their misery is not more real than that with their happiness. We enter into their gratitude toward those faithful friends who did not desert them in their difficulties; and we heartily go along with their resentment against those perfidious traitors who injured, abandoned, or deceived them. In every passion of which the mind of man is susceptible, the emotions of the bystander always correspond to what, by bringing the case home to himself, he imagines should be the sentiments of the sufferer.

5.

Pity and compassion are words appropriated to signify our fellow feeling with the sorrow of others. Sympathy, though its meaning was, perhaps, originally the same, may now, however, without much impropriety, be made use of to denote our fellow feeling with any passion whatever.

6.

Upon some occasions sympathy may seem to arise merely from the view of a certain emotion in another person. The passions, upon some occasions, may seem to be transfused from one man to another, instantaneously and antecedent to any knowledge of what excited them in the person principally concerned. Grief and joy, for example, strongly expressed in the look and gestures of anyone, at once affect the spectator with some degree of a like painful or agreeable emotion. A smiling face is, to everybody that sees it, a cheerful object; as a sorrowful countenance, on the other hand, is a melancholy one.

7.

This, however, does not hold universally, or with regard to every passion. There are some passions of which the expressions excite no sort of sympathy but before we are acquainted with what gave occasion to them serve rather to disgust and provoke us against them. The furious behavior of an angry man is more likely to exasperate us against himself than against his enemies. As we are unacquainted with his provocation, we cannot bring his case home to ourselves, nor conceive any thing like the passions that it excites. But we plainly see what is the situation of those with whom he is angry and to what violence they may be exposed from so enraged an adversary. We readily, therefore, sympathize with their fear or resentment and are immediately disposed to take part against the man from whom they appear to be in so much danger.

8.

If the very appearances of grief and joy inspire us with some degree of the like emotions, it is because they suggest to us the general idea of some good or bad fortune that has befallen the person in whom we observe them: and in these passions this is sufficient to have some little influence upon us. The effects of grief and joy terminate in the person who feels those emotions, of which the expressions do not, like those of resentment, suggest to us the idea of any other person for whom we are concerned and whose interests are opposite to his. The general idea of good or bad fortune, therefore, creates some concern for the person who has met with it, but the general idea of provocation excites no sympathy with the anger of the man who has received it. Nature, it seems, teaches us to be more averse to enter into this passion, and, till informed of its cause, to be disposed rather to take part against it.

9.

Even our sympathy with the grief or joy of another, before we are informed of the cause of either, is always extremely imperfect. General lamentations, which express nothing but the anguish of the sufferer, create rather a curiosity to inquire into his situation, along with some disposition to sympathize with him, than any actual sympathy that is very sensible. The first question that we ask is, what has befallen you? Till this be answered, though we are uneasy both from the vague idea of his misfortune, and still more from torturing ourselves with conjectures about what it may be, yet our fellow feeling is not very considerable.

10.

Sympathy, therefore, does not arise so much from the view of the passion as from that of the situation that excites it. We sometimes feel for another a passion of which he himself seems to be altogether incapable; because, when we put ourselves in his case, that passion arises in our breast from the imagination, though it does not in his from the reality. We blush for the impudence and rudeness of another, though he himself appears to have no sense of the impropriety of his own behavior; because we cannot help feeling with what confusion we ourselves should be covered had we behaved in so absurd a manner.

11.

Of all the calamities to which the condition of mortality exposes mankind, the loss of reason appears, to those who have the least spark of humanity, by far the most dreadful, and they behold that last stage of human wretchedness with deeper commiseration than any other. But the poor wretch, who is in it, laughs and sings perhaps, and is altogether insensible of his own misery. The anguish that humanity feels, therefore, at the sight of such an object, cannot be the reflection of any sentiment of the sufferer. The compassion of the spectator must arise altogether from the consideration of what he himself would feel if he was reduced to the same unhappy situation, and, what perhaps is impossible, was at the same time able to regard it with his present reason and judgment.

12.

What are the pangs of a mother when she hears the moanings of her infant that during the agony of disease cannot express what it feels? In her idea of what it suffers, she joins, to its real helplessness, her own consciousness of that helplessness and her own terrors for the unknown consequences of its disorder; and out of all these, forms, for her own sorrow, the most complete image of misery and distress. The infant, however, feels only the uneasiness of the present instant, which can never be great. With regard to the future, it is perfectly secure, and in its thoughtlessness and want of foresight possesses an antidote against fear and anxiety, the great tormentors of the human breast, from which reason and philosophy will, in vain, attempt to defend it when it grows up to a man.

13.

We sympathize even with the dead, and overlooking what is of real importance in their situation, that awful futurity that awaits them, we are chiefly affected by those circumstances that strike our senses but can have no influence upon their happiness. It is miserable, we think, to be deprived of the light of the sun; to be shut out from life and conversation; to be laid in the cold grave, a prey to corruption and the reptiles of the earth; to be no more thought of in this world, but to be obliterated, in a little time, from the affections, and almost from the memory, of their dearest friends and relations. Surely, we imagine, we can never feel too much for those who have suffered so dreadful a calamity. The tribute of our fellow feeling seems doubly due to them now, when they are in danger of being forgotten by everybody; and, by the vain honors that we pay to their memory, we endeavor, for our own misery, artificially to keep alive our melancholy remembrance of their misfortune. That our sympathy can afford them no consolation seems to be an addition to their calamity; and to think that all we can do is unavailing, and that what alleviates all other distress—the regret, the love, and the lamentations of their friends—can yield no comfort to them serves only to exasperate our sense of their misery. The happiness of the dead, however, most assuredly, is affected by none of these circumstances; nor is it the thought of these things that can ever disturb the profound security of their repose. The idea of that dreary and endless melancholy, which the fancy naturally ascribes to their condition, arises altogether from our joining to the change that has been produced upon them, our own consciousness of that change, from our putting ourselves in their situation, and from our lodging, if I may be allowed to say so, our own living souls in their inanimate bodies, and thence conceiving what would be our emotions in this case. It is from this very illusion of the imagination that the foresight of our own dissolution is so terrible to us and that the idea of those circumstances, which undoubtedly can give us no pain when we are dead, makes us miserable while we are alive. And from thence arises one of the most important principles in human nature, the dread of death, the great poison to the happiness, but the great restraint upon the injustice of mankind, which, while it afflicts and mortifies the individual, guards and protects the society.

Chapter 2: Of the Pleasure of Mutual Sympathy

1.

But whatever may be the cause of sympathy, or however it may be excited, nothing pleases us more than to observe in other men a fellow feeling with all the emotions of our own breast; nor are we ever so much shocked as by the appearance of the contrary. Those who are fond of deducing all our sentiments from certain refinements of self-love think themselves at no loss to account, according to their own principles, both for this pleasure and this pain. Man, say they, conscious of his own weakness, and of the need that he has for the assistance of others, rejoices whenever he observes that they adopt his own passions, because he is then assured of that assistance, and grieves whenever he observes the contrary, because he is then assured of their opposition. But both the pleasure and the pain are always felt so instantaneously, and often upon such frivolous occasions, that it seems evident that neither of them can be derived from any such self-interested consideration. A man is mortified when, after having endeavored to divert the company, he looks round and sees that nobody laughs at his jests but himself. On the contrary, the mirth of the company is highly agreeable to him, and he regards this correspondence of their sentiments with his own as the greatest applause.

2.

Neither does his pleasure seem to arise altogether from the additional vivacity that his mirth may receive from sympathy with theirs, nor his pain from the disappointment he meets with when he misses this pleasure; though both the one and the other, no doubt, do in some measure. When we have read a book or poem so often that we can no longer find any amusement in reading it by ourselves, we can still take pleasure in reading it to a companion. To him it has all the graces of novelty; we enter into the surprise and admiration that it naturally excites in him but that it is no longer capable of exciting in us; we consider all the ideas that it presents rather in the light in which they appear to him than in that in which they appear to ourselves, and we are amused by sympathy with his amusement, which thus enlivens our own. On the contrary, we should be vexed if he did not seem to be entertained with it, and we could no longer take any pleasure in reading it to him. It is the same case here. The mirth of the company, no doubt, enlivens our own mirth, and their silence, no doubt, disappoints us. But though this may contribute both to the pleasure that we derive from the one, and to the pain that we feel from the other, it is by no means the sole cause of either; and this correspondence of the sentiments of others with our own appears to be a cause of pleasure and the want of it a cause of pain, which cannot be accounted for in this manner. The sympathy, which my friends express with my joy, might, indeed, give me pleasure by enlivening that joy: but that which they express with my grief could give me none, if it served only to enliven that grief. Sympathy, however, enlivens joy and alleviates grief. It enlivens joy by presenting another source of satisfaction; and it alleviates grief by insinuating into the heart almost the only agreeable sensation that it is at that time capable of receiving.

3.

It is to be observed accordingly that we are still more anxious to communicate to our friends our disagreeable than our agreeable passions, that we derive still more satisfaction from their sympathy with the former than from that with the latter, and that we are still more shocked by the want of it.

4.

How are the unfortunate relieved when they have found out a person to whom they can communicate the cause of their sorrow? Upon his sympathy they seem to disburden themselves of a part of their distress: he is not improperly said to share it with them. He not only feels a sorrow of the same kind with that which they feel, but as if he had derived a part of it to himself, what he feels seems to alleviate the weight of what they feel. Yet by relating their misfortunes they in some measure renew their grief. They awaken in their memory the remembrance of those circumstances that occasioned their affliction. Their tears accordingly flow faster than before, and they are apt to abandon themselves to all the weakness of sorrow. They take pleasure, however, in all this, and, it is evident, are sensibly relieved by it; because the sweetness of his sympathy more than compensates the bitterness of that sorrow, which, in order to excite this sympathy, they had thus enlivened and renewed. The cruelest insult, on the contrary, that can be offered to the unfortunate is to appear to make light of their calamities. To seem not to be affected with the joy of our companions is but want of politeness; but not to wear a serious countenance when they tell us their afflictions is real and gross inhumanity.

5.

Love is an agreeable, resentment, a disagreeable, passion; and accordingly we are not half so anxious that our friends should adopt our friendships as that they should enter into our resentments. We can forgive them though they seem to be little affected with the favors that we may have received but lose all patience if they seem indifferent about the injuries that may have been done to us: nor are we half so angry with them for not entering into our gratitude as for not sympathizing with our resentment. They can easily avoid being friends to our friends but can hardly avoid being enemies to those with whom we are at variance. We seldom resent their being at enmity with the first, though upon that account we may sometimes affect to make an awkward quarrel with them; but we quarrel with them in good earnest if they live in friendship with the last. The agreeable passions of love and joy can satisfy and support the heart without any auxiliary pleasure. The bitter and painful emotions of grief and resentment more strongly require the healing consolation of sympathy.

6.

As the person who is principally interested in any event is pleased with our sympathy and hurt by the want of it, so we, too, seem to be pleased when we are able to sympathize with him and to be hurt when we are unable to do so. We run not only to congratulate the successful but to condole with the afflicted; and the pleasure that we find in the conversation of one whom in all the passions of his heart we can entirely sympathize with seems to do more than compensate the painfulness of that sorrow with which the view of his situation affects us. On the contrary, it is always disagreeable to feel that we cannot sympathize with him, and instead of being pleased with this exemption from sympathetic pain, it hurts us to find that we cannot share his uneasiness. If we hear a person loudly lamenting his misfortunes, which, however, upon bringing the case home to ourselves, we feel, can produce no such violent effect upon us, we are shocked at his grief; and, because we cannot enter into it, call it pusillanimity and weakness. It gives us the spleen, on the other hand, to see another too happy or too much elevated, as we call it, with any little piece of good fortune. We are disobliged even with his joy; and, because we cannot go along with it, call it levity and folly. We are even put out of humor if our companion laughs louder or longer at a joke than we think it deserves; that is, than we feel that we ourselves could laugh at it.

Alexis de Tocqueville

Born in Paris to an aristocratic family, Alexis de Tocqueville (1805–1859) studied law and worked briefly as a substitute judge before traveling to the United States in 1831 to study the American penal system. On his journey through eighteen states, he became fascinated with American democracy as a new kind of social order. Returning to France, he pursued á career in politics and published his observations of American society in a two-volume work titled *Democracy in America*, the first volume of which appeared in 1835. The second volume, from which this chapter is taken, was published in 1840.

Selection from *Democracy in America*

On the Use Which the Americans Make of Associations in Civil Life

I do not propose to speak of those political associations by means of which men seek to defend themselves against the despotic action of the majority or the encroachments of royal power. I have treated that subject elsewhere. It is clear that unless each citizen learned to combine with his fellows to preserve his freedom at a time when he individually is becoming weaker and so less able in isolation to defend it, tyranny would be bound to increase with equality. But here I am only concerned with those associations in civil life that have no political object.

In the United States, political associations are only one small part of the immense number of different types of associations found there.

Americans of all ages, all stations in life, and all types of disposition are forever forming associations. There are not only commercial and industrial associations in which all take part, but others of a thousand different types—religious, moral, serious, futile, very general and very limited, immensely large and very minute. Americans combine to give fetes, found seminaries, build churches, distribute books, and send missionaries to the antipodes. Hospitals, prisons, and schools take shape in that way. Finally, if they want to proclaim a truth or propagate some feeling by the encouragement of a great example, they form an association. In every case, at the head of any new undertaking, where in France you would find the government or in England some territorial magnate, in the United States you are sure to find an association.

I have come across several types of association in America of which, I confess, I had not previously the slightest conception, and I have often admired the extreme skill they show in proposing a common object for the exertions of very many and in inducing them voluntarily to pursue it.

Since that time I have traveled in England, a country from which the Americans took some of their laws and many of their customs, but it seemed to me that the principle of association was not used nearly so constantly or so adroitly there.

A single Englishman will often carry through some great undertaking, whereas Americans form associations for no matter how small a matter. Clearly the former regard association as a powerful means of action, but the latter seem to think of it as the only one.

Thus the most democratic country in the world now is that in which men have in our time carried to the highest perfection the art of pursuing in common the objects of common desires and have applied this new technique to the greatest number of purposes. Is that just an accident, or is there really some necessary connection between associations and equality?

In aristocratic societies, while there is a multitude of individuals who can do nothing on their own, there is also a small number of very rich and powerful men, each of whom can carry out great undertakings on his own.

In aristocratic societies men have no need to unite for action, since they are held firmly together.

Every rich and powerful citizen is in practice the head of a permanent and enforced association composed of all those whom he makes help in the execution of his designs.

But among democratic peoples all the citizens are independent and weak. They can do hardly anything for themselves, and none of them is in a position to force his fellows to help him. They would all therefore find themselves helpless if they did not learn to help each other voluntarily.

If the inhabitants of democratic countries had neither the right nor the taste for uniting for political objects, their independence would run great risks, but they could keep both their wealth and their knowledge for a long time. But if they did not learn some habits of acting together in the affairs of daily life, civilization itself would be in peril. A people in which individuals had lost the power of carrying through great enterprises by themselves, without acquiring the faculty of doing them together, would soon fall back into barbarism.

Unhappily, the same social conditions that render associations so necessary to democratic nations also make their formation more difficult there than elsewhere.

When several aristocrats want to form an association, they can easily do so. As each of them carries great weight in society, a very small number of associates may be enough. So, being few, it is easy to get to know and understand one another and agree on rules.

But that is not so easy in democratic nations, where, if the association is to have any power, the associates must be very numerous.

I know that many of my contemporaries are not the least embarrassed by this difficulty. They claim that as the citizens become weaker and more helpless, the government must become proportionately more skillful and active, so that society should do what is no longer possible for individuals. They think that answers the whole problem, but I think they are mistaken.

A government could take the place of some of the largest associations in America, and some particular states of the Union have already attempted that. But what political power could ever carry on the vast multitude of lesser undertakings that associations daily enable American citizens to control?

It is easy to see the time coming in which men will be less and less able to produce, by each alone, the commonest bare necessities of life. The tasks of government must therefore perpetually increase, and its efforts to cope with them must spread its net ever wider. The more government takes the place of associations, the more will individuals lose the idea of forming associations and need the government to come to their help. That is a vicious circle of cause and effect. Must the public administration cope with every industrial undertaking beyond the competence of one individual citizen? And if ultimately, as a result of the minute subdivision of landed property, the land itself is so infinitely parceled out that it can only be cultivated by associations of laborers, must the head of the government leave the helm of state to guide the plow?

The morals and intelligence of a democratic people would be in as much danger as its commerce and industry if ever a government wholly usurped the place of private associations.

Feelings and ideas are renewed, the heart enlarged, and the understanding developed only by the reciprocal action of men one upon another.

I have shown how these influences are reduced almost to nothing in democratic countries; they must therefore be artificially created, and only associations can do that.

When aristocrats adopt a new idea or conceive a new sentiment, they lend it something of the conspicuous station they themselves occupy, and so the mass is bound to take notice of them, and they easily influence the minds and hearts of all around.

In democratic countries only the governing power is naturally in a position so to act, but it is easy to see that its action is always inadequate and often dangerous.

A government, by itself, is equally incapable of refreshing the circulation of feelings and ideas among a great people, as it is of controlling every industrial undertaking. Once it leaves the sphere of politics to launch out on this new track, it will, even without intending this, exercise an intolerable tyranny. For a government can only dictate precise rules. It imposes the sentiments and ideas that it favors, and it is never easy to tell the difference between its advice and its commands.

Things will be even worse if the government supposes that its real interest is to prevent the circulation of ideas. It will then stand motionless and let the weight of its deliberate somnolence lie heavy on all.

It is therefore necessary that it should not act alone.

Among democratic peoples associations must take the place of the powerful private persons whom equality of conditions has eliminated.

As soon as several Americans have conceived a sentiment or an idea that they want to produce before the world, they seek each other out, and when found, they unite. Thenceforth they are no longer isolated individuals, but a power conspicuous from the distance whose actions serve as an example; when it speaks, men listen.

The first time that I heard in America that one hundred thousand men had publicly promised never to drink alcoholic liquor, I thought it more of a joke than a serious matter and for the moment did not see why these very abstemious citizens could not content themselves with drinking water by their own firesides.

In the end I came to understand that these hundred thousand Americans, frightened by the progress of drunkenness around them, wanted to support sobriety by their patronage. They were acting in just the same way as some great territorial magnate who dresses very plainly to encourage a contempt of luxury among simple citizens. One may fancy that if they had lived in France, each of these hundred thousand would have made individual representations to the government asking it to supervise all the public houses throughout the realm.

Nothing, in my view, more deserves attention than the intellectual and moral associations in America. American political and industrial associations easily catch our eyes, but the others tend not to be noticed. And even if we do notice them we tend to misunderstand them, hardly ever having seen anything similar before. However, we should recognize that the latter are as necessary as the former to the American people; perhaps more so.

In democratic countries knowledge of how to combine is the mother of all other forms of knowledge; on its progress depends that of all the others.

Among laws controlling human societies there is one more precise and clearer, it seems to me, than all the others. If men are to remain civilized or to become civilized, the art of association must develop and improve among them at the same speed as equality of conditions spreads.

W. E. B. Du Bois

William Edward Burghardt Du Bois (1868–1963) was born in Great Barrington, Massachusetts, and became the first African American to receive a PhD from Harvard University. He was instrumental in founding the National Association for the Advancement of Colored People in 1909, and he edited its magazine, *Crisis*, until 1934. Throughout his life, Du Bois became increasingly critical of capitalism and the United States, and in 1961, two years before his death, he moved to Ghana and joined the Communist Party. Du Bois's most famous book, *The Souls of Black Folk*, was published in 1903. Over the next fifty years he published *The Negro*, *Black Reconstruction in America*, *Color and Democracy*, and *The World and Africa*.

Selection from *The Souls of Black Folk*

I have thus far sought to make clear the physical, economic, and political relations of the Negroes and whites in the South, as I have conceived them, including, for the reasons set forth, crime and education. But after all that has been said on these more tangible matters of human contact, there still remains a part essential to a proper description of the South that it is difficult to describe or fix in terms easily understood by strangers. It is, in fine, the atmosphere of the land, the thought and feeling, the thousand and one little actions that go to make up life. In any community or nation it is these little things that are most elusive to the grasp and yet most essential to any clear conception of the group life taken as a whole. What is thus true of all communities is peculiarly true of the South, where, outside of written history and outside of printed law, there has been going on for a generation as deep a storm and stress of human souls, as intense a ferment of feeling, as intricate a writhing of spirit, as ever a people experienced. Within and without the somber veil of color vast social forces have been at work—efforts for human betterment, movements toward disintegration and despair, tragedies and comedies in social and economic life, and a swaying and lifting and sinking of human hearts that have made this land a land of mingled sorrow and joy, of change and excitement and unrest.

The center of this spiritual turmoil has ever been the millions of black freedmen and their sons, whose destiny is so fatefully bound up with that of the nation. And yet the casual observer visiting the South sees at first little of this. He notes the growing frequency of dark faces as he rides along—but otherwise the days slip lazily on, the sun shines, and this little world seems as happy and contented as other worlds he has visited. Indeed, on the question of questions—the Negro problem—he hears so little that there almost seems to be a conspiracy of silence; the morning papers seldom mention it, and then usually in a far-fetched academic way, and indeed almost everyone seems to forget and ignore the darker half of the land, until the astonished visitor is inclined to ask if after all there is any problem here. But if he lingers long enough there comes the awakening: perhaps in a sudden whirl of passion that leaves him gasping at its bitter intensity; more likely in a gradually dawning sense of things he had not at first noticed. Slowly but surely his eyes begin to catch the shadows of the color line: here he meets crowds of Negroes and whites; then he is suddenly aware that he cannot discover a single dark face; or again at the close of a day's wandering he may find himself in some strange assembly, where all faces are tinged brown or black, and where he has the vague, uncomfortable feeling of the stranger. He realizes at last that silently, resistlessly, the world about flows by him in two great streams: they ripple on in the same sunshine, they approach and mingle their waters in seeming care-lessness—then they divide and flow wide apart. It is done quietly; no mistakes are made, or if one occurs, the swift arm of the law and of public opinion swings down for a moment, as when the other day a black man and a white woman were arrested for talking together on Whitehall Street in Atlanta.

Now if one notices carefully one will see that between these two worlds, despite much physical contact and daily intermingling, there is almost no community of intellectual life or point of transference where the thoughts and feelings of one race can come into direct contact and sympathy with the thoughts and feelings of the other. Before and directly after the war, when all the best of the Negroes were domestic servants in the best of the white families, there were bonds of intimacy, affection, and sometimes blood relationship, between the races. They lived in the same home, shared in the family life, often attended the same church, and talked and conversed with one another. But the increasing civilization of the Negro since then has naturally meant the development of higher classes: there are increasing numbers of ministers, teachers, physicians, merchants, mechanics, and independent farmers, who by nature and training are the aristocracy and leaders of the blacks. Between them, however, and the best element of the whites, there is little or no intellectual commerce. They go to separate churches, they live in separate sections, they are strictly separated in all public gatherings, they travel separately, and they are beginning to read different papers and books. To most libraries, lectures, concerts, and museums, Negroes are either not admitted at all or on terms peculiarly galling to the pride of the very classes who might otherwise be attracted. The daily paper chronicles the doings of the black world from afar with no great regard for accuracy; and so on, throughout the category of means for intellectual communication—schools, conferences, efforts for social betterment, and the like—it is usually true that the very representatives of the two races, who for mutual benefit and the welfare of the land ought to be in complete under-standing and sympathy, are so far strangers that one side thinks all whites are narrow and prejudiced, and the other thinks educated Negroes dangerous and insolent. Moreover, in a land where the tyranny of public opinion and the intolerance of criticism is for obvious historical reasons so strong as in the South, such a situation is extremely difficult to correct. The white man, as well as the Negroes bound and barred by the color line, and many a scheme of friendliness and philanthropy, of broad-minded sympathy and generous fellowship between the two has dropped stillborn because some busybody has forced the color question to the front and brought the tremendous force of unwritten law against the innovators.

It is hardly necessary for me to add very much in regard to the social contact between the races. Nothing has come to replace that finer sympathy and love between some masters and house servants that the radical and more uncompro-mising drawing of the color line in recent years has caused almost completely to disappear. In a world where it means so much to take a man by the hand and sit beside him, to look frankly into his eyes and feel his heart beating with red blood; in a world where a social cigar or a cup of tea together means more than legislative halls and magazine articles and speeches—one can imagine the consequences of the almost utter absence of such social amenities between estranged races, whose separation extends even to parks and streetcars.

Here there can be none of that social going down to the people—the opening of heart and hand of the best to the worst, in generous acknowledg-ment of a common humanity and a common destiny. On the other hand, in matters of simple almsgiving, where there can be no question of social con-tact, and in the succor of the aged and sick, the South, as if stirred by a feeling of its unfortunate limitations, is generous to a fault. The black beggar is never turned away without a good deal more than a crust, and a call for help for the unfortunate meets quick response. I remember, one cold winter, in Atlanta, when I refrained from contributing to a public relief fund lest Negroes should be discriminated against, I afterward inquired of a friend: "Were any black people receiving aid?" "Why," said he, "they were *all* black."

And yet this does not touch the kernel of the problem. Human advance-ment is not a mere question of almsgiving, but rather of sympathy and coop-eration among classes who would scorn charity. And here is a land where, in the higher walks of life, in all the higher striving for the good and noble and true, the color line comes to separate natural friends and coworkers; while at the bottom of the social group, in the saloon, the gambling hell, and the brothel, that same line wavers and disappears.

I have sought to paint an average picture of real relations between the sons of master and man in the South. I have not glossed over matters for policy's sake, for I fear we have already gone too far in that sort of thing. On the other hand, I have sincerely sought to let no unfair exaggerations creep in. I do not doubt that in some Southern communities conditions are better than those I have indicated; while I am no less certain that in other communities they are far worse.

Nor does the paradox and danger of this situation fail to interest and perplex the best conscience of the South. Deeply religious and intensely democratic as are the mass of the whites, they feel acutely the false position in which the Negro problems place them. Such an essentially honest-hearted and generous people cannot cite the caste-leveling precepts of Christianity, or believe in equality of opportunity for all men, without coming to feel more and more with each generation that the present drawing of the color line is a flat contradiction to their beliefs and professions. But just as often as they come to this point, the present social condition of the Negro stands as a menace and a portent before even the most open-minded: if there were nothing to charge against the Negro but his blackness or other physical peculiarities, they argue, the problem would be comparatively simple; but what can we say to his ignorance, shiftlessness, poverty, and crime? CAN A SELF-RESPECTING GROUP HOLD ANYTHING BUT THE LEAST POSSIBLE FELLOWSHIP WITH SUCH PERSONS AND SURVIVE? AND SHALL WE LET A MAWKISH SENTIMENT SWEEP AWAY THE CULTURE OF OUR FATHERS OR THE HOPE OF OUR CHILDREN? The argument so put is of great strength, but it is not a whit stronger than the argument of thinking Negroes: granted, they reply, that the condition of our masses is bad; there is certainly on the one hand adequate historical cause for this, and unmistakable evidence that no small number have, in spite of tremendous disadvantages, risen to the level of American civilization. And when, by proscription and prejudice, these same Negroes are classed with and treated like the lowest of their people, simply *because* they are Negroes, such a policy not only discourages thrift and intelligence among black men but puts a direct premium on the very things you complain of—inefficiency and crime. Draw lines of crime, of incompetency, of vice, as tightly and uncompromisingly as you will, for these things must be proscribed; but a color line not only does not accomplish this purpose but thwarts it.

In the face of two such arguments, the future of the South depends on the ability of the representatives of these opposing views to see and appreciate and sympathize with each other's position—for the Negro to realize more deeply than he does at present the need of uplifting the masses of his people, for the white people to realize more vividly than they have yet done the deadening and disastrous effect of a color prejudice that classes Phillis Wheatley and Sam Hose in the same despised class.

It is not enough for the Negroes to declare that color prejudice is the sole cause of their social condition, nor for the white South to reply that their social condition is the main cause of prejudice. They both act as reciprocal cause and effect, and a change in neither alone will bring the desired effect. Both must change, or neither can improve to any great extent. The Negro cannot stand the present reactionary tendencies and unreasoning drawing of the color line indefinitely without discouragement and retrogression. And the condition of the Negro is ever the excuse for further discrimination. Only by a union of intelligence and sympathy across the color line in this critical period of the republic shall justice and right triumph,

> "That mind and soul according well,
> May make one music as before,
> But vaster."

Langston Hughes

Born in Joplin, Missouri, Langston Hughes (1902–1967) grew up in Lawrence, Kansas, and Cleveland, Ohio. By the time he entered Columbia University in 1921, Hughes had begun to make a name for himself as a poet. After leaving Columbia to work on ships and his writing, Hughes graduated from Lincoln University in Pennsylvania. He became one of the leading figures in the Harlem Renaissance and in the African American literary tradition more generally, publishing fiction, drama, journalism, autobiography, translation, and poetry. "Theme for English B" was first published in 1951.

Theme for English B

The instructor said,

> *Go home and write*
> *a page tonight.*
> *And let that page come out of you—*
> *Then, it will be true.*

I wonder if it's that simple?
I am twenty-two, colored, born in Winston-Salem.
I went to school there, then Durham, then here
to this college on the hill above Harlem.
I am the only colored student in my class.
The steps from the hill lead down into Harlem,
through a park, then I cross St. Nicholas,
Eighth Avenue, Seventh, and I come to the Y,
the Harlem Branch Y, where I take the elevator
up to my room, sit down, and write this page:

It's not easy to know what is true for you or me
at twenty-two, my age. But I guess I'm what
I feel and see and hear, Harlem, I hear you:
hear you, hear me—we two—you, me, talk on this page.
(I hear New York, too.) Me—who?
Well, I like to eat, sleep, drink, and be in love.
I like to work, read, learn, and understand life.
I like a pipe for a Christmas present,
or records—Bessie, bop, or Bach.
I guess being colored doesn't make me *not* like
the same things other folks like who are other races.
So will my page be colored that I write?

Being me, it will not be white.
But it will be
a part of you, instructor.
You are white—
yet a part of me, as I am a part of you.
That's American.
Sometimes perhaps you don't want to be a part of me.
Nor do I often want to be a part of you.
But we are, that's true!
As I learn from you,
I guess you learn from me—
although you're older—and white—
and somewhat more free.

This is my page for English B.

Toni Morrison

Born in Lorain, Ohio, Toni Morrison (b. 1931) is the daughter of working-class African American parents who migrated from the South. She graduated from Howard University and received a master's degree from Cornell University. She has published many widely successful novels, including *The Bluest Eye, Sula, Song of Solomon, Tar Baby, Beloved, Jazz,* and *Love.* Morrison was awarded the Nobel Prize for literature in 1993. "Recitatif," Morrison's only published short story, first appeared in the anthology *Confirmation.*

Recitatif

My mother danced all night and Roberta's was sick. That's why we were taken to St. Bonny's. People want to put their arms around you when you tell them you were in a shelter, but it really wasn't bad. No big long room with one hundred beds like Bellevue. There were four to a room, and when Roberta and me came, there was a shortage of state kids, so we were the only ones assigned to 406 and could go from bed to bed if we wanted to. And we wanted to, too. We changed beds every night and for the whole four months we were there we never picked one out as our own permanent bed.

It didn't start out that way. The minute I walked in and the Big Bozo introduced us, I got sick to my stomach. It was one thing to be taken out of your own bed early in the morning—it was something else to be stuck in a strange place with a girl from a whole other race. And Mary, that's my mother, she was right. Every now and then she would stop dancing long enough to tell me something important and one of the things she said was that they never washed their hair and they smelled funny. Roberta sure did. Smell funny, I mean. So when the Big Bozo (nobody ever called her Mrs. Itkin, just like nobody ever said St. Bonaventure)—when she said, "Twyla, this is Roberta. Roberta, this is Twyla. Make each other welcome," I said, "My mother won't like you putting me in here."

"Good," said Bozo. "Maybe then she'll come and take you home."

How's that for mean? If Roberta had laughed I would have killed her, but she didn't. She just walked over to the window and stood with her back to us.

"Turn around," said the Bozo. "Don't be rude. Now Twyla. Roberta. When you hear a loud buzzer, that's the call for dinner. Come down to the first floor. Any fights and no movie." And then, just to make sure we knew what we would be missing, "*The Wizard of Oz*."

Roberta must have thought I meant that my mother would be mad about my being put in the shelter. Not about rooming with her, because as soon as Bozo left she came over to me and said, "Is your mother sick too?"

"No," I said. "She just likes to dance all night."

"Oh." She nodded her head and I liked the way she understood things so fast. So for the moment it didn't matter that we looked like salt and pepper standing there and that's what the other kids called us sometimes. We were eight years old and got Fs all the time. Me because I couldn't remember what I read or what the teacher said. And Roberta because she couldn't read at all and didn't even listen to the teacher. She wasn't good at anything except jacks, at which she was a killer: pow scoop pow scoop pow scoop.

We didn't like each other all that much at first, but nobody else wanted to play with us because we weren't real orphans with beautiful dead parents in the sky. We were dumped. Even the New York City Puerto Ricans and the upstate Indians ignored us. All kinds of kids were in there, black ones, white ones, even two Koreans. The food was good, though. At least I thought so. Roberta hated it and left whole pieces of things on her plate: Spam, Salisbury steak—even Jell-O with fruit cocktail in it, and she didn't care if I ate what she wouldn't. Mary's idea of supper was popcorn and a can of Yoo-Hoo. Hot mashed potatoes and two weenies was like Thanksgiving for me.

It really wasn't bad, St. Bonny's. The big girls on the second floor pushed us around now and then. But that was all. They wore lipstick and eyebrow pencil and wobbled their knees while they watched TV. Fifteen, sixteen, even, some of them were. They were put-out girls, scared runaways most of them. Poor little girls who fought their uncles off but looked tough to us, and mean. God, did they look mean. The staff tried to keep them separate from the younger children, but sometimes they caught us watching them in the orchard where they played radios and danced with each other. They'd light out after us and pull our hair or twist our arms. We were scared of them, Roberta and me, but neither of us wanted the other one to know it. So we got a good list of dirty names we could shout back when we ran from them through the orchard. I used to dream a lot and almost always the orchard was there. Two acres, four maybe, of these little apple trees. Hundreds of them. Empty and crooked like beggar women when I first came to St. Bonny's but fat with flowers when I left. I don't know why I dreamt about that orchard so much. Nothing really happened there. Nothing all that important, I mean. Just the big girls dancing and playing the radio. Roberta and me watching. Maggie fell down there once. The kitchen woman with legs like parentheses. And the big girls laughed at her. We should have helped her up, I know, but we were scared of those girls with lipstick and eyebrow pencil. Maggie couldn't talk. The kids said she had her tongue cut out, but I think she was just born that way: mute. She was old and sandy colored and she worked in the kitchen. I don't know if she was nice or not. I just remember her legs like parentheses and how she rocked when she walked. She worked from early in the morning till two o'clock, and if she was late, if she had too much cleaning and didn't get out till two-fifteen or so, she'd cut through the orchard so she wouldn't miss her bus and have to wait another hour. She wore this really stupid little hat—a kid's hat with ear flaps—and she wasn't much taller than we were. A really awful little hat. Even for a mute, it was dumb—dressing like a kid and never saying anything at all.

"But what about if somebody tries to kill her?" I used to wonder about that. "Or what if she wants to cry? Can she cry?"

"Sure," Roberta said. "But just tears. No sounds come out."

"She can't scream?"

"Nope. Nothing."

"Can she hear?"

"I guess."

"Let's call her," I said. And we did.

"Dummy! Dummy!" She never turned her head.

"Bowlegs! Bowlegs!" Nothing. She just rocked on, the chin straps of her baby-boy hat swaying from side to side. I think we were wrong. I think she could hear and didn't let on. And it shames me even now to think there was somebody in there after all who heard us call her those names and couldn't tell on us.

We got along all right, Roberta and me. Changed beds every night, got Fs in civics and communication skills and gym. The Bozo was disappointed in us, she said. Out of 130 of us state cases, 90 were under twelve. Almost all were real orphans with beautiful dead parents in the sky. We were the only ones dumped and the only ones with Fs in three classes including gym. So we got along—what with her leaving whole pieces of things on her plate and being nice about not asking questions.

I think it was the day before Maggie fell down that we found out our mothers were coming to visit us on the same Sunday. We had been at the shelter twenty-eight days (Roberta twenty-eight and a half) and this was their first visit with us. Our mothers would come at ten o'clock in time for chapel, then lunch with us in the teachers' lounge. I thought if my dancing mother met her sick mother it might be good for her. And Roberta thought her sick mother would get a big bang out of a dancing one. We got excited about it and curled each other's hair. After breakfast we sat on the bed watching the road from the window. Roberta's socks were still wet. She washed them the night before and put them on the radiator to dry. They hadn't, but she put them on anyway because their tops were so pretty—scalloped in pink. Each of us had a purple construction-paper basket that we had made in craft class. Mine had a yellow crayon rabbit on it. Roberta's had eggs with wiggly lines of color. Inside were cellophane grass and just the jellybeans because I'd eaten the two marshmallow eggs they gave us. The Big Bozo came herself to get us. Smiling, she told us we looked very nice and to come downstairs. We were so surprised by the smile we'd never seen before, neither of us moved.

"Don't you want to see your mommies?"

I stood up first and spilled the jellybeans all over the floor. Bozo's smile disappeared while we scrambled to get the candy up off the floor and put it back in the grass.

She escorted us downstairs to the first floor, where the other girls were lining up to file into the chapel. A bunch of grown-ups stood to one side. Viewers mostly. The old biddies who wanted servants and the fags who wanted company looking for children they might want to adopt. Once in a while a grandmother. Almost never anybody young or anybody whose face wouldn't scare you in the night. Because if any of the real orphans had young relatives they wouldn't be real orphans. I saw Mary right away. She had on those green slacks I hated and hated even more now because didn't she know we were going to chapel? And that fur jacket with the pocket linings so ripped she had to pull to get her hands out of them. But her face was pretty—like always—and she smiled and waved like she was the little girl looking for her mother, not me.

I walked slowly, trying not to drop the jelly beans and hoping the paper handle would hold. I had to use my last Chiclet because by the time I finished cutting everything out, all the Elmer's was gone. I am left-handed and the scissors never worked for me. It didn't matter, though; I might just as well have chewed the gum. Mary dropped to her knees and grabbed me, mashing the basket, the jelly beans, and the grass into her ratty fur jacket.

"Twyla, baby. Twyla, baby!"

I could have killed her. Already I heard the big girls in the orchard the next time saying, "Twyyyyyla, baby!" But I couldn't stay mad at Mary while she was smiling and hugging me and smelling of Lady Esther dusting powder. I wanted to stay buried in her fur all day.

To tell the truth I forgot about Roberta. Mary and I got in line for the traipse into chapel and I was feeling proud because she looked so beautiful even in those ugly green slacks that made her behind stick out. A pretty mother on earth is better than a beautiful dead one in the sky even if she did leave you all alone to go dancing.

I felt a tap on my shoulder, turned, and saw Roberta smiling. I smiled back, but not too much lest somebody think this visit was the biggest thing that ever happened in my life. Then Roberta said, "Mother, I want you to meet my roommate, Twyla. And that's Twyla's mother."

I looked up it seemed for miles. She was big. Bigger than any man and on her chest was the biggest cross I'd ever seen. I swear it was six inches long each way. And in the crook of her arm was the biggest Bible ever made.

Mary, simpleminded as ever, grinned and tried to yank her hand out of the pocket with the raggedy lining—to shake hands, I guess. Roberta's mother looked down at me and then looked down at Mary too. She didn't say anything, just grabbed Roberta with her Bible-free hand and stepped out of line, walking quickly to the rear of it. Mary was still grinning because she's not too swift when it comes to what's really going on. Then this light bulb goes off in her head and she says "That bitch!" really loud and us almost in the chapel now. Organ music whining; the Bonny Angels singing sweetly. Everybody in the world turned around to look. And Mary would have kept it up—kept calling names if I hadn't squeezed her hands as hard as I could. That helped a little, but she still twitched and crossed and uncrossed her legs all through service. Even groaned a couple of times. Why did I think she would come there and act right? Slacks. No hat like the grandmothers and viewers, and groaning all the while. When we stood for hymns she kept her mouth shut. Wouldn't even look at the words on the page. She actually reached in her purse for a mirror to check her lipstick. All I could think of was that she really needed to be killed. The sermon lasted a year, and I knew the real orphans were looking smug again.

We were supposed to have lunch in the teachers' lounge, but Mary didn't bring anything, so we picked fur and cellophane grass off the mashed jelly beans and ate them. I could have killed her. I sneaked a look at Roberta. Her mother had brought chicken legs and ham sandwiches and oranges and a whole box of chocolate-covered grahams. Roberta drank milk from a thermos while her mother read the Bible to her.

Things are not right. The wrong food is always with the wrong people. Maybe that's why I got into waitress work later—to match up the right people with the right food. Roberta just let those chicken legs sit there, but she did bring a stack of grahams up to me later when the visit was over. I think she was sorry that her mother would not shake my mother's hand. And I liked that and I liked the fact that she didn't say a word about Mary groaning all the way through the service and not bringing any lunch.

Roberta left in May when the apple trees were heavy and white. On her last day we went to the orchard to watch the big girls smoke and dance by the radio. It didn't matter that they said, "Twyyyyyla, baby." We sat on the ground and breathed. Lady Esther. Apple blossoms. I still go soft when I smell one or the other. Roberta was going home. The big cross and the big Bible was coming to get her and she seemed sort of glad and sort of not. I thought I would die in that room of four beds without her and I knew Bozo had plans to move some other dumped kid in there with me. Roberta promised to write every day, which was really sweet of her because she couldn't read a lick so how could she write anybody? I would have drawn pictures and sent them to her but she never gave me her address. Little by little she faded. Her wet socks with the pink scalloped tops and her big serious-looking eyes—that's all I could catch when I tried to bring her to mind.

I was working behind the counter at the Howard Johnson's on the Thruway just before the Kingston exit. Not a bad job. Kind of a long ride from Newburgh, but okay once I got there. Mine was the second night shift, eleven to seven. Very light until a Greyhound checked in for breakfast around six-thirty. At that hour the sun was all the way clear of the hills behind the restaurant. The place looked better at night—more like shelter—but I loved it when the sun broke in, even if it did show all the cracks in the vinyl and the speckled floor looked dirty no matter what the mop boy did.

It was August and a bus crowd was just unloading. They would stand around a long while: going to the john, and looking at gifts and junk-for-sale machines, reluctant to sit down so soon. Even to eat. I was trying to fill the coffeepots and get them all situated on the electric burners when I saw her. She was sitting in a booth smoking a cigarette with two guys smothered in head and facial hair. Her own hair was so big and wild I could hardly see her face. But the eyes. I would know them anywhere. She had on a powder-blue halter and shorts outfit and earrings the size of bracelets. Talk about lipstick and eyebrow pencil. She made the big girls look like nuns. I couldn't get off the counter until seven o'clock, but I kept watching the booth in case they got up to leave before that. My replacement was on time for a change, so I counted and stacked my receipts as fast as I could and signed off. I walked over to the booth, smiling and wondering if she would remember me. Or even if she wanted to remember me. Maybe she didn't want to be reminded of St. Bonny's or to have anybody know she was ever there. I know I never talked about it to anybody.

I put my hands in my apron pockets and leaned against the back of the booth facing them.

"Roberta? Roberta Fisk?"

She looked up, "Yeah?"

"Twyla."

She squinted for a second and then said, "Wow."

"Remember me?"

"Sure. Hey. Wow."

"It's been a while," I said, and gave a smile to the two hairy guys.

"Yeah. Wow. You work here?"

"Yeah," I said. "I live in Newburgh."

"Newburgh? No kidding?" She laughed then, a private laugh that included the guys but only the guys, and they laughed with her. What could I do but laugh too and wonder why I was standing there with my knees showing out from under that uniform. Without looking I could see the blue-and-white triangle on my head, my hair shapeless in a net, my ankles thick in white oxfords. Nothing could have been less sheer than my stockings. There was this silence that came down right after I laughed. A silence it was her turn to fill up. With introductions, maybe, to her boyfriends or an invitation to sit down and have a Coke. Instead she lit a cigarette off the one she'd just finished and said, "We're on our way to the Coast. He's got an appointment with Hendrix." She gestured casually toward the boy next to her.

"Hendrix? Fantastic," I said. "Really fantastic. What's she doing now?"

Roberta coughed on her cigarette and the two guys rolled their eyes up at the ceiling.

"Hendrix. Jimi Hendrix, asshole. He's only the biggest—Oh, wow. Forget it."

I was dismissed without anyone saying good-bye, so I thought I would do it for her.

"How's your mother?" I asked. Her grin cracked her whole face. She swallowed. "Fine," she said. "How's yours?"

"Pretty as a picture," I said and turned away. The backs of my knees were damp. Howard Johnson's really was a dump in the sunlight.

James is as comfortable as a house slipper. He liked my cooking and I liked his big loud family. They have lived in Newburgh all of their lives and talk about it the way people do who have always known a home. His grandmother has a porch swing older than his father and when they talk about streets and avenues and buildings they call them names they no longer have. They still call the A&P Rico's because it stands on property, once a mom-and-pop store owned by Mr. Rico. And they call the new community college Town Hall because it once was. My mother-in-law puts up jelly and cucumbers and buys butter wrapped in cloth from a dairy. James and his father talk about fishing and baseball and I can see them all together on the Hudson in a raggedy skiff. Half the population of Newburgh is on welfare now, but to my husband's family it was still some upstate paradise of a time long past. A time of ice-houses and vegetable wagons, coal furnaces and children weeding gardens. When our son was born my mother-in-law gave me the crib blanket that had been hers.

But the town they remembered had changed. Something quick was in the air. Magnificent old houses, so ruined they had become shelter for squatters and rent risks, were bought and renovated. Smart IBM people moved out of their suburbs back into the city and put shutters up and herb gardens in their backyards. A brochure came in the mail announcing the opening of a Food Emporium. Gourmet food, it said—and listed items the rich IBM crowd would want. It was located in a new mall at the edge of town and I drove out to shop there one day—just to see. It was late in June. After the tulips were gone and the Queen Elizabeth roses were open everywhere. I trailed my cart along the aisle tossing in smoked oysters and Robert's sauce and things I knew would sit in my cupboard for years. Only when I found some Klondike ice cream bars did I feel less guilty about spending James's fireman's salary so foolishly. My father-in-law ate them with the same gusto little Joseph did.

Waiting in the checkout line I heard a voice say, "Twyla!"

The classical music piped over the aisles had affected me and the woman leaning toward me was dressed to kill. Diamonds on her hand, a smart white summer dress. "I'm Mrs. Benson," I said.

"Ho. Ho. The Big Bozo," she sang.

For a split second I didn't know what she was talking about. She had a bunch of asparagus and two cartons of fancy water.

"Roberta!"

"Right."

"For heaven's sake. Roberta."

"You look great," she said.

"So do you. Where are you? Here? In Newburgh?"

"Yes. Over in Annandale."

I was opening my mouth to say more when the cashier called my attention to her empty counter.

"Meet you outside." Roberta pointed her finger and went into the express line.

I placed the groceries and kept myself from glancing around to check Roberta's progress. I remembered Howard Johnson's and looking for a chance to speak only to be greeted with a stingy "wow." But she was waiting for me and her huge hair was sleek now, smooth around a small, nicely shaped head. Shoes, dress, everything lovely and summery and rich. I was dying to know what happened to her, how she got from Jimi Hendrix to Annandale, a neighborhood full of doctors and IBM executives. Easy, I thought. Everything is so easy for them. They think they own the world.

"How long," I asked her. "How long have you been here?"

"A year. I got married to a man who lives here. And you, you're married too, right? Benson, you said."

"Yeah. James Benson."

"And is he nice?"

"Oh, is he nice?"

"Well, is he?" Roberta's eyes were steady as though she really meant the question and wanted an answer.

"He's wonderful, Roberta. Wonderful."

"So you're happy."

"Very."

"That's good," she said and nodded her head. "I always hoped you'd be happy. Any kids? I know you have kids."

"One. A boy. How about you?"

"Four."

"Four?"

She laughed. "Stepkids. He's a widower."

"Oh."

"Got a minute? Let's have a coffee."

I thought about the Klondikes melting and the inconvenience of going all the way to my car and putting the bags in the trunk. Served me right for buying all that stuff I didn't need. Roberta was ahead of me.

"Put them in my car. It's right here."

And then I saw the dark blue limousine.

"You married a Chinaman?"

"No." She laughed. "He's the driver."

"Oh, my. If the Big Bozo could see you now."

We both giggled. Really giggled. Suddenly, in just a pulse beat, twenty years disappeared and all of it came rushing back. The big girls (whom we called gar girls—Roberta's misheard word for the evil stone faces described in a civics class) there dancing in the orchard, the ploppy mashed potatoes, the double weenies, the Spam with pineapple. We went into the coffee shop holding on to one another and I tried to think why we were glad to see each other this time and not before. Once, twelve years ago, we passed like strangers. A black girl and a white girl meeting in a Howard Johnson's on the road and having nothing to say. One in a blue-and-white triangle waitress hat, the other on her way to see Hendrix. Now we were behaving like sisters separated for much too long. Those four short months were nothing in time. Maybe it was the thing itself, just being there, together. Two little girls who knew what nobody else in the world knew—how not to ask questions. How to believe what had to be believed. There was politeness in that reluctance and generosity as well. Is your mother sick too? No, she dances all night. Oh—and an understanding nod.

We sat in a booth by the window and fell into recollection like veterans.

"Did you ever learn to read?"

"Watch." She picked up the menu. "Special of the day. Cream of corn soup. Entrées. Two dots and a wriggly line. Quiche. Chef salad, scallops. . . ."

I was laughing and applauding when the waitress came up.

"Remember the Easter baskets?"

"And how we tried to *introduce* them?"

"Your mother with that cross like two telephone poles."

"And yours with those tight slacks."

We laughed so loudly heads turned and made the laughter hard to suppress.

"What happened to the Jimi Hendrix date?"

Roberta made a blow-out sound with her lips.

"When he died I thought about you."

"Oh, you heard about him finally?"

"Finally. Come on, I was a small-town country waitress."

"And I was a small-town country dropout. God, were we wild. I still don't know how I got out of there alive."

"But you did."

"I did. I really did. Now I'm Mrs. Kenneth Norton."

"Sounds like a mouthful."

"It is."

"Servants and all?"

Roberta held up two fingers.

"Ow! What does he do?"

"Computers and stuff. What do I know?"

"I don't remember a hell of a lot from those days, but Lord, St. Bonny's is as clear as daylight. Remember Maggie? The day she fell down and those gar girls laughed at her?"

Roberta looked up from her salad and stared at me. "Maggie didn't fall," she said.

"Yes, she did. You remember."

"No, Twyla. They knocked her down. Those girls pushed her down and tore her clothes. In the orchard."

"I don't—that's not what happened."

"Sure it is. In the orchard. Remember how scared we were?"

"Wait a minute. I don't remember any of that."

"And Bozo was fired."

"You're crazy. She was there when I left. You left before me."

"I went back. You weren't there when they fired Bozo."

"What?"

"Twice. Once for a year when I was about ten, another for two months when I was fourteen. That's when I ran away."

"You ran away from St. Bonny's?"

"I had to. What do you want? Me dancing in that orchard?"

"Are you sure about Maggie?"

"Of course I'm sure. You've blocked it, Twyla. It happened. Those girls had behavior problems, you know."

"Didn't they, though. But why can't I remember the Maggie thing?"

"Believe me. It happened. And we were there."

"Who did you room with when you went back?" I asked her as if I would know her. The Maggie thing was troubling me.

"Creeps. They tickled themselves in the night."

My ears were itching and I wanted to go home suddenly. This was all very well but she couldn't just comb her hair, wash her face, and pretend everything was hunky-dory. After the Howard Johnson's snub. And no apology. Nothing.

"Were you on dope or what that time at Howard Johnson's?" I tried to make my voice sound friendlier than I felt.

"Maybe, a little. I never did drugs much. Why?"

"I don't know, you acted sort of like you didn't want to know me then."

"Oh, Twyla, you know how it was in those days: black—white. You know how everything was."

But I didn't know. I thought it was just the opposite. Busloads of blacks and whites came into Howard Johnson's together. They roamed together then: students, musicians, lovers, protesters. You got to see everything at Howard Johnson's, and blacks were very friendly with whites in those days. But sitting there with nothing on my plate but two hard tomato wedges wondering about the melting Klondikes it seemed childish remembering the slight. We went to her car and, with the help of the driver, got my stuff into my station wagon.

"We'll keep in touch this time," she said.

"Sure," I said, "Sure. Give me a call."

"I will," she said, and then, just as I was sliding behind the wheel, she leaned into the window. "By the way. Your mother. Did she ever stop dancing?"

I shook my head. "No. Never."

Roberta nodded.

"And yours? Did she ever get well?"

She smiled a tiny sad smile. "No. She never did. Look, call me, okay?"

"Okay," I said, but I knew I wouldn't. Roberta had messed up my past somehow with that business about Maggie. I wouldn't forget a thing like that. Would I?

Strife came to us that fall. At least that's what the paper called it. Strife. Racial strife. The word made me think of a bird—a big shrieking bird out of 1,000,000,000 BC. Flapping its wings and cawing. Its eye with no lid always bearing down on you. All day it screeched and at night it slept on the rooftops. It woke you in the morning, and from the *Today* show to the eleven o'clock news it kept you an awful company. I couldn't figure it out from one day to the next. I knew I was supposed to feel something strong, but I didn't know what, and James wasn't any help. Joseph was on the list of kids to be transferred from the junior high school to another one at some far-out-of-the-way place and I thought it was a good thing until I heard it was a bad thing. I mean I didn't know. All the schools seemed dumps to me, and the fact that one was nicer looking didn't hold much weight. But the papers were full of it and then the kids began to get jumpy. In August, mind you. Schools weren't even open yet. I thought Joseph might be frightened to go over there, but he didn't seem scared so I forgot about it, until I found myself driving along Hudson Street out there by the school they were trying to integrate and saw a line of women marching. And who do you suppose was in line, big as life, holding a sign in front of her bigger than her mother's cross? MOTHERS HAVE RIGHTS TOO! it said.

I drove on and then changed my mind. I circled the block, slowed down, and honked my horn.

Roberta looked over and when she saw me she waved. I didn't wave back, but I didn't move either. She handed her sign to another woman and came over to where I was parked.

"Hi."

"What are you doing?"

"Picketing. What's it look like?"

"What for?"

"What do you mean, 'What for?' They want to take my kids and send them out of the neighborhood. They don't want to go."

"So what if they go to another school? My boy's being bused too, and I don't mind. Why should you?"

"It's not about us, Twyla. Me and you. It's about our kids."

"What's more *us* than that?"

"Well, it is a free country."

"Not yet, but it will be."

"What the hell does that mean? I'm not doing anything to you."

"You really think that?"

"I know it."

"I wonder what made me think you were different."

"I wonder what made me think you were different."

"Look at them," I said. "Just look. Who do they think they are? Swarming all over the place like they own it. And now they think they can decide where my child goes to school. Look at them, Roberta. They're Bozos."

Roberta turned around and looked at the women. Almost all of them were standing still now, waiting. Some were even edging toward us. Roberta looked at me out of some refrigerator behind her eyes. "No, they're not. They're just mothers."

"And what am I? Swiss cheese?"

"I used to curl your hair."

"I hated your hands in my hair."

The women were moving. Our faces looked mean to them of course and they looked as though they could not wait to throw themselves in front of a police car or, better yet, into my car and drag me away by my ankles. Now they surrounded my car and gently, gently began to rock it. I swayed back and forth like a sideways yo-yo. Automatically I reached for Roberta, like the old days in the orchard, when they saw us watching them and we had to get out of there, and if one of us fell the other pulled her up and if one of us was caught the other stayed to kick and scratch, and neither would leave the other behind. My arm shot out of the car window but no receiving hand was there. Roberta was looking at me sway from side to side in the car and her face was still. My purse slid from the car seat down under the dashboard. The four policemen who had been drinking Tab in their car finally got the message and strolled over, forcing their way through the women. Quietly, firmly they spoke. "Okay, ladies. Back in line or off the streets."

Some of them went away willingly; others had to be urged away from the car doors and the hood. Roberta didn't move. She was looking steadily at me. I was fumbling to turn on the ignition, which wouldn't catch because the gearshift was still in drive. The seats of the car were a mess because the swaying had thrown my grocery coupons all over and my purse was sprawled on the floor.

"Maybe I am different now, Twyla. But you're not. You're the same little state kid who kicked a poor old black lady when she was down on the ground. You kicked a black lady and you have the nerve to call me a bigot."

The coupons were everywhere and the guts of my purse were bunched under the dashboard. What was she saying? Black? Maggie wasn't black.

"She wasn't black," I said.

"Like hell she wasn't, and you kicked her. We both did. You kicked a black lady who couldn't even scream."

"Liar!"

"You're the liar! Why don't you just go on home and leave us alone, huh?"

She turned away and I skidded away from the curb.

The next morning I went into the garage and cut the side out of the carton our portable TV had come in. It wasn't nearly big enough, but after a while I had a decent sign: red spray-painted letters on a white background—AND SO DO CHILDREN****. I meant just to go down to the school and tack it up somewhere so those cows on the picket line across the street could see it, but when I got there, some ten or so others had already assembled—protesting the cows across the street. Police permits and everything. I got in line and we strutted in time on our side while Roberta's group strutted on theirs. That first day we were all dignified, pretending the other side didn't exist. The second day there was name calling and finger gestures. But that was about all. People changed signs from time to time, but Roberta never did and neither did I. Actually my sign didn't make sense without Roberta's. "And so do children what?" one of the women on my side asked me. Have rights, I said, as though it was obvious.

Roberta didn't acknowledge my presence in any way, and I got to thinking maybe she didn't know I was there. I began to pace myself in the line, jostling people one minute and lagging behind the next, so Roberta and I could reach the end of our respective lines at the same time and there would be a moment in our turn when we would face each other. Still, I couldn't tell whether she saw me and knew my sign was for her. The next day I went early before we were scheduled to assemble. I waited until she got there before I exposed my new creation. As soon as she hoisted her MOTHERS HAVE RIGHTS TOO! I began to wave my new one, which said, HOW WOULD YOU KNOW? I know she saw that one, but I had gotten addicted now. My signs got crazier each day, and the women on my side decided that I was a kook. They couldn't make heads or tails out of my brilliant screaming posters.

I brought a painted sign in queenly red with huge black letters that said, IS YOUR MOTHER WELL? Roberta took her lunch break and didn't come back for the rest of the day or any day after. Two days later I stopped going too and couldn't have been missed because nobody understood my signs anyway.

It was a nasty six weeks. Classes were suspended and Joseph didn't go to anybody's school until October. The children—everybody's children—soon got bored with that extended vacation they thought was going to be so great. They looked at TV until their eyes flattened. I spent a couple of mornings tutoring my son, as the other mothers said we should. Twice I opened a text from last year that he had never turned in. Twice he yawned in my face. Other mothers organized living room sessions so the kids would keep up. None of the kids could concentrate, so they drifted back to *The Price Is Right* and *The Brady Bunch*. When the school finally opened there were fights once or twice and some sirens roared through the streets every once in a while. There were a lot of photographers from Albany. And just when ABC was about to send up a news crew, the kids settled down like nothing in the world had happened. Joseph hung my HOW WOULD YOU KNOW? sign in his bedroom. I don't know what became of AND SO DO CHILDREN****. I think my father-in-law cleaned some fish on it. He was always puttering around in our garage. Each of his five children lived in Newburgh, and he acted as though he had five extra homes.

I couldn't help looking for Roberta when Joseph graduated from high school, but I didn't see her. It didn't trouble me much what she had said to me in the car. I mean the kicking part. I know I didn't do that; I couldn't do that. But I was puzzled by her telling me Maggie was black. When I thought about it I actually couldn't be certain. She wasn't pitch-black, I knew, or I would have remembered that. What I remember was the kiddie hat and the semicircle legs. I tried to reassure myself about the race thing for a long time until it dawned on me that the truth was already there, and Roberta knew it. I didn't kick her; I didn't join in with the gar girls and kick that lady, but I sure did want to. We watched and never tried to help her and never called for help. Maggie was my dancing mother. Deaf, I thought, and dumb. Nobody inside. Nobody who would hear you if you cried in the night. Nobody who could tell you anything important that you could use. Rocking, dancing, swaying as she walked. And when the gar girls pushed her down and started roughhousing, I knew she wouldn't scream, couldn't—just like me—and I was glad about that.

We decided not to have a tree, because Christmas would be at my mother-in-law's house, so why have a tree at both places? Joseph was at SUNY New Paltz and we had to economize, we said. But at the last minute, I changed my mind. Nothing could be that bad. So I rushed around town looking for a tree, something small but wide. By the time I found a place, it was snowing and very late. I dawdled like it was the most important purchase in the world and the tree man was fed up with me. Finally I chose one and had it tied onto the trunk of the car. I drove away slowly because the sand trucks were not out yet and the streets could be murder at the beginning of a snowfall. Downtown the streets were wide and rather empty except for a cluster of people coming out of the Newburgh Hotel. The one hotel in town that wasn't built out of cardboard and Plexiglas. A party, probably. The men huddled in the snow were dressed in tails and the women had on furs. Shiny things glittered from underneath their coats. It made me tired to look at them. Tired, tired, tired. On the next corner was a small diner with loops and loops of paper bells in the window. I stopped the car and went in. Just for a cup of coffee and twenty minutes of peace before I went home and tried to finish everything before Christmas Eve.
    "Twyla?"
    There she was. In a silvery evening gown and dark fur coat. A man and another woman were with her, the man fumbling for change to put in the cigarette machine. The woman was humming and tapping on the counter with her fingernails. They all looked a little bit drunk.
    "Well. It's you."
    "How are you?"
    I shrugged. "Pretty good. Frazzled. Christmas and all."
    "Regular?" called the woman from the counter.
    "Fine," Roberta called back and then, "Wait for me in the car."
    She slipped into the booth beside me. "I have to tell you something, Twyla. I made up my mind if I ever saw you again, I'd tell you."
    "I'd just as soon not hear anything, Roberta. It doesn't matter now, anyway."
    "No," she said. "Not about that."
    "Don't be long," said the woman. She carried two regulars to go and the man peeled his cigarette pack as they left.
    "It's about St. Bonny's and Maggie."

"Oh, please."

"Listen to me. I really did think she was black. I didn't make that up. I really thought so. But now I can't be sure. I just remember her as old, so old. And because she couldn't talk—well, you know, I thought she was crazy. She'd been brought up in an institution like my mother was and like I thought I would be too. And you were right. We didn't kick her. It was the gar girls. Only them. But, well, I wanted to. I really wanted them to hurt her. I said we did it, too. You and me, but that's not true. And I don't want you to carry that around. It was just that I wanted to do it so bad that day—wanting to is doing it."

Her eyes were watery from the drinks she'd had, I guess. I know it's that way with me. One glass of wine and I start bawling over the littlest thing.

"We were kids, Roberta."

"Yeah. Yeah. I know, just kids."

"Eight."

"Eight."

"And lonely."

"Scared, too."

She wiped her cheeks with the heel of her hand and smiled. "Well, that's all I wanted to say."

I nodded and couldn't think of any way to fill the silence that went from the diner past the paper bells on out into the snow. It was heavy now. I thought I'd better wait for the sand trucks before starting home.

"Thanks, Roberta."

"Sure."

"Did I tell you? My mother, she never did stop dancing."

"Yes. You told me. And mine, she never got well." Roberta lifted her hands from the tabletop and covered her face with her palms. When she took them away she really was crying. "Oh, shit, Twyla. Shit, shit, shit. What the hell happened to Maggie?"

Robert Frost

Robert Frost (1874–1963) was born in San Francisco and at age eleven moved to Massachusetts, where he graduated from high school. He attended Dartmouth and Harvard but did not earn a degree from either college. As a young adult, Frost worked as a mill hand, teacher, reporter, and farmer, writing but seldom publishing poems. In his early thirties he penned two collections, *A Boy's Will* and *North of Boston*, which earned him international acclaim. During his lifetime, Frost published nine collections of poetry and won numerous awards and honors, including four Pulitzer Prizes. Toward the end of his life he was called upon as a cultural emissary of the United States, and he recited his work "The Gift Outright" at President John F. Kennedy's inauguration in 1961. "Mending Wall," reprinted here, first appeared in *North of Boston*.

Mending Wall

Something there is that doesn't love a wall,
That sends the frozen-ground-swell under it
And spills the upper boulders in the sun,
And make gaps even two can pass abreast.
The work of hunters is another thing:
I have come after them and made repair
Where they have left not one stone on a stone,
But they would have the rabbit out of hiding,
To please the yelping dogs. The gaps I mean,
No one has seen them made or heard them made,
But at spring mending-time we find them there.
I let my neighbor know beyond the hill;
And on a day we meet to walk the line
And set the wall between us once again.

We keep the wall between us as we go.
To each the boulders that have fallen to each.
And some are loaves and some so nearly balls
We have to use a spell to make them balance:
"Stay where you are until our backs are turned!"
We wear our fingers rough with handling them.
Oh, just another kind of outdoor game,
One on a side. It comes to little more:
There where it is we do not need the wall:
He is all pine and I am apple orchard.
My apple trees will never get across
And eat the cones under his pines, I tell him.
He only says, "Good fences make good neighbors."

Spring is the mischief in me, and I wonder
If I could put a notion in his head:
"*Why* do they make good neighbors? Isn't it
Where there are cows? But here there are no cows.
Before I built a wall I'd ask to know
What I was walling in or walling out,
And to whom I was like to give offense.
Something there is that doesn't love a wall,
That wants it down." I could say "Elves" to him,
But it's not elves exactly, and I'd rather
He said it for himself. I see him there,
Bringing a stone grasped firmly by the top
In each hand, like an old-stone savage armed.
He moves in darkness as it seems to me,
Not of woods only and the shade of trees.
He will not go behind his father's saying,
And he likes having thought of it so well
He says again, "Good fences make good neighbors."

PART II

Serving

In the morning, before Patrice edited—or vandalized—her calendar, it said this: Martin Luther King Jr. Day, National Day of Service. In the evening, after her intervention, Patrice's calendar read differently: Martin Luther King Jr. Day, National Day of What?

Patrice, an AmeriCorps program manager, had spent the day with the volunteers she supervised, painting the walls of a run-down school. Though the school's students had the holiday off, some of them were there painting as well—a kind of detention.

Two ninth-grade boys sat across from Patrice at lunch. They asked her about the "AmeriCorps" on her paint-splattered tee shirt, and, when Patrice told them what AmeriCorps was, they asked her more questions. How old was she? Did she go to college? Did she have a choice about doing—what do you call it—AmeriCorps? Was she married? Why was she at their school? What was wrong with her?

"Why?" Patrice asked. "Where should I be?"

"I don't know," one said, "maybe traveling."

"Or working a real job and making some money," said the other.

"This is better than either of those," Patrice said. They looked at her with disbelief. "I'm helping," Patrice continued, "serving . . . making a difference."

"Who are you helping?" the one with the beginning of a mustache asked.

"You," Patrice said, "your classmates, your younger brothers and sisters—"

"Yeah, but helping how?" he interrupted.

"Teaching, setting other people up to teach."

"Are you teaching today?" Mustache asked with a smirk.

"Indirectly, but mainly I'm painting."

"Today's a holiday," Mustache said, "and you're here, in my broke school, *painting.*"

"Exactly," said Patrice.

"And you think you're helping me," he said, crumpling up his empty lunch bag.

"Believe it or not, I do."

Mustache looked at his friend, who was putting on his jacket.

"Well," said Mustache as he got up from the table to go, "Happy Martin Luther King Jr. Day."

"Right," his friend added. "And we thank you for your service."

At the end of the day, after the walls were painted and the speeches were given and all the volunteers had gone home, Patrice went to her calendar, pen in hand. She scratched out "service" and wrote in "what?"

Even for Patrice, whose livelihood is service, the meaning of service can get lost. What exactly, for Patrice or for any of us, is service? For starters, service is a bland word that refers to a wide range of activities, some bland and some not. I can serve you dinner, I can serve in the military, I can serve to open a point in a tennis match, I can serve as an alderman, I can serve time, I can serve God, I can serve those in need. How can the same word—*serve*—apply in all these different cases? How can the same word fit all these different cases and still retain some distinctive meaning of its own?

A look at the first, simplest example—serving dinner—offers a clue about the activity as a whole. To say, "Dinner is served," means dinner is out there, has been put out there, for others to use, eat, enjoy. This may be a useful way to think about service. Like Patrice, when I am serving I am putting myself and my activity out in the world to benefit others.

In doing this, however, I am also likely trying to benefit myself. I serve you dinner and thereby serve myself some other good: perhaps the intrinsic satisfaction of feeding another human being, or the ongoing pleasures of my relationship with you, or the ennobling sense that I am remedying an injustice, or even some specific favor I hope to get in return for serving this specific meal.

Service, including public or community service, has this odd feature of serving at least two different ends, one expressly named and one tacitly assumed. Service announces itself as beneficial to the world, and also, at the same time, it seems to contain—but does not announce—benefits for the servant as well.

The readings in the following section consider both kinds of benefits—the benefits to the server and to those served—as well as the difficulties that attend many acts of service. They raise fundamental questions about service, questions so basic and obvious that we sometimes forget to ask them, or so challenging that we sometimes turn away.

The section begins with **Mary E. Wilkins Freeman**'s short story "Luella Miller," a kind of horror tale: the title character inspires others to serve her, but it appears that those who serve Luella lose themselves in the process. *Are there limits to the service we should offer others?*

The character at the center of **Margaret Sutherland**'s "Dry Dock" volunteers to assist a rough group of men in talking about books, but it is hard to know what she seeks or how she will know when she has found it. *Why does anyone volunteer in the first place? Do our motives for volunteering matter, as long as we volunteer?*

Jan Beatty's short, tough poem, "Saving the Crippled Boy," amplifies questions about why might we try to serve and even to save other people. *When we try to save people, what are we saving them for—or from? How do our attempts to save them affect us?*

Henri Barbusse's short story "The Eleventh" introduces an even more unsettling question: *What about the people we do not serve? What happens to them—and what happens to us, when we confront them?*

In different ways, the essays included here by **William James** and **Jane Addams** make their own clear case for what service can offer, especially to young people. Reading these essays, we are invited to ponder several questions: *Do the arguments that James and Addams made for service in their own time still speak to us today? How could these arguments be made even more forceful or powerful as a call to service?*

In "The Drum Major Instinct," **Martin Luther King Jr.** offers a stirring appeal, with biblical allusions, to those who might serve. *How can we harness this instinct to seek recognition for ourselves so that it serves good ends?*

King doesn't name the Book of Ruth, but this short scriptural book, like King's speech, raises questions about whether service might be its own reward. *How much does service depend on what we receive in return for it?*

Walt Whitman, in a selection from *Specimen Days*, makes a case not only for service generally but for direct, human interaction. *How does direct service compare to the giving of material goods? When we minister to others out of sympathy, do we give well?*

Gwendolyn Brooks's "The Lovers of the Poor" suggests that direct human interaction might come with its own set of difficulties. *When we encounter those who are receiving service from us, how should we treat them? What does love have to do with service?*

The section concludes with **Adam Davis**'s "What We Don't Talk About

When We Don't Talk About Service," an essay that raises questions about inequality and service and what we may or may not learn when we serve. *Does service address inequalities in our society? What might be the civic impact of candid discussions about inequality and service?*

Mary E. Wilkins Freeman

Mary E. Wilkins Freeman (1852–1930) was a prolific and popular American writer, producing many volumes of short stories, as well as novels, plays, books of poetry, and collections for children. As a young woman, she finished one year of study at Mount Holyoke Female Seminary and briefly taught school. She then began writing pieces for children's magazines and, in time, moved on to stories and novels for adults. Two collections, *A Humble Romance and Other Stories* (1887) and *A New England Nun and Other Stories* (1891), brought her wide acclaim. The following story, "Luella Miller," was published in *Everybody's Magazine* in 1902.

Luella Miller

Close to the village street stood the one-story house in which Luella Miller, who had an evil name in the village, had dwelt. She had been dead for years, yet there were those in the village who, in spite of the clearer light that comes on a vantage point from a long-past danger, half believed in the tale that they had heard from their childhood. In their hearts, although they scarcely would have owned it, was a survival of the wild horror and frenzied fear of their ancestors who had dwelt in the same age with Luella Miller. Young people even would stare with a shudder at the old house as they passed, and children never played around it as was their wont around an untenanted building. Not a window in the old Miller house was broken: the panes reflected the morning sunlight in patches of emerald and blue, and the latch of the sagging front door was never lifted, although no bolt secured it. Since Luella Miller had been carried out of it, the house had had no tenant except one friendless old soul who had no choice between that and the far-off shelter of the open sky. This old woman, who had survived her kindred and friends, lived in the house one week, then one morning no smoke came out of the chimney, and a body of neighbors, a score strong, entered and found her dead in her bed. There were dark whispers as to the cause of her death, and there were those who testified to an expression of fear so exalted that it showed forth the state of the departing soul upon the dead face. The old woman had been hale and hearty when she entered the house, and in seven days she was dead; it seemed that she had fallen a victim to some uncanny power. The minister talked in the pulpit with covert severity against the sin of superstition; still the belief prevailed. Not a soul in the village but would have chosen the almshouse rather than that dwelling. No vagrant, if he heard the tale, would seek shelter beneath that old roof, unhallowed by nearly half a century of superstitious fear.

There was only one person in the village who had actually known Luella Miller. That person was a woman well over eighty, but a marvel of vitality and unextinct youth. Straight as an arrow, with the spring of one recently let loose from the bow of life, she moved about the streets, and she always went to church, rain or shine. She had never married and had lived alone for years in a house across the road from Luella Miller's.

This woman had none of the garrulousness of age, but never in all her life had she ever held her tongue for any will save her own, and she never spared the truth when she essayed to present it. She it was who bore testimony to the life, evil, though possibly wittingly or designedly so, of Luella Miller, and to her personal appearance. When this old woman spoke—and she had the gift of description, although her thoughts were clothed in the rude vernacular of her native village—one could seem to see Luella Miller as she had really looked. According to this woman, Lydia Anderson by name, Luella Miller had been a beauty of a type rather unusual in New England. She had been a slight, pliant sort of creature, as ready with a strong yielding to fate and as unbreakable as a willow. She had glimmering lengths of straight, fair hair, which she wore softly looped round a long, lovely face. She had blue eyes full of soft pleading, little slender, clinging hands, and a wonderful grace of motion and attitude.

"Luella Miller used to sit in a way nobody else could if they sat up and studied a week of Sundays," said Lydia Anderson, "and it was a sight to see her walk. If one of them willows over there on the edge of the brook could start up and get its roots free of the ground, and move off, it would go just the way Luella Miller used to. She had a green shot silk she used to wear, too, and a hat with green ribbon streamers, and a lace veil blowing across her face and out sideways, and a green ribbon flyin' from her waist. That was what she came out bride in when she married Erastus Miller. Her name before she was married was Hill. There was always a sight of *l*'s in her name, married or single. Erastus Miller was good lookin', too, better lookin' than Luella. Sometimes I used to think that Luella wa'n't so handsome after all. Erastus just about worshiped her. I used to know him pretty well. He lived next door to me, and we went to school together. Folks used to say he was waitin' on me, but he wa'n't. I never thought he was except once or twice when he said things that some girls might have suspected meant somethin'. That was before

Luella came here to teach the district school. It was funny how she came to get it, for folks said she hadn't any education, and that one of the big girls, Lottie Henderson, used to do all the teachin' for her, while she sat back and did embroidery work on a cambric pocket handkerchief. Lottie Henderson was a real smart girl, a splendid scholar, and she just set her eyes by Luella, as all the girls did. Lottie would have made a real smart woman, but she died when Luella had been here about a year—just faded away and died: nobody knew what aided her. She dragged herself to that schoolhouse and helped Luella teach till the very last minute. The committee all knew how Luella didn't do much of the work herself, but they winked at it. It wa'n't long after Lottie died that Erastus married her. I always thought he hurried it up because she wa'n't fit to teach. One of the big boys used to help her after Lottie died, but he hadn't much government, and the school didn't do very well, and Luella might have had to give it up, for the committee couldn't have shut their eyes to things much longer. The boy that helped her was a real honest, innocent sort of fellow, and he was a good scholar, too. Folks said he overstudied, and that was the reason he was took crazy the year after Luella married, but I don't know. And I don't know what made Erastus Miller go into consumption of the blood the year after he was married: consumption wa'n't in his family. He just grew weaker and weaker and went almost bent double when he tried to wait on Luella, and he spoke feeble, like an old man. He worked terrible hard till the last trying to save up a little to leave Luella. I've seen him out in the worst storms on a wood sled—he used to cut and sell wood—and he was hunched up on top lookin' more dead than alive. Once I couldn't stand it: I went over and helped him pitch some wood on the cart—I was always strong in my arms. I wouldn't stop for all he told me to, and I guess he was glad enough for the help. That was only a week before he died. He fell on the kitchen floor while he was gettin' breakfast. He always got the breakfast and let Luella lay abed. He did all the sweepin' and the washin' and the ironin' and most of the cookin'. He couldn't bear to have Luella lift her finger, and she let him do for her. She lived like a queen for all the work she did. She didn't even do her sewin'. She said it made her shoulder ache to sew, and poor Erastus's sister Lily used to do all her sewin'. She wa'n't able to, either; she was never strong in her back, but she did it beautifully. She had to, to suit Luella, she was so dreadful particular. I never saw anythin' like the fagotin' and hemstichin' that Lily Miller did for Luella. She made all Luella's weddin' outfit, and that green silk dress, after Maria Babbit cut it. Maria she cut it for nothin', and she did a lot more cuttin' and fittin' for nothin' for Luella, too. Lily Miller went to live with Luella after Erastus died. She gave up her home, though she was real attached to it and wa'n't a mite afraid to stay alone. She rented it and she went to live with Luella right away after the funeral."

Then this old woman, Lydia Anderson, who remembered Luella Miller, would go on to relate the story of Lily Miller. It seemed that on the removal of Lily Miller to the house of her dead brother, to live with his widow, the village people first began to talk. This Lily Miller had been hardly past her first youth, and a most robust and blooming woman, rosy cheeked, with curls of strong, black hair overshadowing round, candid temples and bright dark eyes. It was not six months after she had taken up her residence with her sister-in-law that her rosy color faded and her pretty curves became wan hollows. White shadows began to show in the black rings of her hair, and the light died out of her eyes, her features sharpened, and there were pathetic lines at her mouth, which yet wore always an expression of utter sweetness and even happiness. She was devoted to her sister; there was no doubt that she loved her with her whole heart and was perfectly content in her service. It was her sole anxiety lest she should die and leave her alone.

"The way Lily Miller used to talk about Luella was enough to make you mad and enough to make you cry," said Lydia Anderson. "I've been in there sometimes toward the last when she was too feeble to cook and carried her some blancmange or custard—somethin' I thought she might relish, and she'd thank me, and when I asked her how she was, say she felt better than she did yesterday, and asked me if I didn't think she looked better, dreadful pitiful, and say poor Luella had an awful time takin' care of her and doin' the work—she wa'n't strong enough to do anythin'—when all the time Luella wa'n't liftin' her finger and poor Lily didn't get any care except what the neighbors gave her, and Luella eat up everythin' that was carried in for Lily. I had it real straight that she did. Luella used to just sit and cry and do nothin'. She did act real fond of Lily, and she pined away considerable, too. There was those that thought she'd go into a decline herself. But after Lily died, her aunt Abby Mixter came, and then Luella picked up and grew as fat and rosy as ever. But poor Aunt Abby begun to droop just the way Lily had, and I guess somebody wrote to her married daughter, Mrs. Sam Abbot, who lived in Barre, for she wrote her mother that she must leave right away and come and make her a visit, but Aunt Abby wouldn't go. I can see her now. She was a real good-lookin' woman, tall and large, with a big, square face and a high forehead that looked of itself kind of benevolent and good. She just tended out on Luella as if she had been a baby, and when her married daughter sent for her she wouldn't stir one inch. She'd always thought a lot of her daughter, too, but she said Luella needed her and her married daughter didn't. Her daughter kept writin' and writin', but it didn't do any good. Finally she came, and when she saw how bad her mother looked, she broke down and cried and all but went on her knees to have her come away. She spoke her mind out to Luella, too. She told her that she'd killed her husband and everybody that had anythin' to do with her, and she'd thank her to leave her mother alone. Luella went into hysterics, and Aunt Abby was so frightened that she called me after her daughter went. Mrs. Sam Abbot she went away fairly cryin' out loud in the buggy, the neighbors heard her, and well she might, for she never saw her mother again alive. I went in that night when Aunt Abby called for me, standin' in the door with her little green-checked shawl over her head. I can see her now. 'Do come over here, Miss Anderson,' she sung out, kind of gasping for breath. I didn't stop for anythin'. I put over as fast as I could, and when I got there, there was Luella laughin' and cryin' all together, and Aunt Abby trying to hush her, and all the time she herself was white as a sheet and shakin' so she could hardly stand. 'For the land sakes, Mrs. Mixter,' says I, 'you look worse than she does. You ain't fit to be up out of your bed.'

"'Oh, there ain't anythin' the matter with me,' says she. Then she went on talkin' to Luella. 'There, there, don't, don't, poor little lamb,' says she. 'Aunt Abby is here. She ain't goin' away and leave you. Don't, poor little lamb.'

"'Do leave her with me, Mrs. Mixter, and you get back to bed,' says I, for Aunt Abby had been layin' down considerable lately, though somehow she contrived to do the work.

"'I'm well enough,' says she. 'Don't you think she had better have the doctor, Miss Anderson?'

"'The doctor,' says I, 'I think *you* had better have the doctor. I think you need him much worse than some folks I could mention.' And I looked right straight at Luella Miller laughin' and cryin' and goin' on as if she was the center of all creation. All the time she was actin' so—seemed as if she was too sick to sense anythin'—she was keepin' a sharp lookout as to how we took it out of the corner of one eye. I see her. You could never cheat me about Luella Miller. Finally I got real mad and I run home and I got a bottle of valerian I had, and I poured some boilin' hot water on a handful of catnip, and I mixed up that catnip tea with most half a wineglass of valerian, and I went with it over to Luella's. I marched right up to Luella, a-holdin' out of that cup, all smokin'. 'Now,' says I, 'Luella Miller, *you swaller this!*'

"'What is—what is it, oh, what is it?' she sort of screeches out. Then she goes off a-laughin' enough to kill.

"'Poor lamb, poor little lamb,' says Aunt Abby, standin' over her, all kind of tottery, and tryin' to bathe her head with camphor.

"'*You swaller this right down*,' says I. And I didn't waste any ceremony. I just took hold of Luella Miller's chin and I tipped her head back, and I caught her mouth open with laughin', and I clapped that cup to her lips, and I fairly hollered at her: 'Swaller, swaller, swaller!' and she gulped it right down. She had to, and I guess it did her good. Anyhow, she stopped cryin' and laughin' and let me put her to bed, and she went to sleep like a baby inside of half an hour. That was more than poor Aunt Abby did. She lay awake all that night and I stayed with her, though she tried not to have me; said she wa'n't sick enough for watchers. But I stayed, and I made some good cornmeal gruel and

I fed her a teaspoon every little while all night long. It seemed to me as if she was jest dyin' from bein' all wore out. In the mornin' as soon as it was light I run over to the Bisbees and sent Johnny Bisbee for the doctor. I told him to tell the doctor to hurry, and he come pretty quick. Poor Aunt Abby didn't seem to know much of anythin' when he got there. You couldn't hardly tell she breathed, she was so used up. When the doctor had gone, Luella came into the room lookin' like a baby in her ruffled nightgown. I can see her now. Her eyes were as blue and her face all pink and white like a blossom, and she looked at Aunt Abby in the bed sort of innocent and surprised. 'Why,' says she, 'Aunt Abby ain't got up yet?'

"'No, she ain't,' says I, pretty short.

"'I thought I didn't smell the coffee,' says Luella.

"'Coffee,' says I. 'I guess if you have coffee this mornin' you'll make it yourself.'

"'I never made the coffee in all my life,' says she, dreadful astonished. 'Erastus always made the coffee as long as he lived, and then Lily she made it, and then Aunt Abby made it. I don't believe I *can* make the coffee, Miss Anderson.'

"'You can make it or go without, jest as you please,' says I.

"'Ain't Aunt Abby goin' to get up?' says she.

"'I guess she won't get up,' says I, 'sick as she is.' I was gettin' madder and madder. There was somethin' about that little pink-and-white thing standin' there and talkin' about coffee, when she had killed so many better folks than she was, and had jest killed another, that made me feel 'most as if I wished somebody would up and kill her before she had a chance to do any more harm.

"'Is Aunt Abby sick?' says Luella, as if she was sort of aggrieved and injured.

"'Yes,' says I, 'she's sick, and she's goin' to die, and then you'll be left alone, and you'll have to do for yourself and wait on yourself, or do without things.' I don't know but I was sort of hard, but it was the truth, and if I was any harder than Luella Miller had been I'll give up. I ain't never been sorry that I said it. Well, Luella, she up and had hysterics again at that, and I jest let her have 'em. All I did was to bundle her into the room on the other side of the entry where Aunt Abby couldn't hear her, if she wa'n't past it—I don't know but she was—and set her down hard in a chair and told her not to come back into the other room, and she minded. She had her hysterics in there till she got tired. When she found out that nobody was comin' to coddle her and do for her she stopped. At least I suppose she did. I had all I could do with poor Aunt Abby tryin' to keep the breath of life in her. The doctor had told me that she was dreadful low, and give me some very strong medicine to give to her in drops real often, and told me real particular about the nourishment.

Well, I did as he told me real faithful till she wa'n't able to swaller any longer. Then I had her daughter sent for. I had begun to realize that she wouldn't last any time at all. I hadn't realized it before, though I spoke to Luella the way I did. The doctor he came, and Mrs. Sam Abbot, but when she got there it was too late; her mother was dead. Aunt Abby's daughter just give one look at her mother layin' there, then she turned sort of sharp and sudden and looked at me.

" 'Where is she?' says she, and I knew she meant Luella.

" 'She's out in the kitchen,' says I. 'She's too nervous to see folks die. She's afraid it will make her sick.'

"The doctor he speaks up then. He was a young man. Old Doctor Park had died the year before, and this was a young fellow just out of college. 'Mrs. Miller is not strong,' says he, kind of severe, 'and she is quite right in not agitating herself.'

" 'You are another, young man; she's got her pretty claw on you,' thinks I, but I didn't say anythin' to him. I just said over to Mrs. Sam Abbot that Luella was in the kitchen, and Mrs. Sam Abbot she went out there, and I went, too, and I never heard anythin' like the way she talked to Luella Miller. I felt pretty hard to Luella myself, but this was more than I ever would have dared to say. Luella she was too scared to go into hysterics. She jest flopped. She seemed to jest shrink away to nothin' in that kitchen chair, with Mrs. Sam Abbot standin' over her and talkin' and tellin' her the truth. I guess the truth was most too much for her and no mistake, because Luella presently actually did faint away, and there wa'n't any sham about it, the way I always suspected there was about them hysterics. She fainted dead away and we had to lay her flat on the floor, and the doctor he came runnin' out and he said somethin' about a weak heart dreadful fierce to Mrs. Sam Abbot, but she wa'n't a mite scared. She faced him jest as white as even Luella was layin' there lookin' like death and the doctor feelin' of her pulse.

" 'Weak heart,' says she, 'weak heart; weak fiddlesticks! There ain't nothin' weak about that woman. She's got strength enough to hang onto other folks till she kills 'em. Weak? It was my poor mother that was weak: this woman killed her as sure as if she had taken a knife to her.'

"But the doctor he didn't pay much attention. He was bendin' over Luella layin' there with her yellow hair all streamin' and her pretty pink-and-white face all pale, and her blue eyes like stars gone out, and he was holdin' onto her hand and smoothin' her forehead, and tellin' me to get the brandy in Aunt Abby's room, and I was sure as I wanted to be that Luella had got somebody else to hang onto, now Aunt Abby was gone, and I thought of poor Erastus Miller, and I sort of pitied the poor young doctor, led away by a pretty face, and I made up my mind I'd see what I could do.

"I waited till Aunt Abby had been dead and buried about a month, and the doctor was goin' to see Luella steady and folks were beginnin' to talk; then one evenin', when I knew the doctor had been called out of town and wouldn't be round, I went over to Luella's. I found her all dressed up in a blue muslin with white polka dots on it, and her hair curled jest as pretty, and there wa'n't a young girl in the place could compare with her. There was somethin' about Luella Miller seemed to draw the heart right out of you, but she didn't draw it out of *me*. She was settin' rocking in the chair by her sittin' room window, and Maria Brown had gone home. Maria Brown had been in to help her, or rather to do the work, for Luella wa'n't helped when she didn't do anythin'. Maria Brown was real capable and she didn't have any ties; she wa'n't married, and lived alone, so she'd offered. I couldn't see why she should do the work any more than Luella; she wa'n't any too strong; but she seemed to think she could and Luella seemed to think so, too, so she went over and did all the work—washed, and ironed, and baked, while Luella sat and rocked. Maria didn't live long afterward. She began to fade away just the same fashion the others had. Well, she was warned, but she acted real mad when folks said anythin': said Luella was a poor, abused woman, too delicate to help herself, and they'd ought to be ashamed, and if she died helpin' them that couldn't help themselves she would—and she did.

"'I s'pose Maria has gone home,' says I to Luella, when I had gone in and sat down opposite her.

"'Yes, Maria went half an hour ago, after she had got supper and washed the dishes,' says Luella, in her pretty way.

"'I suppose she has got a lot of work to do in her own house tonight,' says I, kind of bitter, but that was all thrown away on Luella Miller. It seemed to her right that other folks that wa'n't any better able than she was herself should wait on her, and she couldn't get it through her head that anybody should think it *wa'n't* right.

"'Yes,' says Luella, real sweet and pretty, 'yes, she said she had to do her washin' tonight. She has let it go for a fortnight along of comin' over here.'

"'Why don't she stay home and do her washin' instead of comin' over here and doin' *your* work, when you are just as well able, and enough sight more so, than she is to do it?' says I.

"Then Luella she looked at me like a baby who has a rattle shook at it. She sort of laughed as innocent as you please. 'Oh, I can't do the work myself, Miss Anderson,' says she. 'I never did. Maria *has* to do it.'

"Then I spoke out: 'Has to do it!' says I. 'Has to do it!' She don't have to do it, either. Maria Brown has her own home and enough to live on. She ain't beholden to you to come over here and slave for you and kill herself.'

"Luella she jest set and stared at me for all the world like a doll baby that was so abused that it was comin' to life.

"'Yes,' says I, 'she's killin' herself. She's goin' to die just the way Erastus did, and Lily, and your Aunt Abby. You're killin' her jest as you did them. I don't know what there is about you, but you seem to bring a curse,' says I. 'You kill everybody that is fool enough to care anythin' about you and do for you.'

"She stared at me and she was pretty pale.

"'And Maria ain't the only one you're goin' to kill,' says I. 'You're goin' to kill Doctor Malcom before you're done with him.'

"Then a red color came flamin' all over her face. 'I ain't goin' to kill him, either,' says she, and she begun to cry.

"'Yes, you *be!*' says I. Then I spoke as I had never spoke before. You see, I felt it on account of Erastus. I told her that she hadn't any business to think of another man after she'd been married to one that had died for her: that she was a dreadful woman; and she was, that's true enough, but sometimes I have wondered lately if she knew it—if she wa'n't like a baby with scissors in its hand cuttin' everybody without knowin' what it was doin'.

"Luella she kept gettin' paler and paler, and she never took her eyes off my face. There was somethin' awful about the way she looked at me and never spoke one word. After a while I quit talkin' and I went home. I watched that night, but her lamp went out before nine o'clock, and when Doctor Malcom came drivin' past and sort of slowed up he see there wa'n't any light and he drove along. I saw her sort of shy out of meetin' the next Sunday, too, so he shouldn't go home with her, and I begun to think mebbe she did have some conscience after all. It was only a week after that that Maria Brown died—sort of sudden at the last, though everybody had seen it was comin'. Well, then there was a good deal of feelin' and pretty dark whispers. Folks said the days of witchcraft had come again, and they were pretty shy of Luella. She acted sort of offish to the doctor and he didn't go there, and there wa'n't anybody to do anythin' for her. I don't know how she *did* get along. I wouldn't go in there and offer to help her—not because I was afraid of dyin' like the rest, but I thought she was just as well able to do her own work as I was to do it for her, and I thought it was about time that she did it and stopped killin' other folks. But it wa'n't very long before folks began to say that Luella herself was goin' into a decline jest the way her husband, and Lily, and Aunt Abby, and the others had, and I saw myself that she looked pretty bad. I used to see her goin' past from the store with a bundle as if she could hardly crawl, but I remembered how Erastus used to wait and 'tend when he couldn't hardly put one foot before the other, and I didn't go out to help her.

"But at last one afternoon I saw the doctor come drivin' up like mad with his medicine chest, and Mrs. Babbit came in after supper and said that Luella was real sick.

"'I'd offer to go in and nurse her,' says she, 'but I've got my children to consider and mebbe it ain't true what they say, but it's queer how many folks that have done for her have died.'

"I didn't say anythin', but I considered how she had been Erastus's wife and how he had set his eyes by her, and I made up my mind to go in the next mornin', unless she was better, and see what I could do; but the next mornin' I see her at the window, and pretty soon she came steppin' out as spry as you please, and a little while afterward Mrs. Babbit came in and told me that the doctor had got a girl from out of town, a Sarah Jones, to come there, and she said she was pretty sure that the doctor was goin' to marry Luella.

"I saw him kiss her in the door that night myself, and I knew it was true. The woman came that afternoon, and the way she flew around was a caution. I don't believe Luella had swept since Maria died. She swept and dusted, and washed and ironed; wet clothes and dusters and carpets were flyin' over there all day, and every time Luella set her foot out when the doctor wa'n't there, there was that Sarah Jones helpin' of her up and down the steps, as if she hadn't learned to walk.

"Well, everybody knew that Luella and the doctor were goin' to be married, but it wa'n't long before they began to talk about his lookin' so poorly, jest as they had about the others; and they talked about Sarah Jones, too.

"Well, the doctor did die, and he wanted to be married first, so as to leave what little he had to Luella, but he died before the minister could get there, and Sarah Jones died a week afterward.

"Well, that wound up everything for Luella Miller. Not another soul in the whole town would lift a finger for her. There got to be a sort of panic. Then she began to droop in good earnest. She used to have to go to the store herself, for Mrs. Babbit was afraid to let Tommy go for her, and I've seen her goin' past and stoppin' every two or three steps to rest. Well, I stood it as long as I could, but one day I see her comin' with her arms full and stoppin' to lean against the Babbit fence, and I run out and took her bundles and carried them to her house. Then I went home and never spoke one word to her though she called after me dreadful kind of pitiful. Well, that night I was taken sick with a chill, and I was sick as I wanted to be for two weeks. Mrs. Babbit had seen me run out to help Luella and she came in and told me I was goin' to die on account of it. I didn't know whether I was or not, but I considered I had done right by Erastus's wife.

"That last two weeks Luella she had a dreadful hard time, I guess. She was pretty sick, and as near as I could make out nobody dared go near her. I don't know as she was really needin' anythin' very much, for there was enough to eat in her house and it was warm weather, and she made out to cook a little flour gruel every day, I know, but I guess she had a hard time, she that had been so petted and done for all her life.

"When I got so I could go out, I went over there one morning. Mrs. Babbit had just come in to say she hadn't seen any smoke and she didn't know but it was somebody's duty to go in, but she couldn't help thinkin' of her children, and I got right up, though I hadn't been out of the house for two weeks, and I went in there, and Luella she was layin' on the bed, and she was dyin'.

"She lasted all that day and into the night. But I sat there after the new doctor had gone away. Nobody else dared to go there. It was about midnight that I left her for a minute to run home and get some medicine I had been takin', for I begun to feel rather bad.

"It was a full moon that night, and just as I started out of my door to cross the street back to Luella's, I stopped short, for I saw something."

Lydia Anderson at this juncture always said with a certain defiance that she did not expect to be believed, and then proceeded in a hushed voice:

"I saw what I saw, and I know I saw it, and I will swear on my deathbed that I saw it. I saw Luella Miller and Erastus Miller, and Lily, and Aunt Abby, and Maria, and the doctor, and Sarah, all goin' out of her door, and all but Luella shone white in the moonlight, and they were all helpin' her along till she seemed to fairly fly in the midst of them. Then it all disappeared. I stood a minute with my heart poundin', then I went over there. I thought of goin' for Mrs. Babbit, but I thought she'd be afraid. So I went alone, though I knew what had happened. Luella was layin' real peaceful, dead on her bed."

This was the story that the old woman, Lydia Anderson, told, but the sequel was told by the people who survived her, and this is the tale that has become folklore in the village.

Lydia Anderson died when she was eighty-seven. She had continued wonderfully hale and hearty for one of her years until about two weeks before her death.

One bright moonlight evening she was sitting beside a window in her parlor when she made a sudden exclamation and was out of the house and across the street before the neighbor who was taking care of her could stop her. She followed as fast as possible and found Lydia Anderson stretched on the ground before the door of Luella Miller's deserted house, and she was quite dead.

The next night there was a red gleam of fire athwart the moonlight and the old house of Luella Miller was burned to the ground. Nothing is now left of it except a few old cellar stones and a lilac bush, and in summer a helpless trail of morning glories among the weeds, which might be considered emblematic of Luella herself.

Margaret Sutherland

A native of Auckland, New Zealand, Margaret Sutherland (b. 1941) has
written several novels and story collections, including *The Fledgling*,
The Love Contract, and *Dark Places, Deep Regions* (in which this
selection appeared in 1980). Sutherland, the New Zealand winner of the
Katherine Mansfield Award and the Freda Buckland Literary Award, has
been a Literary Fellow at the University of Auckland and is a contributor
to the *Oxford Anthology of New Zealand Writing Since 1945.*

Dry Dock

I went to that grim, nineteenth-century reminder of a hospital to offer
myself as a voluntary worker for a mixture of reasoned motives. With
others of my "type" I shared that easy, liberal sympathy for alcoholics
and the mad, whose illnesses can be viewed as a form of inverse sanity in a
mainly crazy society. As a writer, I tell myself I'm allowed to be inquisitive; I
would have liked to know why people pulled out from the mainstream of life,
sometimes forever.

The roots of superstition and macabre curiosity go deeper. We are drawn
to what we fear; as I was drawn, like a child to a haunted house. A woman
screamed all through the preliminary interview, in which I was allocated to
work with a group of male alcoholics. The charge therapist murmured, "A
new admission," and smiled, reassuringly. I offered back my calmest face. But
a human scream is a spine-chilling sound, and it made me afraid.

As I pull into the hospital grounds and park in view of its ivy-colored brick
facade, I feel fear again. I put it down to my inexperience. I'm neither teacher
nor literary expert; as I go through the main doors I clutch like talismans
the notes I've prepared, "On Books and Writing." I wait in the foyer while
the receptionist puts through a call for the charge therapist. The hospital is
quiet today.

She appears, strong and cheerful, a little out of breath. "The men are
waiting . . . you're not nervous?" And she laughs, bustles ahead through the

corridor-burrows, a white rabbit, starch a-crackle.

The sun porch smells of tobacco and men. They sit in rows, like spectators at the movies. Some doze as though the program is too dull to hold attention. Outside traffic streams along the highway.

"Are we all ready?" The charge therapist ushers me in.

"The young lady who's so kindly come to talk about books, everyone."

In slow motion they stand up. A few nod sheepishly as they go out. Four men stay.

"I hope I'm not late," I say.

Not late, reply their expressions, not early. . . .

To start the session I begin to read aloud a marked passage that, at home and addressed to the kitchen wall, seemed appropriate. Tractor-trailers thunder by; the charge therapist goes to close the windows.

A bell rings. We troop to the yard where the tea wagon stands in a drafty corner. Someone gives me a cup of tea with far too much sugar. Someone else fetches four chocolate cookies; two for the charge therapist, two for me. He offers them in nicotine-marked fingers. I set my diet aside. I hear the charge therapist soliciting. "Mr. Tofua? Won't you join us for the rest of the talk? Mr. Ambrose, do come?"

Mr. Ambrose and Mr. Tofua shuffle, murmur, disperse like uneasy pigeons.

"I'm Mac," says Mac. "Had a leucotomy, sent my memory haywire. I get headaches." He has a kind face.

"Come anyway," persuades the charge therapist. And being kind, Mac does. There are still six in the sun porch. The man with the military moustache has reneged.

"Many people want to write," I state firmly. The charge therapist nods. So does Michael, the Irishman, who wears a tattooed serpent on his arm. His nose is pitted like orange peel, his complexion suggests a man used by rough weather.

"I'll show you my little book one day, Missus," he says.

I ask what it's about, and he rotates a finger in a hairy ear.

"Life," he says. "The facts of life."

I pass out paper and pencils and ask everyone to write a paragraph. Dismayed, they ask for a topic. I suggest the first thing that comes to mind.

"Write about the first thing that comes to mind."

Michael licks his pencil. The sun porch shivers as trucks grind past. When they've finished, Alex of the jesuitical sandals volunteers to read aloud. He has no teeth. He's written about mountains and I feel ashamed. I've expected him to write, "By Christ what I'd give for a drink."

Today the charge therapist is busy with prize-giving and distribution of medals.

"The men will look after you," she says.

They sit in rows, facing the traffic stream. They might have sat, so, all week. Mac brings from behind his back a paperback, *Planet of the Apes*, as a schoolboy offers flowers.

"It's the way we're going, Missus."

A new man sits in the corner as though someone has arranged him there. I ask if he'd like to join in.

"I'm not much of a reader," he says. "Never seen much in books."

"You won't mind if we read out loud?"

"Don't affect me one way or the other." Honestly bored, he goes to sleep.

"Background," I begin, to a setting of traffic rumble that drowns my voice. Michael rubs his nose. When the bell rings for tea break he stops me, offers a dog-eared photograph, asks if I can pick him out. I opt for the largest ears and he blushes, pleased.

"Taken '42."

I ask if he'll do the same for me in thirty years' time; he grins. Even a photograph offers no clue at all to my curiosity. If I said, "Who are you, really, Michael?" he'd grin again.

"I'll show you my book one day; you might find it useful, Missus."

Alex has done the exercise we talked about last week. He looks diffident as he pulls it from his pocket; a large ruled page, tobacco impregnated.

"Didn't come out the way I wanted."

"It never does," I say with empathy.

"I had a headache," Reg says.

Today the sun porch seems almost crowded. A face gray, seamed like a sculpture of age above a canary handmade sweater. A villainous-looking Maori opens bloodshot eyes, offers a sweet, bleary smile. Hastily I open *Contemporary Maori Writing* and pass the marked page to Reg. The degree of his literacy is small but it doesn't matter; the Maori has gone back to sleep. His snores accompany the highway din.

We talk about character. They don't mind humoring me. Reg has put on a green tie and shined his shoes. In the yard he comes up to me, in his odd, stilted walk, with a cup of lukewarm, milky tea. He says he's going out in a few weeks and I say, "That's good." He looks doubtful.

"The doctors were none too pleased to see me back so soon. But I like it here. Very nice place. Plenty happening. Plenty going on. Gymnasium. Squash courts. I don't care for exercise myself. But you always know what to do in a place like this. After a place like this, it's no fun, going out. You're supposed to find a job, all that. You get on the grog. The food here is very nice. Some of them complain, but it's very nice. Always something going on. Nice place."

Graciously, he takes my cup and stalks away across the grim and drafty yard.

The charge therapist has been sympathetic about the noise. For the last session we struggle to the occupational therapy room. The man in the canary sweater bobs ahead, like a bird in church. Pottery, patchwork, and rug weaving brighten the shelves of the handicraft room.

I say, "We'd better have a discussion today, the topic's dialogue."

Everyone falls silent. I pass around paper, pencils. The pages stay white.

"You'd think it would be easy," Alex shakes his head. "It's the hardest of the lot."

We turn to other people's words to pass the time. I came here with thoughts of well-meant altruism . . . that was one intention they've accepted and, paradoxically, given back to me. I feel grateful that they've come with their headaches and diffidence, their backgrounds of Rotoroa and tough seagoing experience, a little band of aging men whose last ambitions slipped away in private ebbs of failure, frustration . . . but I'm guessing, dramatizing again, as writers love to do. Maybe they drink because they want to drink. Maybe I'm condescending when I wonder, "Why an alcoholic, you, Michael, when there are any number of painkillers and escape routes?" But I write, so that's what I do think when he holds out the notebook, as I say goodbye, shake his hand.

"Take it, Missus. Everything's taken care of in this place, I won't be needing it. But it might be useful for you, out there."

His hand is hard and horny as it grips mine. Yet I know I've really not come near, not touched. I hold the notebook with respect, as one should, accepting another's trust. People sometimes prefer to trust obliquely; words that are committed to the page have such a final feel. I wonder if Michael has an answer traced in the large, careful script I've come to recognize in past weeks. This hospital has been a place of dead-end corridors, closed doors.

Alex sees me to the hospital entrance. I turn back to wave; he's standing there, in the handmade green socks, brown sandals he always wears. In the car I can't wait; I open Michael's book. Inside are lists, under a printed heading, FACTS OF LIFE. The first page says:

> Diameter of sun approx 864,000 miles
> Earth 96,000,000 miles from sun
> Population of America 1971, 195 millions
> Diameter of moon = 2,160 miles
> 3000 million miles to Pluto

I look back to the hospital doors, but Alex has disappeared as though he's never been. I can just make out the sun porch window and peopled rows of chairs that look out on the moving traffic stream.

Jan Beatty

Jan Beatty (b. 1952) has published two collections of poetry: *Mad River*, which won the Agnes Lynch Starrett Prize, and *Boneshaker*. Beatty has worked in maximum security prisons and as a welfare caseworker and abortion counselor. She was also the host of *Prosody*, a Pittsburgh-based radio show. She received the Pablo Neruda Prize for Poetry and the State Street Chapbook Prize, among other awards. "Saving the Crippled Boy" appears in *Mad River*.

Saving the Crippled Boy

Tenth-grade field trip, I'm stuck
in the back of the chartered bus
with one-armed Bob Saunders, ten
rows away from the waves of my friends.
There I was, sharing the seat
with his hook of a hand,
his flesh-colored armlike arm,
was it plastic, what was it made of,
we were sixteen, but it wasn't just
his arm—he was short, his hair
was greasy, he wouldn't talk to anyone.
And who would ever love him, had he ever
kissed a girl, would he ever kiss anyone?
Years before I knew about *mercy fucks*,
somewhere between New York City and Hampton,
it started, and we necked all the way home
from Springdale, the whole time, the bolts
in his arm clicked on the rim of the bus window,

Bob's tongue poking and pushing like
a hyperactive worm in my mouth, me afraid
his arm would flap over me like a hard dead person,
the whole time my good deed burying me, I wanted
to save him, just to save him, and now we were
both alone, covered with our benchwarmers,
Bob half on top of me in the cold vinyl seat,
I felt him get hard—small and hard, and
what had this become, I wanted blazing sanctimony,
saving the crippled boy with each plunge of
my normal tongue, but now I was saying, *Look,*
this is what you can't have, not for real,
this is for today, and I grew small and hard,
and thought of my boyfriend at home, my best
friend, Patty, and my sick, ailing heart.

Henri Barbusse

Although he was an established poet, novelist, and short story writer, Henri Barbusse (1873–1935) volunteered to serve in the French army in World War I, only to emerge from the trenches an ardent pacifist. His wartime memoir, *Le Feu*, received the Prix Goncourt, one of France's most prestigious literary awards. Active after the war in peace organizations, Barbusse became a communist and moved to the Soviet Union, where he died in 1935 while at work on a biography of Stalin. "The Eleventh," an early piece, was published in 1908 in *Us Others: Stories of Fate, Love and Pity*.

The Eleventh

The master, who had a pale head with long marblelike hair, and whose spectacles shone in solemnity, came to a standstill on his morning round opposite my little table at the door of Room 28 and condescended to announce to me that I was henceforth appointed to let in the ten poor people who every month were admitted to the hospitality of the house. Then he went on, so tall and so white among the assiduous flock of students that they seemed to be carrying a famous statuette from room to room.

I stammered the thanks that he did not hear. My twenty-five-year-old heart felt a happy pride in reflecting that I had been chosen to preside in one of the noblest traditions of the house in which, a humble assistant, I was wandering forlornly among wealthy invalids.

On the first day of every month the luxurious palace-hospital became the paradise of ten vagabonds. One of its outer doors was opened to admit the first ten who came, whoever they were, wherever they had fallen from or escaped. And for a whole month those ten human derelicts enjoyed the entire hospitality of the comfortable institution, just as much so as the master's most valuable patients, as much as the archdukes and multimillionaires. For them, too, were the lofty halls whose walls were not only white but glistening, the huge corridors like covered streets, which in summer or in winter had the coolness or the mildness of spring. For them also, the immense garden beds set among green velvet, like bunches of flowers so enlarged by magic that one walked among them. For them equally, the outer walls, far off but impassable, which shield one against wide-open space, against rambling roads, against the plains that come to an end no more than the sky. For thirty days the refugees busied themselves only with doing nothing, only worked when they ate, and were no longer afraid of the unknown or of the coming day. They who were remorseful learned to forget things, and they who were bereaved, to forget people.

When by chance they met each other, they simply had to turn their heads away hurriedly. There was not in all the house, by order of the master, a mirror in which they would have found their bad dream again. At the day's end came the dormitory, peaceful as a cemetery, a nice cemetery, where one is not dead, where one waits—where one lives, but without knowing it.

At eight o'clock on the first day of the following month all ten of them went away, cast back into the world one by one, as into the sea. Immediately after, ten others entered, the first ten of the file that, since the night before, had been washed up against the wall of the house as upon the shores of an island. The first ten, no more, no less, no favors, no exceptions, no injustices; one rule only—they who had already been were never again admitted. The arrivals were asked nothing else—not even for the confession of their names.

And on the first day of the month, as soon as nine o'clock had sounded, exactly together from the Anglican church and the Catholic chapel of the house, I opened the little poor door.

A crowd of beings was massed against the door-wing and the wall. Hardly had the former turned in the shadow when the tattered heap rushed forward as though sucked in.

My helper had to throw himself forward to enforce a little order upon the greedy invasion. We had to detach by force, to tear away from the mass each one of the besiegers, who were pressed side by side and elbow to elbow, fastened to each other like fantastic friends. The eight entered, the ninth, the tenth.

And then the door was quickly closed, but not so quickly that it prevented me from seeing, only a step from me, him upon whom it closed, the eleventh, the unlucky one, the accursed.

He was a man of uncertain age; in his gray and withered face lackluster eyes floated. He looked at me so despairingly that he seemed to smile. The touch of that extraordinary disappointment made me start, of that face that was mute as a wound. I glimpsed in a flash—the time that the door took to shut—all the effort he had made to get there, even if too late, and how much he too deserved to come in!

Then I busied myself with the others; but a few minutes later, still affected by the distress I had read on the face of the outcast, I half opened the door to see if he were still there. No one. He and the three or four others—uncertain rags that had fluttered behind him—had gone to the four winds of heaven, carried away along the roads like dead leaves. A little shiver went through me, a shiver almost of mourning for the conquered.

At night, as I was falling asleep, my thoughts went again to them, and I wondered why they stayed there till the last moment, they who arrived only when ten had already taken their places at the door. What did they hope for? Nothing. Yet they were hoping all the same, and therein was a mean miracle of the heart.

We had reached the month of March. On the last day of the old month, toward nightfall, a rather frightened murmur crept from the side of the high road, close to the door. Leaning over a balcony, I could make men out there, stirring like insects. These were the suppliants.

The next morning we opened to these phantoms whom the magical story of the house had called across the world, who had awakened and unburied themselves from the lowest and most awful of depths to get there. We welcomed the ten who first came forward; we were obliged to drive back into life the eleventh.

He was standing, motionless, and offering himself from the other side of the door. I looked at him and then lowered my eyes. He had a terrible look, with his hollow face and lashless eyelids. There breathed from him a reproach of unbearable artlessness.

When the door divided us forever, I regretted him and should have liked to see him again. I turned toward the others, swarming in gladness on the flagstones, almost with resignation, wondering at my own firm conviction that the other, sooner than these, ought to have come in with us.

And it was so every time. Every time I became more indifferent to the crowd of admitted and satisfied and devoted my gaze still more to him who was refused salvation. And every time he seemed to me the most pitiable case, and I felt that I was myself smitten in the person of the one condemned.

In June, it was a woman. I saw her understand and begin to cry. I trembled as I furtively scanned her; to crown all, the weeper's eyelids were blood red as wounds.

In July, the appointed victim was incomparably regrettable by reason of his great age; and no living being was so compassionable as he who was repulsed the month after, so young was he. Another time, he who had to be snatched from the group of the elect besought me with his poor hands, encircled with the remains of frayed linen, like lint. The one whom fate sacrificed the following month showed me a menacing fist. The entreaty of the one made me afraid, and the threat of the other pitiful.

I could almost have begged his pardon, the "eleventh" of October. He drew himself up stiffly; his neck was wrapped high in a grayish tie that looked like a bandage; he was thin, and his coat fluttered in the wind like a flag. But what could I have said to the unfortunate who succeeded him thirty days later? He blushed, stammered a nervous apology, and withdrew after bowing with tragic politeness—piteous remnant of an earlier lot.

And thus a year passed. Twelve times I let in the vagrants whom the stones had worn out, the workmen for whom all work was hopeless, the criminals subdued. Twelve times I let in some of those who clung to the stones of the wall as on to reefs of the seacoast. Twelve times I turned others away, similar ones, whom I confusedly preferred.

An idea beset me—that I was taking part in an abominable injustice. Truly there was no sense in dividing all those poor folk like that into friends and enemies. There was only one arbitrary reason—abstract, not admissible; a matter of a figure, a sign. At bottom, this was neither just nor even logical.

Soon I could no longer continue in this series of errors. I went to the master and begged him to give me some other post, so that I should not have to do the same evil deed again every month.

William James

The psychologist and philosopher William James (1842–1910) attended schools in New York and Rhode Island, England, France, Scotland, and Germany and was also privately tutored. His educational interests, like his schooling, moved around, shifting from painting to chemistry to medicine to psychology to philosophy. A towering figure in American letters in the latter half of the nineteenth century, James wrote *The Principles of Psychology*, *Varieties of Religious Experience*, and *Pragmatism*. This essay is based on a speech given at Stanford University in 1906.

The Moral Equivalent of War

The war against war is going to be no holiday excursion or camping party. The military feelings are too deeply grounded to abdicate their place among our ideals until better substitutes are offered than the glory and shame that come to nations as well as to individuals from the ups and downs of politics and the vicissitudes of trade. There is something highly paradoxical in the modern man's relation to war. Ask all our millions, north and south, whether they would vote now (were such a thing possible) to have our war for the Union expunged from history, and the record of a peaceful transition to the present time substituted for that of its marches and battles, and probably hardly a handful of eccentrics would say yes. Those ancestors, those efforts, those memories and legends, are the most ideal part of what we now own together, a sacred spiritual possession worth more than all the blood poured out. Yet ask those same people whether they would be willing in cold blood to start another civil war now to gain another similar possession, and not one man or woman would vote for the proposition. In modern eyes, precious though wars may be, they must not be waged solely for the sake of the ideal harvest. Only when forced upon one, only when an enemy's injustice leaves us no alternative, is a war now thought permissible.

It was not thus in ancient times. The earlier men were hunting men, and to hunt a neighboring tribe, kill the males, loot the village, and possess the females was the most profitable, as well as the most exciting, way of living. Thus were the more martial tribes selected, and in chiefs and peoples a pure pugnacity and love of glory came to mingle with the more fundamental appetite for plunder.

Modern war is so expensive that we feel trade to be a better avenue to plunder; but modern man inherits all the innate pugnacity and all the love of glory of his ancestors. Showing war's irrationality and horror is of no effect upon him. The horrors make the fascination. War is the *strong* life; it is life in extremis; war taxes are the only ones men never hesitate to pay, as the budgets of all nations show us.

History is a bath of blood. The *Iliad* is one long recital of how Diomedes and Ajax, Sarpedon and Hector *killed*. No detail of the wounds they made is spared us, and the Greek mind fed upon the story. Greek history is a panorama of jingoism and imperialism—war for war's sake, all the citizens being warriors. It is horrible reading, because of the irrationality of it all—save for the purpose of making "history"—and the history is that of the utter ruin of a civilization in intellectual respects perhaps the highest the earth has ever seen.

Those wars were purely piratical. Pride, gold, women, slaves, excitement, were their only motives. In the Peloponnesian war for example, the Athenians ask the inhabitants of Melos (the island where the Venus de Milo was found), hitherto neutral, to own their lordship. The envoys meet and hold a debate that Thucydides gives in full, and that, for sweet reasonableness of form, would have satisfied Matthew Arnold. "The powerful exact what they can," said the Athenians, "and the weak grant what they must." When the Meleans say that sooner than be slaves they will appeal to the gods, the Athenians reply: "Of the gods we believe and of men we know that, by a law of their nature, wherever they can rule they will. This law was not made by us, and we are not the first to have acted upon it; we did but inherit it, and we know that you and all mankind, if you were as strong as we are, would do as we do. So much for the gods; we have told you why we expect to stand as high in their good opinion as you." Well, the Meleans still refused, and their town was taken. "The Athenians," Thucydides quietly says, "thereupon put to death all who were of military age and made slaves of the women and children. They then colonized the island, sending thither five hundred settlers of their own."

Alexander's career was piracy pure and simple, nothing but an orgy of power and plunder, made romantic by the character of the hero. There was no rational principle in it, and the moment he died his generals and governors attacked one another. The cruelty of those times is incredible. When Rome finally conquered Greece, Paulus Aemilius was told by the Roman Senate to reward his soldiers for their toil by "giving" them the old kingdom of Epirus. They sacked seventy cities and carried off a hundred and fifty thousand inhabitants as slaves. How many they killed I know not; but in Etolia they killed all the senators, five hundred and fifty in number. Brutus was "the noblest Roman of them all," but to reanimate his soldiers on the eve of Philippi he similarly promises to give them the cities of Sparta and Thessalonica to ravage, if they win the fight.

Such was the gory nurse that trained societies to cohesiveness. We inherit the warlike type; and for most of the capacities of heroism that the human race is full of, we have to thank this cruel history. Dead men tell no tales, and if there were any tribes of other type than this they have left no survivors. Our ancestors have bred pugnacity into our bone and marrow, and thousands of years of peace won't breed it out of us. The popular imagination fairly fattens on the thought of wars. Let public opinion once reach a certain fighting pitch, and no ruler can withstand it. In the Boer War both governments began with bluff but couldn't stay there; the military tension was too much for them. In 1898 our people had read the word *war* in letters three inches high for three months in every newspaper. The pliant politician McKinley was swept away by their eagerness, and our squalid war with Spain became a necessity.

At the present day, civilized opinion is a curious mental mixture. The military instincts and ideals are as strong as ever but are confronted by reflective criticisms that sorely curb their ancient freedom. Innumerable writers are showing up the bestial side of military service. Pure loot and mastery seem no longer morally avowable motives, and pretexts must be found for attributing them solely to the enemy. England and we, our army and navy authorities repeat without ceasing, arm solely for "peace," Germany and Japan who are bent on loot and glory. *Peace* in military mouths today is a synonym for "war expected." The word has become a pure provocative, and no government wishing peace sincerely should allow it ever to be printed in a newspaper. Every up-to-date dictionary should say that *peace* and *war* mean the same thing, now *in posse*, now *in actu*. It may even reasonably be said that the intensely sharp competitive *preparation* for war by the nations *is the real war*, permanent, unceasing; and that the battles are only a sort of public verification of the mastery gained during the "peace" interval.

It is plain that on this subject civilized man has developed a sort of double personality. If we take European nations, no legitimate interest of any one of them would seem to justify the tremendous destructions that a war to compass it would necessarily entail. It would seem as though common sense and reason ought to find a way to reach agreement in every conflict of honest interests. I myself think it our bounden duty to believe in such international rationality as possible. But, as things stand, I see how desperately hard it is to bring the peace party and the war party together, and I believe that the difficulty is due to certain deficiencies in the program of pacifism that set the militarist imagination strongly, and to a certain extent justifiably, against it. In the whole discussion both sides are on imaginative and sentimental ground. It is but one utopia against another, and everything one says must be abstract and hypothetical. Subject to this criticism and caution, I will try to characterize in abstract strokes the opposite imaginative forces and point out what to my own very fallible mind seems the best utopian hypothesis, the most promising line of conciliation.

In my remarks, pacificist though I am, I will refuse to speak of the bestial side of the war regime (already done justice to by many writers) and consider only the higher aspects of militaristic sentiment. Patriotism no one thinks discreditable; nor does anyone deny that war is the romance of history. But inordinate ambitions are the soul of every patriotism, and the possibility of violent death the soul of all romance. The militarily patriotic and romantic-minded everywhere, and especially the professional military class, refuse to admit for a moment that war may be a transitory phenomenon in social evolution. The notion of a sheep's paradise like that revolts, they say, our higher imagination. Where then would be the steeps of life? If war had ever stopped, we should have to reinvent it, on this view, to redeem life from flat degeneration.

Reflective apologists for war at the present day all take it religiously. It is a sort of sacrament. Its profits are to the vanquished as well as to the victor; and quite apart from any question of profit, it is an absolute good, we are told, for it is human nature at its highest dynamic. Its "horrors" are a cheap price to pay for rescue from the only alternative supposed, of a world of clerks and teachers, of coeducation and zoophily, of "consumer's leagues" and "associated charities," of industrialism unlimited, and feminism unabashed. No scorn, no hardness, no valor any more! Fie upon such a cattle yard of a planet!

So far as the central essence of this feeling goes, no healthy-minded person, it seems to me, can help to some degree partaking of it. Militarism is the great preserver of our ideals of hardihood, and human life with no use for hardihood would be contemptible. Without risks or prizes for the darer, history would be insipid indeed; and there is a type of military character that everyone feels that the race should never cease to breed, for everyone is sensitive to its superiority. The duty is incumbent on mankind of keeping military characters in stock—of keeping them, if not for use, then as ends in themselves and as pure pieces of perfection—so that Roosevelt's weaklings and mollycoddles may not end by making everything else disappear from the face of nature.

This natural sort of feeling forms, I think, the innermost soul of army writings. Without any exception known to me, militarist authors take a highly mystical view of their subject and regard war as a biological or sociological necessity, uncontrolled by ordinary psychological checks and motives. When the time of development is ripe the war must come, reason or no reason, for the justifications pleaded are invariably fictitious. War is, in short, a permanent human *obligation*. General Homer Lea, in his recent book *The Valor of Ignorance*, plants himself squarely on this ground. Readiness for war is for him the essence of nationality, and ability in it the supreme measure of the health of nations.

Nations, General Lea says, are never stationary—they must necessarily expand or shrink, according to their vitality or decrepitude. Japan now is culminating; and by the fatal law in question it is impossible that her statesmen should not long since have entered, with extraordinary foresight, upon a vast policy of conquest—the game in which the first moves were her wars with China and Russia and her treaty with England, and of which the final objective is the capture of the Philippines, the Hawaiian Islands, Alaska, and the whole of our coast west of the Sierra passes. This will give Japan what her ineluctable vocation as a state absolutely forces her to claim, the possession of the entire Pacific Ocean; and to oppose these deep designs we Americans have, according to our author, nothing but our conceit, our ignorance, our commercialism, our corruption, and our feminism. General Lea makes a minute technical comparison of the military strength that we at present could oppose to the strength of Japan and concludes that the islands, Alaska, Oregon, and Southern California would fall almost without resistance, that San Francisco must surrender in a fortnight to a Japanese investment, that in three or four months the war would be over, and our republic, unable to regain what it had heedlessly neglected to protect sufficiently, would then "disintegrate," until perhaps some Caesar should arise to weld us again into a nation.

A dismal forecast indeed! Yet not unplausible, if the mentality of Japan's statesmen be of the Caesarian type of which history shows so many examples, and that is all that General Lea seems able to imagine. But there is no reason to think that women can no longer be the mothers of Napoleonic or Alexandrian characters; and if these come in Japan and find their opportunity, just such surprises as *The Valor of Ignorance* paints may lurk in ambush for us. Ignorant as we still are of the innermost recesses of Japanese mentality, we may be foolhardy to disregard such possibilities.

Other militarists are more complex and more moral in their considerations. The *Philosophie des Krieges*, by S. R. Steinmetz, is a good example. War, according to this author, is an ordeal instituted by God, who weighs the nations in its balance. It is the essential form of the state, and the only function in which peoples can employ all their powers at once and convergently. No victory is possible save as the resultant of a totality of virtues, no defeat for which some vice or weakness is not responsible. Fidelity, cohesiveness, tenacity, heroism, conscience, education, inventiveness, economy, wealth, physical health, and vigor—there isn't a moral or intellectual point of superiority that doesn't tell, when God holds his assizes and hurls the peoples upon one another. *Die Weltgeschichte ist das Weltgericht*; and Dr. Steinmetz does not believe that in the long run chance and luck play any part in apportioning the issues.

The virtues that prevail, it must be noted, are virtues anyhow, superiorities that count in peaceful as well as in military competition; but the strain on them, being infinitely intenser in the latter case, makes war infinitely more searching as a trial. No ordeal is comparable to its winnowings. Its dread hammer is the welder of men into cohesive states, and nowhere but in such states can human nature adequately develop its capacity. The only alternative is "degeneration."

Dr. Steinmetz is a conscientious thinker, and his book, short as it is, takes much into account. Its upshot can, it seems to me, be summed up in Simon Patten's words, that mankind was nursed in pain and fear, and that the transition to a "pleasure economy" may be fatal to a being wielding no powers of defense against its disintegrative influences. If we speak of the "fear of emancipation from the fear regime," we put the whole situation into a single phrase; fear regarding ourselves now taking the place of the ancient fear of the enemy.

Turn the fear over as I will in my mind, it all seems to lead back to two unwillingnesses of the imagination, one aesthetic, and the other moral; unwillingness, first, to envisage a future in which army life, with its many elements of charm, shall be forever impossible, and in which the destinies of peoples shall nevermore be decided quickly, thrillingly, and tragically, by force, but only gradually and insipidly by "evolution"; and, second, unwillingness to see the supreme theater of human strenuousness closed, and the splendid military aptitudes of men doomed to keep always in a state of latency and never show themselves in action. These insistent unwillingnesses, no less than other aesthetic and ethical insistencies, have, it seems to me, to be listened to and respected. One cannot meet them effectively by mere counterinsistency on war's expensiveness and horror. The horror makes the thrill; and when the question is of getting the extremest and supremest out of human nature, talk of expense sounds ignominious. The weakness of so much merely negative criticism is evident—pacificism makes no converts from the military party. The military party denies neither the bestiality nor the horror, nor the expense; it only says that these things tell but half the story. It only says that war is *worth* them; that, taking human nature as a whole, its wars are its best protection against its weaker and more cowardly self and that mankind cannot *afford* to adopt a peace economy.

Pacificists ought to enter more deeply into the aesthetical and ethical point of view of their opponents. Do that first in any controversy, says J. J. Chapman, *then move the point*, and your opponent will follow. So long as antimilitarists propose no substitute for war's disciplinary function, no *moral equivalent* of war, analogous, as one might say, to the mechanical equivalent of heat, so long as they fail to realize the full inwardness of the situation. And as a rule they do fail. The duties, penalties, and sanctions pictured in the utopias they paint are all too weak and tame to touch the military-minded. Tolstoy's pacificism is the only exception to this rule, for it is profoundly pessimistic as regards all this world's values and makes the fear of the Lord furnish the moral spur provided elsewhere by the fear of the enemy. But our socialistic peace advocates all believe absolutely in this world's values; and instead of the fear of the Lord and the fear of the enemy, the only fear they reckon with is the fear of poverty if one be lazy. This weakness pervades all the socialistic literature with which I am acquainted. Even in Lowes Dickinson's exquisite dialogue, high wages and short hours are the only forces invoked for overcoming man's distaste for repulsive kinds of labor. Meanwhile men at large still live as they always have lived, under a pain-and-fear economy—for those of us who live in an ease-economy are but an island in the stormy ocean—and the whole atmosphere of present-day utopian literature tastes mawkish and dishwatery to people who still keep a sense for life's more bitter flavors. It suggests, in truth, ubiquitous inferiority.

Inferiority is always with us, and merciless scorn of it is the keynote of the military temper. "Dogs, would you live forever?" shouted Frederick the Great. "Yes," say our utopians, "let us live forever, and raise our level gradually." The best thing about our "inferiors" today is that they are as tough as nails, and physically and morally almost as insensitive. Utopianism would see them soft and squeamish, while militarism would keep their callousness but transfigure it into a meritorious characteristic, needed by "the service," and redeemed by that from the suspicion of inferiority. All the qualities of a man acquire dignity when he knows that the service of the collectivity that owns him needs them. If proud of the collectivity, his own pride rises in proportion. No collectivity is like an army for nourishing such pride; but it has to be confessed that the only sentiment that the image of pacific cosmopolitan industrialism is capable of arousing in countless worthy breasts is shame at the idea of belonging to *such* a collectivity. It is obvious that the United States of America as they exist today impress a mind like General Lea's as so much human blubber. Where is the sharpness and precipitousness, the contempt for life, whether one's own or another's? Where is the savage "yes" and "no," the unconditional duty? Where is the conscription? Where is the blood tax? Where is anything that one feels honored by belonging to?

Having said thus much in preparation, I will now confess my own utopia. I devoutly believe in the reign of peace and in the gradual advent of some sort of a socialistic equilibrium. The fatalistic view of the war function is to me nonsense, for I know that war-making is due to definite motives and subject to prudential checks and reasonable criticisms, just like any other form of enterprise. And when whole nations are the armies, and the science of destruction vies in intellectual refinement with the sciences of production, I see that war becomes absurd and impossible from its own monstrosity. Extravagant ambitions will have to be replaced by reasonable claims, and nations must make common cause against them. I see no reason why all this should not apply to yellow as well as to white countries, and I look forward to a future when acts of war shall be formally outlawed as between civilized peoples.

All these beliefs of mine put me squarely into the antimilitarist party. But I do not believe that peace either ought to be or will be permanent on this globe, unless the states pacifically organized preserve some of the old elements of army discipline. A permanently successful peace economy cannot be a simple pleasure economy. In the more or less socialistic future toward which mankind seems drifting we must still subject ourselves collectively to those severities that answer to our real position upon this only partly hospitable globe. We must make new energies and hardihoods continue the manliness to which the military mind so faithfully clings. Martial virtues must be the enduring cement; intrepidity, contempt of softness, surrender of private interest, obedience to command, must still remain the rock upon which states are built—unless, indeed, we wish for dangerous reactions against commonwealths fit only for contempt and liable to invite attack whenever a center of crystallization for military-minded enterprise gets formed anywhere in their neighborhood.

The war party is assuredly right in affirming and reaffirming that the martial virtues, although originally gained by the race through war, are absolute and permanent human goods. Patriotic pride and ambition in their military form are, after all, only specifications of a more general competitive passion. They are its first form, but that is no reason for supposing them to be its last form. Men now are proud of belonging to a conquering nation, and without a murmur they lay down their persons and their wealth, if by so doing they may fend off subjection. But who can be sure that *other aspects of one's country* may not, with time and education and suggestion enough, come to be regarded with similarly effective feelings of pride and shame? Why should men not some day feel that it is worth a blood tax to belong to a collectivity superior in *any* ideal respect? Why should they not blush with indignant shame if the community that owns them is vile in any way whatsoever? Individuals, daily more numerous, now feel this civic passion. It is only a question of blowing on the spark till the whole population gets incandescent, and on the ruins of the old morals of military honor, a stable system of morals of civic honor builds itself up. What the whole community comes to believe in grasps the individual as in a vise. The war function has grasped us so far; but constructive interests may some day seem no less imperative and impose on the individual a hardly lighter burden.

Let me illustrate my idea more concretely. There is nothing to make one indignant in the mere fact that life is hard, that men should toil and suffer pain. The planetary conditions once for all are such, and we can stand it. But that so many men, by mere accidents of birth and opportunity, should have a life of *nothing else* but toil and pain and hardness and inferiority imposed upon them, should have *no* vacation, while others natively no more deserving never get any taste of this campaigning life at all—*this* is capable of arousing indignation in reflective minds. It may end by seeming shameful to all of us that some of us have nothing but campaigning, and others nothing but unmanly ease. If now—and this is my idea—there were, instead of military conscription, a conscription of the whole youthful population to form for a certain number of years a part of the army enlisted against nature, the injustice would tend to be evened out, and numerous other goods to the commonwealth would follow. The military ideals of hardihood and discipline would be wrought into the growing fiber of the people; no one would remain blind as the luxurious classes now are blind, to man's relations to the globe he lives on, and to the permanently sour and hard foundations of his higher life. To coal and iron mines; to freight trains; to fishing fleets in December; to dishwashing, clothes washing, and window washing; to road building and tunnel making; to foundries and stokeholes; and to the frames of skyscrapers, would our gilded youths be drafted off, according to their choice, to get the childishness knocked out of them, and to come back into society with healthier sympathies and soberer ideas. They would have paid their blood tax, done their own part in the immemorial human warfare against nature; they would tread the earth more proudly, the women would value them more highly, they would be better fathers and teachers of the following generation.

Such a conscription, with the state of public opinion that would have required it, and the many moral fruits it would bear, would preserve in the midst of a pacific civilization the manly virtues that the military party is so afraid of seeing disappear in peace. We should get toughness without callousness, authority with as little criminal cruelty as possible, and painful work done cheerily because the duty is temporary, and threatens not, as now, to degrade the whole remainder of one's life. I spoke of the "moral equivalent" of war. So far, war has been the only force that can discipline a whole community, and until an equivalent discipline is organized, I believe that war must have its way. But I have no serious doubt that the ordinary prides and shames of social man, once developed to a certain intensity, are capable of organizing such a moral equivalent as I have sketched, or some other just as effective for preserving manliness of type. It is but a question of time, of skillful propagandism, and of opinion-making men seizing historic opportunities.

The martial type of character can be bred without war. Strenuous honor and disinterestedness abound elsewhere. Priests and medical men are in a fashion educated to it, and we should all feel some degree of it imperative if we were conscious of our work as an obligatory service to the state. We should be *owned*, as soldiers are by the army, and our pride would rise accordingly. We could be poor, then, without humiliation, as army officers now are. The only thing needed henceforward is to inflame the civic temper as past history has inflamed the military temper. H. G. Wells, as usual, sees the center of the situation. "In many ways," he says, military organization is the most peaceful of activities. When the contemporary man steps from the street, of clamorous insincere advertisement, push, adulteration, underselling and intermittent employment into the barrack yard, he steps on to a higher social plane, into an atmosphere of service and cooperation and of infinitely more honorable emulations. Here at least men are not flung out of employment to degenerate because there is no immediate work for them to do. They are fed and drilled and trained for better services. Here at least a man is supposed to win promotion by self-forgetfulness and not by self-seeking. And beside the feeble and irregular endowment of research by commercialism, its little shortsighted snatches at profit by innovation and scientific economy, see how remarkable is the steady and rapid development of method and appliances in naval and military affairs! Nothing is more striking than to compare the progress of civil conveniences that has been left almost entirely to the trader, to the progress in military apparatus during the last few decades. The house appliances of today, for example, are little better than they were fifty years ago. A house of today is still almost as ill ventilated, badly heated by wasteful fires, clumsily arranged and furnished as the house of 1858. Houses a couple of hundred years old are still satisfactory places of residence, so little have our standards risen. But the rifle or battleship of fifty years ago was beyond all comparison inferior to those we possess; in power, in speed, in convenience alike. No one has a use now for such superannuated things.

Wells adds that he thinks that the conceptions of order and discipline, the tradition of service and devotion, of physical fitness, unstinted exertion, and universal responsibility, which universal military duty is now teaching European nations, will remain a permanent acquisition, when the last ammunition has been used in the fireworks that celebrate the final peace. I believe as he does. It would be simply preposterous if the only force that could work ideals of honor and standards of efficiency into English or American natures should be the fear of being killed by the Germans or the Japanese. Great indeed is fear; but it is not, as our military enthusiasts believe and try to make us believe, the only stimulus known for awakening the higher ranges of men's spiritual energy. The amount of alteration in public opinion that my utopia postulates is vastly less than the difference between the mentality of those black warriors who pursued Stanley's party on the Congo with their cannibal war cry of "Meat! Meat!" and that of the "general staff" of any civilized nation. History has seen the latter interval bridged over: the former one can be bridged over much more easily.

Jane Addams

A native of Cedarville, Illinois, Jane Addams (1860–1935) moved to Chicago as a young woman and founded Hull-House, a residential community that offered a wide range of help and hospitality to immigrants on the city's West Side. It would become the most famous "settlement house" in America. Addams lived and worked at Hull-House for the rest of her life, while also writing and speaking on an ever-widening stage. The following speech was delivered in 1892 in Plymouth, Massachusetts, at the School of Applied Ethics, as part of a symposium on the theme of philanthropy and social progress.

The Subjective Necessity
of Social Settlements

This paper is an attempt to analyze the motives that underlie a movement based not only upon conviction but upon genuine emotion, wherever educated young people are seeking an outlet for that sentiment of universal brotherhood, which the best spirit of our times is forcing from an emotion into a motive. These young people accomplish little toward the solution of this social problem and bear the brunt of being cultivated into unnourished, oversensitive lives. They have been shut off from the common labor by which they live that is a great source of moral and physical health. They feel a fatal want of harmony between their theory and their lives, a lack of coordination between thought and action. I think it is hard for us to realize how seriously many of them are taking to the notion of human brotherhood, how eagerly they long to give tangible expression to the democratic ideal. These young men and women, longing to socialize their democracy, are animated by certain hopes that may be thus loosely formulated; that if in a democratic country nothing can be permanently achieved save through the masses of the people, it will be impossible to establish a higher political life than the people themselves crave; that it is difficult to see how the notion of a higher civic life can be fostered save through common intercourse; that the blessings that we associate with a life of refinement and cultivation can be made universal and must be made universal if they are to be permanent; that the good we secure for ourselves is precarious and uncertain, is floating in midair, until it is secured for all of us and incorporated into our common life. It is easier to state these hopes than to formulate the line of motives, which I believe to constitute the trend of the subjective pressure toward the settlement. There is something primordial about these motives, but I am perhaps overbold in designating them as a great desire to share the race life. We all bear traces of the starvation struggle that for so long made up the life of the race. Our very organism holds memories and glimpses of that long life of our ancestors that still goes on among so many of our contemporaries. Nothing so deadens the sympathies and shrivels the power of enjoyment as the persistent keeping away from the great opportunities for helpfulness and a continual ignoring of the starvation struggle that makes up the life of at least half the race. To shut one's self away from that half of the race life is to shut one's self away from the most vital part of it; it is to live out but half the humanity to which we have been born heir and to use but half our faculties. We have all had longings for a fuller life that should include the use of these faculties. These longings are the physical complement of the "intimations of immortality," on which no ode has yet been written. To portray these would be the work of a poet, and it is hazardous for any but a poet to attempt it.

You may remember the forlorn feeling that occasionally seizes you when you arrive early in the morning a stranger in a great city: the stream of laboring people goes past you as you gaze through the plate-glass window of your hotel; you see hard workingmen lifting great burdens; you hear the driving and jostling of huge carts and your heart sinks with a sudden sense of futility. The door opens behind you and you turn to the man who brings you in your breakfast with a quick sense of human fellowship. You find yourself praying that you may never lose your hold on it all. A more poetic prayer would be that the great mother breasts of our common humanity, with its labor and suffering and its homely comforts, may never be withheld from you. You turn helplessly to the waiter and feel that it would be almost grotesque to claim from him the sympathy you crave because civilization has placed you apart, but you resent your position with a sudden sense of snobbery. Literature is full of portrayals of these glimpses: they come to shipwrecked men on rafts; they overcome the differences of an incongruous multitude when in the presence of a great danger or when moved by a common enthusiasm. They are not, however, confined to such moments, and if we were in the habit of telling them to each other, the recital would be as long as the tales of children are, when they sit down on the green grass and confide to each other how many times they have remembered that they lived once before. If these childish tales are the stirring of inherited impressions, just so surely is the other the striving of inherited powers.

"It is true that there is nothing after disease, indigence, and a sense of guilt, so fatal to health and to life itself as the want of a proper outlet for active faculties." I have seen young girls suffer and grow sensibly lowered in vitality in the first years after they leave school. In our attempt then to give a girl pleasure and freedom from care we succeed, for the most part, in making her pitifully miserable. She finds "life" so different from what she expected it to be. She is besotted with innocent little ambitions and does not understand this apparent waste of herself, this elaborate preparation, if no work is provided for her. There is a heritage of noble obligation that young people accept and long to perpetuate. The desire for action, the wish to right wrong and alleviate suffering, haunts them daily. Society smiles at it indulgently instead of making it of value to itself. The wrong to them begins even farther back, when we restrain the first childish desires for "doing good" and tell them that they must wait until they are older and better fitted. We intimate that social obligation begins at a fixed date, forgetting that it begins with birth itself. We treat them as children who, with strong-growing limbs, are allowed to use their legs but not their arms, or whose legs are daily carefully exercised that after a while their arms may be put to high use. We do this in spite of the protest of the best educators, Locke and Pestalozzi. We are fortunate in the meantime if their unused members do not weaken and disappear. They do sometimes. There are a few girls who, by the time they are "educated," forget their old childish desires to help the world and to play with poor little girls "who haven't playthings." Parents are often inconsistent: they deliberately expose their daughters to knowledge of the distress in the world; they send them to hear missionary addresses on famines in India and China; they accompany them to lectures on the suffering in Siberia; they agitate together over the forgotten region of East London. In addition to this, from babyhood the altruistic tendencies of these daughters are persistently cultivated. They are taught to be self-forgetting and self-sacrificing, to consider the good of the whole before the good of the ego. But when all this information and culture show results, when the daughter comes back from college and begins to recognize her social claim to the "submerged tenth," and to evince a disposition to fulfill it, the family claim is strenuously asserted; she is told that she is unjustified, ill advised in her efforts. If she persists, the family too often are injured and unhappy unless the efforts are called missionary and the religious zeal of the family carry them over their sense of abuse. When this zeal does not exist, the result is perplexing. It is a curious violation of what we would fain believe a fundamental law—that the final return of the deed is upon the head of the doer. The deed is that of exclusiveness and caution, but the return, instead of falling upon the head of the exclusive and cautious, falls upon a young head full of generous and unselfish plans. The girl loses something vital out of her life to which she is entitled. She is restricted and unhappy; her elders, meanwhile, are unconscious of the situation and we have all the elements of a tragedy.

We have in America a fast-growing number of cultivated young people who have no recognized outlet for their active faculties. They hear constantly of the great social maladjustment, but no way is provided for them to change it, and their uselessness hangs about them heavily. Huxley declares that the sense of uselessness is the severest shock that the human system can sustain, and that if persistently sustained, it results in atrophy of function. These young people have had advantages of college, of European travel, and of economic study, but they are sustaining this shock of inaction. They have pet phrases, and they tell you that the things that make us all alike are stronger than the things that make us different. They say that all men are united by needs and sympathies far more permanent and radical than anything that temporarily divides them and sets them in opposition to each other. If they affect art, they say that the decay in artistic expression is due to the decay in ethics, that art when shut away from the human interests and from the great mass of human-ity is self-destructive. They tell their elders with all the bitterness of youth that if they expect success from them in business or politics or in whatever lines their ambition for them has run, they must let them consult all of humanity; that they must let them find out what the people want and how they want it. It is only the stronger young people, however, who formulate this. Many of them dissipate their energies in so-called enjoyment. Others not content with that go on studying and go back to college for their second degrees; not that they are especially fond of study, but because they want something definite to do, and their powers have been trained in the direction of mental accumulation. Many are buried beneath this mental accumulation that lowered vitality and discontent. Walter Besant says they have had the vision that Peter had when he saw the great sheet let down from heaven, wherein was neither clean nor unclean. He calls it the sense of humanity. It is not philanthropy nor benevo-lence but a thing fuller and wider than either of these.

This young life, so sincere in its emotion and good phrase and yet so undi-rected, seems to me as pitiful as the other great mass of destitute lives. One is supplementary to the other, and some method of communication can surely be devised. Mr. Barnett, who urged the first settlement—Toynbee Hall, in East London—recognized this need of outlet for the young men of Oxford and Cambridge and hoped that the settlement would supply the communication. It is easy to see why the settlement movement originated in England, where the years of education are more constrained and definite than they are here, where class distinctions are more rigid. The necessity of it was greater there, but we are fast feeling the pressure of the need and meeting the necessity for settlements in America. Our young people feel nervously the need of putting theory into action and respond quickly to the settlement form of activity.

Other motives that I believe make toward the settlement are the result of a certain renaissance going forward in Christianity. The impulse to share the lives of the poor, the desire to make social service, irrespective of propaganda, express the spirit of Christ is as old as Christianity itself. We have no proof from the records themselves that the early Roman Christians, who strained their simple art to the point of grotesqueness in their eagerness to record a "good news" on the walls of the catacombs, considered this good news a religion. Jesus had no set of truths labeled religious. On the contrary, his doctrine was that all truth is one, that the appropriation of it is freedom. His teaching had no dogma to mark it off from truth and action in general. He himself called it a revelation—a life. These early Roman Christians received the Gospel message, a command to love all men, with a certain joyous simplicity. The image of the Good Shepherd is blithe and gay beyond the gentlest shepherd of Greek mythology; the hart no longer pants but rushes to the water brooks. The Christians looked for the continuous revelation but believed what Jesus said, that this revelation, to be retained and made manifest, must be put into terms of action; that action is the only medium man has for receiving and appropriating truth; that the doctrine must be known through the will.

That Christianity has to be revealed and embodied in the line of social progress is a corollary to the simple proposition that man's action is found in his social relationships in the way in which he connects with his fellows; that his motives for action are the zeal and affection with which he regards his fellows. By this simple process was created a deep enthusiasm for humanity, which regarded man as at once the organ and the object of revelation; and by this process came about the wonderful fellowship, the true democracy of the early church, that so captivates the imagination. The early Christians were preeminently nonresistant. They believed in love as a cosmic force. There was no iconoclasm during the minor peace of the church. They did not yet denounce nor tear down temples, nor preach the end of the world. They grew to a mighty number, but it never occurred to them, either in their weakness or in their strength, to regard other men for an instant as their foes or as aliens. The spectacle of the Christians loving all men was the most astounding Rome had ever seen. They were eager to sacrifice themselves for the weak, for children, and for the aged; they identified themselves with slaves and did not avoid the plague; they longed to share the common lot that they might receive the constant revelation. It was a new treasure that the early Christians added to the sum of all treasures, a joy hitherto unknown in the world—the joy of finding the Christ who lieth in each man but who no man can unfold save in fellowship. A happiness ranging from the heroic to the pastoral enveloped them. They were to possess a revelation as long as life had new meaning to unfold, new action to propose.

I believe that there is a distinct turning among many young men and women toward this simple acceptance of Christ's message. They resent the assumption that Christianity is a set of ideas that belong to the religious consciousness, whatever that may be. They insist that it cannot be proclaimed and instituted apart from the social life of the community and that it must seek a simple and natural expression in the social organism itself. The settlement movement is only one manifestation of that wider humanitarian movement that throughout Christendom, but preeminently in England, is endeavoring to embody itself not in a sect but in society itself.

I believe that this turning, this renaissance of the early Christian humanitarianism, is going on in America, in Chicago, if you please, without leaders who write or philosophize, without much speaking, but with a bent to express in social service and in terms of action the spirit of Christ. Certain it is that spiritual force is found in the settlement movement, and it is also true that this force must be evoked and must be called into play before the success of any settlement is assured. There must be the overmastering belief that all that is noblest in life is common to men as men, in order to accentuate the likenesses and ignore the differences that are found among the people whom the settlement constantly brings into juxtaposition. It may be true, as the positivists insist, that the very religious fervor of man can be turned into love for his race, and his desire for a future life into content to live in the echo of his deeds; Paul's formula of seeking for the Christ who lieth in each man and founding our likenesses on him seems a simpler formula to many of us.

In a thousand voices singing the Hallelujah Chorus in Handel's *Messiah*, it is possible to distinguish the leading voices, but the differences of training and cultivation between them and the voices of the chorus are lost in the unity of purpose and in the fact that they are all human voices lifted by a high motive. This is a weak illustration of what a settlement attempts to do. It aims, in a measure, to develop whatever of social life its neighborhood may afford, to focus and give form to that life, to bring to bear upon it the results of cultivation and training; but it receives in exchange for the music of isolated voices the volume and strength of the chorus. It is quite impossible for me to say in what proportion or degree the subjective necessity that led to the opening of Hull-House combined the three trends: first, the desire to interpret democracy in social terms; second, the impulse beating at the very source of our lives, urging us to aid in the race progress; and, third, the Christian movement toward humanitarianism. It is difficult to analyze a living thing; the analysis is at best imperfect. Many more motives may blend with the three trends; possibly the desire for a new form of social success due to the nicety of imagination, which refuses worldly pleasures unmixed with the joys of self-sacrifice; possibly a love of approbation, so vast that it is not content with the treble clapping of delicate hands but wishes also to hear the brass notes from toughened palms, may mingle with these.

The settlement, then, is an experimental effort to aid in the solution of the social and industrial problems that are engendered by the modern conditions of life in a great city. It insists that these problems are not confined to any one portion of a city. It is an attempt to relieve, at the same time, the overaccumulation at one end of society and the destitution at the other; but it assumes that this overaccumulation and destitution is most sorely felt in the things that pertain to social and educational privileges. From its very nature it can stand for no political or social propaganda. It must, in a sense, give the warm welcome of an inn to all such propaganda, if perchance one of them be found an angel. The one thing to be dreaded in the settlement is that it lose its flexibility, its power of quick adaptation, its readiness to change its methods as its environment may demand. It must be open to conviction and must have a deep and abiding sense of tolerance. It must be hospitable and ready for experiment. It should demand from its residents a scientific patience in the accumulation of facts and the steady holding of their sympathies as one of the best instruments for that accumulation. It must be grounded in a philosophy whose foundation is on the solidarity of the human race, a philosophy that will not waver when the race happens to be represented by a drunken woman or an idiot boy. Its residents must be emptied of all conceit of opinion and all self-assertion and ready to arouse and interpret the public opinion of their neighborhood. They must be content to live quietly side by side with their neighbors, until they grow into a sense of relationship and mutual interests. Their neighbors are held apart by differences of race and language that the residents can more easily overcome. They are bound to see the needs of their neighborhood as a whole, to furnish data for legislation, and to use their influence to secure it. In short, residents are pledged to devote themselves to the duties of good citizenship and to the arousing of the social energies that too largely lie dormant in every neighborhood given over to industrialism. They are bound to regard the entire life of their city as organic, to make an effort to unify it, and to protest against its overdifferentiation.

It is always easy to make all philosophy point one particular moral and all history adorn one particular tale; but I may be forgiven the reminder that the best speculative philosophy sets forth the solidarity of the human race; that the highest moralists have taught that without the advance and improvement of the whole, no man can hope for any lasting improvement in his own moral or material individual condition; and that the subjective necessity for social settlements is therefore identical with that necessity, which urges us on toward social and individual salvation.

Martin Luther King Jr.

Martin Luther King Jr. (1929–1968), the leading figure of the civil rights movement in America, is revered around the world as a martyr for racial equality, social justice, and nonviolence. Born in Atlanta, he enrolled at Morehouse College at the age of fifteen. Four years later, he had completed his degree and was ordained a Baptist minister. He later received a PhD in systematic theology from Boston University. In 1964, King was awarded the Nobel Peace Prize. King delivered this sermon in Ebenezer Baptist Church on February 4, 1968, two months before his assassination in Memphis.

The Drum Major Instinct

This morning I would like to use as a subject from which to preach "the drum major instinct." And our text for the morning is taken from a very familiar passage in the tenth chapter as recorded by Saint Mark; beginning with the thirty-fifth verse of that chapter, we read these words: "And James and John the sons of Zebedee came unto him saying, 'Master, we would that thou shouldest do for us whatsoever we shall desire.' And he said unto them, 'What would ye that I should do for you?' And they said unto him, 'Grant unto us that we may sit one on thy right hand, and the other on thy left hand in thy glory.' But Jesus said unto them, 'Ye know not what ye ask. Can ye drink of the cup that I drink of and be baptized with the baptism that I am baptized with?' And they said unto him, 'We can.' And Jesus said unto them, 'Ye shall indeed drink of the cup that I drink of, and with the baptism that I am baptized with all shall ye be baptized. But to sit on my right hand and on my left hand is not mine to give, but it shall be given to them for whom it is prepared.'"

And then, Jesus goes on toward the end of that passage to say, "But so shall it not be among you, but whosoever will be great among you, shall be your servant; and whosoever of you will be the chiefest shall be servant of all." The setting is clear. James and John are making a specific request of the master. They had dreamed, as most Hebrews dreamed, of a coming king of Israel who would set Jerusalem free. And establish his kingdom on Mount Zion, and in righteousness rule the world. And they thought of Jesus as this kind of king, and they were thinking of that day when Jesus would reign supreme as this new king of Israel. And they were saying now, "when you establish your kingdom, let one of us sit on the right hand, and the other on the left hand of your throne."

Now very quickly, we would automatically condemn James and John, and we would say they were selfish. Why would they make such a selfish request? But before we condemn them too quickly, let us look calmly and honestly at ourselves, and we will discover that we too have those same basic desires for recognition, for importance, that same desire for attention, that same desire to be first. Of course the other disciples got mad with James and John, and you could understand why, but we must understand that we have some of the same James and John qualities. And there is, deep down within all of us, an instinct. It's a kind of drum major instinct—a desire to be out front, a desire to lead the parade, a desire to be first. And it is something that runs a whole gamut of life.

And so before we condemn them, let us see that we all have the drum major instinct. We all want to be important, to surpass others, to achieve distinction, to lead the parade. Alfred Adler, the great psychoanalyst, contends that this is the dominant impulse. Sigmund Freud used to contend that sex was the dominant impulse, and Adler came with a new argument saying that this quest for recognition, this desire for attention, this desire for distinction is the basic impulse, the basic drive of human life—this drum major instinct.

And you know, we begin early to ask life to put us first. Our first cry as a baby was a bid for attention. And all through childhood the drum major impulse or instinct is a major obsession. Children ask life to grant them first place. They are a little bundle of ego. And they have innately the drum major impulse, or the drum major instinct.

Now in adult life, we still have it, and we really never get by it. We like to do something good. And you know, we like to be praised for it. Now if you don't believe that, you just go on living life, and you will discover very soon that you like to be praised. Everybody likes it, as a matter of fact. And somehow this warm glow we feel when we are praised, or when our name is in print, is something of the vitamin A to our ego. Nobody is unhappy when they are praised, even if they know they don't deserve it, and even if they don't believe it. The only unhappy people about praise is when that praise is going too much toward somebody else. But everybody likes to be praised because of this real drum major instinct.

Now the presence of the drum major instinct is why so many people are joiners. You know there are some people who just join everything. And it's really a quest for attention, and recognition, and importance. And they get names that give them that impression. So you get your groups, and they become the grand patron, and the little fellow who is henpecked at home needs a chance to be the most worthy of the most worthy of something. It is the drum major impulse and longing that runs the gamut of human life. And so we see it everywhere, this quest for recognition. And we join things, overjoin really, that we think that we will find that recognition in.

Now the presence of this instinct explains why we are so often taken by advertisers. You know those gentlemen of massive verbal persuasion. And they have a way of saying things to you that kind of gets you into buying. In order to be a man of distinction, you must drink this whiskey. In order to make your neighbors envious, you must drive this type of car. In order to be lovely to love, you must wear this kind of lipstick or this kind of perfume. And you know, before you know it you're just buying that stuff. That's the way the advertisers do it.

I got a letter the other day. It was a new magazine coming out. And it opened up, "Dear Dr. King. As you know, you are on many mailing lists. And you are categorized as highly intelligent, progressive, a lover of the arts and the sciences, and I know you will want to read what I have to say." Of course I did. After you said all of that and explained me so exactly, of course I wanted to read it.

But very seriously, it goes through life, the drum major instinct is real. And you know what else it causes to happen? It often causes us to live above our means. It's nothing but the drum major instinct. Do you ever see people buy cars that they can't even begin to buy in terms of their income? You've seen people riding around in Cadillacs and Chryslers who don't earn enough to have a good Model-T Ford. But it feeds a repressed ego.

You know economists tell us that your automobiles should not cost more than half of your annual income. So if you're making an income of five thousand dollars, your car shouldn't cost more than about twenty-five hundred. That's just good economics. And if it's a family of two, and both members of the family make ten thousand dollars, they would have to make out with one car. That would be good economics, although it's often inconvenient. But so often . . . haven't you seen people making five thousand dollars a year and driving a car that costs six thousand? And they wonder why their ends never meet. That's a fact.

Now the economists also say that your house shouldn't cost, if you're buying a house, it shouldn't cost more than twice your income. That's based on the economy, and how you would make ends meet. So, if you have an income of five thousand dollars, it's kind of difficult in this society. But say it's a family with an income of ten thousand dollars, the house shouldn't cost more than twenty thousand. But I've seen folk making ten thousand dollars, living in a forty- and fifty-thousand-dollar house. And you know they just barely make it. They get a check every month somewhere, and they owe all of that out before it comes in; never have anything to put away for rainy days.

But now the problem is, it is the drum major instinct. And you know, you see people over and over again with the drum major instinct taking them over. And they just live their lives trying to outdo the Joneses. They got to get this coat because this particular coat is a little better and a little better-looking than Mary's coat. And I got to drive this car because it's something about this car that makes my car a little better than my neighbor's car. I know a man who used to live in a thirty-five-thousand-dollar house. And other people started building thirty-five-thousand-dollar houses, so he built a seventy-thousand-dollar house, and he built a hundred-thousand-dollar house. And I don't know where he's going to end up if he's going to live his life trying to keep up with the Joneses.

There comes a time that the drum major instinct can become destructive. And that's where I want to move now. I want to move to the point of saying that if this instinct is not harnessed, it becomes a very dangerous, pernicious instinct. For instance, if it isn't harnessed, it causes one's personality to become distorted. I guess that's the most damaging aspect of it—what it does to the personality. If it isn't harnessed, you will end up day in and day out trying to deal with your ego problem by boasting.

Have you ever heard people that—you know, and I'm sure you've met them—that really become sickening because they just sit up all the time talking about themselves. And they just boast, and boast, and boast, and that's the person who has not harnessed the drum major instinct.

And then it does other things to the personality. It causes you to lie about who you know sometimes. There are some people who are influence peddlers. And in their attempt to deal with the drum major instinct, they have to try to identify with the so-called big-name people. And if you're not careful, they will make you think they know somebody that they don't really know. They know them well, they sip tea with them. And they . . . this and that. That . . . that happens to people.

And the other thing is that it causes one to engage ultimately in activities that are merely used to get attention. Criminologists tell us that some people are driven to crime because of this drum major instinct. They don't feel that they are getting enough attention through the normal channels of social behavior, and others turn to antisocial behavior in order to get attention, in order to feet important. And so they get that gun. And before they know it they rob the bank in a quest for recognition, in a quest for importance.

And then the final great tragedy of the distorted personality is the fact that when one fails to harness this instinct, he ends by trying to push others down in order to push himself up. And whenever you do that, you engage in some of the most vicious activities. You will spread evil, vicious, lying gossip on people, because you are trying to pull them down in order to push yourself up.

And the great issue of life is to harness the drum major instinct.

Now the other problem is when you don't harness the drum major instinct, this uncontrolled aspect of it, is that it leads to snobbish exclusivism. Now you know, this is the danger of social clubs and fraternities. I'm in a fraternity; I'm in two or three. For sororities, and all of these, I'm not talking against them; I'm saying it's the danger. The danger is that they can become forces of classism and exclusivism where somehow you get a degree of satisfaction because you are in something exclusive, and that's fulfilling something, you know. And I'm in this fraternity, and it's the best fraternity in the world and everybody can't get fraternity. So it ends up, you know, a very exclusive kind of thing.

And you know, that can happen with the church. I've known churches get in that bind sometimes. I've been to churches you know, and they say, "We have so many doctors and so many schoolteachers, and so many lawyers, and so many businessmen in our church." And that's fine, because doctors need to go to church, and lawyers, and businessmen, teachers—they ought to be in church. But they say that, even the preacher sometime will go on through it, they say that as if the other people don't count. And the church is the one place where a doctor ought to forget that he's a doctor. The church is the one place where a PhD ought to forget that he's a PhD. The church is the one place that a schoolteacher ought to forget the degree she has behind her name. The church is the one place where the lawyer ought to forget that he's a lawyer. And any church that violates the "whosoever will, let him come" doctrine is a dead, cold church, and nothing but a little social club with a thin veneer of religiosity.

When the church is true to its nature, it says, "Whosoever will, let him come." And it does not propose to satisfy the perverted uses of the drum major instinct. It's the one place where everybody should be the same standing before a common master and savior. And a recognition grows out of this—that all men are brothers because they are children of a common father.

The drum major instinct can lead to exclusivism in one's thinking and can lead one to feel that because he has some training, he's a little better than that person that doesn't have it, or because he has some economic security, that he's a little better than the person who doesn't have it. And that's the uncontrolled, perverted use of the drum major instinct.

Now the other thing is that it leads to tragic—and we've seen it happen so often—tragic race prejudice. Many have written about this problem—Lillian Smith used to say it beautifully in some of her books. And she would say it to the point of getting men and women to see the source of the problem. Do you know that a lot of the race problem grows out of the drum major instinct? A need that some people have to feel superior. A need that some people have to feel that they are first and to feel that their white skin ordained them to be first. And they have said it over and over again in ways that we see with our own eyes. In fact, not too long ago, a man down in Mississippi said that God was a charter member of the White Citizens Council. And so God being the charter member means that everybody who's in that has a kind of divinity, a kind of superiority.

And think of what has happened in history as a result of this perverted use of the drum major instinct. It has led to the most tragic prejudice, the most tragic expressions of man's inhumanity to man.

I always try to do a little converting when I'm in jail. And when we were in jail in Birmingham the other day, the white wardens all enjoyed coming around to the cell to talk about the race problem. And they were showing us where we were so wrong demonstrating. And they were showing us where segregation was so right. And they were showing us where intermarriage was so wrong. So I would get to preaching, and we would get to talking—calmly, because they wanted to talk about it. And then we got down one day to the point—that was the second or third day—to talk about where they lived, and how much they were earning. And when those brothers told me what they were earning, I said now, "You know what? You ought to be marching with us. You're just as poor as Negroes." And I said, "You are put in the position of supporting your oppressor. Because through prejudice and blindness, you fail to see that the same forces that oppress Negroes in American society oppress poor white people. And all you are living on is the satisfaction of your skin being white, and the drum major instinct of thinking that you are somebody big because you are white. And you're so poor you can't send your children to school. You ought to be out here marching with every one of us every time we have a march."

Now that's a fact. That the poor white has been put into this position—where through blindness and prejudice, he is forced to support his oppressors, and the only thing he has going for him is the false feeling that he is superior because his skin is white. And can't hardly eat and make his ends meet week in and week out.

And not only does this thing go into the racial struggle, it goes into the struggle between nations. And I would submit to you this morning that what is wrong in the world today is that the nations of the world are engaged in a bitter, colossal contest for supremacy. And if something doesn't happen to stop this trend I'm sorely afraid that we won't be here to talk about Jesus Christ and about God and about brotherhood too many more years. If somebody doesn't bring an end to this suicidal thrust that we see in the world today, none of us are going to be around, because somebody's going to make the mistake through our senseless blundering of dropping a nuclear bomb somewhere, and then another one is going to drop. And don't let anybody fool you; this can happen within a matter of seconds. They have twenty-megaton bombs in Russia right now that can destroy a city as big as New York in three seconds with everybody wiped away and every building. And we can do the same thing to Russia and China.

But this is where we are drifting, and we are drifting there, because nations are caught up with the drum major instinct. I must be first. I must be supreme. Our nation must rule the world. And I am sad to say that the nation in which we live is the supreme culprit. And I'm going to continue to say it to America, because I love this country too much to see the drift that it has taken.

God didn't call America to do what she's doing in the world now. God didn't call America to engage in a senseless, unjust war, [such] as the war in Vietnam. And we are criminals in that war. We have committed more war crimes almost than any nation in the world, and I'm going to continue to say it. And we won't stop it because of our pride and our arrogance as a nation.

But God has a way of even putting nations in their place. The God that I worship has a way of saying, "Don't play with me." He has a way of saying, as the God of the Old Testament used to say to the Hebrews, "Don't play with me, Israel. Don't play with me, Babylon. Be still and know that I'm God. And if you don't stop your reckless course, I'll rise up and break the backbone of your power." And that can happen to America. Every now and then I go back and read Gibbon's *Decline and Fall of the Roman Empire*. And when I come and look at America, I say to myself, the parallels are frightening.

And we have perverted the drum major instinct. But let me rush on to my conclusion, because I want you to see what Jesus was really saying. What was the answer that Jesus gave these men? It's very interesting. One would have thought that Jesus would have said, "You are out of your place. You are selfish. Why would you raise such a question?"

But that isn't what Jesus did. He did something altogether different. He said in substance, "Oh, I see, you want to be first. You want to be great. You want to be important. You want to be significant. Well you ought to be. If you're going to be my disciple, you must be." But he reordered priorities. And he said, "Yes, don't give up this instinct. It's a good instinct if you use it right. It's a good instinct if you don't distort it and pervert it. Don't give it up. Keep feeling the need for being important. Keep feeling the need for being first. But I want you to be first in love. I want you to be first in moral excellence. I want you to be first in generosity. That is what I want you to do."

And he transformed the situation by giving a new definition of greatness. And you know how he said it? He said now, "Brethren, I can't give you greatness. And really, I can't make you first." This is what Jesus said to James and John. You must earn it. True greatness comes not by favoritism but by fitness. And the right hand and the left are not mine to give; they belong to those who are prepared.

And so Jesus gave us a new norm of greatness. If you want to be important —wonderful. If you want to be recognized—wonderful. If you want to be great—wonderful. But recognize that he who is greatest among you shall be your servant. That's your new definition of greatness. And this morning, the thing that I like about it . . . by giving that definition of greatness, it means that everybody can be great. Because everybody can serve. You don't have to have a college degree to serve. You don't have to make your subject and your verb agree to serve. You don't have to know about Plato and Aristotle to serve. You don't have to know Einstein's theory of relativity to serve. You don't have to know the second theory of thermodynamics in physics to serve. You only need a heart full of grace. A soul generated by love. And you can be that servant.

I know a man, and I just want to talk about him a minute, and maybe you will discover who I'm talking about as I go down the way, because he was a great one. And he just went about serving. He was born in an obscure village, the child of a poor peasant woman. And then he grew up in still another obscure village, where he worked as a carpenter until he was thirty years old. Then for three years, he just got on his feet, and he was an itinerant preacher. And then he went about doing some things. He didn't have much. He never wrote a book. He never held an office. He never had a family. He never owned a house. He never went to college. He never visited a big city. He never went two hundred miles from where he was born. He did none of the usual things that the world would associate with greatness. He had no credentials but himself.

He was thirty-three when the tide of public opinion turned against him. They called him a rabble rouser. They called him a troublemaker. They said he was an agitator. He practiced civil disobedience; he broke injunctions. And so he was turned over to his enemies and went through the mockery of a trial. And the irony of it all is that his friends turned him over to them. One of his closest friends denied him. Another of his friends turned him over to his enemies. And while he was dying, the people who killed him gambled for his clothing, the only possession that he had in the world. When he was dead, he was buried in a borrowed tomb, through the pity of a friend.

Nineteen centuries have come and gone, and today, he stands as the most influential figure that ever entered human history. All of the armies that ever marched, all the navies that ever sailed, all the parliaments that ever sat, and all the kings that ever reigned put together have not affected the life of man on this earth as much as that one solitary life. His name may be a familiar one. But today I can hear them talking about him. Every now and then somebody says, "He's king of kings." And again I can hear somebody saying, "He's lord of lords." Somewhere else I can hear somebody saying, "In Christ there is no east or west." And they go on and talk about. . . . "In him there's no north and south but one great fellowship of love throughout the whole wide world." He didn't have anything. He just went around serving and doing good.

This morning, you can be on his right hand and his left hand if you serve. It's the only way in.

Every now and then I guess we all think realistically about that day when we will be victimized with what is life's final common denominator—that something we call death. We all think about it. And every now and then I think about my own death, and I think about my own funeral.

And I don't think of it in a morbid sense. Every now and then I ask myself, "What is it that I would want said?" And I leave the word to you this morning.

If any of you are around when I have to meet my day, I don't want a long funeral. And if you get somebody to deliver the eulogy, tell them not to talk too long. Every now and then I wonder what I want them to say. Tell them not to mention that I have a Nobel Peace Prize; that isn't important. Tell them not to mention that I have three or four hundred other awards; that's not important. Tell him not to mention where I went to school.

I'd like somebody to mention that day that Martin Luther King Jr. tried to give his life serving others. I'd like for somebody to say that day that Martin Luther King Jr. tried to love somebody. I want you to say that day that I tried to be right on the war question. I want you to be able to say that day that I did try to feed the hungry. And I want you to be able to say that day that I did try, in my life, to clothe those who were naked. I want you to say, on that day, that I did try, in my life, to visit those who were in prison. I want you to say that I tried to love and serve humanity.

Yes, if you want to say that I was a drum major, say that I was a drum major for justice; say that I was a drum major for peace; I was a drum major for righteousness. And all of the other shallow things will not matter. I won't have any money to leave behind. I won't have the fine and luxurious things of life to leave behind. But I just want to leave a committed life behind.

And that's all I want to say . . . if I can help somebody as I pass along, if I can cheer somebody with a word or song, if I can show somebody he's traveling wrong, then my living will not be in vain. If I can do my duty as a Christian ought, if I can bring salvation to a world once wrought, if I can spread the message as the master taught, then my living will not be in vain.

Yes, Jesus, I want to be on your right side or your left side, not for any selfish reason. I want to be on your right or your best side, not in terms of some political kingdom or ambition, but I just want to be there in love and in justice and in truth and in commitment to others, so that we can make of this old world a new world.

The Book of Ruth appears in the Hebrew Bible between Judges and I Samuel. It is presented here in its entirety from the New Revised Standard Version translation.

The Book of Ruth

1 In the days when the judges ruled, there was a famine in the land, and a certain man of Bethlehem in Judah went to live in the country of Moab, he and his wife and two sons. ²The name of the man was Elimelech and the name of his wife Naomi, and the names of his two sons were Mahlon and Chilion; they were Ephrathites from Bethlehem in Judah. They went into the country of Moab and remained there. ³But Elimelech, the husband of Naomi, died, and she was left with her two sons. ⁴These took Moabite wives; the name of the one was Orpah and the name of the other Ruth. When they had lived there about ten years, ⁵both Mahlon and Chilion also died, so that the woman was left without her two sons and her husband.

⁶Then she started to return with her daughters-in-law from the country of Moab, for she had heard in the country of Moab that the LORD had considered his people and given them food. ⁷So she set out from the place where she had been living, she and her two daughters-in-law, and they went on their way to go back to the land of Judah. ⁸But Naomi said to her two daughters-in-law, "Go back each of you to your mother's house. May the LORD deal kindly with you, as you have dealt with the dead and with me. ⁹The LORD grant that you may find security, each of you in the house of your husband." Then she kissed them, and they wept aloud. ¹⁰They said to her, "No, we will return with you to your people." ¹¹But Naomi said, "Turn back, my daughters, why will you go with me? Do I still have sons in my womb that they may become your husbands? ¹²Turn back, my daughters, go your way, for I am too old to have a husband. Even if I thought there was hope for me, even if I should have a husband tonight and bear sons, ¹³would you then wait until they were grown? Would you then refrain from marrying? No, my daughters, it has been far more bitter for me than for you, because the hand of the LORD has turned against me." ¹⁴Then they wept aloud again. Orpah kissed her mother-in-law, but Ruth clung to her.

¹⁵So she said, "See, your sister-in-law has gone back to her people and to her gods; return after your sister-in-law." ¹⁶But Ruth said,

"Do not press me to leave you
  or to turn back from following
    you!
Where you go, I will go;
  Where you lodge, I will lodge;
your people shall be my people,
  and your God my God.
[17] Where you die, I will die—
  there will I be buried.
May the LORD do thus and so to me,
  and more as well,
  if even death parts me from you!"

[18] When Naomi saw that she was determined to go with her, she said no more to her.

[19] So the two of them went on until they came to Bethlehem. When they came to Bethlehem, the whole town was stirred because of them; and the women said, "Is this Naomi?" [20] She said to them,

"Call me no longer Naomi,
  call me Mara,
  for the Almighty has dealt bitterly with
    me.
[21] I went away full,
  but the LORD has brought me back
    empty;
why call me Naomi
  when the LORD has dealt harshly with
    me,
  and the Almighty has brought
    calamity upon me?"

[22] So Naomi returned together with Ruth the Moabite, her daughter-in-law, who came back with her from the country of Moab. They came to Bethlehem at the beginning of the barley harvest.

2 Now Naomi had a kinsman on her husband's side, a prominent rich man, of the family of Elimelech, whose name was Boaz. [2] And Ruth the Moabite said to Naomi, "Let me go to the field and glean among the ears of grain, behind someone in whose sight I may find favor." She said to her, "Go, my daughter." [3] So she went. She came and gleaned in the field behind the reapers. As it happened, she came to the part of the field belonging to Boaz, who was of the family of Elimelech. [4] Just then Boaz came from Bethlehem. He said to the reapers, "The LORD be with you." They answered, "The LORD bless you." [5] Then Boaz said to his servant who was in charge of the reapers, "To whom does this young woman belong?" [6] The servant who was in charge of the reapers answered, "She is the Moabite who came back with Naomi from the country of Moab. [7] She said, 'Please, let me glean and gather among the sheaves behind the reapers.' So she came, and she has been on her feet from early this morning until now, without resting even for a moment."

[8] Then Boaz said to Ruth, "Now listen, my daughter, do not go to glean in another field or leave this one, but keep close to my young women. [9] Keep your eyes on the field that is being reaped, and follow behind them. I have ordered the young men not to bother you. If you get thirsty, go to the vessels and drink from what the young men have drawn." [10] Then she fell prostrate, with her face to the ground, and said to him, "Why have I found favor in your sight, that you should take notice of me, when I am a foreigner?" [11] But Boaz answered her, "All that you have done for your mother-in-law since the death of your husband has been fully told me, and how you left your father and mother and your native land and came to a people that you did not know before. [12] May the LORD

reward you for your deeds, and may you have a full reward from the LORD, the God of Israel, under whose wings you have come for refuge!" ¹³Then she said, "May I continue to find favor in your sight, my LORD, for you have comforted me and spoken kindly to your servant, even though I am not one of your servants."

¹⁴At mealtime Boaz said to her, "Come here, and eat some of this bread, and dip your morsel in the sour wine." So she sat beside the reapers, and he heaped up for her some parched grain. She ate until she was satisfied, and she had some left over. ¹⁵When she got up to glean, Boaz instructed his young men, "Let her glean even among the standing sheaves, and do not reproach her. ¹⁶You must also pull out some handfuls for her from the bundles, and leave them for her to glean, and do not rebuke her."

¹⁷So she gleaned in the field until evening. Then she beat out what she had gleaned, and it was about an ephah of barley. ¹⁸She picked it up and came into the town, and her mother-in-law saw how much she had gleaned. Then she took out and gave her what was left over after she herself had been satisfied. ¹⁹Her mother-in-law said to her, "Where did you glean today? And where have you worked? Blessed be the man who took notice of you." So she told her mother-in-law with whom she had worked and said, "The name of the man with whom I worked today is Boaz." ²⁰Then Naomi said to her daughter-in-law, "Blessed be he by the LORD, whose kindness has not forsaken the living or the dead!" Naomi also said to her, "The man is a relative of ours, one of our nearest kin." ²¹Then Ruth the Moabite said, "He even said to me, 'Stay close by my

servants, until they have finished all my harvest.'" ²²Naomi said to Ruth, her daughter-in-law, "It is better, my daughter, that you go out with his young women, otherwise you might be bothered in another field." ²³So she stayed close to the young women of Boaz, gleaning until the end of the barley and wheat harvests; and she lived with her mother-in-law.

3 Naomi, her mother-in-law, said to her, "My daughter, I need to seek some security for you, so that it may be well with you. ²Now here is our kinsman Boaz, with whose young women you have been working. See, he is winnowing barley tonight at the threshing floor. ³Now wash and anoint yourself, and put on your best clothes and go down to the threshing floor; but do not make yourself known to the man until he has finished eating and drinking. ⁴When he lies down, observe the place where he lies; then, go and uncover his feet and lie down; and he will tell you what to do." ⁵She said to her, "All that you tell me I will do."

⁶So she went down to the threshing floor and did just as her mother-in-law had instructed her. ⁷When Boaz had eaten and drunk, and he was in a contented mood, he went to lie down at the end of the heap of grain. Then she came stealthily and uncovered his feet and lay down. ⁸At midnight the man was startled and turned over, and there, lying at his feet, was a woman! ⁹He said, "Who are you?" And she answered, "I am Ruth, your servant; spread your cloak over your servant, for you are next-of-kin." ¹⁰He said, "May you be blessed by the LORD,

my daughter; this last instance of your loyalty is better than the first; you have not gone after young men, whether poor or rich. [11] And now, my daughter, do not be afraid, I will do for you all that you ask, for all the assembly of my people know that you are a worthy woman. [12] But now, though it is true that I am a near kinsman, there is another kinsman more closely related than I. [13] Remain this night, and in the morning, if he will act as next-of-kin for you, good; let him do it. If he is not willing to act as next-of-kin for you, then, as the LORD lives, I will act as next-of kin for you. Lie down until the morning."

[14] So she lay at his feet until morning but got up before one person could recognize another; for he said, "It must not be known that the woman came to the threshing floor." [15] Then he said, "Bring the cloak you are wearing and hold it out." So she held it, and he measured out six measures of barley and put it on her back; then he went into the city. [16] She came to her mother-in-law, who said, "How did things go with you, my daughter?" Then she told her all that the man had done for her, [17] saying, "He gave me these six measures of barley, for he said, 'Do not go back to your mother-in-law empty-handed.'" [18] She replied, "Wait, my daughter, until you learn how the matter turns out, for the man will not rest, but will settle the matter today."

4 No sooner had Boaz gone up to the gate and sat down there than the next-of-kin, of whom Boaz had spoken, came passing by. So Boaz said, "Come over, friend; sit down here." And he went over and sat down. [2] Then Boaz took ten men of the elders of the city and said, "Sit down here"; so they sat down. [3] He then said to the next-of-kin, "Naomi, who has come back from the country of Moab, is selling the parcel of land that belonged to our kinsman Elimelech. [4] So I thought I would tell you of it and say: Buy it in the presence of those sitting here, and in the presence of the elders of my people. If you will redeem it, redeem it; but if you will not, tell me, so that I may know; for there is no one prior to you to redeem it, and I come after you." So he said, "I will redeem it." [5] Then Boaz said, "The day you acquire the field from the hand of Naomi, you are also acquiring Ruth the Moabite, the widow of the dead man, to maintain the dead man's name on his inheritance." [6] At this, the next-of-kin said, "I cannot redeem it for myself without damaging my own inheritance. Take my right of redemption yourself, for I cannot redeem it."

[7] Now this was the custom in former times in Israel concerning redeeming and exchanging: to confirm a transaction, the one took off a sandal and gave it to the other; this was the manner of attesting in Israel. [8] So when the next-of-kin said to Boaz, "Acquire it for yourself," he took off his sandal. [9] Then Boaz said to the elders and all the people, "Today you are witnesses that I have acquired from the hand of Naomi all that belonged to Elimelech and all that belonged to Chilion and Mahlon. [10] I have also acquired Ruth the Moabite, the wife of Mahlon, to be my wife, to maintain the dead man's name on his inheritance, in order that the name of the dead may not be cut off from his kindred and from the gate of his native place; today you

are witnesses." [11]Then all the people who were at the gate, along with the elders, said, "We are witnesses. May the LORD make the woman who is coming into your house like Rachel and Leah, who together built up the house of Israel. May you produce children in Ephrathah and bestow a name in Bethlehem; [12]and, through the children that the LORD will give you by this young woman, may your house be like the house of Perez, whom Tamar bore to Judah."

[13]So Boaz took Ruth and she became his wife. When they came together, the LORD made her conceive, and she bore a son. [14]Then the women said to Naomi, "Blessed be the LORD, who has not left you this day without next-of-kin; and may his name be renowned in Israel! [15]He shall be to you a restorer of life and a nourisher of your old age; for your daughter-in-law who loves you, who is more to you than seven sons, has borne him." [16]Then Naomi took the child and laid him in her bosom and became his nurse. [17]The women of the neighborhood gave him a name, saying, "A son has been born to Naomi." They named him Obed; he became the father of Jesse, the father of David.

[18]Now these are the descendants of Perez: Perez became the father of Hezron, [19]Hezron of Ram, Ram of Amminadab, [20]Amminadab of Nahshon, Nahshon of Salmon, [21]Salmon of Boaz, Boaz of Obed, [22]Obed of Jesse, and Jesse of David.

Walt Whitman

Raised in Brooklyn, New York, Walt Whitman (1819–1892) left school at age eleven, working as an office boy, printer's apprentice, teacher, and journalist before publishing his influential collection of poems, *Leaves of Grass,* in 1855. In his younger days an avatar of Romantic individualism and America's democratic exuberance, Whitman was deeply affected by the American Civil War. After witnessing suffering at the front in 1862, Whitman volunteered as a nurse in military hospitals in Washington DC. Whitman's other notable books include *Drum Taps, Democratic Vistas,* and *Specimen Days,* from which this selection is taken.

Selection from *Specimen Days*

Some Specimen Cases

J une 18th—In one of the hospitals I find Thomas Haley, Company M, 4th New York Cavalry—a regular Irish boy, a fine specimen of youthful physical manliness—shot through the lungs—inevitably dying—came over to this country from Ireland to enlist—has not a single friend or acquaintance here—is sleeping soundly at this moment (but it is the sleep of death)—has a bullet hole straight through the lung. I saw Tom when first brought here, three days since, and didn't suppose he could live twelve hours (yet he looks well enough in the face to a casual observer). He lies there with his frame exposed above the waist, all naked, for coolness, a fine built man, the tan not bleach'd from his checks and neck. It is useless to talk to him, as with his sad hurt, and the stimulants they give him, and the utter strangeness of every object, face, furniture, etc., the poor fellow, even when awake, is like some frighten'd, shy animal. Much of the time he sleeps, or half sleeps. (Sometimes I thought he knew more than he show'd.) I often come and sit by him in perfect silence; he will breathe for ten minutes as softly and evenly as a young babe asleep. Poor youth, so handsome, athletic, with profuse beautiful shining hair. One time as I sat looking at him while he lay asleep, he suddenly, without the least start, awaken'd, open'd his eyes, gave me a long steady look, turning his face very slightly to gaze easier—one long, clear, silent look—a slight sigh—then turn'd back and went into his doze again. Little he knew, poor death-stricken boy, the heart of the stranger that hover'd near.

W. H. E., Co. R, 2d N. J.—His disease is pneumonia. He lay sick at the wretched hospital below Aquia Creek, for seven or eight days before brought here. He was detail'd from his regiment to go there and help as nurse, but was soon taken down himself. Is an elderly, sallow-faced, rather gaunt, gray-hair'd man, a widower, with children. He express'd a great desire for good, strong green tea. An excellent lady, Mrs. W., of Washington, soon sent him a package; also a small sum of money. The doctor said give him the tea at pleasure; it lay on the table by his side, and he used it every day. He slept a great deal; could not talk much, as he grew deaf. Occupied bed 15, ward I, Armory. (The same lady above, Mrs. W., sent the men a large package of tobacco.)

J. G. lies in bed 52, ward I; is of Company B, 7th Pennsylvania. I gave him a small sum of money, some tobacco, and envelopes. To a man adjoining also gave twenty-five cents; he flush'd in the face when I offer'd it—refused at first, but as I found he had not a cent, and was very fond of having the daily papers to read, I prest it on him. He was evidently very grateful but said little.

J. T. L., of Company F., 9th New Hampshire, lies in bed 37, ward I. Is very fond of tobacco. I furnish him some; also with a little money. Has gangrene of the feet; a pretty bad case; will surely have to lose three toes. Is a regular specimen of an old-fashion'd, rude, hearty, New England countryman, impressing me with his likeness to that celebrated singed cat, who was better than she look'd.

Bed 3, ward E, Armory, has a great hankering for pickles, something pungent. After consulting the doctor, I gave him a small bottle of horseradish; also some apples; also a book. Some of the nurses are excellent. The woman nurse in this ward I like very much. (Mrs. Wright—a year afterward I found her in Mansion House Hospital, Alexandria—she is a perfect nurse.)

In one bed a young man, Marcus Small, Company K, 7th Maine—sick with dysentery and typhoid fever—pretty critical case—I talk with him often—he thinks he will die—looks like it indeed. I write a letter for him home to East Livermore, Maine—I let him talk to me a little, but not much, advise him to keep very quiet—do most of the talking myself—stay quite a while with him, as he holds on to my hand—talk to him in a cheering, but slow, low and measured manner—talk about his furlough and going home as soon as he is able to travel.

Thomas Lindly, 1st Pennsylvania cavalry, shot very badly through the foot—poor young man, he suffers horribly, has to be constantly dosed with morphine, his face ashy and glazed, bright young eyes—I give him a large handsome apple, lay it in sight, tell him to have it roasted in the morning, as he generally feels easier then, and can eat a little breakfast. I write two letters for him.

Opposite, an old Quaker lady is sitting by the side of her son, Amer Moore, 2d U.S. Artillery—shot in the head two weeks since, very low, quite rational—from hips down paralyzed—he will surely die. I speak a very few words to him every day and evening—he answers pleasantly—wants nothing (he told me soon after he came about his home affairs, his mother had been an invalid, and he fear'd to let her know his condition). He died soon after she came.

Gifts—Money—Discrimination

As a very large proportion of the wounded came up from the front without a cent of money in their pockets, I soon discover'd that it was about the best thing I could do to raise their spirits and show them that somebody cared for them, and practically felt a fatherly or brotherly interest in them, to give them small sums in such cases, using tact and discretion about it. I am regularly supplied with funds for this purpose by good women and men in Boston, Salem, Providence, Brooklyn, and New York. I provide myself with a quantity of bright new ten-cent and five-cent bills, and, when I think it incumbent, I give twenty-five or thirty cents, or perhaps fifty cents, and occasionally a still larger sum to some particular case. As I have started this subject, I take opportunity to ventilate the financial question. My supplies, altogether voluntary, mostly confidential, often seeming quite providential, were numerous and varied. For instance, there were two distant and wealthy ladies, sisters, who sent regularly, for two years, quite heavy sums, enjoining that their names should be kept secret. The same delicacy was indeed a frequent condition. From several I had carte blanche. Many were entire strangers. From these sources, during from two to three years, in the manner described, in the hospitals, I bestowed, as almoner for others, many, many thousands of dollars. I learn'd one thing conclusively—that beneath all the ostensible greed and heartlessness of our times there is no end to the generous benevolence of men and women in the United States, when once sure of their object. Another thing became clear to me—while *cash* is not amiss to bring up the rear, tact and magnetic sympathy and unction are, and ever will be, sovereign still.

Gwendolyn Brooks

Born in Topeka, Kansas, Gwendolyn Brooks (1917–2000) moved with her family only several weeks later to Chicago. She graduated from Wilson Junior College in 1936, and in 1945 published her first book of poetry, *A Street in Bronzeville*, on the strength of which she was awarded a Guggenheim Fellowship. In 1949 she published *Annie Allen*, and won the Pulitzer Prize for poetry the next year. Brooks went on to publish many more books of poetry, a novel, and an autobiography and to serve as the poet laureate of Illinois in 1968. "The Lovers of the Poor" first appeared in *The Bean Eaters*.

The Lovers of the Poor

arrive. The Ladies from the Ladies' Betterment
  League
Arrive in the afternoon, the late light slanting
In diluted gold bars across the boulevard brag
Of proud, seamed faces with mercy and murder hinting
Here, there, interrupting, all deep and debonair,
The pink paint on the innocence of fear;
Walk in a gingerly manner up the hall.
Cutting with knives served by their softest care,
Served by their love, so barbarously fair.
Whose mothers taught: You'd better not be cruel!
You had better not throw stones upon the wrens!
Herein they kiss and coddle and assault
Anew and dearly in the innocence
With which they baffle nature. Who are full,
Sleek, tender-clad, fit, fiftyish, a-glow, all
Sweetly abortive, hinting at fat fruit,

144

Judge it high time that fiftyish fingers felt
Beneath the lovelier planes of enterprise.
To resurrect. To moisten with milky chill.
To be a random hitching post or plush.
To be, for wet eyes, random and handy hem.
              Their guild is giving money to the poor.
The worthy poor. The very very worthy
And beautiful poor. Perhaps just not too swarthy?
Perhaps just not too dirty nor too dim
Nor—passionate. In truth, what they could wish
Is—something less than derelict or dull.
Not staunch enough to stab, though, gaze for gaze!
God shield them sharply from the beggar-bold!
The noxious needy ones whose battle's bald
Nonetheless for being voiceless, hits one down.
              But it's all so bad! and entirely too much for them.
The stench; the urine, cabbage, and dead beans,
Dead porridges of assorted dusty grains,
The old smoke, *heavy* diapers, and, they're told,
Something called chitterlings. The darkness. Drawn
Darkness, or dirty light. The soil that stirs.
The soil that looks the soil of centuries.
And for that matter the *general* oldness. Old
Wood. Old marble. Old tile. Old old old.
Not homekind Oldness! Not Lake Forest, Glencoe.
Nothing is sturdy, nothing is majestic,
There is no quiet drama, no rubbed glaze, no
Unkillable infirmity of such
A tasteful turn as lately they have left,
Glencoe, Lake Forest, and to which their cars
Must presently restore them. When they're done
With dullards and distortions of this fistic
Patience of the poor and put-upon.

They've never seen such a make-do-ness as
Newspaper rugs before! In this, this "flat,"
Their hostess is gathering up the oozed, the rich
Rugs of the morning (tattered! the bespattered . . .),
Readies to spread clean rugs for afternoon.
Here is a scene for you. The Ladies look,
In horror, behind a substantial citizeness
Whose trains clank out across her swollen heart.
Who, arms akimbo, almost fills a door.
All tumbling children, quilts dragged to the floor
And tortured thereover, potato peelings, soft-
Eyed kitten, hunched-up, haggard, to-be-hurt.
          Their League is allotting largesse to the Lost.
But to put their clean, their pretty money, to put
Their money collected from delicate rose-fingers
Tipped with their hundred flawless rose-nails seems . . .
          They own Spode, Lowestoft, candelabra,
Mantels, and hostess gowns, and sunburst clocks,
Turtle soup, Chippendale, red satin "hangings,"
Aubussons and Hattie Carnegie. They Winter
In Palm Beach; cross the Water in June; attend,
When suitable, the nice Art Institute;
Buy the right books in the best bindings; saunter
On Michigan, Easter mornings, in sun or wind.
Oh Squalor! This sick four-story hulk, this fiber
With fissures everywhere! Why, what are bringings
Of loathe-love largesse? What shall peril hungers
So old old, what shall flatter the desolate?
Tin can, blocked fire escape and chitterling
And swaggering seeking youth and the puzzled wreckage
Of the middle passage, and urine and stale shames
And, again, the porridges of the underslung
And children children children. Heavens! That
Was a rat, surely, off there, in the shadows? Long
And long-tailed? Gray? The Ladies from the Ladies'

Betterment League agree it will be better
To achieve the outer air that rights and steadies,
To hie to a house that does not holler, to ring
Bells elsetime, better presently to cater
To no more Possibilities, to get
Away. Perhaps the money can be posted.
Perhaps they two may choose another Slum!
Some serious sooty half-unhappy home!—
Where loathe-love likelier may be invested.

       Keeping their scented bodies in the center
Of the hall as they walk down the hysterical hall,
They allow their lovely skirts to graze no wall,
Are off at what they manage of a canter,
And, resuming all the clues of what they were,
Try to avoid inhaling the laden air.

Adam Davis

Adam Davis (b. 1970) directs Justice Talking, a reading and discussion series for AmeriCorps volunteers administered by the Illinois Humanities Council, and the Camp of Dreams, a Chicago nonprofit organization providing year-round programming to young people. Davis is the editor, with Elizabeth Lynn, of *The Civically Engaged Reader.*

What We Don't Talk About
When We Don't Talk About Service

There is this odd thing happening: a vogue for service. Look around and you can't help but see it: more community service, more service learning, more compulsory volunteering. Elementary schools, high schools, and colleges across the country have adopted community service programs quickly, seamlessly, and with relatively little opposition or argument. Students are no longer simply concerned with their classes or even with their clubs—now they are collecting clothes, ladling out meals, wrapping gifts, building houses, tutoring younger kids, chatting with elders, and serving the community in numerous other ways as well. And the trend goes far beyond students: young people in record numbers are applying to City Year, Teach for America, and other AmeriCorps organizations; retirees are volunteering with various service organizations; and professionals, too, at and away from work, are engaging in community service. This trend toward service, unlike many trends, is generally praised, though often in imprecise terms. Service Is Good (SIG), we seem to assume—good for those of us doing the serving, good for those of us being served, good for everyone. It has become so clear that Service Is Good (SIG) that we can demand service activity—even "voluntary" service activity—as we require classes in math, science, and the humanities. We can demand it after school or work and on weekends. We can demand it from our brightest young people, our busiest professionals, and our most experienced elders.

It seems to be so clear that Service Is Good (SIG) that we do not need to question service or to talk about it; we only need to do it. It even seems that talking about service might be a problem—first, because if you're talking about service, you might not be doing service, and second, because if you're talking about service, you might start to wonder about its goodness.

But neither possibility, I believe, is something to fear. We ought to wonder about service, and we ought to talk about service with those we're serving with and perhaps also with those we're serving. It may (or even must) be worthwhile to call the goodness of service into question, and with that, to ask why we so rarely ask questions about service. For the length of this piece, then, I want to call into question the assumption or conclusion that Service Is Good (SIG). I want to look briefly at what we mean by service and what we mean by goodness and also at activities we engage in but refrain from discussing. And then I want to suggest that talk, not in place of but in addition to service, might also be good.

Service

The kind of service at issue here is community service, that is, "voluntary" service, which usually implies service to those in need. Neither the waiter (who serves those with means) nor the criminal (who may serve those in need but doesn't exactly choose to do so) is engaging in precisely the kind of service activity I'm talking about. What separates our form of service from other forms of service is above all its voluntary character, which is revealed or confirmed by the fact that service work is nonremunerative, or barely remunerative. People either don't get paid or get paid badly to do this kind of service work, but that's okay; it's not, we're told, about the money. AmeriCorps volunteers, for example, receive a stipend and some help with tuition, but in general that's not why, really why, they're doing it. We don't do service to make money but because service is good in and of itself. To put it another way, community service isn't service *work*; even if checks are cut and hours are counted, community service somehow exists outside the realm of wages and timecards. On its own terms, for reasons internal to the activity itself, Service (S), we say, Is Good (IG).

If we don't serve for money, why do we serve? There are no doubt more reasons to engage in service than can be cataloged, and every act of service probably involves some combination of reasons, but here I'll try to identify and separate out what I see as the most fundamental and common reasons. And it seems sensible, on account of their richer lexicon, their history of service, and their expertise, to begin with the devout among us. The devout might say that we serve because we love God. Or they might say: there but for the grace of God go I, and since the grace of God has temporarily given me more than it has given you, I will freely choose to serve you. In both cases, the explanation for service derives from the belief that we are all children of God and we are all in need. I happen to have more by way of earthly goods than you at this moment, and so I will share. But both of us are in need of spiritual goods, in need of God, and by serving others we serve God.

Earthier but still pious folks might say that we serve because we love others; we serve because we want to help others; we serve because we share with others. Here the emphasis is not on the next world but on this world, though again the impulse to serve derives from a principle of commonality, of what we share. We may or may not all be children of God, according to this approach, but we are all children of the earth, and so, whether we choose to admit it or not, we share. This world is small, so your ills are my ills; your goods are my goods.

The potentially more cynical companion to this view is that we serve not because we share with others but because we identify with others. I know what it's like to be in your shoes. In fact, thanks to my imagination, I *am* in your shoes. I choose to serve you because I see you suffering, I can't help but imagine myself suffering, and I don't want to suffer. By alleviating your suffering, I take care of myself. This is a potentially cynical view because the server emphasizes her own good rather than that of whomever she serves. It's good for you, yes, but I'm doing it because it's good for me.

We become significantly more cynical when we turn to those who explain service by appealing to the reputation it wins for the server. Here the good of the server remains primary, but the good of the served is tertiary rather than secondary. I ladle food onto your plate because others who see me do so will think better of me. And, oh yeah, you won't be quite so hungry.

With this last explanation, we move back toward the devout, though from the other side. Now it is not love that explains humble service but guilt. I am bad, I am evil, I am a sinner—and I know my sinful nature is seen. By serving I acknowledge my consciousness of my sinful nature and mitigate it somewhat. I suck, please let me serve you, perhaps I will suck somewhat less.

Why serve? Here are five reductive answers: (1) we are God's children; (2) we share the earth; (3) I find myself in you; (4) I win praise by serving you; (5) I suck.

Goodness

In each of the above cases, we explain service by referring, usually in a tacit way, to a good or some goods. But the location and content of these goods appear to change as we move from one set of reasons to the next. Here I mean only to point out that service might be good for me (doing the serving), it might be good for them (being served), it might be good for us (as a society), or, weirdly enough, it might be good for God (though this would seem to be presumptuous to the point of impiety). Some might also make the case that service is simply good, in some abstract and objective way, without necessarily being good for anyone. Service, to repeat, might be good for the server, good for the served, good for all of us, good for God, or objectively good.

Whomever service is good *for* (or wherever the goods produced by service reside), we should also note that different reasons for service appeal to different understandings of what the good consists (or the goods consist) of. Service Is Good (SIG) because of the aid it brings to those served, because of the habits (of discipline, humility, and generosity) it instills (probably in the server rather than the served), because of the pleasure it provides (again, most likely to the server), because of the sense of unity it begets among all parties involved, because it is divinely sanctioned, because of its capacity to move the way things are toward how they ought to be. That is, service might produce goods that are necessary, educational, pleasurable, beautiful, holy, or right.

Service activity, then, might produce goods external to the transaction itself, internal to the transaction itself, both, or neither. Any particular act of service could be demeaning to the served and uncomfortable for the server, but it may at the same time provide the served with what she needs. You serve me a meal at a soup kitchen, and this puts my need on display, which demeans me and makes you uncomfortable, yet my hunger is appeased. We might therefore call this act of service good chiefly because of the positive consequences of the act, the external goods, and despite the difficulties internal to the act.

Or the reverse could be true: an act of service could lead to no positive external outcome—or even to a negative external outcome for both parties— but might fill both the server and the served with a feeling of dignity or justice, pleasure or love. You serve me a meal at a soup kitchen, and this pleases me (it's nice to be given a free meal) and makes you feel holy (it's nice to choose to give someone a free meal), but relative to everyone else at the kitchen, I'm not really in need. I come out of there having learned how I might preserve a little more cash to bet with, you come out feeling you've done your part to save the world, and so this act of service feels good to the parties involved but would most likely not be called good according to any reliable external standard.

This distinction between external and internal goods is in many ways too extreme, because sought-after goods are rarely only internal or only external, but the distinction might begin to help us see that service activity is complex. And only after we acknowledge the complexity of service—with its multiple parties and various goods—can we begin to sort out better acts of service from worse.

If, on the other hand, we remain at the acronymic level—SIG—we may find ourselves shortchanging all three abbreviated terms (service, is, and good). It is simply the case that some service activity—ill-conceived or unwanted or badly executed or questionably motivated service—might not be good. Some—and perhaps all—service activity might be both good and bad. At the very least, then, we should recognize that no matter where one comes down on the goodness of service, service, in principle and in practice, is not simple (SINS). In short, the belief that service is good (SIG) should not mean that we blind ourselves to the complexity of service—SINS.

Anyone who has served or been served by another—in short, anyone—can testify to the range of feelings such an exchange produces: serving someone, I might feel close to that person or ashamed at how close I am to someone I do not know, or I might expect more signs of gratitude, or I might feel any number of other things; being served, I might feel close to the person serving me, or ashamed, or grateful but estranged, or any number of other things. This range of possible feelings attests to the fact that service is complex as well as deep. If, on account of its apparently voluntary, unpaid character, service can seem like play, it can also, on account of its emotional and moral significance, seem more serious than anything else we could conceive of or do.

Yet service is something we rarely discuss.

What We Do; What We Do Not Discuss

Many of us pick our noses. Few of us talk about it. Our silence on the subject of nose picking seems to be related to the unsavory character of the activity. It is bad; we don't discuss it.

All of us wipe (I hope). Few of us talk about it. Our silence on the subject of wiping, however, does not derive from our collective disapproval of the activity. In fact, I think we would all say, if pushed, that wiping is good (WIG). But we only want people to do it, not to discuss it. To discuss it would be in bad taste (consider this paragraph).

We could talk about the very first thing we do when we sit down in the driver's seat of our cars, but we don't. We don't discuss this because nobody cares, because it's insignificant, because it's boring.

We could talk about what we imagine while the attractive person behind the counter serves us coffee, but we don't. We don't discuss this because, again, it is bad, or in bad taste, or boring.

Then, too, many of us follow an unwritten rule not to talk about politics or religion. But this impulse to avoid talk of politics or religion does not develop because the avoided subject is bad, or in bad taste, or boring; rather, politics and religion are things we care about, and because we care about them, we might disagree with each other, even disagree hotly, and if we disagree hotly, something must be wrong. So we don't talk about them.

Many of us also do not talk about money—about how much we make, how much we pay to live where we live, how much our families do or do not have. We don't talk about money, I want to suggest, because of our peculiar blend of democratic political culture and capitalist ethos. (There may also be some residual aristocratic notion that talk of money is vulgar, or cheap, though that would mainly explain why the wealthy among us remain reticent here.) We think of ourselves as democrats, or as citizens of a democracy, so we like to think that we are all equal, whatever that might mean. But we also think of ourselves as free marketers, and we seem to believe that those who have money have earned it, or deserve it, and so money can seem like a measure of merit. To talk of money would then be to talk of difference, and not just any difference, but difference of worth and power. To talk of money would be to put our inequality in front of us.

Now we return to our silence on service. To talk of service, to really look at it, would require us to look closely at inequality. This is a difficult and uncomfortable place to look.

Inequality and Service

Here is an exaggerated pass at the relation between inequality and service: I serve you because I want to; I choose to. You receive my service because you have to; you need it. I live in the realm of freedom; you live in the realm of necessity. Serving you, I confirm my relative superiority. Being served, you confirm your inferiority. By my apparent act of humility, I raise myself up. "The happiness," as Nietzsche writes, "of slight superiority," only we don't say so.

Instead we say very little about why we and especially our kids serve. It's good, that's why; our kids learn valuable lessons and those they serve receive valuable help. But these lessons are complicated and the help is not always helpful. To pretend otherwise is to pass on a dirty little secret with the tacit message that it best be kept secret.

What is the dirty little secret? Maybe this: we cherish inequality. We don't say this, of course, and we may not even think it, but we show it by what we do and especially what we accept. Look at schools, jobs, cars, clothes, teeth, bellies, eyes. Look anywhere at all and you'll see signs, indisputable signs, of inequality.

We are told that "all men are created equal," and we are taught to believe it. We may be taught to believe this more deeply than any other single thing. But this claim—"all men are created equal"—is a self-evident falsehood. It is simply and obviously not the case that men—people—are created equal: we do not possess equal gifts and we do not find ourselves with equal opportunities to make our way in the world. We are equal only with respect to our end. Our beginnings, our points of entry, could not be more unequal, and the beginning, as Aristotle tells us, is more than half. The beginning, as any newspaper or attentive glance can tell us, is much more than half.

Here again we return to service. Those who serve set out to help, yes, but they also set out to bridge a gap, to remedy the consequences of inequality. To the extent that we engage in service because we think it's good for those we're serving—and here we have learned to tread carefully: we're not improving those we serve; we're only improving the conditions in which they find themselves (again, the wishful insistence that all *are* created equal)—we seem by our activity to declare that the gap is wrong. We who have more—more money or more time or more education or more energy or more freedom—should close the distance between ourselves and those we serve. We should move toward equality.

Do acts of service move us toward equality? Might some acts of service enshrine and even extend the very gap they mean to bridge? Where will the server be, five years from any particular service transaction? Where will the served be? How has this transaction, this series of transactions, contributed to the socioeconomic and perhaps especially to the psychological positions in which these people find themselves? What do we learn when we serve? What do we learn when we are served?

What don't we talk about when we don't talk about service?

We do not like to be seen as hypocrites and we certainly do not like to see ourselves as hypocrites. So when we say that everyone is equal, we want to believe it. But equality is threatening; it might rob my loved ones of their security; it might rob me of my freedom, my relative rank. It feels good to look down, better still if I can tell myself I'm ready to serve those less fortunate (that is, less) than me. That way I'm not just better, I'm also good.

Service Is Not Simple

I have not meant to suggest that service is bad, or at least not that it is necessarily bad, or that inequality is bad, or, for that matter, good. Instead I want to suggest that inequality is present and in many ways desired and that this accounts in large part for the fact that service is not simple (SINS), no matter what we pretend.

The crux of this piece, however, might be simple. Here it is: by pretending service is simple (SIS), we risk turning service bad—bad for the served and for the server. And by pretending service is simple (SIS), we saddle ourselves with a burden we do not acknowledge. It may originate as a salutary burden, for it derives from and endeavors to satisfy our aspiration to live more justly, to do right by those we are with and among. But it remains a burden, and the less we acknowledge it, the heavier it gets.

PART III

Giving

The donor wanted his money back. It was his money, after all. He had made it, building that company from scratch. And then he had given it to his alma mater, for a dining hall. The hall hadn't been built—well, not in the way they said it would. Not by the proposed architect. Not in the promised place on the main quad. Not even for the purpose they had settled on nearly ten years ago, over endless dinners and glasses of wine. So what if they suddenly needed a dormitory more? He wanted his money back.

The alma mater didn't see it quite the same way. It was their money, after all. He had given it. And they had used it as best they could, in light of changing students and changing times. The dormitory had a dining hall in it. The first architect had died. The new location fit the revised campus master plan. They had done their best, and they weren't giving the money back.

In some ways this story is an unusual one. Most of us don't give gifts that measure in the millions, much less try to take them back. But in other ways the story may feel quite familiar. We have all given gifts we wished we *could* take back. We have all received gifts we could not use as intended. We have all struggled with the complexities of giving and receiving.

Sometimes the smallest of gifts will yield joys large and strange, out of all proportion to the gift itself. Other times, the largest of gifts will take us down paths of resentment and regret. Much of the time, and perhaps even in the best of cases, acts of giving and receiving lead into quiet perplexity and self-doubt. *Should I have given that dollar to the man on the street? What were my motives for donating money to my alma mater or the state police? Why am I giving at all? Is this for me or them, and does it even matter?*

The readings in this section display a wide range of minds at work on these and other questions about the sometimes sweet, sometimes sour, but always perplexing human experience of giving and receiving.

In the opening story, "Where Were We," **Dave Eggers** explores what happens as two young men travel around the world giving away an unexpected windfall of money as fast as they possibly can. *Why is it that some forms of giving do not feel right?*

Traveling around his own neighborhood, solitary walker **Jean-Jacques Rousseau** explores the unhappy consequences of impulsive giving. *Why do we give in the first place? What is pleasant about such giving, and how does an initially pleasurable activity turn unpleasant and onerous?*

Rousseau's examination of the bitter aftertaste of giving is followed by **Maya Angelou**, who instead implores us to savor "the sweetness of Charity." *What is charity, and why is it sometimes called sweet? Should we savor that sweetness?*

In a short excerpt from an interview with Robert Bly, **Pablo Neruda** recalls a childhood exchange of trinkets. *Why do certain gift exchanges remain with us long after the gifts themselves—and their givers—have disappeared?*

Andrew Carnegie, hardly interested in trinkets, ponders the use of large fortunes. In *The Gospel of Wealth*, Part I, he tells us exactly how to give them away. *How can wealth be used to bridge the gap between rich and poor? Should we give away our money while we are alive—and only to "those who can help themselves"?*

Ralph Waldo Emerson, for one, will have none of Carnegie's advice. In a brief, pungent passage from "Self-Reliance," he counsels us to listen to ourselves and to give only to those who belong to us. *Is it good and right to give only to those persons to whom you belong, and who belong to you? How would you know that someone belongs to you, or you to them?*

A Buddhist parable from **Sogyal Rinpoche** follows, calling us back to the mystery of compassion for other living beings. *What is compassion, and how might solitude and spiritual practice prepare us to understand its true nature?*

In "A Bed for the Night," German playwright and poet **Bertolt Brecht** invites us to witness another act of compassion, but (don't put down the book yet, reader!) he also artfully reminds us of its limits. *What is the delicate balance between the relief of suffering and the reform of social injustice?*

In the essay "Four Traditions of Philanthropy," **Elizabeth Lynn** and **D. Susan Wisely** suggest that relief, social reform, and other traditions of giving each have an important place in American philanthropy. *What are the comparative strengths and weaknesses of these traditions? Is civic engagement itself a tradition of philanthropy?*

Next, medieval Jewish philosopher and physician **Moses Maimonides** guides us through eight degrees of giving, leaving us to ponder where we fit as givers—and how we should feel about that. *Are there higher and lower degrees of giving? What distinctions are worth making concerning the relations of giver and receiver?*

And in closing, Russian poet **Anna Akhmatova** turns giving on its head, inviting us to appreciate the strength we receive from those who beg for our help. *What kind of strength does it take to beg for help? What kind of strength does it give others to be asked? Is it better to give than to receive?*

Dave Eggers

Dave Eggers was born in Chicago in 1970, grew up in Lake Forest, Illinois, and attended the University of Illinois. He achieved quick fame in 2000 with his first book, *A Heartbreaking Work of Staggering Genius*, and has since published *You Shall Know Our Velocity!* and *How We Are Hungry*. He is the editor of *McSweeney's* and the founder of 826 Valencia, a San Francisco writing lab for young people that has spawned similar centers in other cities throughout the United States. This selection, adapted from *You Shall Know Our Velocity!* first appeared in the August 12, 2002, issue of the *New Yorker* magazine.

Where Were We

The light was screaming through the windows, and I opened my portal's eyelid a quick few inches and we were coming at Africa at three hundred miles per hour. The neat shadow of the plane swept over Dakar's shoreline, the city's buildings glowing in tan and white and standing still as the water and wind came to them with all die world's fury—and then died. We were somewhere else. What were we doing here? We had no idea. Hand was awake.

"Senegal," I said.

"Senegal," Hand said.

We had pictured Senegal green, but this was tan.

"West Africa, I guess, is tan," he said.

"I really figured on green for Senegal."

There was no gangway to the terminal, just a stairway to the tarmac. The air was warm and the wind was warm; the sky was clear, blue but bleached, and the sun hung still, bored and unchallenged. The baggage handlers, with green kneepads, watched us through their goggles, hands resting on their heads.

"We're in Africa," Hand said.

We stepped into the airport.

"This is an African airport," he said.

It was tiny, and open everywhere. It looked like a mini-mall. We sat on the cool linoleum floor and filled out our customs forms.

"I can't believe I got to Africa," Hand said. I'd known Hand since I was seven. I'd never been further than Nevada; he'd been as far as Toronto.

"I know," I said.

"How did we get to Africa?" he said. "Already I don't want to leave. Did you feel that air? It's different. It's African air. It's like mixed with the sun more. Like our air isn't mixed as well with the sun. Here they mix it perfectly. The sun's in the wind; the sun's in your breath."

"I'm glad you could come," I said.

We passed customs and the cabbies didn't touch us, because we had no bags. A large woman in brilliant yellow appeared and asked us something.

"What?" we said.

"Wheech 'otel?"

"The Independent," Hand said, cribbing it from a backlighted ad above us.

"I take you," she said, pointing to a small bus out front. We asked her if we could get some money first. "Fine," she said, with an annoyed look at her watch. We were hers already, her children, and we were holding her up.

We cashed two thousand dollars in traveler's checks—swoop! swik! swoop!—and stopped in the bathroom to hide it. I gave half to Hand, who split it five times and found pockets for each portion. I buried stacks in pockets, in my backpack, in my socks.

We were the only passengers in the bus. The landscape on the way in to the city was dry and dusty, the color of stripped pine. Billboards featured Senegalese citizens frowning upon littering and public urination and encouraged the drinking of milk.

When the minibus stopped at a light, our open windows filled up with faces, mothers with babies pointing into their infants' tiny mouths.

"Bebbe! Bebbe!" they yelled. The babies were swarmed by flies. Boys hawked candy and mobile phones. Everything was too fast. We weren't ready.

"Give 'em something!" Hand yelled.

"You!"

"You!"

We had money and wanted to give it to them but everything had been too sudden, and I was preoccupied by the traffic, the babies were too close—and so I managed only to smile apologetically, like a locksmith who'd failed to open a door. I moved away from the window.

"Bebbe! Bebbe!"

"Meester! Meester!"

The shuttle woman was watching us struggle. Why wasn't she telling us not to give them money? I smiled more, flustered. Hand was looking flustered, too, though he was still only half awake and his bed head was ridiculous, but finally the shuttle lurched forward. A gold sedan slipped in front of us, its driver on the phone and gesturing with fists. Soon the road was narrow and wound through the city. Men carried bike tires or sold meat from carts, while others hoisted sacks of oranges into passing cars. No one was sweating, and no one was smoking. Outside a gated compound, a tousled-haired white tourist in an enormous Fubu football jersey was talking to two uniformed men with assault rifles while a group of students from Italy—Hand was sure it was Italy—in crisp white tops and black pants and skirts lightly dusted, whinnied by on mopeds. All of Dakar's residents, it seemed, were selling objects, or moving them from one location to another—a city of small favors and short errands.

We'd called the airlines that offered round-the-world tickets. The tickets allowed unrestricted flying in one direction. You usually have twelve months to go around the globe, but we'd do it in a week. The tickets cost three thousand dollars each, a number out of the reach of people like us under normal circumstances, but I had got some money about a year before, in a windfall kind of way, and had been both grateful and constantly confused by it. And now I wanted to get rid of it, or most of it, and I believed this purging would provide clarity, and that doing it in a quick global flurry would make it—well, I actually don't know why Hand and I combined these two ideas. We just figured we would go all the way around, once, in a week, starting in Chicago, ideally hitting Saskatchewan first, then Mongolia, then Siberia, then Yemen, then Rwanda, then Madagascar—maybe those last two switched around—then Greenland, then home.

"This'll be good," said Hand.

"It will," I said.

"How much are we getting rid of again?"

"I think thirty-eight thousand."

"Is that including the tickets?"

"Yeah."

"So we're actually giving away what—thirty-two thousand dollars?"

"Something like that," I said.

"How are you going to bring it? Cash?"

"Traveler's checks."

"And then we give it to who?"

"I don't know yet. I think it'll be obvious when we get there."

We could easily make our way around the world in a week, with maybe five stops along the way—the hours elapsed would in part be voided by the crossing of time zones. We would oppose the turning of the planet and refuse the setting of the sun.

The itinerary changed on each of the days we had to decide, on the phone, with me in Chicago consulting a laminated pocket atlas and Hand in St. Louis with his globe, a huge thing, the size of a beach ball, which spun wildly between poles—he'd bumped into it one late night, and it was no longer smooth.

We called an airline representative. She thought we were assholes. If we wanted to get around the world in a week, she said, we'd be in the air ninety-five percent of the trip.

We decided to skip the preplanned round-the-world tickets. We'd start in Mongolia and just go from there. We'd get there and then just hit the airports when we were ready to leave. The new plan felt good. It was more in keeping with the overall idea, anyway—that of unmitigated movement, of serving any impulse. It couldn't cost all that much more, we figured. How much could it cost? We had no idea. All we wanted was to get around the world in a week with half a day in Franz Josef Land at least.

The hotel, in the left-middle of Dakar, was dark inside, the lobby low and sleek and smooth with black marble, all of it cool, safe, immaculate. The reception man laughed at Hand's French and gave us his English. We asked for two beds and we dropped our bags in the room. The view was bright, and facing both the city of yellows and whites and the sea, all violet and sugar. We'd been screwed at O'Hare trying to get to Mongolia, and Senegal was the next flight out to somewhere we knew nothing about, so we'd taken it.

"I thought you said you spoke French," I said.

"I do. Some."

"Your dad's French, right?"

"Not, like, from France. He's not *from France*."

"What are you wearing?"

"What?"

He was wearing a shirt declaring "I am proud of my black heritage."

"Where'd you get that?"

"Thrift store."

"No one's going to get the joke here. Or whatever it is. It's not even a joke."

"No one will know. And it's not a joke. I liked the shirt. Did you see the back?"

I nodded slowly, to communicate the pain it caused me. The back said "Rogers Park Women's Volleyball."

We left the hotel looking for a travel agent to book a flight out. We wanted information on all flights leaving Senegal; we wanted Madagascar or Rwanda, tomorrow. On the street we were besieged, men striding with us, matching our pace, walking backward, asking, "Where are you from? English?" while shaking Hand's hand. Looking at me: "Spanish?" I always get "Spanish," with the dark hair, the eyelashes. I have the sort of eyelashes that imply I'm wearing eyeliner, and the good fortune this has occasionally worked is nothing compared to the stares, the constant Robert Smith comparisons. And now my face was stranger, still healing, slowly, from a beating I'd taken—long story—weeks before.

"American."

"Ameri*kahn*, ah. Welcome to Dakar! You have accident! Your face! Need mask like Phantom! Ha-ha! You like Dakar? How long you been in Dakar?"

"Twenty minutes."

"Oh ha-ha. Twenty minutes! Very good. Joke! Welcome! Welcome! Do you need taxi? Tour? I—"

And we ducked into the travel agency.

"Where do you want to go?" asked the agent, a stately woman in cosmic blue.

"We are not sure," Hand said, in English. "We want to see our options. Do you have that kind of in-for-ma-tion? All of the avail-a-ble flights?"

This is when Hand started speaking with a Senegalese accent, without contractions and with breaks between syllables. It was almost a British accent, but a slower version, with him nodding a lot.

"Sir, where is it you want to go?" she asked. She, too, thought we were assholes.

"We want to see all of the options and then to choose from them," he said.

The woman stared. "You have to tell me where you want to go."

"Can you not first show us the flights?"

"No. I cannot."

We thanked her and walked back to the hotel and the business center to get on the Web. We checked planes leaving from Dakar. Nothing, almost nothing, without Paris first. We couldn't get to Rwanda without Paris. We couldn't get to Yemen without Paris. We could get to Madagascar, but only through South Africa. To get anywhere would take a full day or more. And visas. We couldn't even cross into the Gambia, stuck inside Senegal like a tumor, without a visa. Just getting across the continent, to Cairo, could occupy our whole week. Could we just drive from Dakar to Cairo? We couldn't. Mauritania wanted a visa, same with Mali. Neither was recommended for drivers.

"Fuck."

"We're fucked."

"*Yes!*"

There was a man on a computer behind us. It was his "Yes." He was dressed for tennis, white socks Van Horned around his calves. Hand turned to him.

"My friend's in the Paris-to-Dakar rally," the man said.

"The big car-race thing?" Hand said.

"Yeah. He's in seventh place." He looked American, but his accent had something in it. He was looking at a page of results.

"Wow. Motorcycle or car?" Hand said. Hand was interested.

"Motorcycle," the man said. "He's very good."

Hand knew about the race. Hand knew things like this. He knew how many guerrilla-killed gorillas there were each year in the Congo, and how many tons of cocaine were imported weekly from Colombia, how they did it and how pure it was, and who ran which cartel with the help of which U.S. agencies and for how long. And how Spinoza was actually autistic—he'd read this recently but couldn't remember where, but it was true! They'd studied DNA!—and that you could grow the bones of dwarfs by attaching external bone-growing devices that looked like medieval torture instruments. It worked! he would yell; he'd seen a documentary, and one guy had grown almost a foot, though some dwarfs objected, calling him some sort of Uncle Tom. . . . On and on, for twenty years I'd heard this shit, from first grade, when he claimed you'd get worms if you touched your penis—and always this mixture of the true, the almost true, and the apocryphal—he'd veer within this emporium of anecdote like an angry drunk, but he stood steadfastly behind all of his stories, never with a twinge of doubt or even allowances for your own.

"Where are you from?" Hand asked the tennis man.

"Chile."

"Your English is very American."

"I live in Fort Lauderdale," he said.

Chilean but living in Florida and now in Senegal waiting for a friend riding a bike from Paris. He was like us, I thought, flattering myself and Hand —world travelers who defied God and beat time in planes and rented cars.

As Hand and this man talked, I tried more connections on the Web travel sites. Dakar to the Congo: no. Dakar to Kenya: yes, but wildly expensive and through Paris. Dakar to Mongolia: no. This was so wrong. Why wouldn't there be planes going from Senegal to Mongolia? I'd always assumed, vaguely, that the rest of the world was even better connected than the United States, that passage between all countries outside of America was constant and easy—that all other nations were huddled together, trading information and commiserating, like smokers outside a building. We left.

Minutes later, we were girding for death. What was this cop doing in our car? Or was he a soldier? He was taking us to the place where tourists were killed. If nuns could be killed in Colombia, we could be killed in Africa. Even in Senegal, which hadn't been billed as particularly dangerous, at least according to the few minutes of Web research we'd done at the hotel. But what did we really know? Nothing. We were fools, and now we were driving to our deaths in a rental car. Janet Jackson was tinkling from the speakers, asking what we had done for her of late.

The cop was sitting in the back seat, directing our turnings. He was tall, about forty-five, thin, wearing a tan uniform and what looked like Foster Grants. He had been standing in the road directing traffic when he told us to stop. We pulled over, and Hand's French hadn't worked. The man could not get our crime through Hand's head. Exasperated, finally he opened the back door.

Now he was directing us through alleys near the center of Dakar. One of us was going to be dragged around by his penis.

Hand and I needed to put together some sort of plan and were speaking in very speedy English, in case the man knew any.

"Thisiswhentheydragyouaroundbyyourpenis," I said.

"Notfunny. Shouldwetrytobribehimnow?"

"Nonotyetwaitasec."

In Senegal, you weren't supposed to trust the police. Were you? Or maybe that's Peru—

We passed small walled fortresses with driveways flanked by armed guards.

"Youthinkwe'regoingtothepolicestation?"

"Ihavenoidea."

Hand was periodically turning to the man and trying more French. I tensed. It was Hand who dozens of times had brought us near the brink of injury or expulsion or infection or death; Hand who three weeks ago had fairly directly brought the wrath of three Wisconsin fuckers upon me as he and I were supposed to be packing up Jack's stuff. Jack, who otherwise would have been here with us, was killed six months ago, on the highway, ten miles from his house. And now we were here. I don't know if that explains anything.

The policeman barked orders, with his big dry hand, the one not in my bag, near my ear, pointing left or right at every turn. We seemed to be circling. It was arbitrary. We were dead.

The cop signaled us to pull over. I did, behind a taxi, in front of a bar. The cop pointed to a street sign. This was, we realized, exactly where he had stopped us in the first place. We'd made some kind of elaborate and misshapen loop to get back here. The sign was a blue circle, bordered in red, indicating that the road prohibited the traveling on it of anything but buses and taxis.

Ah. Hand and I made exaggerated sounds of understanding and approval. "Aaaahhhh!" Hand said. We were happy to be alive. We had broken a law and that's . . . okay! Now we'd pay a fine and be off. We all smiled and laughed. We laughed and nodded our heads. Stupid us! I wanted to hug the man but didn't know local custom.

We would live.

"I am so sorry," the man at the hotel's rental counter said. The car had died two blocks from the sign. "I knew this might happen, but I hoped it would not be so soon."

I blinked into the sun and wondered just what the hell we were doing. Out there were the Senegalese, and beyond them the Gambia, and the sun was already finding the uppermost points of its arc, and we were still in the hotel lobby. Where was teleporting, for fuck's sake? They promised us teleporting decades ago. Why were we spending billions on unmanned missions to Mars when we could be betting the cash on teleporting? Fuck regular movement. Fuck cars, rental cars, and wheels and engineering, and big metal machines that were always too loud and used this ridiculous kind of fuel, so goddamn medieval—

In the hotel room, waiting for a new car, we both fell asleep and when we woke it was five.

"Piss."

"What a waste."

"We've done nothing."

No delta, no mangroves, no Gambia.

We were hungry.

We ran into the Chilean American tennis man in the lobby—

"What's his name again?" I whispered.

"Raymond."

"Hey, Raymond!" I said.

"Hello, my friends!"

—and had a taxi take us six blocks to the Italian place he liked. The cabbie asked for the equivalent of fifty cents, and I gave him ten dollars; he said thank you, thank you, and told us that he'd wait until we were done to take us back, or anywhere else, anytime, while we stayed in his country, you friends!

The restaurant was empty but for four drunk and round Italians at the bar talking to the drunk Italian hostess.

"She's gorgeous, isn't she?" Raymond said. "That's why I had to come back."

Hand, blond and tall and dark-eyed, I guess you'd say doe-eyed, was well liked by women. He agreed. "She is nice. But I'm really starting to have a thing for the Senegalese women."

"You, too?" said Raymond. "I know. They are superb." He stretched out the "perb" for what seemed like five lascivious minutes. Raymond raised his finger, about to make a point. "But," he said, closing his eyes slowly and raising his chin, "they are all whores."

Hand and I stared at Raymond. We were stuck with this man, even though it was becoming obvious that he was not of our stripe. He was a bigger asshole than we were. Friendships, even temporary ones like this, were based on proximity and chance, and so rarely made any sense at all.

The music piped in was a short, ever-repeating loop of Dire Straits, Pink Floyd, Eagles, and *White Album* Beatles. We had fettuccine and Senegalese beer. We learned that Raymond worked in cell phones. Something involving GPS and cell phones and how, soon enough, everyone would know—for their own safety, he insisted—where everyone else in the world was, by tracking cell phones. This was, he insisted, for good, not evil. Not for surveillance, not for spying, not for control, for safety! For the children. For grandparents and wives.

After dinner, Hand asked the cabbie, who'd been waiting without radio or newspaper, to take us to see live music. "You know," said Hand, "like Youssou N'Dour." We'd read in the hotel-lobby guidebook that Youssou N'Dour lived in Dakar and owned a club. The cabbie seemed to understand, began driving, and a few minutes later pulled up in front of an outdoor café.

"Here is the location of the music that is live?" asked Hand.

Raymond looked at Hand. Hand needed reining in.

"Yes, yes," said the driver, waving us out of the car. "You like, you like." We got out.

It looked fine, a French-café sort of place, outdoor seating, inside warmly lit. But there was no music at all; just wrought-iron tables and a floor of white tile, a black slate bar with a bowl of Manet oranges. We walked in anyway. We'd get a drink and leave.

All eyes jumped to us. There were groups of men and groups of women. The men were tourists and the women were local. I went to the bathroom, and the small round scallop-shaped soap I traded between my wet hands smelled of home.

I found Raymond and Hand at a table outside, with two women, lighter skinned than most Senegalese, both with long, braided hair. Raymond stood and gave me his chair and grabbed another for himself. The girls surveyed me briefly and looked away.

There were drinks for everyone. I was introduced to the two, whose names I pretended to understand and whose limp hands I held momentarily and then dropped. They looked about twenty, twenty-two. They were sisters, and I felt again, as I had so many times with Hand and Jack—who together formed a loud perfect rockabilly duo of rollicking charm—like deadweight.

"They're from Sierra Leone," said Raymond.

"Refugees," added Hand.

They were just short of glorious, with large dark eyes and crooked, oversized teeth. Raymond and Hand were trying to speak French with them.

"We speak little French," the older one said. "Speak English. In Sierra Leone we speak English."

"So you are liking it here in the Dakar?" Hand asked.

The older one nodded. Hand ordered more drinks and then leaned toward them. He was about to dig in.

"So what's the situation like in Sierra Leone now? Is Charles Taylor still lurking around? I should know this, I guess, but it's been a while since I read about it. Have you seen any of the violence around the diamond trade?"

They looked dumbfounded, turning to Raymond, as if he might translate. Hand continued. "What did you do for a living? Are you students? When did you guys leave? I mean, are your parents still there?"

The sisters looked at each other.

"What?" the older said, smiling.

"Your parents? In Sierra Leone?"

"Yes. Live there."

"So how old are you two?" Raymond asked.

"What?"

"How old are you?"

The older one, to whom Raymond had directed the question, laughed and looked at her sister. She shook her head. She didn't understand.

"How many years are you?" Hand tried.

The older held up her hands in a "stop" sort of motion, closed them, then did it again.

"Twenty," Hand said.

She nodded.

Raymond laughed.

"Your English is not very good, is it?" Hand said.

"What?" she said.

Raymond said it in French.

"Speak English!" the girl said. "We are from Sierra Leone!"

Where was this going? No one could know. Soon I stopped listening.

I watched the sidewalk over the café's low hedge. The place was stocked with chubby European or American men, mostly middle-aged and cheerful. Some had garnered the attentions of the available women, others waited patiently with friends. By the door was a man with no legs, sitting on a mat.

Now the younger sister was laughing about something Hand had said, making a point of grabbing his arm with both hands and burying her head in his shoulder to demonstrate the great mirth he'd generated. Hand rolled his eyes to me, like a cat had jumped into his lap. More drinks were ordered.

"So we go to disco now?" the older said to Raymond.

Hand and Raymond looked at each other, then at me. I shrugged.

I walked to the cab, not caring if they came with us or not. I was groped by the man without legs. He wanted money. Raymond and Hand appeared, without the women. An old woman with a tin cup placed herself in front of us, sticking the cup a few inches from my mouth. Another woman from the bar appeared, too. We were surrounded. We backed into the cab. Raymond got in the front seat and closed his door. Hand got in the rear and I sunk in after him, but the no-legged man was now halfway in the car and the door wouldn't close. I could smell his breath—worlds contained within.

"Just give him something," said Raymond, laughing. It wasn't funny. This was the kind of thing that happened in India, or in the Bible.

I gave the man the coins in my pocket, and while counting them he backed away long enough for us to get the door closed. The old woman appeared at the open window, thrusting her head inside. The car was moving, but her head was fully in our cab. Raymond's hand was on her shoulder, pushing her away. He shoved, but too roughly—she fell back into the shrubbery with a shriek.

We were off.

"Jesus," I said.

"That was wretched," said Hand.

"These people are poor," said Raymond, without turning around, talking through the wind pouring through his window.

"But that's just not right," Hand said.

"Listen," Raymond said, now turning to us. "You're here. You came here. You left the hotel. You walk these streets, you allow your path to be chosen by me, by"—jerking a thumb toward the cabbie—"this driver. You invite things to happen. You open the door. You inhale. And if you inhale the chaos you give the chaos, the chaos gives back. You know this?"

I felt my forehead tighten, indicating I was thinking—often my forehead starts thinking before I do. I committed what he'd said to memory—it was a jigsaw dumped on a rug, but I was hoping I could put it back together, later.

We rode in silence for a few minutes.

"That didn't even make sense," Hand muttered.

"The imbalance is there," Raymond continued. My tolerance for Raymond was waning. "We know we're stronger, but we ignore this. You watch *Star Trek*, how they—what's the word for their beaming up and down?"

"Teleporting," I said, shocked at how this thought had just plowed right into my own backyard.

"Right," Raymond said. "They teleport in and out of troubled planets?"

"Wait," Hand said, actually raising his palm to Raymond's face. "You get *Star Trek* in Chile?"

"Of course."

Hand snorted, impressed. "Okay, go on."

"So this teleporting was based on a cold-war mentality. This was the American foreign-policy model then. This was based on the American strength, the American ability to move and to change the worlds they touched."

The cabbie pulled up in front of a club called Hollywood.

"Is this the live music?" I asked.

"Yes, yes, you love there!" he said, shooing us inside. "I wait here."

It was a small disco, pink and purple, full of large-framed movie stills in black-and-white. Two or three life-size pictures of James Dean and Marilyn Monroe, and one each of Tom Selleck, Sandra Bullock, and Charlie Sheen, but also, strangely, seven different shots of Val Kilmer in *Top Gun*. The place was empty apart from twelve young white men with crewcuts. Sailors.

"I could do that," Hand said.

"Be a sailor? You're high," I said.

"For a year I could do that."

"Just for the pants. That's why you'd do it."

Hand was intercepted by a tall thin woman in a halter top and pleather pants. She led him to a small dance floor, lit from below and facing a mirror. Debbie Harry was singing "Heart of Glass."

"This is Engela," Hand said after the song had finished. "She's studying to become a lawyer."

Hand bought shots for them both. He drank his; she left hers; so he drank it, too. She played with Hand's ear. Two sailors were on the dance floor, without women, admiring their own legs moving inside their tight, tapered, delicately bleached jeans.

I went to the bar for a shot of anything. The woman serving me was wearing a white sports bra that looked like it had been mauled by tigers. I turned again. Hand was showing his friend something. A piece of paper. A picture. What was it?

I grabbed it.

"What the fuck are you doing?" I yelled. It was a picture of Jack. Hand stood and looked at me, heavy-lidded with pity.

"I told her we were looking for our friend," he said.

"What does that mean?"

He was drunk already.

"You know what it means," he said.

"That doesn't even make sense," I said.

"So what the fuck?" he said.

"Don't ever show that picture to some random waitress again," I said.

"Guys!" Raymond said, with an arm between us. "Easy."

We were home by one. In the cool black lobby we waited with Raymond for the elevator.

"So where to next?" he asked. "Tomorrow."

"Not sure yet," Hand said. "You?"

"I go to Portugal, with my friend. A vacation after his race."

"You think he'll win?" I asked.

"Win? Not a chance. But that's not the point."

I thought it was the point. "Why not?" I asked.

"The point is to offer yourself to death and see if you're chosen."

"Jesus," I said. The elevator arrived.

"Not him."

"Who?"

"I don't believe in Jesus," Raymond said. "I think He would be horrified that we called Jesus Christ His son."

He was losing me. Hand steered us back onto the main trail. "So, Portugal," he said.

"That should be nice," I said. I don't know why I said this. I didn't think of Portugal as nice, though I'd never seen a picture, or couldn't remember one.

"Well," said Raymond, "I dread it, frankly. I love being here. I love wearing my clothes in these new places. It's the only thing I love, maybe—travel. I am finished with women," he said, chin jutting with an adolescent sort of defiance.

"We're liking it so far," Hand said. "The trip and all. But—"

"So why not stay in Senegal?" Raymond said. "In a week you will meet everyone. You will be kings."

"I guess," I said. "But we're liking the moving." I set my head on the elevator wall, wondering why I had used a pronoun that included Hand, whom I now hated. I was so tired my eyes felt distended.

Raymond's floor rang and the doors opened.

"There is travel and there are babies," he said, stepping out. "Everything else is drudgery and death."

I had been given eighty thousand dollars to screw in a light bulb. There's almost no way to dress it up; that's what it was. I was working for a contracting company. We'd just built a sunroom for a family on Orchard, and it turned out the owner worked at this ad agency, and while putting together logo proposals for a light-bulb maker, she'd used a silhouette of me on my stepladder, and tried it out on the company, and the company said, "Sure." I said, "Sure," too. In lieu of cash they offered me stock, stock that could mature, with a split or two, they said, into ten, twelve million, so good were these new light bulbs. They were brilliant, I told them. Their bulbs were fucking great, I said. Then I gave them the routing number for the eighty thousand dollars, their cash offer and apparently the going rate for people transformed into silhouettes to sell things. I felt briefly, mistakenly, powerful: my outline burned into the minds of millions! But then I came back down, crashing.

Jack was twenty-six and had died a few months after the money came. Jack was smarter than us and better than us in everything. When we were kids, everyone assumed we were as dumb as we acted. Soon enough, though, everyone realized that Jack was different from me and Hand, that he had calm where I had chaos and wisdom where Hand had just a huge gaping mouth. But he was not cool; he didn't have the gene. We wanted him to speed, but Jack would not speed. He drove with his hands perfectly at ten and two, which afforded him the most control, but it blocked, completely, his view of the speedometer. Every few seconds he would have to raise his thumbs, as if giving a double thumbs-up, granting himself a view of the gauge. It drove us nuts.

So when I first heard that there had been an accident, for a second I was happy, because Jack could never have been driving fast enough for a car accident; I pictured car crashes as involving only cars going very fast, two cars colliding, both at top speed. Not a truck coming from behind, doing eighty, downhill, hitting Jack's car, the momentum driving the wheels up and over Jack's, grinding it flat as it passed, twelve wheels at once practically, all of it happening in half a second.

This was six months ago, and in those months everything was pulling at my eyes. Songs were knocking me from wall to wall, certain songs in certain progressions roughed up my throat, brought me near tears without delivering me to any kind of catharsis. I was shaking my head at how perfect some song was, and then I was in the car, on the way to Kmart to buy a lesson kit, convinced I could teach myself piano and, with my exceptional taste, make an album, and then I would double back and think, Fuck, I should learn to fly airplanes. That's the thing I really want to do. *Fly planes.* But it would take years, and I needed it quicker. What I wanted to do was take a course in the bar, take it and then practice law, all without having done law school at all. Or maybe I should just open the police-souvenir store, as I'd planned in eighth grade, or the general store in New Mexico with the local handicrafts. And marry a woman cop. She would be huge and strong and named Heather.

I was arguing with strangers constantly now, though only in my cloudy skull, while adopting this hollow admonishing tone, which even I couldn't stand:

—You, driving the Lexus.

—Me?

—Yes, you. You paid too much.

It helped me work through problems, solving things, reaching conclusions that were final, edifying, and even, occasionally, mutually agreeable.

—You, on the motorcycle.

—Yes.

—It's only a matter of time.

—I know.

—It would be fun, I guess, if it weren't constant, and so loud.

We woke up late. It was 9 a.m. "What a waste," Hand said. "We could have slept in the car on our way somewhere."

"We'll be fine."

"We really have to move."

We drove to the airport and made for the Air Afrique desk. Behind the counter were three queens—grand, dressed in the most florid and glorious wares, skin luminous like polished lanterns.

We asked what they had flying out.

"Where are you going?" they asked.

"What do you have flying out?" I said.

"You do not know where you are going?"

"Well, yes and no."

They had a flight to Mauritania, but Mauritania wanted a visa.

"Anything else?"

"There is a flight tomorrow to Casablanca."

Morocco didn't require a visa. But we'd have to stay in Senegal one more night. Which meant more waste, and the diminished likelihood of our making it around the world. But we had no choice. We'd stay one more night.

We left the airport, heading for the coast, for Saly, where there were beaches. First we had to swim. Then to the Gambia and back. We could make it, we figured, but we'd have to speed.

We were lost before we left the airport. In front of an abandoned hangar we stopped for directions. There were about thirty men, half of them in suits, standing in the parking lot. A contingent of five approached the car. We explained where we needed to go, Saly, and instead of directing us two of them began arguing, each with his hands on the backdoor handle. We asked again for directions. Directions only, we said.

Then a young man was in the back seat.

"I take you there," he said.

"What?" Hand said.

"I show you the way, then you pay me, no problem."

Hand looked at me, I looked at Hand.

"I show you, you pay me, no problem," he said again.

His name was Abass. He was about twenty-five, wearing a nylon sweat-suit; he sat where the officer had sat. In a few minutes, he had us on the road to Saly and had rendered himself redundant.

"Shouldntwejustdrophimoffnow?" I asked.

"Ithinkthatwouldberude. Maybewewanttotalktohimandpickhisbrain—"

He stayed. We liked him. He liked James Brown, and Hand had a James Brown tape, so we played James Brown. He liked, most of all, Wu-Tang Clan, but we didn't have any Wu-Tang Clan. We had Dolly Parton.

The road was an endless marketplace; the kind of road bearing strip malls and fast-food outlets in the United States but here tire shops, open-air refrigerator outlets, and fruit stands. Three gangly boys playing Foosball at a table five feet from the road. Small buses, bright blue, overfilled with people. The bus never actually stopped. The children were filthy, but the Mobils and Shells were pristine, as were the adults. Everywhere there were people in dashikis, long enough to brush the road's unpaved shoulder but still unbesmirched.

The light was the familiar dusty white. I decided that when we got to Saly we'd give Abass half of what we had on us—about twelve hundred dollars.

"You have wife?" Hand asked.

"No, no. Soon," he said.

"Kids?"

"No, no. Soon."

"Girlfriend?"

"Yeah! Yeah!"

"Nice girlfriend?"

"Yeah!" he said, holding up three fingers. Three girlfriends.

What would he do with the money?

Start a business? Buy his way out of Senegal? I didn't have the tools to imagine.

At a stoplight, a man was selling orange juice. We flagged him over to buy three drinks. But it wasn't orange juice. It was brake fluid. Behind him, an enormous pile of fish, the shape of an anthill, lay rotting in the sun.

"We should let him get off here," I said.

Hand made the offer. Abass shook his head and smiled.

"He wants to go to Saly," Hand said.

We drove on. Hand and Abass were talking about something that prompted, from Hand, many expressions of surprise. He turned to me.

"I think he said his father was the ambassador to Zaire."

"Tell him congratulations," I said, wondering why the son of an ambassador was in our car riding to Saly.

Hand and Abass exchanged words.

"He's dead ten years," Hand explained.

We expressed our condolences. I handed Abass a chocolate-chip energy bar. He pointed out the window, at a French Army truck going the other way.

"Ask him his last name," I said.

Hand asked.

"Diallo," Abass said.

"Really?" Hand said.

Another French troop truck.

"Tell him," I said, "we have a very famous Diallo in America."

Hand told him. Abass was interested.

"Abass wants to know," Hand said, "what our Diallo did to become famous."

We drove in silence. We'd never be able to explain it, and I didn't want to spoil the mood.

"Tell him he's a singer," I said.

At Saly, we turned off. This was a resort complex, and the foliage was lusher here, the street sides uncluttered—like a Floridian national park. We pulled into a hotel called Savana Saly and in the lot stepped out and stretched.

I was getting the money ready—this particular wad drawn from my inner waist pocket, under my belt—when Abass told us how much he wanted.

"What?" said Hand. Abass spoke quickly and sternly. They exchanged words. "I think he wants eighty dollars."

"Eighty dollars for getting us on the highway?"

"I guess so."

"That's too much," Hand told Abass. He glared at Hand. Now he was not our friend. Eighty dollars for three turns and an hour on the highway. He spit more words to Hand.

"He says he has to get a cab back to Dakar," Hand said.

There was no way he was getting a cab back to Dakar. He'd take the bus and pocket the eighty dollars. We didn't like him. He knew we'd feel awful paying him less than what he asked, but eighty dollars was wrong. I looked up and the sky gave me no tether. We'd been driving too long and we hadn't eaten—

I wanted a ceiling, but it was too thin and porous. I wanted something accountable above—

"Hey!"

"What? What?"

"You're back."

"Sorry."

I gave Abass the eighty dollars but not the hundreds I had planned on. He took the money and wrote his name and number on a piece of paper, urging us to call if we needed help getting back to Dakar. We said we'd be sure to call. The fucker.

He walked to the highway. Hand and I stood in the lot watching his back.

"That's too bad," Hand said.

At the reception desk, French tourists sat on their suitcases, waiting for deliverance. They stared at us dismissively.

We went to swim. The beach was slim and rocky, the water a vibrating cobalt blue. The bathers were old and white, flesh melting downward, the men in bikinis, many of the women topless and drooping without caution. Hand ran, jumped on and off a huge gray gumdrop rock and into the sea.

"Fuck!" he yelled. He stood waist deep; his hands shot to his face. "It's fucking cold!"

I stepped in; it was brutal. The air was about ninety, but the water was crisp, bracing. The cold of an upper Wisconsin lake, in June.

I spread my towel and I laid my head on the sand. A bird, fifty feet above, fell from the sky like a plane. It crashed through the water, broken, but in a second rose, fish in beak, and flew toward the white shore or the green hills above.

I burrowed my head deeper into the terry cloth and closed my eyes. Only on sand like this did I ever feel as though I could sleep forever, that sleep could be a destination, like a warm island full of food. The comfort was limitless, and I knew I was mouthing the words "Fantastic, so good, fantastic, so good," into the towel but couldn't help it. The sun had half my face, one eye, a shoulder, and the rest was mine. I felt the heat of the light pressing into me, in my neck, my crown, the side of my calf, nudging with strong bony forefingers.

We dressed quickly so we could drive through the countryside and tape money to donkeys. We'd been in Senegal for thirty hours and hadn't given anything away.

The plan was Hand's. As we drove, hair still wet, we looked for donkeys so we could tape money to them for their owners to find. We wondered what the donkey owners would think. We had no idea. Money taped to a donkey? It was a great idea. But each time we saw a donkey there was someone standing nearby.

"We have to find one alone, so the owner will be surprised," Hand said.

"Right."

Periodically, we'd pass through a village, the buildings, squat and clay, abutting the road, kids running out of open doorways. But we couldn't find a fucking donkey. Cows would be just as good, we thought, but every time we stopped and approached a cow on foot, a car would come down the road, or a bright-blue bus, or a farmer, and we'd abort. At one point, when we really thought we were going to do it, had the money in a pouch and the tape all around it and a cow picked out and were only a few feet away, it wasn't a car that came but a whole caravan of men, French, we guessed, on four-wheel ATVs, eleven of them, in a row, half with white girlfriends strapped around their waists, all with aviator glasses, a few with scarves.

"Good Lord God, no," Hand said.

We gave up on taping money to animals. We were now looking for people. Anyone to unload the money on. We found a group of boys working in a field, raking hay and throwing it into a large wooden wagon attached to a mule. Five boys—

"Brothers, probably," said Hand. We stopped on the side of the road.

"They're gonna see us," I said.

"Then get out and give 'em some money, idiot."

"Not yet. I gotta make sure."

"Here," Hand said, spreading a map between us. "This is like a fucking stakeout or something."

—working together, without pause. They were perfect. All I had to do was get out of the car, walk a hundred feet, and hand them part of the fourteen hundred dollars (Hand had found more in his shoe) we had left. We had to get rid of this money. Tomorrow we would cash more checks—swoop! swoop!—and start over. We were already so far behind.

"That one guy looks like a dad," I said.

"No, he's just a little older than the others."

"I can't give it to them if the dad's there."

"Why?"

"Because the dad won't take it."

"Bullshit."

"No, it's a pride thing. He won't take the money in front of his sons."

"Not here, stupid. These guys know they need it and that we can afford it. They're not taking it from a neighbor, they're taking it from people who it means, you know, next to nothing to."

"You do it."

"No, you. It's your money."

"No, it's not. That's the point."

"Just go."

"I can't. Maybe we should wait. The dad'll go get some water or something. Or you could create a diversion."

We sat, watching.

"This is predatory," I said.

"Yeah, but it's okay."

"Let's go. We'll find someone better."

We drove, though I wasn't sure it would ever feel right. It was wrong to stalk them, and even more wrong not to give them the money, a life-changing amount of money here, where the average yearly earnings were, we'd read, about sixteen hundred dollars. It was all so wrong, and now we were a mile away. To the right, beyond the amber fields and a thin row of trees, the Atlantic shimmered like a dime.

The sun was low and the air was cooling. We approached a huge warehouse. The place was immense, and shuttered, its parking lot covered in grass. There were no other buildings for miles.

We parked the car behind the warehouse, hiding it from the road. We imagined the possibility of roaming marauders who would strip our car bare and then move on. With the car hidden, we could walk through the fields and head to the ocean, less than a mile west.

The ground was hard and brown and dotted with seashells, white and broken. After a few minutes, we could see the ocean. It was the lightest blue, a dry and sun-faded blue. A few hundred yards from the shore, there was a group of small houses, all the same design and standing in formation. About fifteen of them, cottage-size and neatly arrayed, on a sort of plateau, separated from us and from the beach beyond by a moat, sixteen feet down and filled with what seemed to be—

"Sewage," I said.

The builders, it looked like, had run out of money. This was a resort-to-be, but without any sign of recent work. Only these small windowless homes.

We got as close as we could before the moat asserted itself. The water in the moat was too deep and dirty to wade through, and too wide to jump.

A man walked into view on the other side of the moat, among the houses. He was holding some kind of electric device in his hand, black and with a long antenna. He stared.

"Security," Hand said. "They've got someone guarding the place."

"We should leave."

We were watching the man and he was watching us.

We turned and shuffled away. Was he armed? He could shoot us if he wanted to and no one would ever know. We sat behind a pair of thick shrubs.

I stood, and the man was gone.

"Let's go," Hand said.

We walked alongside the moat, hoping to find a place to cross. We soon saw a clothesline threaded between a porch and a tree. Shirts and pants hung from it, and on the porch there were towels and an Indiana University umbrella.

"Jesus," I said. "Someone's living here."

"We could plant some money in there," Hand said. "Put it in a pair of pants."

"Yeah, on the clothesline. That'd be good."

We went around the entire moat and at the end found an area where we could get down the bluff, about fifty feet, on to the beach, and over the water. There was a rocky sort of path, and after taking off our shoes, in case we landed somehow in the moat, we descended, sliding and jumping, and soon found ourselves jogging slightly, as if descending stairs in a hurry. Then we were jumping, and the path was now dotted with large flat rocks, like overturned dinner plates, and we were jumping at a speed that I should have found alarming but somehow didn't, and we were doing so barefoot, which might have increased the alarm but instead made it easier, because my bare feet would land on the rock and kind of wrap around it, simianlike, in a way that a shoe or sneaker or sandal couldn't. There was no time to think, which was plenty of time—I had a few fractions of a second in midair, between rocks, to calculate the location of the next rock-landing options, the stability of each, the flattest surface among them. Then the rocks ended, and I jumped into the sand with a *shhhht*.

We hopped from the middle to the side, into wet mud, the ground like wet velour. Then up a bluff, only twenty feet or so, and we were now in the resort.

The man appeared again. He wasn't a man. He was about seventeen. In his hand was a transistor radio, fuzzily broadcasting the news.

"Bonjour," said Hand.

"Bonjour," said the teenager.

They shook hands, the boy's grip limp and uninterested. He looked at me quickly. In French, Hand asked if he was the guard. He shook his head. He was staying at a hotel nearby, he said, waving down the shore, and was just walking.

He didn't speak much French, he said. He and Hand laughed. I laughed. We stood for a moment. The boy looked at his radio and tuned the dial.

Hand said goodbye. The boy said goodbye, and we walked on, toward the beach.

"Let's skip the beach," Hand said. "I want to get back to that house and see who lives there."

"We'll do the clothesline."

It didn't look as though anyone was home, so we could sneak in, dump the money, and leave. That was almost better, we agreed, than taping it to a donkey.

We crept around the house, our own skulking making the place seem more sinister. There was the dark and vacuumed smell of clay. This was the sort of place where bodies were found. Or guns. We peeked around. Through the open front door we could see the corner of a bed and a calendar on the wall.

"You go," I said.

"You."

"You."

"You."

"You."

Hand stepped around until he was peering through the front porch of the house.

"Bonjour!" he said.

A man stepped through the door and into the light. It was the transistor-radio teenager from before. He wasn't happy.

Hand shook the boy's hand again. The boy was on his porch and we were below, grinning with shame. We said sorry a few times, for intruding, then Hand said, "So is it you leeve here?"

The man didn't understand.

"It's nice here, yes?" Hand said. "You're smart to stay here." He gestured to the house. "It's very nice."

The boy stared at Hand. Hand turned to me, and I understood. I took the money from my Velcro pocket, slowly, the way a criminal would lay down a gun before a cop. I took the stack of bills and aimed them at the boy. He didn't move.

"Sorry," I said, looking down.

"Can we . . ." said Hand, gesturing his arms like pistons, in a give-and-take sort of way.

"We want to . . ." I tried.

"Will you take?" Hand said, pointing to the money as you would to a broken toy offered to a skeptical child.

The boy took the bills. We smiled. We both made gestures meaning, Yes, it's yours. We can't use it. Please don't worry about it. Thank you for taking it off our hands. You have done us the greatest of favors.

The boy glanced at the stack and smiled at us grimly. He turned and with two steps was back in his house.

The warm wind was good. We were giddy. There was a hole in my shirt, in the left underarm, and the air darted through on tiny wings. We were walking quickly back to the car.

"There's nothing wrong with that," said Hand.

"There can't be," I said.

"We gave the guy money."

"How much was it, you figure?"

"It was most of what I had left. About eight hundred dollars."

"He took it. We left."

"Nothing wrong with that."

"Not a thing. It was simple. It was good."

We retrieved the car from behind the warehouse. The day had been long, and soon we would rest. We needed to eat, and I wanted beer. I wanted four beers and many potatoes, then sleep.

"I want to marry this country," I said.

"It's a good country," Hand said.

"I want to spend a lifetime here."

"Yeah."

"I could do it."

"Right."

And my mind leaped ahead, skipping and whistling. In the first year, I'd master French, the second join some kind of traveling medical entourage, dressing wounds and disseminating medicine. We'd do inoculations, birth control, hold the line on AIDS. After that, I'd marry a Senegalese woman and we'd raise our kids while working shoulder to shoulder—all of us— at the clinic. The kids would check people in, maybe do some minimal fil- ing—they'd do their homework in the waiting room. I'd visit America now and then, once every few years, in Senegal I'd read the English-speaking papers once a month or so. We'd live on the coast.

"Sounds good," said Hand.

"But that's one lifetime."

"Yeah."

"But while doing that one I'd want to be able to have done other stuff. Whole other lives. The one where I sail—"

"I know, on a boat you made yourself."

"Yeah, for a couple of years, through the Mediterranean, the Red Sea, the Caspian Sea."

"Can you sail? You can't sail."

We passed two more white people on ATVs.

"You know quantum theory, right?"

This is how he started; it was always friendly enough, but—

"Sure," I lied.

"Well, there's this guy named Deutsch who's taken quantum theory and applied it to everything. To all life. You know Max Planck, right?"

"Go on," I said. Hand was such a prick.

"Anyway," he continued. "Quantum physics says that atoms aren't so hard and fast, just sitting there like fake fruit or something, touchable and solid. They're mercurial. They come and go. They appear and disappear. They occupy different places at once. They can be teleported. Scientists have actually done this."

"They've teleported atoms."

"Yeah. Of course."

No one tells me anything. "I can't believe I missed that," I said.

"They also slowed the speed of light."

"I did hear that."

"Slowed it to a Sunday crawl."

"That's what I heard."

We drove as the sky went pink, then barn red, passing small villages emptying in the night, people standing around small fires.

Hand went on, "So if these atoms can exist in different places at once—and I don't think any physicists argue about that—this guy Deutsch argues that everything can exist in a bunch of places at once. We're all made of the same electrons and protons, right, so if they exist in many places at once, and can be teleported, then there must be multiple us's, and multiple worlds, simultaneously."

"Jesus."

"That's the multiverse."

"Oh. That's a nice name for it."

We passed a clearing with a basketball court, the backboard bent forward like a priest granting communion. Two young boys, one wearing red and one in blue, were scrapping under it, each ball bounce beating a rugful of dust.

"We have to stop," I said. We were already past the court.

"Why? To watch?"

"We have to play. Haven't you ever driven past a court and—"

"Those kids were about twelve."

"Then we won't keep score."

They stopped as they saw us approach. Hand called for the ball. How did they know he wouldn't leave with it? They threw it.

Hand bounced the ball, and it landed on a rock and ricocheted away. The boys laughed. Hand chased it down and returned and did some bizarre Bob Cousy lay-up, underhand and goofy; the ball dropped through the dented red rim. Hand shot the ball three times from the free-throw area, without luck. Now I laughed with the boys. I gave one of them a handshake, making up an elaborate series of subshakes involving wrists and fingers and lots of snapping. He thought I knew what I was doing.

The light kept leaking from the sky. Another boy showed up, bigger and more confident. He had newish sneakers and knee-length basketball shorts, a Puma T-shirt. He was serious. He smiled, shook our hands, but then he bore down and didn't look us in the eye. It was our two against their three, and there was dust everywhere. The tall boy was determined to win. The game got closer. I tried to switch teams, to relieve the nationalistic tension, but the boys refused.

It was ridiculous for Hand and me to be playing like this; we weren't the players—Jack was, Jack was the best pure player our school had ever seen, rhythm and speed impossible, it seemed, in someone we knew, someone from Wisconsin whose father sold seeds. We played Jack, were humored by him, but when he wanted to he turned it up and broke us like twigs.

Very soon there were ten kids watching, then twenty, all boys, half of them barefoot. Every time the ball bounced off the court and away, toward the village, two more boys emerged to reclaim it.

It was dark now. We were passing the ball, and it was hitting our chests before we could see it. We called the game.

We walked back to the car and brought out the water we had left, took pulls, and handed it to the boy in red. He handed it to the tall one, who sipped and gave it to the blue boy, who finished it. Another boy, of about thirteen, pushed through the crowd around the car, arched his back, and said with clarity and force, "My father is in the army. My name is Steven."

And then he walked away, back to the village.

The tall Puma boy spoke some English; his name, he said, was Denis. "Where do you live?" he asked.

"Chicago," I said.

"The Bulls!" he said. "You see Bulls?"

Hand told him we'd been to games, even while Jordan was still active. And this was almost true. We'd been to one game, with Jordan playing the first half of a blowout.

Denis's mouth formed an exaggerated oval. "Was he good?" he asked. Hand grinned: Yes. Denis said he'd love to come to America, see basketball, see his cousin, who lived in New Mexico. I told him New Mexico was very pretty. "Très bien," I said.

"But," said Hand, still on the Bulls, "Pippen is the more elegant player."

Hand said this all the time, partly, surely, because it enraged anyone in Chicago who heard it.

Denis shook his head and smiled. He didn't agree but kept mum.

We didn't know if we would give them money. We got in the car and debated. They hadn't asked, but it seemed they knew the possibility existed, that we could spare it. I still had some American hundreds in my shoes, but would that spoil everything? Would we pollute something pure—a simple game between travelers and hosts—by afterward throwing money at them? But maybe they did expect money. Maybe this was a common occurrence: Americans pull up, grab the ball, show them what's what, drop cash, and head back to the Saly hotels—

"Let's not," Hand said.

"Okay." The boys surrounded us, waving. We began to drive back to the highway, as the boys went their separate ways. I stopped the car, alongside Denis, the Bulls fan who wanted to go to New Mexico.

I rolled down my window and said "Hey," to the boy. He approached the window. I reached into my sock and grabbed what I could. I handed him three hundred dollars in three American bills.

"See you in Chicago," I said.

The boy thanked us. "If I get to Chicago, it is because of you," he said.

"See you there," Hand said to Denis. To me: "We should get going."

We said goodbye to Denis, and his eyes were liquid with feeling, and we loved him, but there was a man in our back seat.

"This is my brother," said Denis. "He needs a ride to Mbuu."

I looked at Hand. Denis's brother was in the car, and it was too late; we had no choice. Mbuu was on our way. We said hello to Denis's brother. His name was Pierre.

His chatter was never-ending. Mbuu was twenty minutes away, and Pierre did not stop talking. Denis's brother had seen his brother's receipt of cash, and wanted some of his own.

Pierre used Abass's line, that he needed cab fare to get back. Hand explained his demands to me. We laughed.

The man began talking again, but he had changed tacks: now he needed the money to go to Zaire.

He and Hand barked back and forth for a while, making little headway. When Hand had talked him away from the Zaire plan, the brother became hungry. He thrust his palm between us.

"We have any food?" Hand asked me. From my backpack, I produced a granola bar. The brother accepted it, didn't open it, and did not stop talking; he was a machine. We were approaching Mbuu, and he was getting desperate.

"Jesus," I said, "is there any way we can ask him to stop talking?"

We were in Mbuu, a dark adobe village. There were no constant lines—everything was moving. The walls were moving; they were human. There were people everywhere, and everyone was shifting. The homes were open storefronts. Our headlights flashed over hundreds of people, walking, watching TV—large groups or families visible through glassless windows, all in the open-air storefronts, eating their dinners, drinking at the street-side bar, everyone so close.

We stopped and said goodbye to Denis's brother. He paused in the car, waiting. We stared at him. His eyes spoke.

—You owe me.

—We don't.

—This is wrong.

—It's not wrong.

—You're not sure. You're confused.

—Yes, I am confused.

—It's all wrong.

—I agree.

He stepped out and closed the door. We got back on the road.

"I don't feel bad about that," Hand said.

"I hated that fucker."

And nothing else in the world had changed.

The next day, we woke up early to get back to and out of Dakar at noon. We'd left Chicago forty-eight hours ago. The road was clear for us, and Hand swung the radio volume right and we were delirious.

We sped through the savanna and suburbs and made it to the airport by eleven. At the Air Afrique desk, the three stunning queens, in blue and yellow and green, wanted four hundred dollars each, in cash, for the ticket to Casablanca, so I put my name on more traveler's checks at the money-change desk—me! me! swoop! swoop!—and came back and presented the money, two inches thick, to the eldest of the three women.

"Ah, so you the big boss?" she asked.

"The big boss! You!" she repeated.

"Yes, the big boss, this one!" said another of the women.

"But it was you who wanted cash," I said. I was confused. I didn't want to be the big boss.

"Some man beat the big boss," said the third.

Then they all laughed. For a long time. I wondered if they hazed everyone like this. These women were cruel. I looked at Hand. His eyes were alight with something else.

"Ladies," said Hand, "do women like you ever date people like us? What would it take?"

"What?" the senior one said.

Hand tried it again in French. They all laughed. This one just knocked them out. Now we were both shamed. These three were something. I left as they continued to cackle; Hand joined me soon after, chin on his chest.

We had three hours in the air. Morocco we'd do better. We'd meet more people quicker. Our car would go faster. We'd do more in a day than we'd done in Senegal and we'd get out of there and on to Mongolia within twenty-four hours. We'd learned and we would not waste the time again. I went to sleep and woke up when the pilot was urging us to put our seat belts on again. We descended into Morocco. Which was green. As far as we could see, from the air, it was green.

"Isn't this a desert—the whole country?" Hand asked, leaning over the aisle and toward me. Everywhere below, squares of farmland stitched together with orange thread. Already we knew nothing we thought we knew. And as we got closer to the earth, it bore less and less resemblance to anything we'd expected.

"I thought desert, too," I said.

"We got it backwards. Or they did. Senegal should be green. Morocco brown."

"It's gorgeous down there," Hand said.

"Christ. It really is."

Jean-Jacques Rousseau

The son of a Genevan watchmaker, Jean-Jacques Rousseau (1712–1778) became a central figure of the French Enlightenment and inspired political revolutionaries on two continents. He wrote what has come to be classified as political theory and anthropology, as well as a wildly successful novel, a resonant treatise on education, and one of the first distinctively modern autobiographies. As a young man, Rousseau roamed around Europe, attempting various unsuccessful routes to fame and fortune (including the invention of a new system of musical notation). As an older man, in addition to publishing several influential books, Rousseau copied music and devoted much of his energy to botany. This selection comes from the Sixth Walk of his last work, *The Reveries of the Solitary Walker*, published four years after his death.

Selection from
The Reveries of the Solitary Walker

There is hardly any of our automatic impulses whose cause we could not find in our heart, if we only knew how to look for it. Yesterday, crossing the new boulevard to go look for plants on the Gentilly side of the Bièvre, I made a turn to the right in coming up to the Enfer tollgate and, getting out into the countryside, I went along the road to Fontainebleau up to the bluffs beside this little river. In itself, this route was of no significance; but on recalling that I had automatically made the same detour several times, I looked within myself for its cause and I could not keep from laughing when I managed to unravel it.

At a corner of the boulevard near the Enfer tollgate exit, there is a woman who sets up a stand every day in the summer to sell fruit, herb tea, and rolls. This woman has a very nice, but lame, little boy who, hobbling along on his crutches, goes about quite graciously asking passersby for alms. I had become slightly acquainted with this little fellow; each time I passed, he did not fail to come pay his little compliment, always followed by my little offering. At first I

187

was charmed to see him; I gave to him very goodheartedly and for some time continued to do so with the same pleasure, quite frequently even prompting and listening to his little prattle, which I found enjoyable. This pleasure, having gradually become a habit, was inexplicably transformed into a kind of duty I soon felt to be annoying, especially because of the preliminary harangue to which I had to listen and in which he never failed to call me Monsieur Rousseau many times, to show that he knew me well. But to the contrary, that only taught me that he knew me no more than those who had instructed him. From that time on I passed by there less willingly, and finally I automatically got in the habit of making a detour when I came close to this crossing.

That is what I discovered by reflecting on it; for until then, none of this had clearly entered my thoughts. This observation recalled to me a multitude of others, one after the other, which entirely convinced me that the true and primary motives of most of my actions are not as clear even to me as I had long imagined. I know and feel that to do good is the truest happiness the human heart can savor; but it is a long time now since this happiness has been put out of my reach, and it is not in such a wretched lot as mine that one can hope to perform wisely and fruitfully a single really good action. The greatest care of those who rule my fate having been to make everything appear only false and deceptive to me, an occasion for virtue is never anything but a lure they hold out to draw me into the snare they want to enlace me in. I know that; I know that the only good that might henceforth be within my power is to abstain from acting from fear of doing evil without wanting to and without knowing it.

But there were happier times when, following the impulses of my heart, I could sometimes make another heart content; and I owe myself the honorable testimony that, whenever I was able to savor this pleasure, I found it sweeter than any other. This tendency was intense, true, pure, and nothing in my most secret inner self ever belied it. However, I have often felt the burden of my own good deeds by the chain of duties they later entailed. Then the pleasure disappeared, and the continuation of the very attentiveness that had charmed me at first no longer struck me as anything but an almost unbearable annoyance. During my brief moments of prosperity, many people appealed to me; and despite the multitude of favors they asked of me, none of them was ever turned away. But from these first good deeds, which my heart poured out effusively, were forged chains of subsequent liabilities I had not foreseen and whose yoke I could no longer shake off. In the eyes of those who received them, my first favors were only a pledge for those that were supposed to follow; and as soon as some unfortunate man had hooked me with my own good deed, that was it from then on. This first free and voluntary good deed became an unlimited right to all those he might need afterward, without even my lack of power being enough to release me from his claim. That is how very delightful enjoyments were transformed into onerous subjections for me ever afterward.

***

I know that there is a kind of contract, and even the holiest of all, between the benefactor and the beneficiary. They form a sort of society with each other, more restricted than the one that unites men in general. And if the beneficiary tacitly pledges himself to gratitude, the benefactor likewise pledges himself to preserve for the other, as long as he does not make himself unworthy of it, the same goodwill he has just shown him and to renew its acts for him whenever he is able to and whenever it is required. Those are not stated conditions, but they are natural effects of the relationship that has just been set up between them. He who refuses a spontaneous favor the first time it is asked of him gives the one he has refused no right to complain. But he who, in a similar case, refuses the same person the same kindness he heretofore accorded him, frustrates a hope he has authorized him to conceive. He deceives and belies an expectation he has engendered. In this refusal, we feel an inexplicable injustice and greater harshness than in the other; but it is no less the effect of an independence the heart loves and renounces only with effort. When I pay a debt, it is a duty I fulfill; when I give a gift, it is a pleasure I give myself. Now, the pleasure of fulfilling our duties is one of those that only the habit of virtue engenders; those that come to us immediately from nature do not rise so high.

Maya Angelou

Maya Angelou (b. 1928) was born Marguerite Johnson in St. Louis, Missouri. A single mother at age eighteen, she worked in her early years as a cook, San Francisco's first African American cable car conductor, and a nightclub dancer, in which capacity she took the name Maya Angelou. She went on to become a successful singer and actress. Angelou was active in the civil rights movement of the 1960s and in 1970 published her first book, the autobiographical *I Know Why the Caged Bird Sings*. She has since published additional volumes of autobiography, poetry, plays, essays, and children's books. The following reflection appeared in the essay collection *Wouldn't Take Nothing for My Journey Now*, published in 1993.

The Sweetness of Charity

The New Testament informs the reader that it is more blessed to give than to receive. I have found that among its other benefits, giving liberates the soul of the giver. The size and substance of the gift should be important to the recipient, but not to the donor, save that the best thing one can give is that which is appreciated. The giver is as enriched as is the recipient, and more important, that intangible but very real psychic force of good in the world is increased.

When we cast our bread upon the waters, we can presume that someone downstream whose face we will never know will benefit from our action, as we who are downstream from another will profit from that grantor's gift.

Since time is the one immaterial object that we cannot influence—neither speed up nor slow down, add to nor diminish—it is an imponderably valuable gift. Each of us has a few minutes a day or few hours a week that we could donate to an old folks' home or a children's hospital ward. The elderly whose pillows we plump or whose water pitchers we refill may or may not thank us for our gift, but the gift is upholding the foundation of the universe. The children to whom we read simple stories may or may not show gratitude, but each boon we give strengthens the pillars of the world.

While our gifts and the recipients should be considered, our bounty, once decided upon, should be without concern, overflowing one minute and forgotten the next.

Recently I was asked to speak before a group of philanthropists and was astonished at their self-consciousness. The gathered donors give tens of millions of dollars annually to medical research, educational development, art support, and social reform. Yet to a person they seemed a little, just a little, ashamed of themselves. I pondered their behavior and realized that someone had told someone that not only was it degrading to accept charity but it was equally debasing to give it. And sad to say, someone had believed that statement. Hence, many preferred to have it known that they dispense philanthropy rather than charity.

I like charitable people and like to think of myself as charitable, as being of a generous heart and a giving nature—being a friend indeed to anyone in need. Why, I pondered, did the benefactors not feel as I?

Some benefactors may desire distance from the recipients of their largess because there is a separation between themselves and the resources they distribute. As inheritors or managers of fortune rather than direct earners, perhaps they feel exiled from the gifts; then it follows that they feel exiled from the recipient.

It is sad when people who give to the needy feel estranged from the objects of their generosity. They can take little, if any, relish from their acts of charity; therefore, [they] are generous out of duty rather than delight.

If we change the way we think of charity, our personal lives will be richer and the larger world will be improved. When we give cheerfully and accept gratefully, everyone is blessed. "Charity . . . is kind; . . . envieth not; . . . vaunteth not itself, is not puffed up."

Pablo Neruda

Pablo Neruda (1904–1973) was born Neftalí Ricardo Reyes Basoalto in Parral, Chile. When he was thirteen, he contributed a few articles and his first published poem to *El Mañana*. In 1920, he contributed to the literary journal *Selva Austral* under the name Pablo Neruda, which he adopted in memory of Czech poet Jan Neruda. From the late 1920s on, Neruda traveled extensively and became active in several political causes. He published many books of poetry, as well as memoirs and prose. Neruda received the Nobel Prize in Literature in 1971 and died in 1973. This selection comes from an interview with Robert Bly, which first appeared in a volume edited by Bly, *Vallejo and Neruda: Selected Poems*.

The Lamb and the Pinecone

One time, investigating in the backyard of our house in Temuco the tiny objects and minuscule beings of my world, I came upon a hole in one of the boards of the fence. I looked through the hole and saw a landscape like that behind our house, uncared for and wild. I moved back a few steps, because I sensed vaguely that something was about to happen. All of a sudden a hand appeared—a tiny hand of a boy about my own age. By the time I came close again, the hand was gone, and in its place there was a marvelous white sheep.

The sheep's wool was faded. Its wheels had escaped. All of this only made it more authentic. I had never seen such a wonderful sheep. I looked back through the hole but the boy had disappeared. I went into the house and brought out a treasure of my own: a pinecone, opened, full of odor and resin, which I adored. I set it down in the same spot and went off with the sheep.

I never saw either the hand or the boy again. And I have never again seen a sheep like that either. The toy I lost finally in a fire. But even now, in 1954, almost fifty years old, whenever I pass a toy shop, I look furtively into the window, but it's no use. They don't make sheep like that any more.

I have been a lucky man. To feel the intimacy of brothers is a marvelous thing in life. To feel the love of people whom we love is a fire that feeds our

life. But to feel the affection that comes from those whom we do not know, from those unknown to us, who are watching over our sleep and solitude, over our dangers and our weaknesses—that is something still greater and more beautiful because it widens out the boundaries of our being and unites all living things.

That exchange brought home to me for the first time a precious idea: that all of humanity is somehow together. That experience came to me again much later; this time it stood out strikingly against a background of trouble and persecution.

It won't surprise you then that I attempted to give something resiny, earthlike, and fragrant in exchange for human brotherhood. Just as I once left the pinecone by the fence, I have since left my words on the door of so many people who were unknown to me, people in prison, or hunted, or alone.

That is the great lesson I learned in my childhood, in the backyard of a lonely house. Maybe it was nothing but a game two boys played who didn't know each other and wanted to pass to the other some good things of life. Yet maybe this small and mysterious exchange of gifts remained inside me also, deep and indestructible, giving my poetry light.

Andrew Carnegie

Andrew Carnegie (1835–1919) was born in Scotland and came to the United States in 1848. He went to work at age twelve, laboring in cotton mills, telegraph offices, and railroad companies before launching his own steel company and, with it, the steel industry of Pittsburgh. In 1889, Carnegie published an essay titled "Wealth" in the *North American Review*. The essay was expanded and republished as *The Gospel of Wealth* in 1900. A year later, Carnegie sold his business to J. P. Morgan and devoted the remainder of his life to writing and philanthropy, helping to establish 2,509 Carnegie Libraries in communities around the world. The following selection is Part I of *The Gospel of Wealth*.

The Gospel of Wealth, Part I

The Problem of the Administration of Wealth

The problem of our age is the proper administration of wealth, that the ties of brotherhood may still bind together the rich and poor in harmonious relationship. The conditions of human life have not only been changed, but revolutionized, within the past few hundred years. In former days there was little difference between the dwelling, dress, food, and environment of the chief and those of his retainers. The Indians are today where civilized man then was. When visiting the Sioux, I was led to the wigwam of the chief. It was like the others in external appearance, and even within the difference was trifling between it and those of the poorest of his braves. The contrast between the palace of the millionaire and the cottage of the laborer with us today measures the change that has come with civilization. This change, however, is not to be deplored but welcomed as highly beneficial. It is well, nay, essential, for the progress of the race that the houses of some should be homes for all that is highest and best in literature and the arts, and for all the refinements of civilization, rather than that none should be so. Much better this great irregularity than universal squalor. Without wealth there can be no Maecenas. The "good old times" were not good old times. Neither master nor servant was as well situated then as today. A relapse to old conditions would be disastrous to both—not the least so to him who serves—and would sweep away civilization with it. But whether the change be for good or ill, it is upon us, beyond our power to alter, and, therefore, to be accepted and made the best of. It is a waste of time to criticize the inevitable.

It is easy to see how the change has come. One illustration will serve for almost every phase of the cause. In the manufacture of products we have the whole story. It applies to all combinations of human industry, as stimulated and enlarged by the inventions of this scientific age. Formerly, articles were manufactured at the domestic hearth, or in small shops that formed part of the household. The master and his apprentices worked side by side, the latter living with the master, and therefore subject to the same conditions. When these apprentices rose to be masters, there was little or no change in their mode of life, and they, in turn, educated succeeding apprentices in the same routine. There was, substantially, social equality, and even political equality, for those engaged in industrial pursuits had then little or no voice in the state.

The inevitable result of such a mode of manufacture was crude articles at high prices. Today the world obtains commodities of excellent quality at prices that even the preceding generation would have deemed incredible. In the commercial world similar causes have produced similar results, and the race is benefited thereby. The poor enjoy what the rich could not before afford. What were the luxuries have become the necessaries of life. The laborer has now more comforts than the farmer had a few generations ago. The farmer has more luxuries than the landlord had and is more richly clad and better housed. The landlord has books and pictures rarer and appointments more artistic than the king could then obtain.

The price we pay for this salutary change is, no doubt, great. We assemble thousands of operatives in the factory, and in the mine, of whom the employer can know little or nothing, and to whom he is little better than a myth. All intercourse between them is at an end. Rigid castes are formed, and, as usual, mutual ignorance breeds mutual distrust. Each caste is without sympathy with the other and ready to credit anything disparaging in regard to it. Under the law of competition, the employer of thousands is forced into the strictest economies, among which the rates paid to labor figure prominently, and often there is friction between the employer and the employed, between capital and labor, between rich and poor. Human society loses homogeneity.

The price that society pays for the law of competition, like the price it pays for cheap comforts and luxuries, is also great; but the advantages of this law are also greater still than its cost—for it is to this law that we owe our wonderful material development, which brings improved conditions in its train. But, whether the law be benign or not, we must say of it, as we say of the change in the conditions of men to which we have referred: it is here; we cannot evade it; no substitutes for it have been found; and while the law may be sometimes hard for the individual, it is best for the race, because it ensures the survival of the fittest in every department. We accept and welcome, therefore, as conditions to which we must accommodate ourselves, great inequality of environment; the concentration of business, industrial and commercial, in the hands of a few; and the law of competition between these, as being not only beneficial but essential to the future progress of the race. Having accepted these, it follows that there must be great scope for the exercise of special ability in the merchant and in the manufacturer who has to conduct affairs upon a great scale. That this talent for organization and management is rare among men is proved by the fact that it invariably secures enormous rewards for its possessor, no matter where or under what laws or conditions. The experienced in affairs always rate the *man* whose services can be obtained as a partner as not only the first consideration, but such as render the question of his capital scarcely worth considering: for able men soon create capital; in the hands of those without the special talent required, capital soon takes wings. Such men become interested in firms or corporations using millions; and, estimating only simple interest to be made upon the capital invested, it is inevitable that their income must exceed their expenditure and that they must, therefore, accumulate wealth. Nor is there any middle ground that such men can occupy, because the great manufacturing or commercial concern that does not earn at least interest upon its capital soon becomes bankrupt. It must either go forward or fall behind; to stand still is impossible. It is a condition essential to its successful operation that it should be thus far profitable, and even that, in addition to interest on capital, it should make profit. It is a law, as certain as any of the others named, that men possessed of this peculiar talent for affairs, under the free play of economic forces must, of necessity, soon be in receipt of more revenue than can be judiciously expended upon themselves; and this law is as beneficial for the race as the others.

Objections to the foundations upon which society is based are not in order, because the condition of the race is better with these than it has been with any other that has been tried. Of the effect of any new substitutes proposed we cannot be sure. The socialist or anarchist who seeks to overturn present conditions is to be regarded as attacking the foundation upon which civilization itself rests, for civilization took its start from the day when the capable, industrious workman said to his incompetent and lazy fellow, "If thou dost not sow, thou shalt not reap," and thus ended primitive communism by separating the drones from the bees. One who studies this subject will soon be brought face-to-face with the conclusion that upon the sacredness of property civilization itself depends—the right of the laborer to his hundred dollars in the savings bank, and equally the legal right of the millionaire to his millions. Every man must be allowed "to sit under his own vine and fig tree, with none to make afraid," if human society is to advance, or even to remain so far advanced as it is. To those who propose to substitute communism for this intense individualism, the answer therefore is: the race has tried that. All progress from that barbarous day to the present time has resulted from its displacement. Not evil but good has come to the race from the accumulation of wealth by those who have had the ability and energy to produce it. But even if we admit for a moment that it might be better for the race to discard its present foundation, individualism—that it is a nobler ideal that man should labor not for himself alone but in and for a brotherhood of his fellows and share with them all in common, realizing Swedenborg's idea of heaven, where, as he says, the angels derive their happiness not from laboring for self but for each other—even admit all this, and a sufficient answer is, this is not evolution but revolution. It necessitates the changing of human nature itself—a work of eons, even if it were good to change it, which we cannot know.

It is not practicable in our day or in our age. Even if desirable theoretically, it belongs to another and long-succeeding sociological stratum. Our duty is with what is practicable now—with the next step possible in our day and generation. It is criminal to waste our energies in endeavoring to uproot, when all we can profitably accomplish is to bend the universal tree of humanity a little in the direction most favorable to the production of good fruit under existing circumstances. We might as well urge the destruction of the highest existing type of man because he failed to reach our ideal as to favor the destruction of individualism, private property, the law of accumulation of wealth, and the law of competition; for these are the highest result of human experience, the soil in which society, so far, has produced the best fruit. Unequally or unjustly, perhaps, as these laws sometimes operate, and imperfect as they appear to the idealist, they are, nevertheless, like the highest type of man, the best and most valuable of all that humanity has yet accomplished.

We start, then, with a condition of affairs under which the best interests of the race are promoted but that inevitably gives wealth to the few. Thus far, accepting conditions as they exist, the situation can be surveyed and pronounced good. The question then arises—and if the foregoing be correct, it is the only question with which we have to deal—what is the proper mode of administering wealth after the laws upon which civilization is founded have thrown it into the hands of the few? And it is of this great question that I believe I offer the true solution. It will be understood that fortunes are here spoken of, not moderate sums saved by many years of effort, the returns from which are required for the comfortable maintenance and education of families. This is not wealth, but only competence, which it should be the aim of all to acquire, and which it is for the best interests of society should be acquired.

There are but three modes in which surplus wealth can be disposed of. It can be left to the families of the decedents; or it can be bequeathed for public purposes; or, finally, it can be administered by its possessors during their lives. Under the first and second modes most of the wealth of the world that has reached the few has hitherto been applied. Let us in turn consider each of these modes. The first is the most injudicious. In monarchical countries, the estates and the greatest portion of the wealth are left to the first son, that the vanity of the parent may be gratified by the thought that his name and title are to descend unimpaired to succeeding generations. The condition of this class in Europe today teaches the failure of such hopes or ambitions. The successors have become impoverished through their follies, or from the fall in the value of land. Even in Great Britain the strict law of entail has been found inadequate to maintain a hereditary class. Its soil is rapidly passing into the hands of the stranger. Under republican institutions the division of property among the children is much fairer; but the question that forces itself upon thoughtful men in all lands is, why should men leave great fortunes to their children? If this is done from affection, is it not misguided affection? Observation teaches that, generally speaking, it is not well for the children that they should be so burdened. Neither is it well for the state. Beyond providing for the wife and daughters moderate sources of income, and very moderate allowances indeed, if any, for the sons, men may well hesitate; for it is no longer questionable that great sums bequeathed often work more for the injury than for the good of the recipients. Wise men will soon conclude that, for the best interests of the members of their families, and of the state, such bequests are an improper use of their means.

It is not suggested that men who have failed to educate their sons to earn a livelihood shall cast them adrift in poverty. If any man has seen fit to rear his sons with a view to their living idle lives, or, what is highly commendable, has instilled in them the sentiment that they are in a position to labor for public ends without reference to pecuniary considerations, then, of course, the duty of the parent is to see that such are provided for in moderation. There are instances of millionaires' sons unspoiled by wealth, who, being rich, still perform great services to the community. Such are the very salt of the earth, as valuable as, unfortunately, they are rare. It is not the exception, however, but the rule, that men must regard; and, looking at the usual result of enormous sums conferred upon legatees, the thoughtful man must shortly say, "I would as soon leave to my son a curse as the almighty dollar," and admit to himself that it is not the welfare of the children but family pride that inspires these legacies.

As to the second mode, that of leaving wealth at death for public uses, it may be said that this is only a means for the disposal of wealth, provided a man is content to wait until he is dead before he becomes of much good in the world. Knowledge of the results of legacies bequeathed is not calculated to inspire the brightest hopes of much posthumous good being accomplished by them. The cases are not few in which the real object sought by the testator is not attained, nor are they few in which his real wishes are thwarted. In many cases the bequests are so used as to become only monuments of his folly. It is well to remember that it requires the exercise of not less ability than that which acquires it to use wealth so as to be really beneficial to the community. Besides this, it may fairly be said that no man is to be extolled for doing what he cannot help doing, nor is he to be thanked by the community to which he only leaves wealth at death. Men who leave vast sums in this way may fairly be thought men who would not have left it at all had they been able to take it with them. The memories of such cannot be held in grateful remembrance, for there is no grace in their gifts. It is not to be wondered at that such bequests seem so generally to lack the blessing.

The growing disposition to tax more and more heavily large estates left at death is a cheering indication of the growth of a salutary change in public opinion. The State of Pennsylvania now takes—subject to some exceptions—one-tenth of the property left by its citizens. The budget presented in the British Parliament the other day proposes to increase the death duties; and, most significant of all, the new tax is to be a graduated one. Of all forms of taxation this seems the wisest. Men who continue hoarding great sums all their lives, the proper use of which for public ends would work good to the community from which it chiefly came, should be made to feel that the community, in the form of the state, cannot thus be deprived of its proper share. By taxing estates heavily at death the state marks its condemnation of the selfish millionaire's unworthy life.

It is desirable that nations should go much further in this direction. Indeed, it is difficult to set bounds to the share of a rich man's estate that should go at his death to the public through the agency of the state, and by all means such taxes should be graduated, beginning at nothing upon moderate sums to dependents, and increasing rapidly as the amounts swell, until of the millionaire's hoard, as of Shylock's, at least

> The other half
> Comes to the privy coffer of the state.

This policy would work powerfully to induce the rich man to attend to the administration of wealth during his life, which is the end that society should always have in view, as being by far the most fruitful for the people. Nor need it be feared that this policy would sap the root of enterprise and render men less anxious to accumulate, for, to the class whose ambition it is to leave great fortunes and to be talked about after their death, it will attract even more attention, and, indeed, be a somewhat nobler ambition, to have enormous sums paid over to the state from their fortunes.

There remains, then, only one mode of using great fortunes; but in this we have the true antidote for the temporary unequal distribution of wealth, the reconciliation of the rich and the poor—a reign of harmony, another ideal, differing, indeed, from that of the communist in requiring only the further evolution of existing conditions not the total overthrow of our civilization. It is founded upon the present most intense individualism, and the race is prepared to put it in practice by degrees whenever it pleases. Under its sway we shall have an ideal state, in which the surplus wealth of the few will become, in the best sense, the property of the many, because administered for the common good; and this wealth, passing through the hands of the few, can be made a much more potent force for the elevation of our race than if distributed in small sums to the people themselves. Even the poorest can be made to see this, and to agree that great sums gathered by some of their fellow citizens and spent for public purposes, from which the masses reap the principal benefit, are more valuable to them than if scattered among themselves in trifling amounts through the course of many years.

If we consider the results that flow from the Cooper Institute, for instance, to the best portion of the race in New York not possessed of means, and compare these with those that would have ensued for the good of the masses from an equal sum distributed by Mr. Cooper in his lifetime in the form of wages, which is the highest form of distribution, being for work done and not for charity, we can form some estimate of the possibilities for the improvement of the race that lie embedded in the present law of the accumulation of wealth. Much of this sum, if distributed in small quantities among the people, would have been wasted in the indulgence of appetite, some of it in excess, and it may be doubted whether even the part put to the best use, that of adding to the comforts of the home, would have yielded results for the race, as a race, at all comparable to those that are flowing and are to flow from the Cooper Institute from generation to generation. Let the advocate of violent or radical change ponder well this thought.

We might even go so far as to take another instance—that of Mr. Tilden's bequest of five millions of dollars for a free library in the city of New York; but in referring to this one cannot help saying involuntarily: how much better if Mr. Tilden had devoted the last years of his own life to the proper administration of this immense sum; in which case neither legal contest nor any other cause of delay could have interfered with his aims. But let us assume that Mr. Tilden's millions finally become the means of giving to this city a noble public library, where the treasures of the world contained in books will be open to all forever, without money and without price. Considering the good of that part of the race that congregates in and around Manhattan Island, would its permanent benefit have been better promoted had these millions been allowed to circulate in small sums through the hands of the masses? Even the most strenuous advocate of communism must entertain a doubt upon this subject. Most of those who think will probably entertain no doubt whatever.

Poor and restricted are our opportunities in this life, narrow our horizon, our best work most imperfect; but rich men should be thankful for one inestimable boon. They have it in their power during their lives to busy themselves in organizing benefactions from which the masses of their fellows will derive lasting advantage, and thus dignify their own lives. The highest life is probably to be reached, not by such imitation of the life of Christ as Count Tolstoy gives us, but, while animated by Christ's spirit, by recognizing the changed conditions of this age, and adopting modes of expressing this spirit suitable to the changed conditions under which we live, still laboring for the good of our fellows, which was the essence of his life and teaching, but laboring in a different manner.

This, then, is held to be the duty of the man of wealth: to set an example of modest, unostentatious living, shunning display or extravagance; to provide moderately for the legitimate wants of those dependent upon him; and, after doing so, to consider all surplus revenues that come to him simply as trust funds, which he is called upon to administer, and strictly bound as a matter of duty to administer in the manner that, in his judgment, is best calculated to produce the most beneficial results for the community—the man of wealth thus becoming the mere trustee and agent for his poorer brethren, bringing to their service his superior wisdom, experience, and ability to administer, doing for them better than they would or could do for themselves.

We are met here with the difficulty of determining what are moderate sums to leave to members of the family; what is modest, unostentatious living; what is the test of extravagance. There must be different standards for different conditions. The answer is that it is as impossible to name exact amounts or actions as it is to define good manners, good taste, or the rules of propriety; but, nevertheless, these are verities, well known, although indefinable. Public sentiment is quick to know and to feel what offends these. So in the case of wealth. The rule in regard to good taste in dress of men or women applies here. Whatever makes one conspicuous offends the canon. If any family be chiefly known for display, for extravagance in home, table, or equipage, for enormous sums ostentatiously spent in any form upon itself—if these be its chief distinctions, we have no difficulty in estimating its nature or culture. So likewise in regard to the use or abuse of its surplus wealth, or to generous, freehanded cooperation in good public uses, or to unabated efforts to accumulate and hoard to the last, or whether they administer or bequeath. The verdict rests with the best and most enlightened public sentiment. The community will surely judge, and its judgments will not often be wrong.

The best uses to which surplus wealth can be put have already been indicated. Those who would administer wisely must, indeed, be wise; for one of the serious obstacles to the improvement of our race is indiscriminate charity. It were better for mankind that the millions of the rich were thrown into the sea than so spent as to encourage the slothful, the drunken, the unworthy.

Of every thousand dollars spent in so-called charity today, it is probable that nine hundred and fifty dollars is unwisely spent—so spent, indeed, as to produce the very evils that it hopes to mitigate or cure. A well-known writer of philosophic books admitted the other day that he had given a quarter of a dollar to a man who approached him as he was coming to visit the house of his friend. He knew nothing of the habits of this beggar, knew not the use that would be made of this money, although he had every reason to suspect that it would be spent improperly. This man professed to be a disciple of Herbert Spencer; yet the quarter-dollar given that night will probably work more injury than all the money will do good that its thoughtless donor will ever be able to give in true charity. He only gratified his own feelings, saved himself from annoyance—and this was probably one of the most selfish and very worst actions of his life, for in all respects he is most worthy.

In bestowing charity, the main consideration should be to help those who will help themselves; to provide part of the means by which those who desire to improve may do so; to give those who desire to rise the aids by which they may rise; to assist, but rarely or never to do all. Neither the individual nor the race is improved by almsgiving. Those worthy of assistance, except in rare cases, seldom require assistance. The really valuable men of the race never do, except in case of accident or sudden change. Every one has, of course, cases of individuals brought to his own knowledge where temporary assistance can do genuine good, and these he will not overlook. But the amount that can be wisely given by the individual for individuals is necessarily limited by his lack of knowledge of the circumstances connected with each. He is the only true reformer who is as careful and as anxious not to aid the unworthy as he is to aid the worthy, and, perhaps, even more so, for in almsgiving more injury is probably done by rewarding vice than by relieving virtue.

The rich man is thus almost restricted to following the examples of Peter Cooper; Enoch Pratt, of Baltimore; Mr. Pratt, of Brooklyn; Senator Stanford; and others, who know that the best means of benefiting the community is to place within its reach the ladders upon which the aspiring can rise—free libraries, parks, and means of recreation, by which men are helped in body and mind; works of art, certain to give pleasure and improve the public taste; and public institutions of various kinds, which will improve the general condition of the people; in this manner returning their surplus wealth to the mass of their fellows in the forms best calculated to do them lasting good.

Thus is the problem of rich and poor to be solved. The laws of accumulation will be left free, the laws of distribution free. Individualism will continue, but the millionaire will be but a trustee for the poor, entrusted for a season with a great part of the increased wealth of the community, but administering it for the community far better than it could or would have done for itself. The best minds will thus have reached a stage in the development of the race in which it is clearly seen that there is no mode of disposing of surplus wealth creditable to thoughtful and earnest men into whose hands it flows, save by using it year by year for the general good. This day already dawns. Men may die without incurring the pity of their fellows, still sharers in great business enterprises from which their capital cannot be or has not been withdrawn and that is left chiefly at death for public uses; yet the day is not far distant when the man who dies leaving behind him millions of available wealth, which was free to him to administer during life, will pass away "unwept, unhonored, and unsung," no matter to what uses he leaves the dross that he cannot take with him. Of such as these he public verdict will then be: "the man who dies thus rich dies disgraced."

Such, in my opinion, is the true gospel concerning wealth, obedience to which is destined some day to solve the problem of the rich and the poor, and to bring "peace on earth, among men goodwill."

Ralph Waldo Emerson

Ralph Waldo Emerson (1803–1882) was born in Boston and died in nearby Concord, Massachusetts. Ordained as a Unitarian pastor, he quit the ministry early and chose to devote himself to a life of letters. Beloved nationwide as a lecturer, poet, and essayist, Emerson made Concord his lifelong home and the center of New England Transcendentalism; his published sermons, journals, letters, essays, and poems together add up to forty-one volumes. The following selection is a single paragraph from "Self-Reliance," which he published in 1841 in *Essays, First Series.*

Selection from *Self-Reliance*

Whoso would be a man must be a nonconformist. He who would gather immortal palms must not be hindered by the name of goodness but must explore if it be goodness. Nothing is at last sacred but the integrity of your own mind. Absolve you to yourself, and you shall have the suffrage of the world. I remember an answer that when quite young I was prompted to make to a valued adviser who was wont to importune me with the dear old doctrines of the church. On my saying, "What have I to do with the sacredness of traditions, if I live wholly from within?" my friend suggested—"But these impulses may be from below, not from above." I replied, "They do not seem to me to be such; but if I am the devil's child, I will live then from the devil." No law can be sacred to me but that of my nature. Good and bad are but names very readily transferable to that or this; the only right is what is after my constitution; the only wrong what is against it. A man is to carry himself in the presence of all opposition as if everything were titular and ephemeral but he. I am ashamed to think how easily we capitulate to badges and names, to large societies and dead institutions. Every decent and well-spoken individual affects and sways me more than is right. I ought to go upright and vital and speak the rude truth in all ways. If malice and vanity wear the coat of philanthropy, shall that pass? If an angry bigot assumes this bountiful cause of abolition, and comes to me with his last news from Barbados, why should I not say to him, "Go love thy infant; love thy woodchopper;

be good natured and modest; have that grace; and never varnish your hard, uncharitable ambition with this incredible tenderness for black folk a thousand miles off. Thy love afar is spite at home." Rough and graceless would be such greeting, but truth is handsomer than the affectation of love. Your goodness must have some edge to it—else it is none. The doctrine of hatred must be preached, as the counteraction of the doctrine of love, when that pules and whines. I shun father and mother and wife and brother when my genius calls me. I would write on the lintels of the doorpost, *Whim*. I hope it is somewhat better than whim at last, but we cannot spend the day in explanation. Expect me not to show cause why I seek or why I exclude company. Then again, do not tell me, as a good man did today, of my obligation to put all poor men in good situations. Are they *my* poor? I tell thee, thou foolish philanthropist, that I grudge the dollar, the dime, the cent I give to such men as do not belong to me and to whom I do not belong. There is a class of persons to whom by all spiritual affinity I am bought and sold; for them I will go to prison if need be; but your miscellaneous popular charities; the education at college of fools; the building of meetinghouses to the vain end to which many now stand; alms to sots, and the thousandfold relief societies—though I confess with shame I sometimes succumb and give the dollar, it is a wicked dollar, which by and by I shall have the manhood to withhold.

Sogyal Rinpoche

Sogyal Rinpoche was born in Kham, in eastern Tibet. In response to the Chinese occupation of Tibet, Rinpoche went into exile with his spiritual master and in 1971 traveled to England to study comparative religions at Cambridge University. He became a translator and aide to several leading Tibetan masters and began teaching in the West in 1974. Rinpoche is the founder and spiritual director of Rigpa, a network of Buddhist centers and groups around the world, and the author of *The Tibetan Book of Living and Dying*, from which this selection is taken.

Compassion: The Wish-Fulfilling Jewel

Asanga was one of the most famous Indian Buddhist saints and lived in the fourth century. He went to the mountains to do a solitary retreat, concentrating all his meditation practice on the Buddha Maitreya, in the fervent hope that he would be blessed with a vision of this Buddha and receive teachings from him.

For six years Asanga meditated in extreme hardship but did not even have one auspicious dream. He was disheartened and thought he would never succeed with his aspiration to meet the Buddha Maitreya, so he abandoned his retreat and left his hermitage. He had not gone far down the road when he saw a man rubbing an enormous iron bar with a strip of silk. Asanga went up to him and asked him what he was doing. "I haven't got a needle," the man replied, "so I'm going to make one out of this iron bar." Asanga stared at him, astounded; even if the man were able to manage it in a hundred years, he thought, what would be the point? He said to himself: "Look at the trouble people give themselves over things that are totally absurd. You are doing something really valuable, spiritual practice, and you're not nearly so dedicated." He turned around and went back to his retreat.

Another three years went by, still without the slightest sign from the Buddha Maitreya. "Now I know for certain," he thought, "I'm never going to succeed." So he left again and soon came to a bend in the road where there was a huge rock, so tall it seemed to touch the sky. At the foot of the rock was a man busily rubbing it with a feather soaked in water. "What are you doing?" Asanga asked.

"This rock is so big it's stopping the sun from shining on my house, so I'm trying to get rid of it." Asanga was amazed at the man's indefatigable energy and ashamed at his own lack of dedication. He returned to his retreat.

Three more years passed, and still he had not even had a single good dream. He decided, once and for all, that it was hopeless, and he left his retreat for good. The day wore on, and in the afternoon he came across a dog lying by the side of the road. It had only its front legs, and the whole of the lower part of its body was rotting and covered with maggots. Despite its pitiful condition, the dog was snapping at passersby and pathetically trying to bite them by dragging itself along the ground with its two good legs.

Asanga was overwhelmed with a vivid and unbearable feeling of compassion. He cut a piece of flesh off his own body and gave it to the dog to eat. Then he bent down to take off the maggots that were consuming the dog's body. But he suddenly thought he might hurt them if he tried to pull them out with his fingers, and he realized that the only way to remove them would be on his tongue. Asanga knelt on the ground and, looking at the horrible festering, writhing mass, closed his eyes. He leant closer and put out his tongue . . . The next thing he knew, his tongue was touching the ground. He opened his eyes and looked up. The dog was gone; there in its place was the Buddha Maitreya, ringed by a shimmering aura of light.

"At last," said Asanga. "Why did you never appear to me before?"

Maitreya spoke softly: "It is not true that I have never appeared to you before. I was with you all the time, but your negative karma and obscurations prevented you from seeing me. Your twelve years of practice dissolved them slightly, so that you were at last able to see the dog. Then, thanks to your genuine and heartfelt compassion, all those obscurations were completely swept away, and you can see me before you with your very own eyes. If you don't believe that this is what happened, put me on your shoulder and try and see if anyone else can see me."

Asanga put Maitreya on his right shoulder and went to the marketplace, where he began to ask everyone: "What have I got on my shoulder?" "Nothing," most people said and hurried on. Only one old woman, whose karma had been slightly purified, answered: "You've got the rotting corpse of an old dog on your shoulder, that's all." Asanga at last understood the boundless power of compassion that had purified and transformed his karma, and so made him a vessel fit to receive the vision and instruction of Maitreya. Then the Buddha Maitreya, whose name means "loving kindness," took Asanga to a heavenly realm and there gave him many sublime teachings that are among the most important in the whole of Buddhism.

Bertolt Brecht

Bertolt Brecht (1898–1956) was born into a prosperous and pious middle-class family in Augsburg, Germany. As a young man, he began medical studies in Munich but abandoned them to become a poet and playwright. His first play, *Baal*, was produced in 1923; *The Threepenny Opera* followed in 1928. A communist and advocate of social reform, Brecht saw his plays and other writings banned in Germany in the 1930s. He went into exile in 1933, living first in Scandinavia and then the United States, where he wrote briefly and without much success for Hollywood. Upon his return to Germany in 1948, Brecht became that country's most popular contemporary poet, finding an audience on both sides of the political divide. The following poem, "A Bed for the Night," appeared in his *Collected Poems 1913–1956.*

A Bed for the Night

I hear that in New York
At the corner of 26th Street and Broadway
A man stands every evening during the winter months
And gets beds for the homeless there
By appealing to passers-by.

It won't change the world
It won't improve relations among men
It will not shorten the age of exploitation
But a few men have a bed for the night
For a night the wind is kept from them
The snow meant for them falls on the roadway.

Don't put down the book on reading this, man.

A few people have a bed for the night
For a night the wind is kept from them
The snow meant for them falls on the roadway
But it won't change the world
It won't improve relations among men
It will not shorten the age of exploitation.

Elizabeth Lynn and D. Susan Wisely

Elizabeth Lynn (b. 1958) directs the Project on Civic Reflection at Valparaiso University and is the editor, with Adam Davis, of *The Civically Engaged Reader*. D. Susan Wisely (b. 1945) served the Lilly Endowment for three decades, first as a program officer and later as director of evaluation, before retiring in 2002. The following selection is a revised version of an article that began as an internal staff paper for the Lilly Endowment and appeared most recently in the anthology *The Perfect Gift*, edited by Amy Kass.

Four Traditions of Philanthropy

Central to the history of philanthropy in the United States is a vision of human connectedness. As Ellen Condliffe Lagemann has written, American philanthropy represents a long history of "efforts to establish the values, shape the beliefs, and define the behaviors that would join people to one another."

Yet though philanthropists have sought to cultivate connection among the members of American society, they have not always understood this task in the same way. In the brief history of this nation, we have seen three distinctive philanthropic traditions: relief, improvement, and social reform. Within each of these traditions, the principles and purposes of philanthropy have been defined differently. Philanthropy understood as relief operates on the principle of compassion and seeks to alleviate human suffering. Philanthropy understood as improvement operates on the principle of progress and seeks to maximize individual human potential. Philanthropy understood as reform operates on the principle of justice and seeks to solve social problems. Let's briefly explore each of these traditions.

***

Philanthropy as Relief

Give a man a fish, feed him for a day.
—Anonymous

The tradition of philanthropy as relief represents the most ancient form of philanthropy—what is sometimes called charity. Animated by the principle of compassion, this kind of philanthropy is mainly concerned with alleviating human suffering.

Of all of the traditions contributing to the contemporary practice of philanthropy, the tradition of benevolence is most obviously rooted in a religious worldview. Charity, from the Latin term *caritas*, means other-regarding love, prompted without regard for status or merit, as in God's love for humanity. The benevolent impulse proceeds from the recognition that we are all connected to one another as part of God's creation. Even our accumulated wealth is God's gift, not our own achievement, and therefore is to be shared freely with God's other creatures.

In "On Christian Charity," a now-famous sermon delivered to his fellow Puritans while sailing to America in 1630, John Winthrop gave these principles exemplary expression. Because we are "knit . . . together in the bond of brotherly affection," he said, "it appears plainly that no man is made more honorable than another or more wealthy, etc., out of any particular and singular respect to himself, but for the glory of his creator and the common good of the creature, man." We are therefore commanded to love our neighbors as ourselves. As "members of the same body," he concluded, "we must delight in each other, make others' conditions as our own, rejoice together, mourn together, labor and suffer together."

The tradition of charity has been an important part of American philanthropy from Winthrop's day forward, and it continues today to animate philanthropies large and small, organized and individual, modest and lavish. When a foundation commits funds for the needy, it participates in the tradition of relief. Likewise, when we as individuals make a donation to the Red Cross, provide goods to a food pantry, shovel out an elderly neighbor, or carry food to a fire victim, we too are participating in the tradition of relief.

The tradition of relief has many strengths (imagine a world without it!). It allows us to express love or empathy for others, without regard for status or merit. It highlights our personal obligation to respond to others. It meets clear and pressing needs. And, precisely because it is an act of compassion, a matter of "feeling with" others, charitable philanthropy is responsive to those it serves rather than actively trying to shape or lead them.

At its worst, however, this tradition of benevolence can waste precious resources by failing to address the causes of suffering. It can also cultivate passivity toward the way things are by inviting us to respond to pressing needs rather than change the conditions that created them. Winthrop expressed this attitude of acquiescence to the order of things in the opening words of his sermon, when he declared that "God Almighty . . . hath so disposed of the condition of mankind as in all times some must be rich, some poor; some high and eminent in power and dignity, others mean in subjection." For better or worse, charity is a tradition resigned to the inevitability of social inequality. "The poor you will always have with you" might well be its motto.

Philanthropy as Improvement

Teach a man to fish, feed him for a lifetime.
—Anonymous

The second great tradition of American philanthropy developed at least partly in response to the perceived futility of relief. Questioning the wisdom and effectiveness of "almsgiving," philanthropists like Benjamin Franklin and Andrew Carnegie sought instead to maximize human potential. Their distinctive style of giving established a great American tradition of providing opportunities for individual and civic improvement. To this day, many of us choose to give by underwriting scholarships for talented individuals, sponsoring cultural and artistic activities, or supporting educational and other "improving" organizations.

Andrew Carnegie provides an especially interesting example of philanthropy as improvement. In establishing one of the first modern foundations, he consciously rejected the old tradition of charity. Like those who practice benevolence, Carnegie hoped his philanthropy would foster human connectedness. His essay "The Gospel of Wealth" begins: "The problem of our age is the proper administration of wealth, that the ties of brotherhood may still bind together the rich and poor in harmonious relationship." But he believed that the revolutionary changes wrought by industrialization and urbanization in the last third of the nineteenth century called for a fundamentally new approach to philanthropy.

For Carnegie, as for a number of Victorian philanthropists, the traditional forms of charity and almsgiving perpetuated the very ills they sought to alleviate. Far better, he believed, were charitable efforts that aim at improvement:

> In bestowing charity, the main consideration should be to help those
> who will help themselves; to provide part of the means by which
> those who desire to improve may do so; to give those who desire to
> rise the aids by which they may rise; to assist, but rarely or never to
> do all. Neither the individual nor the race is improved by almsgiv-
> ing. . . . [T]he best means of benefiting the community is to place

> within its reach the ladders upon which the aspiring can rise—free
> libraries, parks, and means of recreation, by which men are helped
> in body and mind; works of art, certain to give pleasure and improve
> the public taste; and public institutions of various kinds, which will
> improve the general condition of the people.

According to Carnegie, proper philanthropy sets out ladders for those who have initiative and climbing skill. Individuals are then responsible for taking advantage of the ladders set before them. The libraries funded by Carnegie are an excellent example of this kind of giving. As is often the case in improvement philanthropy, they were inspired by Carnegie's own boyhood experiences of using a library.

More than a hundred years after Carnegie published "The Gospel of Wealth," the improvement tradition remains a vital part of American philanthropy, practiced especially by individual givers who want to make opportunities of the sort they experienced available to others. This kind of philanthropy has many inviting qualities that ensure its continued vitality. It allows us to express gratitude for special opportunities we have received by extending the same opportunities to others. It emphasizes individual responsibility and encourages individual initiative.

Yet the tradition of improvement, like the tradition of relief, has weaknesses. In the latter half of the twentieth century, American philanthropy increasingly confronted a society in which its improving efforts seemed chiefly to benefit the well-situated and highly motivated members of the community. (Ladders, after all, are useful only to those with climbing skills, and fishing lessons only help those with access to the pond.) The concept of "individual opportunities" is of diminished value if entire groups are effectively blocked—for social, legal, and economic reasons—from taking advantage of such opportunities.

Philanthropy as Social Reform

A Catalyst for Change
—MacArthur Foundation slogan

Carnegie reacted to the flaws in the relief tradition—and philanthropists who came after Carnegie reacted in turn to the flaws in the improvement tradition. A retrospective published in 1981 by the Carnegie Corporation (Carnegie's own foundation) noted that during the 1960s the staff and board had become "painfully aware of the urgent problems of race, poverty, and equality that were besetting the nation." Looking back on a tradition of encouraging educational opportunities, they concluded that "it was not reasonable to expect that schooling alone could create equality of opportunity when equality did not exist in the world of jobs, of social relations, or of politics." Like the Rockefeller and Ford foundations, the Carnegie Corporation shifted its grant-making strategies in a new direction: it began to attack perceived underlying circumstances of inequality. Many of America's largest foundations now dedicated themselves not to charity or improvement but to social reform.

This third great tradition in American philanthropy—the tradition of reform—has roots in America's past: recall the abolitionists of the 1800s, for instance, or the muckrakers of the Progressive Era. Yet the goal of social reform has achieved special prominence in recent years, to the point where it characterizes the self-understanding of most large foundations and of many smaller and more traditional charitable organizations as well.

Philanthropy as social reform is, above all, dedicated to encouraging social change. Its practitioners believe that societal circumstances are often more powerful in shaping human destiny than the actions of individuals themselves; hence, they argue, philanthropy must strive to change the circumstances. Indeed, its motto might well be that of the MacArthur Foundation in the late twentieth century: A Catalyst for Change.

As this motto suggests, the philanthropic tradition of social reform takes a proactive, even directive, role in public life. Rather than responding to the requests of others, it actively attempts to identify and solve public problems, often through experimentation and the innovative use of venture capital. According to proponents of this approach, a foundation has unique resources, freedom, and expertise necessary to experiment on social problems. It should therefore seek innovative solutions that other groups might not be able to discover, but from which the larger society will benefit.

Exemplary expressions of this tradition can be found in the writings of national commissions established in the early 1970s to study the public role of foundations. Consider, for instance, the following statement from the Peterson Commission in 1970: "Our society . . . is in obvious need of philanthropic institutions standing outside the frame of government but in support of the public interest," it declared. "[J]ust as scouts move in advance of a body of troops to probe what lies ahead," so too philanthropic institutions "can spot emergent problems, diagnose them, and test alternative ways to deal with them."

The tradition of social reform has great strengths. It acknowledges the power of societal circumstances and seeks to change them. It intentionally experiments with alternative solutions to social problems and seeks to learn from those solutions. But social experimentation has brought with it some difficulties. Modern foundations have naturally been tempted to see themselves as a kind of "shadow government," not just as supporters of experiments that might inspire further thinking but as the very makers of future social policy. Paul Ylvisaker indicates this tendency in *The Handbook on Private*

Foundations, when he writes that modern philanthropy has been dedicated "to finding systemic solutions to underlying causes of poverty and other social ills, and over time has become a recognized social process, in effect *a set of private legislatures* defining public problems, setting goals and priorities, and allocating resources toward general solutions" (emphasis added). The result can be a kind of arrogance in advocating for social change "on behalf of" the public, and a failure to listen carefully to that public.

Toward a Fourth Philanthropic Response

Only connect!
—E. M. Forster

The three types of philanthropy outlined above are not mutually exclusive. Indeed, most philanthropic organizations participate to some degree in all three traditions. Yet, on the whole, organized American philanthropy has in recent decades moved increasingly in the direction of social reform, relying on individual givers to fund opportunities for self-improvement and relegating the traditionally charitable work of relief to governmental and religious bodies.

The future direction of American philanthropy is less clear. Events of recent years have put new pressure upon foundations to rethink their fundamental strategies for serving the American public. Effective solutions to social problems have proved more elusive than had been hoped. Despite the social reform efforts of both government and philanthropy, ours is more than ever a society divided into rich and poor, a society still very much challenged to alleviate human suffering and to maximize human potential by providing significant opportunities for all its members.

Nor is it clear, in the new century, just *who* should be proposing solutions. We hear calls for different voices in public life—not just the voice of the successful, not just the voice of the expert, but the voice of the citizen. And yet, with the increased complexity and ambitions of the philanthropic enterprise, philanthropy's relation to its public—its capacity to hear and learn from the public—has, if anything, diminished. The philanthropist who funds libraries or experiments with social policy stands at a far greater remove from those served than the relief worker who ladles soup in a soup kitchen.

In response, foundations and other philanthropic organizations have begun to turn toward a fourth philanthropic way, which some people refer to as *civic engagement*. They are investing resources in strengthening relationships and nurturing conversations among citizens, in order to build, as the President of the Public Education Network, Wendy Puriefoy, put it, "more reflective and resourceful local communities." Study circles, neighborhood associations, and the forums sponsored by the Kettering Foundation are examples of this fourth philanthropic response, as is the more ambitious recent initiative of the Annie E. Casey Foundation to "partner" with communities in cultivating local resources for addressing poverty. Ultimately, the goal of these investments may be to relieve, improve, or reform the communities they serve. Yet the focus of the work, and the standard of its success, is building up connections among ordinary citizens.

American interest in civic engagement is not new. In 1889, the same year Andrew Carnegie published his reflections on wealth, Jane Addams started Hull-House in Chicago. Taking inspiration from London's Toynbee Hall, Addams established this settlement house with the conviction that we must connect with one another in order to help one another. In *Democracy and Social Ethics*, published in 1902, she cautions against the indiscriminate giving of relief and the stern policy of justice and points the reader toward another way:

> "To love mercy" and at the same time "to do justly" is the difficult task; to fulfill the first requirement alone is to fall into the error of indiscriminate giving with all its disastrous results; to fulfill the second solely is to obtain the stern policy of withholding, and it results in such a dreary lack of sympathy and understanding that the establishment of justice is impossible. It may be that the combination of the two can never be attained save as we fulfill the third requirement —"to walk humbly with God," which may mean to walk for many dreary miles beside the lowliest of his creatures.

The help Hull-House offered its neighbors took many forms—sometimes relief from pain, sometimes improved individual opportunity, sometimes advocacy for social change. But its first and final value, for Addams, lay in building relationships among citizens so that they could better understand and assist one another. Addams did not call this work philanthropy, much less civic engagement. Yet in her writings and practices one can find many echoes of our contemporary need to build up meaningful connections among citizens.

As Addams would have been the first to acknowledge, civic engagement suffers from the perennial frustrations of democracy. It can be slow, contentious, prone to more talk than action, and difficult to render into measurable outcomes. But it can also empower those who might not otherwise participate in public life. It encourages attention to local needs and, in the language of our own time, recognizes local assets. And it builds community by engaging its citizens with one another and enabling them to work together on their shared concerns.

In Conclusion

Each of the first three philanthropic traditions outlined earlier has made significant contributions to the well-being of the American public. But each, if taken alone, also displays weaknesses. The tradition of relief can encourage a philanthropy that is passive, reacting to pressing needs rather than trying to change the conditions that create those needs. The tradition of improvement can encourage philanthropy that benefits only selected members of the community. The tradition of social reform can lead foundation workers or other donors into unilateral decision making "on behalf of" the public, without much openness to the wisdom or will of that public.

As we enter a new century, when new wisdom is needed, civic engagement may be an especially important philanthropic response. Citizens have untapped wisdom and resources for public service in their own practical experience that, for a variety of reasons, they have not been able to discover or recover. To put it simply, people need opportunities to learn from themselves and about themselves, from others and about others. A foundation can help those whom it would serve to tap these deep veins of wisdom, thereby discerning more clearly appropriate directions for public service in their own particular places and in their own particular ways.

One timely contribution foundations as well as individual donors can make, then, is to promote civic engagement and encourage public moral discourse, by cultivating hospitable spaces for reflection and by bringing diverse people and perspectives into conversation. Rather than trying to force a specific vision of the future (which could turn out to be an unexamined extension of the past), we can create the conditions for conversation, in the hope that new vision and fresh action will eventually emerge. In doing so, we are not forcing our own experimental answers or simply repeating the predictable answers a little louder for all to hear. Instead, we will be furthering public deliberation and promoting discovery of new ways of seeing.

Philanthropy as Relief	Philanthropy as Improvement	Philanthropy as Social Reform	Philanthropy as Civic Engagement
Operates on principle of compassion	Operates on principle of progress	Operates on principle of justice	Operates on principle of participation
Alleviates human suffering	Maximizes human potential	Solves social problems	Builds community

Moses Maimonides

Moses Maimonides (1135–1204) was born Moshe ben Maimon in Córdoba, the first son of a judge in the rabbinical court, shortly before Christians began their reconquest of Spain from its Muslim rulers. He spent his childhood wandering Andalusia with his family to avoid persecution and later moved to Morocco, Israel, and finally Egypt, where he served as chief physician at the court of Saladin. He also became the Nagid, or the supreme head of the Jews. Maimonides produced a great body of written works on Talmudic scholarship, Jewish law, medicine, and philosophy. His major contribution to Jewish life remains the *Mishneh Torah*, his code of Jewish law, which in time became a standard guide to Jewish practice. The following selection is taken from "Gifts to the Poor" in Book Seven (the Book of Agriculture) of the *Mishneh Torah*.

Selection from the *Mishneh Torah*

There are eight degrees of almsgiving, each one superior to the other. The highest degree, than which there is none higher, is one who upholds the hand of an Israelite reduced to poverty by handing him a gift or a loan, or entering into a partnership with him, or finding work for him, in order to strengthen his hand, so that he would have no need to beg from other people. Concerning such a one Scripture says, "Thou shalt uphold him; as a stranger and a settler shall he live with thee" (Leviticus 25:35), meaning uphold him, so that he would not lapse into want.

Below this is he who gives alms to the poor in such a way that he does not know to whom he has given, nor does the poor man know from whom he has received. This constitutes the fulfilling of religious duty for its own sake, and for such there was a chamber of secrets in the temple, whereunto the righteous would contribute secretly, and wherefrom the poor of good families would draw their sustenance in equal secrecy. Close to such a person is he who contributes directly to the alms fund.

One should not, however, contribute directly to the alms fund unless he knows that the person in charge of it is trustworthy, is a sage, and knows how to manage it properly, as was the case of Rabbi Hananiah ben Teradion.

Below this is he who knows to whom he is giving, while the poor man does not know from whom he is receiving. He is thus like a great among the sages who were wont to set out secretly and throw the money down at the doors of the poor. This is a proper way of doing it, and a preferable one if those in charge of alms are not conducting themselves as they should.

Below this is the case where the poor man knows from whom he is receiving, but himself remains unknown to the giver. He is thus like the great among the sages who used to place the money in the fold of a linen sheet that they would throw over their shoulder, whereupon the poor would come behind them and take the money without being exposed to humiliation.

Below this is he who hands alms to the poor man before being asked for them.

Below this is he who hands alms to the poor man after the latter has asked for them.

Below this is he who gives the poor man less than what is proper but with a friendly countenance.

Below this is he who gives alms with a frowning countenance.

Anna Akhmatova

Anna Akhmatova (1889–1966) was born Anna Gorenko in Bolshoy Fountains near Odessa, Ukraine. She began writing poetry at the age of eleven, attended the Smolnyi Institute in St. Petersburg, and became a member of the Acmeist group of poets. Akhmatova's first collection, *Vecher* ("Evening"), appeared in 1912, and her second, *Chyotki* ("Rosary"), brought her wider recognition in 1914. Publication of her work was banned in the Soviet Union, save for occasional and brief periods, between 1925 and 1952. Only in the final years of her life was she able to move unrestricted in the literary world. She died in Moscow, and her collected works were published in 1986, twenty years after her death.

If All Who Have Begged Help

If all who have begged help
From me in this world,
All the holy innocents,
Broken wives, and cripples,
The imprisoned, the suicidal—
If they had sent me one kopeck
I should have become "richer
Than all Egypt" . . .
But they did not send me kopecks,
Instead they shared with me their strength,
And so nothing in the world
Is stronger than I,
And I can bear anything, even this.

1961

PART IV

Leading

Your invitation to attend the leadership summit arrives in the mail on a glossy brochure. *Be a Leader!* it proclaims. *Join the Leadership Network. Meet Other Emerging Leaders. Develop Your Leadership Skills.* Photographs of open skies, misty mountains, tall buildings, and birds in full flight complete the message, along with a lofty quotation and an equally lofty registration fee.

The brochure is flattering to receive. It announces that you, too, are a leader. (How did they ever find out?) Yet the longer you look, the less flattering it feels. There is something circular about the logic of the summit, something hollow at its core. It is not clear whether the program promises to convene or create leaders. It is even less clear what leadership means to the summit organizers, even though the word is invoked in every line. It is a downright mystery just who is to be led. A mountain? A building? A cloud? A bird?

By contrast, the actual work of leadership sneaks up on you with less pomp and more certainty. One day you find yourself exercising power over others, shaping their experience for better or for worse. You may have become a parent, a teacher, a program director, a coach. You may have agreed to serve on a committee or a board. You may have been drawn out of yourself by an event in the community, organized a group in response, and now you are charged with managing the growing momentum. You may have a staff, a congregation, a Cub Scout troop looking to you for guidance. No mountains or birds in sight. What do you do? How do you lead?

The readings in this section do not answer these questions so much as raise and complicate them—much as the actual work of leadership raises and complicates them. Reflecting on the selections, alone and in the company of others, will not make you a Leader with a capital L. But it may help ease the burden and improve the experience of leadership.

This section begins with **Charles Waddell Chesnutt**'s short story "The Wife of His Youth." Mr. Ryder, the story's central character, experiences a personal crisis that is simultaneously a crisis of leadership; in response, he risks both his leadership role and the integrity of the organization he leads. *How can we reconcile the competing claims of our origins and our aspirations?*

In Chapters 11 and 12 of the Second Book of Samuel, King David experiences a different kind of crisis that, like Chesnutt's story, raises questions about the relation between leadership and justice. *As leaders, how do we recognize injustice, and how do we persuade others that it exists? How should we respond to those we see as victims of injustice when they do not see themselves this way?*

Graham Greene's short story "The Destructors" describes the ascent of a young gang leader, who draws his followers into carrying out his vision of something both horrible and beautiful, but perhaps also necessary. *In what way is destruction part of civic work? How should we decide what to destroy and what to preserve?*

Franz Kafka's parable "The Helmsman" depicts a descending leader who, on his way down, questions the position he is losing. *Why do any of us want to lead, and how do we respond when our leadership is challenged?*

Toni Cade Bambara's short story "The Lesson" invites us to consider how—and perhaps why—we should lead reluctant followers. *How might we lead those who do not seem to want to be led? How do we know we are right to do so?*

William Carlos Williams's short story "The Use of Force" raises the stakes; his narrator, a doctor intent on diagnosing the illness of a small child, uses violence to impose his purpose. *When does help require harm, or the perception of harm? How can we ensure that the ends and the means of our interventions are full of care?*

And an excerpt from *The Autobiography of Benjamin Franklin* has **Benjamin Franklin** attempting to lead himself (and, later, others) where he seems least inclined to go. *Is the idea of self-improvement a sound one? What relation is there, if any, between self-improvement and community improvement?*

The section concludes with four readings that raise questions about the relationship between authority and morality. **Ursula K. Le Guin**'s short story "The Ones Who Walk Away from Omelas" is an unsettling depiction of a seemingly ideal society whose well-being depends on a horrifying set of terms. *Why do some of us and not others decide to walk away from a way of life we can no longer tolerate? When—if ever—should we make the decision to leave?*

Billy Collins's poem "The History Teacher" suggests another way of avoiding the responsibilities of leadership and (like Le Guin's story) leaves us asking what the alternative might be. *When does leadership require that we speak the truth, and when does it demand that we withhold it?*

In his Second Inaugural Address, **Abraham Lincoln** presents a compelling alternative: he uses speech to move a divided nation toward charity for all, malice toward none (an exhortation repeated, incidentally, by Charles Waddell Chesnutt's Mr. Ryder). *Is "charity toward all and malice toward none" enough to ask of us? Is it too much to ask?*

The section concludes with **Nathaniel Hawthorne**'s short story "The Minister's Black Veil" whose central character uses a more symbolic exhortation to lead his flock—a choice that proves both mysterious and effective. *As leaders, how much should we reveal of ourselves and how much should we keep hidden?*

Charles Waddell Chesnutt

Born in Cleveland, Ohio, Charles Waddell Chesnutt (1858–1932) grew up in Fayetteville, North Carolina. He became a schoolteacher and then a lawyer, as well as a writer of short stories, novels, and a biography of Frederick Douglass. In 1887, he became the first African American fiction writer to be published in the *Atlantic Monthly*. After publishing two collections of short fiction (*The Conjure Woman* and *The Wife of His Youth and Other Stories of the Color Line*) and three novels, Chesnutt turned his energies from writing to business. This story, "The Wife of His Youth," appeared in the *Atlantic Monthly* in 1898.

The Wife of His Youth

1.

Mr. Ryder was going to give a ball. There were several reasons why this was an opportune time for such an event.

Mr. Ryder might aptly be called the dean of the Blue Veins. The original Blue Veins were a little society of colored persons organized in a certain Northern city shortly after the war. Its purpose was to establish and maintain correct social standards among a people whose social condition presented almost unlimited room for improvement. By accident, combined perhaps with some natural affinity, the society consisted of individuals who were, generally speaking, more white than black. Some envious outsider made the suggestion that no one was eligible for membership who was not white enough to show blue veins. The suggestion was readily adopted by those who were not of the favored few, and since that time the society, though possessing a longer and more pretentious name, had been known far and wide as the "Blue Vein Society," and its members as the "Blue Veins."

The Blue Veins did not allow that any such requirement existed for admission to their circle, but, on the contrary, declared that character and culture were the only things considered; and that if most of their members were light-colored, it was because such persons, as a rule, had had better opportunities to qualify themselves for membership. Opinions differed, too, as to the usefulness of the society. There were those who had been known to assail it violently as a glaring example of the very prejudice from which the colored race had suffered most; and later, when such critics had succeeded in getting on the inside, they had been heard to maintain with zeal and earnestness that the society was a lifeboat, an anchor, a bulwark, and a shield—a pillar of cloud by day and of fire by night, to guide their people through the social wilderness. Another alleged prerequisite for Blue Vein membership was that of free birth; and while there was really no such requirement, it is doubtless true that very few of the members would have been unable to meet it if there had been. If there were one or two of the older members who had come up from the South and from slavery, their history presented enough romantic circumstances to rob their servile origin of its grosser aspects.

While there were no such tests of eligibility, it is true that the Blue Veins had their notions on these subjects and that not all of them were equally liberal in regard to the things they collectively disclaimed. Mr. Ryder was one of the most conservative. Though he had not been among the founders of the society, but had come in some years later, his genius for social leadership was such that he had speedily become its recognized adviser and head, the custodian of its standards, and the preserver of its traditions. He shaped its social policy, was active in providing for its entertainment, and when the interest fell off, as it sometimes did, he fanned the embers until they burst again into a cheerful flame.

There were still other reasons for his popularity. While he was not as white as some of the Blue Veins, his appearance was such as to confer distinction upon them. His features were of a refined type, his hair was almost straight; he was always neatly dressed; his manners were irreproachable and his morals above suspicion. He had come to Groveland a young man, and obtaining employment in the office of a railroad company as messenger had in time worked himself up to the position of stationery clerk, having charge of the distribution of the office supplies for the whole company. Although the lack of early training had hindered the orderly development of a naturally fine mind, it had not prevented him from doing a great deal of reading or from forming decidedly literary tastes. Poetry was his passion. He could repeat whole pages of the great English poets; and if his pronunciation was sometimes faulty, his eye, his voice, his gestures, would respond to the changing sentiment with a precision that revealed a poetic soul and disarmed criticism. He was economical and had saved money; he owned and occupied a very comfortable house on a respectable street. His residence was handsomely furnished, containing among other things a good library, especially rich in poetry; a piano; and some choice engravings. He generally shared his house with some young couple, who looked after his wants and were company for him; for Mr. Ryder was a single man. In the early days of his connection with the Blue Veins he had been regarded as quite a catch, and young ladies and their mothers had maneuvered with much ingenuity to capture him. Not, however, until Mrs. Molly Dixon visited Groveland had any woman ever made him wish to change his condition to that of a married man.

Mrs. Dixon had come to Groveland from Washington in the spring, and before the summer was over she had won Mr. Ryder's heart. She possessed many attractive qualities. She was much younger than he; in fact, he was old enough to have been her father, though no one knew exactly how old he was. She was whiter than he and better educated. She had moved in the best colored society of the country, at Washington, and had taught in the schools of that city. Such a superior person had been eagerly welcomed to the Blue Vein Society and had taken a leading part in its activities. Mr. Ryder had at first been attracted by her charms of person, for she was very good looking and not over twenty-five; then by her refined manners and the vivacity of her wit. Her husband had been a government clerk and at his death had left a considerable life insurance. She was visiting friends in Groveland, and, finding the town and the people to her liking, had prolonged her stay indefinitely. She had not seemed displeased at Mr. Ryder's attentions, but on the contrary had given him every proper encouragement; indeed, a younger and less cautious man would long since have spoken. But he had made up his mind and had only to determine the time when he would ask her to be his wife. He decided to give a ball in her honor, and at some time during the evening of the ball to offer her his heart and hand. He had no special fears about the outcome, but, with a little touch of romance, he wanted the surroundings to be in harmony with his own feelings when he should have received the answer he expected.

Mr. Ryder resolved that this ball should mark an epoch in the social history of Groveland. He knew, of course—no one could know better—the entertainments that had taken place in past years and what must be done to surpass them. His ball must be worthy of the lady in whose honor it was to be given and must, by the quality of its guests, set an example for the future. He had observed of late a growing liberality, almost a laxity, in social matters, even among members of his own set, and had several times been forced to meet in a social way persons whose complexions and callings in life were hardly up to the standard that he considered proper for the society to maintain. He had a theory of his own.

"I have no race prejudice," he would say, "but we people of mixed blood are ground between the upper and the nether millstone. Our fate lies between absorption by the white race and extinction in the black. The one doesn't want us yet but may take us in time. The other would welcome us, but it would be for us a backward step. 'With malice toward none, with charity for all,' we must do the best we can for ourselves and those who are to follow us. Self-preservation is the first law of nature."

His ball would serve by its exclusiveness to counteract leveling tendencies, and his marriage with Mrs. Dixon would help to further the upward process of absorption he had been wishing and waiting for.

2.

The ball was to take place on Friday night. The house had been put in order, the carpets covered with canvas, the halls and stairs decorated with palms and potted plants; and in the afternoon Mr. Ryder sat on his front porch, which the shade of a vine running up over a wire netting made a cool and pleasant lounging place. He expected to respond to the toast "The Ladies" at the supper, and from a volume of Tennyson—his favorite poet—was fortifying himself with apt quotations. The volume was open at "A Dream of Fair Women." His eyes fell on these lines, and he read them aloud to judge better of their effect:

> "At length I saw a lady within call,
> Stiller than chisell'd marble, standing there;
> A daughter of the gods, divinely tall,
> And most divinely fair."

He marked the verse, and turning the page read the stanza beginning—

> "O sweet pale Margaret,
> O rare pale Margaret."

He weighed the passage a moment and decided that it would not do. Mrs. Dixon was the palest lady he expected at the ball, and she was of a rather ruddy complexion, and of lively disposition and buxom build. So he ran over the leaves until his eye rested on the description of Queen Guinevere—

> "She seem'd a part of joyous Spring:
> A gown of grass-green silk she wore,
> Buckled with golden clasps before;
> A light-green tuft of plumes she bore
> Closed in a golden ring.

> •   •   •   •   •   •

> "She look'd so lovely, as she sway'd
> The rein with dainty finger-tips,
> A man had given all other bliss,
> And all his worldly worth for this,
> To waste his whole heart in one kiss
> Upon her perfect lips."

As Mr. Ryder murmured these words audibly, with an appreciative thrill, he heard the latch of his gate click and a light footfall sounding on the steps. He turned his head and saw a woman standing before his door.

She was a little woman, not five feet tall, and proportioned to her height. Although she stood erect, and looked around her with very bright and restless eyes, she seemed quite old; for her face was crossed and recrossed with a hundred wrinkles, and around the edges of her bonnet could be seen protruding here and there a tuft of short gray wool. She wore a blue calico gown of ancient cut, a little red shawl fastened around her shoulders with an old-fashioned brass brooch, and a large bonnet profusely ornamented with faded red and yellow artificial flowers. And she was very black—so black that her toothless gums, revealed when she opened her mouth to speak, were not red but blue. She looked like a bit of the old plantation life, summoned up from the past by the wave of a magician's wand, as the poet's fancy had called into being the gracious shapes of which Mr. Ryder had just been reading.

He rose from his chair and came over to where she stood.

"Good afternoon, madam," he said.

"Good evenin', suh," she answered, ducking suddenly with a quaint curtsy. Her voice was shrill and piping but softened somewhat by age. "Is dis yere whar Mistuh Ryduh lib, suh?" she asked, looking around her doubtfully, and glancing into the open windows, through which some of the preparations for the evening were visible.

"Yes," he replied, with an air of kindly patronage, unconsciously flattered by her manner," I am Mr. Ryder. Did you want to see me?"

"Yas, suh, ef I ain't 'sturbin' of you too much."

"Not at all. Have a seat over here behind the vine, where it is cool. What can I do for you?"

"'Scuse me, suh," she continued, when she had sat down on the edge of a chair, "'scuse me, suh, I's lookin' for my husban'. I heerd you wuz a big man an' had libbed heah a long time, an' I 'lowed you would n' min' ef I'd come roun' an' ax you ef you'd ever heerd of a merlatter man by de name er Sam Taylor 'quirin' roun' in de chu'ches ermongs' de people fer his wife 'Liza Jane?"

Mr. Ryder seemed to think for a moment.

"There used to be many such cases right after the war," he said, "but it has been so long that I have forgotten them. There are very few now. But tell me your story, and it may refresh my memory."

She sat back farther in her chair so as to be more comfortable and folded her withered hands in her lap.

"My name's 'Liza," she began, "'Liza Jane. W'en I wuz young I us'ter b'long ter Marse Bob Smif, down in ole Missoura. I wuz bawn down dere. W'en I wuz a gal I wuz married ter a man named Jim. But Jim died, an' after dat I married a merlatter man named Sam Taylor. Sam wuz freebawn, but his mammy and daddy died, an' de w'ite folks 'prenticed him ter my marster fer ter work fer 'im 'tel he wuz growed up. Sam worked in de fiel', an' I wuz de cook. One day Ma'y Ann, ole miss's maid, came rushin' out ter de kitchen, an' says she, I ''Liza Jane, ole marse gwine sell yo' Sam down de ribber.'

"'Go way f'm yere,' says I; 'my husban' 's free!'

"'Don' make no diff'ence. I heerd ole marse tell ole miss he wuz gwine take yo' Sam 'way wid 'im ter-morrow, fer he needed money, an' he knowed whar he could git a t'ousan' dollars fer Sam an' no questions axed.'

"Wen Sam come home f'm de fiel' dat night, I tole him 'bout ole marse gwine steal 'im, an' Sam run erway. His time wuz mos' up, an' he swo' dat w'en he wuz twenty-one he would come back an' he'p me run erway, er else save up de money ter buy my freedom. An' I know he'd 'a' done it, fer he thought a heap er me, Sam did. But w'en he come back he did n' fin' me, fer I wuz n' dere. Ole marse had heerd dat I warned Sam, so he had me whip' an' sol' down de ribber.

"Den de wah broke out, an' w'en it wuz ober de cullud folks wuz scattered. I went back ter de ole home; but Sam wuz n' dere, an' I could n' l'arn nuffin' 'bout 'im. But I knowed he'd be'n dere to look fer me an' had n' foun' me, an' had gone erway ter hunt fer me.

"I's be'n lookin' fer 'im eber sence," she added simply, as though twenty-five years were but a couple of weeks, "an' I knows he's be'n lookin' fer me. Fer he sot a heap er sto' by me, Sam did, an' I know he's be'n huntin' fer me all dese years—'less'n he's be'n sick er sump'n, so he could n' work, er out'n his head, so he could n' 'member his promise. I went back down de ribber, fer I 'lowed he'd gone down dere lookin' fer me. I's be'n ter Noo Orleens, an' Atlanty, an' Charleston, an' Richmon'; an' w'en I'd be'n all ober de Souf I come ter de Norf. Fer I knows I'll fin' 'im some er dese days," she added softly, "er he'll fin' me, an' den we'll bofe be as happy in freedom as we wuz in de ole days befo' de wah." A smile stole over her withered countenance as she paused a moment, and her bright eyes softened into a faraway look.

This was the substance of the old woman's story. She had wandered a little here and there. Mr. Ryder was looking at her curiously when she finished.

"How have you lived all these years?" he asked.

"Cookin', suh. I's a good cook. Does you know anybody w'at needs a good cook, suh? I's stoppin' wid a cullud fam'ly roun' de corner yonder 'tel I kin git a place."

"Do you really expect to find your husband? He may be dead long ago."

She shook her head emphatically. "Oh no, he ain' dead. De signs an' de tokens tells me. I dremp three nights runnin' on'y dis las' week dat I foun' him."

"He may have married another woman. Your slave marriage would not have prevented him, for you never lived with him after the war, and without that your marriage doesn't count."

"Would n' make no diff'ence wid Sam. He would n' marry no yuther 'ooman 'tel he foun' out 'bout me. I knows it," she added. "Sump'n 's be'n tellin' me all dese years dat I's gwine fin' Sam 'fo' I dies."

"Perhaps he's outgrown you and climbed up in the world where he wouldn't care to have you find him."

"No, indeed, suh," she replied, "Sam ain' dat kin' er man. He wuz good ter me, Sam wuz, but he wuz n' much good ter nobody e'se, fer he wuz one er de triflin'es' han's on de plantation. I 'spec's ter haf ter suppo't 'im w'en I fin' 'im, fer he nebber would work 'less'n he had ter. But den he wuz free, an' he did n' git no pay fer his work, an' I don' blame 'im much. Mebbe he's done better sence he run erway, but I ain' 'spectin' much."

"You may have passed him on the street a hundred times during the twenty-five years, and not have known him; time works great changes."

She smiled incredulously. "I'd know 'im 'mongs' a hund'ed men. Fer dey wuz n' no yuther merlatter man like my man Sam, an' I could n' be mistook. I's toted his picture roun' wid me twenty-five years."

"May I see it?" asked Mr. Ryder. "It might help me to remember whether I have seen the original."

As she drew a small parcel from her bosom he saw that it was fastened to a string that went around her neck. Removing several wrappers, she brought to light an old-fashioned daguerreotype in a black case. He looked long and intently at the portrait. It was faded with time, but the features were still distinct, and it was easy to see what manner of man it had represented.

He closed the case, and with a slow movement handed it back to her.

"I don't know of any man in town who goes by that name," he said, "nor have I heard of any one making such inquiries. But if you will leave me your address, I will give the matter some attention, and if I find out anything I will let you know."

She gave him the number of a house in the neighborhood and went away, after thanking him warmly.

He wrote the address on the flyleaf of the volume of Tennyson, and, when she had gone, rose to his feet and stood looking after her curiously. As she walked down the street with mincing step, he saw several persons whom she passed turn and look back at her with a smile of kindly amusement. When she had turned the corner, he went upstairs to his bedroom and stood for a long time before the mirror of his dressing case, gazing thoughtfully at the reflection of his own face.

3.

At eight o'clock the ballroom was a blaze of light and the guests had begun to assemble; for there was a literary program and some routine business of the society to be gone through with before the dancing. A black servant in evening dress waited at the door and directed the guests to the dressing rooms.

The occasion was long memorable among the colored people of the city; not alone for the dress and display but for the high average of intelligence and culture that distinguished the gathering as a whole. There were a number of schoolteachers, several young doctors, three or four lawyers, some professional singers, an editor, a lieutenant in the United States Army spending his furlough in the city, and others in various polite callings; these were colored, though most of them would not have attracted even a casual glance because of any marked difference from white people. Most of the ladies were in evening costume, and dress coats and dancing pumps were the rule among the men. A band of string music, stationed in an alcove behind a row of palms, played popular airs while the guests were gathering.

The dancing began at half past nine. At eleven o'clock supper was served. Mr. Ryder had left the ballroom some little time before the intermission but reappeared at the supper table. The spread was worthy of the occasion, and the guests did full justice to it. When the coffee had been served, the toastmaster, Mr. Solomon Sadler, rapped for order. He made a brief introductory speech, complimenting host and guests, and then presented in their order the toasts of the evening. They were responded to with a very fair display of after-dinner wit.

"The last toast," said the toastmaster, when he reached the end of the list, "is one which must appeal to us all. There is no one of us of the sterner sex who is not at some time dependent upon woman—in infancy for protection, in manhood for companionship, in old age for care and comforting. Our good host has been trying to live alone, but the fair faces I see around me tonight prove that he too is largely dependent upon the gentler sex for most that makes life worth living—the society and love of friends—and rumor is at fault if he does not soon yield entire subjection to one of them. Mr. Ryder will now respond to the toast—The Ladies."

There was a pensive look in Mr. Ryder's eyes as he took the floor and adjusted his eyeglasses. He began by speaking of woman as the gift of heaven to man, and after some general observations on the relations of the sexes he said: "But perhaps the quality that most distinguishes woman is her fidelity and devotion to those she loves. History is full of examples, but has recorded none more striking than one which only today came under my notice."

He then related, simply but effectively, the story told by his visitor of the afternoon. He gave it in the same soft dialect, which came readily to his lips, while the company listened attentively and sympathetically. For the story had awakened a responsive thrill in many hearts. There were some present who had seen, and others who had heard their fathers and grandfathers tell, the wrongs and sufferings of this past generation, and all of them still felt, in their darker moments, the shadow hanging over them. Mr. Ryder went on—

"Such devotion and confidence are rare even among women. There are many who would have searched a year, some who would have waited five years, a few who might have hoped ten years; but for twenty-five years this woman has retained her affection for and her faith in a man she has not seen or heard of in all that time.

"She came to me today in the hope that I might be able to help her find this long-lost husband. And when she was gone I gave my fancy rein and imagined a case I will put to you.

"Suppose that this husband, soon after his escape, had learned that his wife had been sold away and that such inquiries as he could make brought no information of her whereabouts. Suppose that he was young, and she much older than he; that he was light, and she was black; that their marriage was a slave marriage and legally binding only if they chose to make it so after the war. Suppose, too, that he made his way to the North, as some of us have done, and there, where he had larger opportunities, had improved them, and had in the course of all these years grown to be as different from the ignorant boy who ran away from fear of slavery as the day is from the night. Suppose, even, that he had qualified himself, by industry, by thrift, and by study, to win the friendship and be considered worthy the society of such people as these I see around me tonight, gracing my board and filling my heart with gladness; for I am old enough to remember the day when such a gathering would not have been possible in this land. Suppose, too, that, as the years went by, this man's memory of the past grew more and more indistinct, until at last it was rarely, except in his dreams, that any image of this bygone period rose before his mind. And then suppose that accident should bring to his knowledge the fact that the wife of his youth, the wife he had left behind him—not one who had walked by his side and kept pace with him in his upward struggle, but one upon whom advancing years and a laborious life had set their mark—was alive and seeking him, but that he was absolutely safe from recognition or discovery, unless he chose to reveal himself. My friends, what would the man do? I will presume that he was one who loved honor and tried to deal justly with all men. I will even carry the case further and suppose that perhaps he had set his heart upon another, whom he had hoped to call his own. What would he do, or rather what ought he to do, in such a crisis of a lifetime?

"It seemed to me that he might hesitate, and I imagined that I was an old friend, a near friend, and that he had come to me for advice; and I argued the case with him. I tried to discuss it impartially. After we had looked upon the matter from every point of view, I said to him, in words that we all know—

> This above all: to thine own self be true,
> And it must follow, as the night the day,
> Thou canst not then be false to any man.

Then, finally, I put the question to him, 'Shall you acknowledge her?'

"And now, ladies and gentlemen, friends and companions, I ask you, what should he have done?"

There was something in Mr. Ryder's voice that stirred the hearts of those who sat around him. It suggested more than mere sympathy with an imaginary situation; it seemed rather in the nature of a personal appeal. It was observed, too, that his look rested more especially upon Mrs. Dixon, with a mingled expression of renunciation and inquiry.

She had listened, with parted lips and streaming eyes. She was the first to speak: "He should have acknowledged her."

"Yes," they all echoed, "he should have acknowledged her."

"My friends and companions," responded Mr. Ryder, "I thank you, one and all. It is the answer I expected, for I knew your hearts."

He turned and walked toward the closed door of an adjoining room, while every eye followed him in wondering curiosity. He came back in a moment, leading by the hand his visitor of the afternoon, who stood startled and trembling at the sudden plunge into this scene of brilliant gaiety. She was neatly dressed in gray and wore the white cap of an elderly woman.

"Ladies and gentlemen," he said, "this is the woman, and I am the man, whose story I have told you. Permit me to introduce to you the wife of my youth."

Much of the narrative of II Samuel, which appears in the Hebrew Bible between I Samuel and I Kings, describes David's rule over the nation of Israel. The story is full of war, violence, treachery, infidelity, punishment, repentance, and music. This excerpt is from the New Revised Standard Version translation.

II Samuel, Chapters 11–12

11 In the spring of the year, the time when kings go out to battle, David sent Joab with his officers and all Israel with him; they ravaged the Ammonites and besieged Rabbah. But David remained at Jerusalem.

²It happened, late one afternoon, when David rose from his couch and was walking about on the roof of the king's house, that he saw from the roof a woman bathing; the woman was very beautiful. ³David sent someone to inquire about the woman. It was reported, "This is Bathsheba, daughter of Eliam, the wife of Uriah the Hittite." ⁴So David sent messengers to get her, and she came to him, and he lay with her. (Now she was purifying herself after her period.) Then she returned to her house. ⁵The woman conceived; and she sent and told David, "I am pregnant."

⁶So David sent word to Joab, "Send me Uriah the Hittite." And Joab sent Uriah to David. ⁷When Uriah came to him, David asked how Joab and the people fared, and how the war was going.

⁸Then David said to Uriah, "Go down to your house, and wash your feet." Uriah went out of the king's house, and there followed him a present from the king. ⁹But Uriah slept at the entrance of the king's house with all the servants of his lord and did not go down to his house. ¹⁰When they told David, "Uriah did not go down to his house," David said to Uriah, "You have just come from a journey. Why did you not go down to your house?" ¹¹Uriah said to David, "The ark and Israel and Judah remain in booths; and my lord Joab and the servants of my lord are camping in the open field; shall I then go to my house, to eat and to drink, and to lie with my wife? As you live, and as your soul lives, I will not do such a thing." ¹²Then David said to Uriah, "Remain here today also, and tomorrow I will send you back." So Uriah remained in Jerusalem that day. On the next day, ¹³David invited him to eat and drink in his presence and made him drunk; and

in the evening he went out to lie on his couch with the servants of his lord, but he did not go down to his house.

¹⁴In the morning David wrote a letter to Joab and sent it by the hand of Uriah. ¹⁵In the letter he wrote, "Set Uriah in the forefront of the hardest fighting, and then draw back from him, so that he may be struck down and die." ¹⁶As Joab was besieging the city, he assigned Uriah to the place where he knew there were valiant warriors. ¹⁷The men of the city came out and fought with Joab; and some of the servants of David among the people fell. Uriah the Hittite was killed as well. ¹⁸Then Joab sent and told David all the news about the fighting; ¹⁹and he instructed the messenger, "When you have finished telling the king all the news about the fighting, ²⁰then, if the king's anger rises, and if he says to you, 'Why did you go so near the city to fight? Did you not know that they would shoot from the wall? ²¹Who killed Abimelech son of Jerubbaal? Did not a woman throw an upper millstone on him from the wall, so that he died at Thebez? Why did you go so near the wall?' then you shall say, 'Your servant Uriah the Hittite is dead too.'"

²²So the messenger went and came and told David all that Joab had sent him to tell. ²³The messenger said to David, "The men gained an advantage over us and came out against us in the field; but we drove them back to the entrance of the gate. ²⁴Then the archers shot at your servants from the wall; some of the king's servants are dead; and your servant Uriah the Hittite is dead also." ²⁵David said to the messenger, "Thus you shall say to Joab, 'Do not let this matter trouble you, for the sword devours now one and now another; press your attack on the city and overthrow it.' And encourage him."

²⁶When the wife of Uriah heard that her husband was dead, she made lamentation for him. ²⁷When the mourning was over, David sent and brought her to his house, and she became his wife and bore him a son.

12 But the thing that David had done displeased the LORD, and the LORD sent Nathan to David. He came to him and said to him, "There were two men in a certain city, the one rich and the other poor. ²The rich man had very many flocks and herds; ³but the poor man had nothing but one little ewe lamb, which he had bought. He brought it up, and it grew up with him and with his children; it used to eat of his meager fare, and drink from his cup, and lie in his bosom, and it was like a daughter to him. ⁴Now there came a traveler to the rich man, and he was loath to take one of his own flock or herd to prepare for the wayfarer who had come to him, but he took the poor man's lamb, and prepared that for the guest who had come to him." ⁵Then David's anger was greatly kindled against the man. He said to Nathan, "As the LORD lives, the man who has done this deserves to die; ⁶he shall restore the lamb fourfold, because he did this thing, and because he had no pity."

⁷Nathan said to David, "You are the man!"

Graham Greene

Born in Hertfordshire, England, Graham Greene (1904–1991) studied modern history at Balliol College, Oxford, where he edited "The Oxford Outlook" and completed a novel. He went on to work as an editor with *The Times* of London, although he left that job to pursue writing full-time after the publication of *The Man Within* in 1929. Greene wrote prodigiously, and his work often revolved around themes related to his conversion to Catholicism, his extensive travel, and his involvement with the British Secret Service. "The Destructors" was first published in 1954.

The Destructors

1.

It was on the eve of August Bank Holiday that the latest recruit became the leader of the Wormsley Common Gang. No one was surprised except Mike, but Mike at the age of nine was surprised by everything. "If you don't shut your mouth," somebody once said to him, "you'll get a frog down it." After that Mike kept his teeth tightly clamped except when the surprise was too great.

The new recruit had been with the gang since the beginning of the summer holidays, and there were possibilities about his brooding silence that all recognized. He never wasted a word even to tell his name until that was required of him by the rules. When he said "Trevor" it was a statement of fact, not as it would have been with the others a statement of shame or defiance. Nor did anyone laugh except Mike, who finding himself without support and meeting the dark gaze of the newcomer, opened his mouth and was quiet again. There was every reason why T., as he was afterward referred to, should have been an object of mockery—there was his name (and they substituted the initial because otherwise they had no excuse not to laugh at it), the fact that his father, a former architect and present clerk, had "come down in the world" and that his mother considered herself better than the neighbors. What but an odd quality of danger, of the unpredictable, established him in the gang without any ignoble ceremony of initiation?

The gang met every morning in an impromptu car park, the site of the last bomb of the first blitz. The leader, who was known as Blackie, claimed to have heard it fall, and no one was precise enough in his dates to point out that he would have been one year old and fast asleep on the down platform of Wormsley Common Underground Station. On one side of the car park leant the first occupied house, No. 3, of the shattered Northwood Terrace—literally leant, for it had suffered from the blast of the bomb and the side walls were supported on wooden struts. A smaller bomb and some incendiaries had fallen beyond, so that the house stuck up like a jagged tooth and carried on the further wall relics of its neighbor, a dado, the remains of a fireplace. T., whose words were almost confined to voting yes or no to the plan of operations proposed each day by Blackie, once startled the whole gang by saying broodingly, "Wren built that house, father says."

"Who's Wren?"

"The man who built St. Paul's."

"Who cares?" Blackie said. "It's only Old Misery's."

Old Misery—whose real name was Thomas—had once been a builder and decorator. He lived alone in the crippled house, doing for himself: once a week you could see him coming back across the common with bread and vegetables, and once as the boys played in the car park he put his head over the smashed wall of his garden and looked at them.

"Been to the lav," one of the boys said, for it was common knowledge that since the bombs fell something had gone wrong with the pipes of the house and Old Misery was too mean to spend money on the property. He could do the redecorating himself at cost price, but he had never learnt plumbing. The lav was a wooden shed at the bottom of the narrow garden with a star-shaped hole in the door: it had escaped the blast that had smashed the house next door and sucked out the window frames of No. 3.

The next time the gang became aware of Mr. Thomas was more surprising. Blackie, Mike, and a thin yellow boy, who for some reason was called by his surname, Summers, met him on the common coming back from the market. Mr. Thomas stopped them. He said glumly, "You belong to the lot that play in the car park?"

Mike was about to answer when Blackie stopped him. As the leader he had responsibilities. "Suppose we are?" he said ambiguously.

"I got some chocolates," Mr. Thomas said. "Don't like 'em myself. Here you are. Not enough to go round, I don't suppose. There never is," he added with somber conviction. He handed over three packets of Smarties.

The gang was puzzled and perturbed by this action and tried to explain it away. "Bet someone dropped them and he picked 'em up," somebody suggested.

"Pinched 'em and then got in a bleeding funk," another thought aloud.

"It's a bribe," Summers said. "He wants us to stop bouncing balls on his wall."

"We'll show him we don't take bribes," Blackie said, and they sacrificed the whole morning to the game of bouncing that only Mike was young enough to enjoy. There was no sign from Mr. Thomas.

Next day T. astonished them all. He was late at the rendezvous, and the voting for that day's exploit took place without him. At Blackie's suggestion the gang was to disperse in pairs, take buses at random, and see how many free rides could be snatched from unwary conductors (the operation was to be carried out in pairs to avoid cheating). They were drawing lots for their companions when T. arrived.

"Where you been, T.?" Blackie asked.

"You can't vote now. You know the rules."

"I've been *there*," T. said. He looked at the ground, as though he had thoughts to hide.

"Where?"

"At Old Misery's." Mike's mouth opened and then hurriedly closed again with a click. He had remembered the frog.

"At Old Misery's?" Blackie said. There was nothing in the rules against it, but he had a sensation that T. was treading on dangerous ground. He asked hopefully, "Did you break in?"

"No. I rang the bell."

"And what did you say?"

"I said I wanted to see his house."

"What did he do?"

"He showed it to me."

"Pinch anything?"

"No."

"What did you do it for then?"

The gang had gathered round: it was as though an impromptu court were about to form and try some case of deviation. T. said, "It's a beautiful house," and still watching the ground, meeting no one's eyes, he licked his lips first one way, then the other.

"What do you mean, a beautiful house?" Blackie asked with scorn.

"It's got a staircase two hundred years old like a corkscrew. Nothing holds it up."

"What do you mean, nothing holds it up. Does it float?"

"It's to do with opposite forces, Old Misery said."

"What else?"

"There's paneling."

"Like in the Blue Boar?"

"Two hundred years old."

"Is Old Misery two hundred years old?"

Mike laughed suddenly and then was quiet again. The meeting was in a serious mood. For the first time since T. had strolled into the car park on the first day of the holidays, his position was in danger. It only needed a single use of his real name and the gang would be at his heels.

"What did you do it for?" Blackie asked. He was just, he had no jealousy, he was anxious to retain T. in the gang if he could. It was the word "beautiful" that worried him—that belonged to a class world that you could still see parodied at the Wormsley Common Empire by a man wearing a top hat and a monocle, with a haw-haw accent. He was tempted to say, "My dear Trevor, old chap," and unleash his hellhounds. "If you'd broken in," he said sadly—that indeed would have been an exploit worthy of the gang.

"This was better," T. said. "I found out things." He continued to stare at his feet, not meeting anybody's eye, as though he were absorbed in some dream he was unwilling—or ashamed—to share.

"What things?"

"Old Misery's going to be away all tomorrow and Bank Holiday."

Blackie said with relief, "You mean we could break in?"

"And pinch things?" somebody asked.

Blackie said, "Nobody's going to pinch things. Breaking in—that's good enough, isn't it? We don't want any court stuff."

"I don't want to pinch anything," T. said. "I've got a better idea."

"What is it?"

T. raised eyes as gray and disturbed as the drab August day. "We'll pull it down," he said. "We'll destroy it."

Blackie gave a single hoot of laughter and then, like Mike, fell quiet, daunted by the serious implacable gaze. "What'd the police be doing all the time?" he said.

"They'd never know. We'd do it from inside. I've found a way in." He said with a sort of intensity, "We'd be like worms, don't you see, in an apple. When we came out again there'd be nothing there, no staircase, no panels, nothing but just walls, and then we'd make the walls fall down—somehow."

"We'd go to jug," Blackie said.

"Who's to prove? And anyway we wouldn't have pinched anything." He added without the smallest flicker of glee, "There wouldn't be anything to pinch after we'd finished."

"I've never heard of going to prison for breaking things," Summers said.

"There wouldn't be time," Blackie said. "I've seen housebreakers at work."

"There are twelve of us," T. said. "We'd organize."

"None of us know how . . ."

"I know," T. said. He looked across at Blackie. "Have you got a better plan?"

"Today," Mike said tactlessly, "we're pinching free rides . . ."

"Free rides," T. said. "Kid stuff. You can stand down, Blackie, if you'd rather . . ."

"The gang's got to vote."

"Put it up then."

Blackie said uneasily, "It's proposed that tomorrow and Monday we destroy Old Misery's house."

"Here, here," said a fat boy called Joe.

"Who's in favor?"

T. said, "It's carried."

"How do we start?" Summers asked.

"He'll tell you," Blackie said. It was the end of his leadership. He went away to the back of the car park and began to kick a stone, dribbling it this way and that. There was only one old Morris in the park, for few cars were left there except lorries: without an attendant there was no safety. He took a flying kick at the car and scraped a little paint off the rear mudguard. Beyond, paying no more attention to him than to a stranger, the gang had gathered round T.; Blackie was dimly aware of the fickleness of favor. He thought of going home, of never returning, of letting them all discover the hollowness of T.'s leadership, but suppose after all what T. proposed was possible—nothing like it had ever been done before. The fame of the Wormsley Common car park gang would surely reach around London. There would be headlines in the papers. Even the grown-up gangs who ran the betting at the all-in wrestling and the barrow boys would hear with respect of how Old Misery's house had been destroyed. Driven by the pure, simple, and altruistic ambition of fame for the gang, Blackie came back to where T. stood in the shadow of Old Misery's wall.

T. was giving his orders with decision: it was as though this plan had been with him all his life, pondered through the seasons, now in his fifteenth year crystallized with the pain of puberty. "You," he said to Mike, "bring some big nails, the biggest you can find, and a hammer. Anybody who can, better bring a hammer and a screwdriver. We'll need plenty of them. Chisels too. We can't have too many chisels. Can anybody bring a saw?"

"I can," Mike said.

"Not a child's saw," T. said. "A real saw."

Blackie realized he had raised his hand like any ordinary member of the gang.

"Right, you bring one, Blackie. But now there's a difficulty. We want a hacksaw."

"What's a hacksaw?" someone asked.

"You can get 'em at Woolworth's," Summers said.

The fat boy called Joe said gloomily, "I knew it would end in a collection."

"I'll get one myself," T. said. "I don't want your money. But I can't buy a sledgehammer."

Blackie said, "They are working on No. 15. I know where they'll leave their stuff for Bank Holiday."

"Then that's all," T. said. "We meet here at nine sharp."

"I've got to go to church," Mike said.

"Come over the wall and whistle. We'll let you in."

2.

On Sunday morning all were punctual except Blackie, even Mike. Mike had a stroke of luck. His mother felt ill, his father was tired after Saturday night, and he was told to go to church alone with many warnings of what would happen if he strayed. Blackie had difficulty in smuggling out the saw, and then in finding the sledgehammer at the back of No. 15. He approached the house from a lane at the rear of the garden, for fear of the policeman's beat along the main road. The tired evergreens kept off a stormy sun: another wet Bank Holiday was being prepared over the Atlantic, beginning in swirls of dust under the trees. Blackie climbed the wall into Misery's garden.

There was no sign of anybody anywhere. The lav stood like a tomb in a neglected graveyard. The curtains were drawn. The house slept. Blackie lumbered nearer with the saw and the sledgehammer. Perhaps after all nobody had turned up: the plan had been a wild invention; they had woken wiser. But when he came close to the back door he could hear a confusion of sound hardly louder than a hive in swarm: a clickety-clack, a bang bang, a scraping, a creaking, a sudden painful crack. He thought: it's true, and whistled.

They opened the back door to him and he came in. He had at once the impression of organization, very different from the old happy-go-lucky ways under his leadership. For a while he wandered up and down stairs looking for T. Nobody addressed him: he had a sense of great urgency, and already he could begin to see the plan. The interior of the house was being carefully demolished without touching the outer walls. Summers with hammer and chisel was ripping out the skirting boards in the ground-floor dining room: he had already smashed the panels of the door. In the same room Joe was heaving up the parquet blocks, exposing the soft wood floorboards over the cellar. Coils of wire came out of the damaged skirting and Mike sat happily on the floor clipping the wires.

On the curved stairs two of the gang were working hard with an inadequate child's saw on the banisters—when they saw Blackie's big saw they signaled for it wordlessly. When he next saw them a quarter of the banisters had been dropped into the hall. He found T. at last in the bathroom—he sat moodily in the least cared-for room in the house, listening to the sounds coming up from below.

"You've really done it," Blackie said with awe. "What's going to happen?"

"We've only just begun," T. said.

He looked at the sledgehammer and gave his instructions. "You stay here and break the bath and washbasin. Don't bother about the pipes. They come later."

Mike appeared at the door. "I've finished the wires, T.," he said.

"Good. You've just got to go wandering round now. The kitchen's in the basement. Smash all the china and glass and bottles you can lay hold of. Don't turn on the taps—we don't want a flood—yet. Then go into all the rooms and turn out drawers. If they are locked get one of the others to break them open. Tear up any papers you find and smash all the ornaments. Better take a carving knife with you from the kitchen. The bedroom's opposite here. Open the pillows and tear up the sheets. That's enough for the moment. And you, Blackie, when you've finished in here crack the plaster in the passage up with your sledgehammer."

"What are you going to do?" Blackie asked.

"I'm looking for something special," T. said.

It was nearly lunchtime before Blackie had finished and went in search of T. Chaos had advanced. The kitchen was a shambles of broken glass and china. The dining room was stripped of parquet, the skirting was up, the door had been taken off its hinges, and the destroyers had moved up a floor. Streaks of light came in through the closed shutters where they worked with the seriousness of creators—and destruction after all is a form of creation. A kind of imagination had seen this house as it had now become.

Mike said, "I've got to go home for dinner."

"Who else?" T. asked, but all the others on one excuse or another had brought provisions with them.

They squatted in the ruins of the room and swapped unwanted sandwiches. Half an hour for lunch and they were at work again. By the time Mike returned they were on the top floor, and by six the superficial damage was completed. The doors were all off, all the skirtings raised, the furniture pillaged and ripped and smashed—no one could have slept in the house except on a bed of broken plaster. T. gave his orders—eight o'clock next morning—and to escape notice they climbed singly over the garden wall, into the car park. Only Blackie and T. were left: the light had nearly gone, and when they touched a switch, nothing worked—Mike had done his job thoroughly.

"Did you find anything special?" Blackie asked.

T. nodded. "Come over here," he said, "and look." Out of both pockets he drew bundles of pound notes. "Old Misery's savings," he said. "Mike ripped out the mattress, but he missed them."

"What are you going to do? Share them?"

"We aren't thieves," T. said. "Nobody's going to steal anything from this house. I kept these for you and me—a celebration." He knelt down on the floor and counted them out—there were seventy in all. "We'll burn them," he said, "one by one," and taking it in turns they held a note upward and lit the top corner, so that the flame burnt slowly toward their fingers. The gray ash floated above them and fell on their heads like age. "I'd like to see Old Misery's face when we are through," T. said.

"You hate him a lot?" Blackie asked.

"Of course I don't hate him," T. said. "There'd be no fun if I hated him." The last burning note illuminated his brooding face. "All this hate and love," he said, "it's soft, it's hooey. There's only things, Blackie," and he looked round the room crowded with the unfamiliar shadows of half things, broken things, former things. "I'll race you home, Blackie," he said.

3.

Next morning the serious destruction started. Two were missing—Mike and another boy whose parents were off to Southend and Brighton in spite of the slow warm drops that had begun to fall and the rumble of thunder in the estuary like the first guns of the old blitz. "We've got to hurry," T. said.

Summers was restive. "Haven't we done enough?" he asked. "I've been given a bob for slot machines. This is like work."

"We've hardly started," T. said. "Why, there's all the floors left, and the stairs. We haven't taken out a single window. You voted like the others. We are going to *destroy* this house. There won't be anything left when we've finished."

They began again on the first floor picking up the top floor-boards next the outer wall, leaving the joists exposed. Then they sawed through the joists and retreated into the hall, as what was left of the floor heeled and sank. They had learnt with practice, and the second floor collapsed more easily. By the evening an odd exhilaration seized them as they looked down the great hollow of the house. They ran risks and made mistakes: when they thought of the windows it was too late to reach them. "Cor," Joe said, and dropped a penny down into the dry rubble-filled well. It cracked and spun among the broken glass.

"Why did we start this?" Summers asked with astonishment; T. was already on the ground, digging at the rubble, clearing a space along the outer wall. "Turn on the taps," he said. "It's too dark for anyone to see now, and in the morning it won't matter." The water overtook them on the stairs and fell through the floorless rooms.

It was then they heard Mike's whistle at the back. "Something's wrong," Blackie said. They could hear his urgent breathing as they unlocked the door.

"The bogies?" Summers asked.

"Old Misery," Mike said. "He's on his way." He put his head between his knees and retched. "Ran all the way," he said with pride.

"But why?" T. said. "He told me . . ." He protested with the fury of the child he had never been, "It isn't fair."

"He was down at Southend," Mike said, "and he was on the train coming back. Said it was too cold and wet." He paused and gazed at the water. "My, you've had a storm here. Is the roof leaking?"

"How long will he be?"

"Five minutes. I gave Ma the slip and ran."

"We better clear," Summers said. "We've done enough, anyway."

"Oh no, we haven't. Anybody could do this—" *this* was the shattered hollowed house with nothing left but the walls. Yet walls could be preserved. Façades were valuable. They could build inside again more beautifully than before. This could again be a home. He said angrily, "We've got to finish. Don't move. Let me think."

"There's no time," a boy said.

"There's got to be a way," T. said. "We couldn't have got this far . . ."

"We've done a lot," Blackie said.

"No. No, we haven't. Somebody watch the front."

"We can't do any more."

"He may come in at the back."

"Watch the back too." T. began to plead. "Just give me a minute and I'll fix it. I swear I'll fix it." But his authority had gone with his ambiguity. He was only one of the gang. "Please," he said.

"Please," Summers mimicked him, and then suddenly struck home with the fatal name. "Run along home, Trevor."

T. stood with his back to the rubble like a boxer knocked groggy against the ropes. He had no words as his dreams shook and slid. Then Blackie acted before the gang had time to laugh, pushing Summers backward. "I'll watch the front, T.," he said, and cautiously he opened the shutters of the hall. The gray wet common stretched ahead, and the lamps gleamed in the puddles. "Someone's coming, T. No, it's not him. What's your plan, T.?"

"Tell Mike to go out to the lav and hide close beside it. When he hears me whistle he's got to count ten and start to shout."

"Shout what?"

"Oh, 'Help,' anything."

"You hear, Mike," Blackie said. He was the leader again. He took a quick look between the shutters. "He's coming, T."

"Quick, Mike. The lav. Stay here, Blackie, all of you, till I yell."

"Where are you going, T.?"

"Don't worry. I'll see to this. I said I would, didn't I?"

Old Misery came limping off the common. He had mud on his shoes and he stopped to scrape them on the pavement's edge. He didn't want to soil his house, which stood jagged and dark between the bomb sites, saved so narrowly, as he believed, from destruction. Even the fanlight had been left unbroken by the bomb's blast. Somewhere somebody whistled. Old Misery looked sharply round. He didn't trust whistles. A child was shouting: it seemed to come from his own garden. Then a boy ran into the road from the car park. "Mr. Thomas," he called, "Mr. Thomas."

"What is it?"

"I'm terribly sorry, Mr. Thomas. One of us got taken short, and we thought you wouldn't mind, and now he can't get out."

"What do you mean, boy?"

"He's got stuck in your lav."

"He'd no business . . . Haven't I seen you before?"

"You showed me your house."

"So I did. So I did. That doesn't give you the right to . . ."

"Do hurry, Mr. Thomas. He'll suffocate."

"Nonsense. He can't suffocate. Wait till I put my bag in."

"I'll carry your bag."

"Oh no, you don't. I carry my own."

"This way, Mr. Thomas."

"I can't get in the garden that way. I've got to go through the house."

"But you *can* get in the garden this way, Mr. Thomas. We often do."

"You often do?" He followed the boy with a scandalized fascination. "When? What right . . . ?"

"Do you see . . . ? The wall's low."

"I'm not going to climb walls into my own garden. It's absurd."

"This is how we do it. One foot here, one foot there, and over." The boy's face peered down, an arm shot out, and Mr. Thomas found his bag taken and deposited on the other side of the wall.

"Give me back my bag," Mr. Thomas said. From the loo a boy yelled and yelled. "I'll call the police."

"Your bag's all right, Mr. Thomas. Look. One foot there. On your right. Now just above. To your left." Mr. Thomas climbed over his own garden wall. "Here's your bag, Mr. Thomas."

"I'll have the wall built up," Mr. Thomas said, "I'll not have you boys coming over here, using my loo." He stumbled on the path, but the boy caught his elbow and supported him. "Thank you, thank you, my boy," he murmured automatically. Somebody shouted again through the dark. "I'm coming, I'm coming," Mr. Thomas called. He said to the boy beside him, "I'm not unreasonable. Been a boy myself. As long as things are done regular. I don't mind you playing round the place Saturday mornings. Sometimes I like company. Only it's got to be regular. One of you asks leave and I say yes. Sometimes I'll say no. Won't feel like it. And you come in at the front door and out at the back. No garden walls."

"Do get him out, Mr. Thomas."

"He won't come to any harm in my loo," Mr. Thomas said, stumbling slowly down the garden. "Oh, my rheumatics," he said. "Always get 'em on Bank Holiday. I've got to go careful. There's loose stones here. Give me your hand. Do you know what my horoscope said yesterday? 'Abstain from any dealings in first half of week. Danger of serious crash.' That might be on this path," Mr. Thomas said. "They speak in parables and double meanings." He paused at the door of the loo. "What's the matter in there?" he called. There was no reply.

"Perhaps he's fainted," the boy said.

"Not in my loo. Here, you, come out," Mr. Thomas said, and giving a great jerk at the door he nearly fell on his back when it swung easily open. A hand first supported him and then pushed him hard. His head hit the opposite wall and he sat heavily down. His bag hit his feet. A hand whipped the key out of the lock and the door slammed. "Let me out," he called, and heard the key turn in the lock. "A serious crash," he thought, and felt dithery and confused and old.

A voice spoke to him softly through the star-shaped hole in the door. "Don't worry, Mr. Thomas," it said, "we won't hurt you, not if you stay quiet."

Mr. Thomas put his head between his hands and pondered. He had noticed that there was only one lorry in the car park, and he felt certain that the driver would not come for it before the morning. Nobody could hear him from the road in front, and the lane at the back was seldom used. Anyone who passed there would be hurrying home and would not pause for what they would certainly take to be drunken cries. And if he did call "Help," who, on a lonely Bank Holiday evening, would have the courage to investigate? Mr. Thomas sat on the loo and pondered with the wisdom of age.

After a while it seemed to him that there were sounds in the silence—they were faint and came from the direction of his house. He stood up and peered through the ventilation hole—between the cracks in one of the shutters he saw a light, not the light of a lamp, but the wavering light that a candle might give. Then he thought he heard the sound of hammering and scraping and chipping. He thought of burglars—perhaps they had employed the boy as a scout, but why should burglars engage in what sounded more and more like a stealthy form of carpentry? Mr. Thomas let out an experimental yell, but nobody answered. The noise could not even have reached his enemies.

4.

Mike had gone home to bed, but the rest stayed. The question of leadership no longer concerned the gang. With nails, chisels, screwdrivers, anything that was sharp and penetrating, they moved around the inner walls worrying at the mortar between the bricks. They started too high, and it was Blackie who hit on the damp course and realized the work could be halved if they weakened the joints immediately above. It was a long, tiring, unamusing job, but at last it was finished. The gutted house stood there balanced on a few inches of mortar between the damp course and the bricks.

There remained the most dangerous task of all, out in the open at the edge of the bomb site. Summers was sent to watch the road for passersby, and Mr. Thomas, sitting on the loo, heard clearly now the sound of sawing. It no longer came from his house, and that a little reassured him. He felt less concerned. Perhaps the other noises too had no significance.

A voice spoke to him through the hole. "Mr. Thomas."

"Let me out," Mr. Thomas said sternly.

"Here's a blanket," the voice said, and a long gray sausage was worked through the hole and fell in swathes over Mr. Thomas' head.

"There's nothing personal," the voice said. "We want you to be comfortable tonight."

"Tonight," Mr. Thomas repeated incredulously.

"Catch," the voice said. "Penny buns—we've buttered them, and sausage rolls. We don't want you to starve, Mr. Thomas."

Mr. Thomas pleaded desperately. "A joke's a joke, boy. Let me out and I won't say a thing. I've got rheumatics. I got to sleep comfortable."

"You wouldn't be comfortable, not in your house, you wouldn't. Not now."

"What do you mean, boy?" But the footsteps receded. There was only the silence of night: no sound of sawing. Mr. Thomas tried one more yell, but he was daunted and rebuked by the silence—a long way off an owl hooted and made away again on its muffled flight through the soundless world.

At seven next morning the driver came to fetch his lorry. He climbed into the seat and tried to start the engine. He was vaguely aware of a voice shouting, but it didn't concern him. At last the engine responded and he backed the lorry until it touched the great wooden shore that supported Mr. Thomas' house. That way he could drive right out and down the street without reversing. The lorry moved forward, was momentarily checked as though something were pulling it from behind, and then went on to the sound of a long rumbling crash. The driver was astonished to see bricks bouncing ahead of him, while stones hit the roof of his cab. He put on his brakes. When he climbed out the whole landscape had suddenly altered. There was no house beside the car park, only a hill of rubble. He went round and examined the back of his lorry for damage, and found a rope tied there that was still twisted at the other end round part of a wooden strut.

The driver again became aware of somebody shouting. It came from the wooden erection that was the nearest thing to a house in that desolation of broken brick. The driver climbed the smashed wall and unlocked the door. Mr. Thomas came out of the loo. He was wearing a gray blanket to which flakes of pastry adhered. He gave a sobbing cry. "My house," he said. "Where's my house?"

"Search me," the driver said. His eye lit on the remains of a bath and what had once been a dresser and he began to laugh. There wasn't anything left anywhere.

"How dare you laugh," Mr. Thomas said. "It was my house. My house."

"I'm sorry," the driver said, making heroic efforts, but when he remembered the sudden check to his lorry, the crash of bricks falling, he became convulsed again. One moment the house had stood there with such dignity between the bomb sites like a man in a top hat, and then, bang, crash, there wasn't anything left—not anything. He said, "I'm sorry. I can't help it, Mr. Thomas. There's nothing personal, but you got to admit it's funny."

Franz Kafka

Born in the Jewish ghetto of Prague, Franz Kafka (1883–1924) earned a law degree and became a clerk for an accident insurance company. Though he wrote a number of enigmatic and compelling stories and novels, he published little during his lifetime. As he was dying of tuberculosis, Kafka requested that his unpublished manuscripts be burned. However, his good friend Max Brod preserved these writings, including "A Hunger Artist," *The Castle*, and *The Trial*. This selection, translated by Tania and James Stern, was written between 1917 and 1923.

The Helmsman

"A m I not the helmsman here?" I called out. "You?" asked a tall, dark man and passed his hands over his eyes as though to banish a dream. I had been standing at the helm in the dark night, a feeble lantern burning over my head, and now this man had come and tried to push me aside. And as I would not yield, he put his foot on my chest and slowly crushed me while I still clung to the hub of the helm, wrenching it around in falling. But the man seized it, pulled it back in place, and pushed me away. I soon collected myself, however, ran to the hatchway that gave on to the mess quarters, and cried out: "Men! Comrades! Come here, quick! A stranger has driven me away from the helm!"

Slowly they came up, climbing the companion ladder, tired, swaying, powerful figures. "Am I the helmsman?" I asked. They nodded, but they had eyes only for the stranger, stood around him in a semicircle, and when, in a commanding voice, he said: "Don't disturb me!" they gathered together, nodded at me, and withdrew down the companion ladder. What kind of people are these? Do they ever think, or do they only shuffle pointlessly over the earth?

Toni Cade Bambara

Toni Cade Bambara (1939–1995) was born in New York City. She taught at the City College of New York, Spelman College, Rutgers University, and Duke University and continually struggled to improve the living conditions of minorities and the poor. Her works include two short story collections, *Gorilla, My Love* (from which this selection is taken) and *The Sea Birds Are Still Alive*, as well as a novel, *The Salt Eaters*.

The Lesson

Back in the days when everyone was old and stupid or young and foolish and me and Sugar were the only ones just right, this lady moved on our block with nappy hair and proper speech and no makeup. And quite naturally we laughed at her, laughed the way we did at the junk man who went about his business like he was some bigtime president and his sorry-ass horse his secretary. And we kinda hated her too, hated the way we did the winos who cluttered up our parks and pissed on our handball walls and stank up our hallways and stairs so you couldn't halfway play hide-and-seek without a goddamn gas mask. Miss Moore was her name. The only woman on the block with no first name. And she was black as hell, cept for her feet, which were fish-white and spooky. And she was always planning these boring-ass things for us to do, us being my cousin, mostly, who lived on the block cause we all moved North the same time and to the same apartment then spread out gradual to breathe. And our parents would yank our heads into some kinda shape and crisp up our clothes so we'd be presentable for travel with Miss Moore, who always looked like she was going to church, though she never did. Which is just one of the things the grownups talked about when they talked behind her back like a dog. But when she came calling with some sachet she'd sewed up or some gingerbread she'd made or some book, why then they'd all be too embarrassed to turn her down and we'd get handed over all spruced up. She'd been to college and said it was only right that she should take responsibility for the young ones' education, and she not even related by marriage or blood. So they'd go for it. Specially Aunt Gretchen. She was the main gofer in the family. You got some ole dumb shit foolishness you want somebody to go for, you send for Aunt Gretchen. She been screwed into the go-along for so long, it's a blood-deep natural thing with her. Which is how she got saddled with me and Sugar and Junior in the first place while our mothers were in a la-de-da apartment up the block having a good ole time.

So this one day Miss Moore rounds us all up at the mailbox and it's purdee hot and she's knockin herself out about arithmetic. And school suppose to let up in summer I heard, but she don't never let up. And the starch in my pinafore scratching the shit outta me and I'm really hating this nappy-head bitch and her goddamn college degree. I'd much rather go to the pool or to the show where it's cool. So me and Sugar leaning on the mailbox being surly, which is a Miss Moore word. And Flyboy checking out what everybody brought for lunch. And Fat Butt already wasting his peanut-butter-and-jelly sandwich like the pig he is. And Junebug punchin on Q.T.'s arm for potato chips. And Rosie Giraffe shifting from one hip to the other waiting for somebody to step on her foot or ask her if she from Georgia so she can kick ass, preferably Mercedes's. And Miss Moore asking us do we know what money is, like we a bunch of retards. I mean real money, she say, like it's only poker chips or Monopoly papers we lay on the grocer. So right away I'm tired of this and say so. And would much rather snatch Sugar and go to the Sunset and terrorize the West Indian kids and take their hair ribbons and their money too. And Miss Moore files that remark away for next week's lesson on brotherhood, I can tell. And finally I say we oughta get to the subway cause it's cooler and besides we might meet some cute boys. Sugar done swiped her mama's lipstick, so we ready.

So we heading down the street and she's boring us silly about what things cost and what our parents make and how much goes for rent and how money ain't divided up right in this country. And then she gets to the part about we all poor and live in the slums, which I don't feature. And I'm ready to speak on that, but she steps out in the street and hails two cabs just like that. Then she hustles half the crew in with her and hands me a five-dollar bill and tells me to calculate 10 percent tip for the driver. And we're off. Me and Sugar and Junebug and Flyboy hangin out the window and hollering to everybody, putting lipstick on each other cause Flyboy a faggot anyway, and making farts with our sweaty armpits. But I'm mostly trying to figure how to spend this money. But they all fascinated with the meter ticking and Junebug starts laying bets as to how much it'll read when Flyboy can't hold his breath no more. Then Sugar lays bets as to how much it'll be when we get there. So I'm stuck. Don't nobody want to go for my plan, which is to jump out at the next light and run off to the first bar-b-que we can find. Then the driver tells us to get the hell out cause we there already. And the meter reads eighty-five cents. And I'm stalling to figure out the tip and Sugar say give him a dime. And I decide he don't need it bad as I do, so later for him. But then he tries to take off with

Junebug foot still in the door so we talk about his mama something ferocious. Then we check out that we on Fifth Avenue and everybody dressed up in stockings. One lady in a fur coat, hot as it is. White folks crazy.

"This is the place," Miss Moore say, presenting it to us in the voice she uses at the museum. "Let's look in the windows before we go in."

"Can we steal?" Sugar asks very serious like she's getting the ground rules squared away before she plays. "I beg your pardon," say Miss Moore, and we fall out. So she leads us around the windows of the toy store and me and Sugar screamin, "This is mine, that's mine, I gotta have that, that was made for me, I was born for that," till Big Butt drowns us out.

"Hey, I'm goin to buy that there."

"That there? You don't even know what it is, stupid."

"I do so," he say punchin on Rosie Giraffe. "It's a microscope."

"Whatcha gonna do with a microscope, fool?"

"Look at things."

"Like what, Ronald?" ask Miss Moore. And Big Butt ain't got the first notion. So here go Miss Moore gabbing about the thousands of bacteria in a drop of water and the somethinorother in a speck of blood and the million and one living things in the air around us is invisible to the naked eye. And what she say that for? Junebug go to town on that "naked" and we rolling. Then Miss Moore ask what it cost. So we all jam into the window smudgin it up and the price tag say $300. So then she ask how long'd take for Big Butt and Junebug to save up their allowances. "Too long," I said. "Yeh," adds Sugar, "outgrown it by that time." And Miss Moore say no, you never outgrow learning instruments. "Why, even medical students and interns and," blah, blah, blah. And we ready to choke Big Butt for bringing it up in the first damn place.

"This here costs four hundred eighty dollars," say Rosie Giraffe. So we pile up all over her to see what she pointin out. My eyes tell me it's a chunk of glass cracked with something heavy and different-color inks dripped into the splits, then the whole thing put into a oven or something. But for $480 it don't make sense.

"That's a paperweight made of semiprecious stones fused together under tremendous pressure," she explains slowly, with her hands doing the mining and all the factory work.

"So what's a paperweight?" asks Rosie Giraffe.

"To weigh paper with, dumbbell," say Flyboy, the wise man from the East.

"Not exactly," say Miss Moore, which is what she say when you warm or way off too. "It's to weigh paper down so it won't scatter and make your desk untidy." So right away me and Sugar curtsy to each other and then to Mercedes who is more the tidy type.

"We don't keep paper on top of the desk in my class," say Junebug, figuring Miss Moore crazy or lyin one.

"At home, then," she say. "Don't you have a calendar and a pencil case and a blotter and a letter opener on your desk at home where you do your homework?" And she know damn well what our homes look like cause she nosys around in them every chance she gets.

"I don't even have a desk," say Junebug. "Do we?"

"No. And I don't get no homework neither," say Big Butt.

"And I don't even have a home," say Flyboy like he do at school to keep the white folks off his back and sorry for him. Send this poor kid to camp posters, is his specialty.

"I do," say Mercedes. "I have a box of stationery on my desk and a picture of my cat. My godmother bought the stationery and the desk. There's a big rose on each sheet and the envelopes smell like roses."

"Who wants to know about your smelly-ass stationery," say Rosie Giraffe fore I can get my two cents in.

"It's important to have a work area all your own so that . . ."

"Will you look at this sailboat, please," say Flyboy, cuttin her off and pointin to the thing like it was his. So once again we tumble all over each other to gaze at this magnificent thing in the toy store that is just big enough to maybe sail two kittens across the pond if you strap them to the posts tight. We all start reciting the price tag like we in assembly. "Handcrafted sailboat of fiberglass at one thousand one hundred ninety-five dollars."

"Unbelievable," I hear myself say and am really stunned. I read it again for myself just in case the group recitation put me in a trance. Same thing. For some reason this pisses me off. We look at Miss Moore and she lookin at us, waiting for I dunno what.

Who'd pay all that when you can buy a sailboat set for a quarter at Pop's, a tube of glue for a dime, and a ball of string for eight cents? "It must have a motor and a whole lot else besides," I say. "My sailboat cost me about fifty cents."

"But will it take water?" say Mercedes with her smart ass.

"Took mine to Alley Pond Park once," say Flyboy. "String broke. Lost it. Pity."

"Sailed mine in Central Park and it keeled over and sank. Had to ask my father for another dollar."

"And you got the strap," laugh Big Butt. "The jerk didn't even have a string on it. My old man wailed on his behind."

Little Q.T. was staring hard at the sailboat and you could see he wanted it bad. But he too little and somebody'd just take it from him. So what the hell. "This boat for kids, Miss Moore?"

"Parents silly to buy something like that just to get all broke up," say Rosie Giraffe.

"That much money it should last forever," I figure.

"My father'd buy it for me if I wanted it."

"Your father, my ass," say Rosie Giraffe getting a chance to finally push Mercedes.

"Must be rich people shop here," say Q.T.

"You are a very bright boy," say Flyboy. "What was your first clue?" And he rap him on the head with the back of his knuckles, since Q.T. the only one he could get away with. Though Q.T. liable to come up behind you years later and get his licks in when you half expect it.

"What I want to know is," I say to Miss Moore though I never talk to her, I wouldn't give the bitch that satisfaction, "is how much a real boat costs? I figure a thousand'd get you a yacht any day."

"Why don't you check that out," she say, "and report back to the group?" Which really pains my ass. If you gonna mess up a perfectly good swim day least you could do is have some answers. "Let's go in," she say like she got something up her sleeve. Only she don't lead the way. So me and Sugar turn the corner to where the entrance is, but when we get there I kinda hang back. Not that I'm scared, what's there to be afraid of, just a toy store. But I feel funny, shame. But what I got to be shamed about? Got as much right to go in as anybody. But somehow I can't seem to get hold of the door, so I step away for Sugar to lead. But she hangs back too. And I look at her and she looks at me and this is ridiculous. I mean, damn, I have never ever been shy about doing nothing or going nowhere. But then Mercedes steps up and then Rosie Giraffe and Big Butt crowd in behind and shove, and next thing we all stuffed into the doorway with only Mercedes squeezing past us, smoothing out her jumper and walking right down the aisle. Then the rest of us tumble in like a glued-together jigsaw done all wrong. And people lookin at us. And it's like the time me and Sugar crashed into the Catholic church on a dare. But once we got in there and everything so hushed and holy and the candles and the bowin and the handkerchiefs on all the drooping heads, I just couldn't go through with the plan. Which was for me to run up to the altar and do a tap dance while Sugar played the nose flute and messed around in the holy water. And Sugar kept givin me the elbow. Then later teased me so bad I tied her up in the shower and turned it on and locked her in. And she'd be there till this day if Aunt Gretchen hadn't finally figured I was lyin about the boarder takin a shower.

Same thing in the store. We all walkin on tiptoe and hardly touchin the games and puzzles and things. And I watched Miss Moore who is steady watchin us like she waitin for a sign. Like Mama Drewery watches the sky and sniffs the air and takes note of just how much slant is in the bird formation. Then me and Sugar bump smack into each other, so busy gazing at the toys, specially the sailboat. But we don't laugh and go into our fat-lady bump-stomach routine. We just stare at that price tag. Then Sugar run a finger over the whole boat. And I'm jealous and want to hit her. Maybe not her, but I sure want to punch somebody in the mouth.

"Watcha bring us here for, Miss Moore?"

"You sound angry, Sylvia. Are you mad about something?" Givin me one of them grins like she tellin a grown-up joke that never turns out to be funny. And she's lookin very closely at me like maybe she plannin to do my portrait from memory. I'm mad, but I won't give her that satisfaction. So I slouch around the store being very bored and say, "Let's go."

Me and Sugar at the back of the train watchin the tracks whizzin by large then small then gettin gobbled up in the dark. I'm thinking about this tricky toy I saw in the store. A clown that somersaults on a bar then does chin-ups just cause you yank lightly at his leg. Cost $35. I could see me askin my mother for a $35 birthday clown. "You wanna who that costs what?" she'd say, cocking her head to the side to get a better view of the hole in my head. Thirty-five dollars could buy new bunk beds for Junior and Gretchen's boy. Thirty-five dollars and the whole household could go visit Granddaddy Nelson in the country. Thirty-five dollars would pay for the rent and the piano bill too. Who are these people that spend that much for performing clowns and $1,000 for toy sailboats? What kinda work they do and how they live and how come we ain't in on it? Where we are is who we are, Miss Moore always pointin out. But it don't necessarily have to be that way, she always adds then waits for somebody to say that poor people have to wake up and demand their share of the pie and don't none of us know what kind of pie she talkin about in the first damn place. But she ain't so smart cause I still got her four dollars from the taxi and she sure ain't gettin it. Messin up my day with this shit. Sugar nudges me in my pocket and winks.

Miss Moore lines us up in front of the mailbox where we started from, seem like years ago, and I got a headache for thinkin so hard. And we lean all over each other so we can hold up under the draggy-ass lecture she always finishes us off with at the end before we thank her for borin us to tears. But she just looks at us like she readin tea leaves. Finally she say, "Well, what did you think of FAO Schwarz?"

Rosie Giraffe mumbles, "White folks crazy."

"I'd like to go there again when I get my birthday money," says Mercedes, and we shove her out the pack so she has to lean on the mailbox by herself.

"I'd like a shower. Tiring day," said Flyboy.

Then Sugar surprises me by sayin, "You know, Miss Moore, I don't think all of us here put together eat in a year what that sailboat costs." And Miss Moore lights up like somebody goosed her. "And?" she say, urging Sugar on. Only I'm standin on her foot so she don't continue.

"Imagine for a minute what kind of society it is in which some people can spend on a toy what it would cost to feed a family of six or seven. What do you think?"

"I think," say Sugar pushing me off her feet like she never done before, cause I whip her ass in a minute, "that this is not much of a democracy if you ask me. Equal chance to pursue happiness means an equal crack at the dough, don't it?" Miss Moore is besides herself and I am disgusted with Sugar's treachery. So I stand on her foot one more time to see if she'll shove me. She shuts up, and Miss Moore looks at me, sorrowfully I'm thinkin. And somethin weird is goin on, I can feel it in my chest.

"Anybody else learn anything today?" lookin dead at me. I walk away and Sugar has to run to catch up and don't even seem to notice when I shrug her arm off my shoulder.

"Well, we got four dollars anyway," she said.

"Uh hunh."

"We could go to Hascombs and get half a chocolate layer and then go to the Sunset and still have plenty money for potato chips and ice-cream sodas."

"Uh hunh."

"Race you to Hascombs," she say.

We start down the block and she gets ahead which is okay by me cause I'm goin to the West End and then over to the Drive to think this day through. She can run if she want to and even run faster. But ain't nobody gonna beat me at nuthin.

William Carlos Williams

Born in Rutherford, New Jersey, William Carlos Williams (1883–1963) received his MD from the University of Pennsylvania and practiced medicine while establishing himself as an influential writer of poetry and prose. After an initial association with Ezra Pound and the Imagist poets, Williams set for himself the challenge of inventing a fresh, distinctly American kind of poetry that would concentrate on everyday circumstances and common people. Williams won the National Book Award in 1950 and the Pulitzer Prize in 1963, the year of his death. "The Use of Force" was first published in 1938.

The Use of Force

They were new patients to me; all I had was the name, Olson. Please come down as soon as you can, my daughter is very sick.

When I arrived I was met by the mother, a big startled-looking woman, very clean and apologetic, who merely said, Is this the doctor? and let me in. In the back, she added. You must excuse us, Doctor, we have her in the kitchen where it is warm. It is very damp here sometimes.

The child was fully dressed and sitting on her father's lap near the kitchen table. He tried to get up, but I motioned for him not to bother, took off my overcoat and started to look things over. I could see that they were all very nervous, eyeing me up and down distrustfully. As often, in such cases, they weren't telling me more than they had to, it was up to me to tell them; that's why they were spending three dollars on me.

The child was fairly eating me up with her cold, steady eyes, and no expression to her face whatever. She did not move and seemed, inwardly, quiet; an unusually attractive little thing, and as strong as a heifer in appearance. But her face was flushed, she was breathing rapidly, and I realized that she had a high fever. She had magnificent blond hair, in profusion. One of those picture children often reproduced in advertising leaflets and the photogravure sections of the Sunday papers.

She's had a fever for three days, began the father, and we don't know what it comes from. My wife has given her things, you know, like people do, but it don't do no good. And there's been a lot of sickness around. So we tho't you'd better look her over and tell us what is the matter.

As doctors often do I took a trial shot at it as a point of departure. Has she had a sore throat?

Both parents answered me together, No . . . No, she says her throat don't hurt her.

Does your throat hurt you? added the mother to the child. But the little girl's expression didn't change nor did she move her eyes from my face.

Have you looked?

I tried to, said the mother, but I couldn't see.

As it happens we had been having a number of cases of diphtheria in the school to which this child went during that month and we were all, quite apparently, thinking of that, though no one had as yet spoken of the thing.

Well, I said, suppose we take a look at the throat first. I smiled in my best professional manner and asking for the child's first name I said, come on, Mathilda, open your mouth and let's take a look at your throat.

Nothing doing.

Aw, come on, I coaxed, just open your mouth wide and let me take a look. Look, I said, opening both hands wide, I haven't anything in my hands. Just open up and let me see.

Such a nice man, put in the mother. Look how kind he is to you. Come on, do what he tells you to. He won't hurt you.

At that I ground my teeth in disgust. If only they wouldn't use the word *hurt* I might be able to get somewhere. But I did not allow myself to be hurried or disturbed but speaking quietly and slowly I approached the child again.

As I moved my chair a little nearer suddenly with one catlike movement both her hands clawed instinctively for my eyes and she almost reached them too. In fact she knocked my glasses flying and they fell, though unbroken, several feet away from me on the kitchen floor.

Both the mother and father almost turned themselves inside out in embarrassment and apology. You bad girl, said the mother, taking her and shaking her by one arm. Look what you've done. The nice man . . .

For heaven's sake, I broke in. Don't call me a nice man to her. I'm here to look at her throat on the chance that she might have diphtheria and possibly die of it. But that's nothing to her. Look here, I said to the child, we're going to look at your throat. You're old enough to understand what I'm saying. Will you open it now by yourself or shall we have to open it for you?

Not a move. Even her expression hadn't changed. Her breaths however were coming faster and faster. Then the battle began. I had to do it. I had to have a throat culture for her own protection. But first I told the parents that it was entirely up to them. I explained the danger but said that I would not insist on a throat examination so long as they would take the responsibility.

If you don't do what the doctor says you'll have to go to the hospital, the mother admonished her severely.

Oh yeah? I had to smile to myself. After all, I had already fallen in love with the savage brat, the parents were contemptible to me. In the ensuing struggle they grew more and more abject, crushed, exhausted, while she surely rose to magnificent heights of insane fury of effort bred of her terror of me.

The father tried his best, and he was a big man but the fact that she was his daughter, his shame at her behavior, and his dread of hurting her made him release her just at the critical moment several times when I had almost achieved success, till I wanted to kill him. But his dread also that she might have diphtheria made him tell me to go on, go on though he himself was almost fainting, while the mother moved back and forth behind us raising and lowering her hands in an agony of apprehension.

Put her in front of you on your lap, I ordered, and hold both her wrists.

But as soon as he did the child let out a scream. Don't, you're hurting me. Let go of my hands. Let them go I tell you. Then she shrieked terrifyingly, hysterically. Stop it! Stop it! You're killing me!

Do you think she can stand it, doctor! said the mother.

You get out, said the husband to his wife. Do you want her to die of diphtheria?

Come on now, hold her, I said.

Then I grasped the child's head with my left hand and tried to get the wooden tongue depressor between her teeth. She fought, with clenched teeth, desperately! But now I also had grown furious—at a child. I tried to hold myself down but I couldn't. I know how to expose a throat for inspection. And I did my best. When finally I got the wooden spatula behind the last teeth and just the point of it into the mouth cavity, she opened up for an instant but before I could see anything she came down again and gripping the wooden blade between her molars she reduced it to splinters before I could get it out again.

Aren't you ashamed, the mother yelled at her. Aren't you ashamed to act like that in front of the doctor?

Get me a smooth-handled spoon of some sort, I told the mother. We're going through with this. The child's mouth was already bleeding. Her tongue was cut and she was screaming in wild hysterical shrieks. Perhaps I should have desisted and come back in an hour or more. No doubt it would have been better. But I have seen at least two children lying dead in bed of neglect in such cases, and feeling that I must get a diagnosis now or never I went at it again. But the worst of it was that I too had got beyond reason. I could have torn the child apart in my own fury and enjoyed it. It was a pleasure to attack her. My face was burning with it.

The damned little brat must be protected against her own idiocy, one says to one's self at such times. Others must be protected against her. It is social necessity. And all these things are true. But a blind fury, a feeling of adult shame, bred of a longing for muscular release are the operatives. One goes on to the end.

In a final unreasoning assault I overpowered the child's neck and jaws. I forced the heavy silver spoon back of her teeth and down her throat till she gagged. And there it was—both tonsils covered with membrane. She had fought valiantly to keep me from knowing her secret. She had been hiding that sore throat for three days at least and lying to her parents in order to escape just such an outcome as this.

Now truly she *was* furious. She had been on the defensive before but now she attacked. Tried to get off her father's lap and fly at me while tears of defeat blinded her eyes.

Benjamin Franklin

As a young boy, Benjamin Franklin (1706–1790) became an apprentice printer to his brother. At the age of seventeen, he left his native Boston and began to work as a printer in Philadelphia. He went on to set up his own newspaper, publish *Poor Richard's Almanack*, and establish several civic associations (including a philosophical society, a fire company, a subscription library, and a hospital). A tireless and inquisitive mind, Franklin invented the lightning rod, developed bifocal spectacles, and was elected to the Royal Society in London. He also helped to draft the Declaration of Independence, which he signed; negotiated alliances and treaties with France and Great Britain; and participated in the Federal Constitutional Convention in 1787. He began his autobiography in 1771, though at his death in 1790 he had gone no further than age fifty two.

Selection from *The Autobiography of Benjamin Franklin*

It was about this time [c. 1728] that I conceiv'd the bold and arduous Project of arriving at moral Perfection. I wish'd to live without committing any Fault at any time; I would conquer all that either Natural Inclination, Custom, or Company might lead me into. As I knew, or thought I knew, what was right and wrong, I did not see why I might not *always* do the one and avoid the other. But I soon found I had undertaken a Task of more Difficulty than I had imagined. While my *Attention was taken up* in guarding against one Fault, I was often surpriz'd by another. Habit took the Advantage of Inattention. Inclination was sometimes too strong for Reason. I concluded at length that the mere speculative Conviction that it was our Interest to be compleatly virtuous was not sufficient to prevent our Slipping, and that the contrary Habits must be broken and good ones acquired and established, before we can have any Dependance on a steady uniform Rectitude of Conduct. For this purpose I therefore contriv'd the following Method.

In the various Enumerations of the moral Virtues I had met with in my Reading, I found the Catalogue more or less numerous, as different Writers included more or fewer ideas under the same Name. Temperance, for Example, was by some confin'd to Eating and Drinking, while by others it was extended to mean the moderating every other Pleasure, Appetite, Inclination, or Passion, bodily or mental, even to our Avarice and Ambition. I propos'd to myself, for the sake of Clearness, to use rather more Names with fewer Ideas annex'd to each, than a few Names with more Ideas; and I included under Thirteen Names of Virtues all that at that time occurr'd to me as necessary or desirable, and annex'd to each a short Precept, which fully express'd the Extent I gave to its Meaning.

These Names of Virtues with their Precepts were

1. TEMPERANCE

Eat not to Dulness.
Drink not to Elevation.

2. SILENCE

Speak not but what may benefit others or yourself. Avoid trifling Conversation.

3. ORDER

Let all your Things have their Places. Let each Part of your Business have its Time.

4. RESOLUTION

Resolve to perform what you ought. Perform without fail what you resolve.

5. FRUGALITY

Make no Expence but to do good to others or yourself. i.e., Waste nothing.

6. INDUSTRY

Lose no Time. Be always employ'd in something useful. Cut off all unnecessary Actions.

7. SINCERITY

Use no hurtful Deceit.
Think innocently and justly; and, if you speak, speak accordingly.

8. JUSTICE

Wrong none, by doing Injuries or omitting the Benefits that are your Duty.

9. MODERATION

Avoid Extreams. Forbear resenting Injuries so much as you think they deserve.

10. CLEANLINESS

Tolerate no Uncleanness in Body, Cloaths, or Habitation.

11. TRANQUILITY

Be not disturbed at Trifles, or at Accidents common or unavoidable.

12. CHASTITY

Rarely use Venery but for Health or Offspring; Never to Dulness, Weakness, or the Injury of your own or another's Peace or Reputation.

13. HUMILITY

Imitate Jesus and Socrates.

My Intention being to acquire the *Habitude* of all these Virtues, I judg'd it would be well not to distract my Attention by attempting the whole at once, but to fix it on one of them at a time, and when I should be Master of that, then to proceed to another, and so on till I should have gone thro' the thirteen. And as the previous Acquisition of some might facilitate the Acquisition of certain others, I arrang'd them with that View as they stand above. *Temperance* first, as it tends to procure that Coolness and Clearness of Head, which is so necessary where constant Vigilance was to be kept up, and Guard maintained, against the unremitting Attraction of ancient Habits, and the Force of perpetual Temptations. This being acquir'd and establish'd, *Silence* would be more easy, and my Desire being to gain Knowledge at the same time that I improv'd in Virtue, and considering that in Conversation it was obtain'd rather by the use of the Ears than of the Tongue, and therefore wishing to break a Habit I was getting into of Prattling, Punning, and Joking, which only made me acceptable to trifling Company, I gave *Silence* the second Place. This, and the next, *Order*, I expected would allow me more Time for attending to my Project and my Studies; *Resolution*, once become habitual, would keep me firm in my Endeavours to obtain all the subsequent Virtues; *Frugality* and *Industry*, by freeing me from my remaining Debt, and producing Affluence and Independence, would make more easy the Practice of *Sincerity* and *justice, etc. etc.* Conceiving then that agreable to the Advice of Pythagoras in his Golden Verses daily Examination would be necessary, I contrivd the following Method for conducting that Examination.

I made a little Book in which I allotted a Page for each of the Virtues. I rul'd each Page with red Ink, so as to have seven Columns, one for each Day of the Week, marking each Column with a Letter for the Day. I cross'd these Columns with thirteen red Lines, marking the Beginning of each Line with the first Letter of one of the Virtues, on which Line and in its proper Column I might mark by a little black Spot every Fault I found upon Examination to have been committed respecting that Virtue upon the Day.

I determined to give a Week's strict Attention to each of the Virtues successively. Thus in the first Week my great Guard was to avoid every the least Offence against Temperance, leaving the other Virtues to their ordinary Chance, only marking every Evening the Faults of the Day. Thus if in the first Week I could keep my first Line marked T clear of Spots, I suppos'd the Habit of that Virtue so much strengthen'd and its opposite weaken'd, that I might venture extending my Attention to include the next, and for the following Week keep both Lines clear of Spots. Proceeding thus to the last, I could go thro' a Course compleat in Thirteen Weeks, and four Courses in a Year. And like him who having a Garden to weed does not attempt to eradicate all the bad Herbs at once, which would exceed his Reach and his Strength, but works on one of the Beds at a time, and having accomplish'd the first proceeds to a Second; so I should have (I hoped) the encouraging Pleasure of seeing on my Pages the Progress I made in Virtue, by clearing successively my Lines of their Spots, till in the End by a Number of Courses, I should be happy in viewing a clean Book after a thirteen Weeks daily Examination.

Temperance.						
Eat not to Dulness. Drink not to Elevation.						
S	M	T	W	T	F	S
T						
S	• •	•		•		•	
O	•	•	•		•	•	•
R			•			•	
F		•			•		
I			•				
S							
J							
M							
Cl							
T							
Ch							
H							

. . . The Precept of *Order* requiring that *every Part of my Business should have its allotted Time,* one Page in my little Book contain'd the following Scheme of Employment for the Twenty-four Hours of a natural Day,

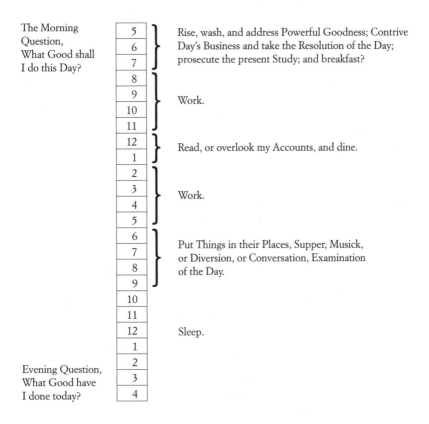

The Morning Question, What Good shall I do this Day?	5	}	Rise, wash, and address Powerful Goodness; Contrive Day's Business and take the Resolution of the Day; prosecute the present Study; and breakfast?
	6		
	7		
	8	}	Work.
	9		
	10		
	11		
	12	}	Read, or overlook my Accounts, and dine.
	1		
	2	}	Work.
	3		
	4		
	5		
	6	}	Put Things in their Places, Supper, Musick, or Diversion, or Conversation, Examination of the Day.
	7		
	8		
	9		
	10		
	11		
	12		Sleep.
	1		
Evening Question, What Good have I done today?	2		
	3		
	4		

I enter'd upon the Execution of this Plan for Self Examination, and continu'd it with occasional Intermissions for some time. I was surpriz'd to find myself so much fuller of Faults than I had imagined, but I had the Satisfaction of seeing them diminish. To avoid the Trouble of renewing now and then my little Book, which by scraping out the Marks on the Paper of old Faults to make room for new Ones in a new Course, became full of Holes: I transferr'd my Tables and Precepts to the Ivory Leaves of a Memorandum Book, on which the Lines were drawn with red Ink that made a durable Stain, and on those Lines I mark'd my Faults with a black Lead Pencil, which Marks I could easily wipe out with a wet Sponge. After a while I went thro' one Course only in a Year, and afterward only one in several Years, till at length I omitted them entirely, being employ'd in Voyages and Business abroad with a Multiplicity of Affairs, that interfered, but I always carried my little Book with me.

My Scheme of *Order*, gave me the most Trouble, and I found, that tho' it might be practicable where a Man's Business was such as to leave him the Disposition of his Time, that of a Journeyman Printer for instance, it was not possible to be exactly observ'd by a Master, who must mix with the World, and often receive People of Business at their own Hours. *Order* too, with regard to Places for Things, Papers, etc. I found extremely difficult to acquire. I had not been early accustomed to *Method*, and having an exceeding good Memory, I was not so sensible of the Inconvenience attending Want of Method. This Article therefore cost me so much painful Attention and my Faults in it vex'd me so much, and I made so little Progress in Amendment, and had such frequent Relapses, that I was almost ready to give up the Attempt, and content myself with a faulty Character in that respect. Like the Man who in buying an Ax of a Smith my neighbour, desired to have the whole of its Surface as bright as the Edge; the Smith consented to grind it bright for him if he would turn the Wheel. He turn'd while the Smith press'd the broad Face of the Ax hard and heavily on the Stone, which made the Turning of it very fatiguing. The Man came every now and then from the Wheel to see how the Work went on; and at length would take his Ax as it was without farther Grinding. No, says the Smith, Turn on, turn on; we shall have it bright by and by; as yet 'tis only speckled. Yes, says the Man; but—*I think I like a speckled Ax best*. And I believe this may have been the Case with many who having for want of some such Means as I employ'd found the Difficulty of obtaining good, and breaking bad Habits, in other Points of Vice and Virtue, have given up the Struggle, and concluded that *a speckled Ax was best*. For something that pretended to be Reason was every now and then suggesting to me that such extream Nicety as I exacted of my self might be a kind of Foppery in Morals, which if it were known would make me ridiculous; that a perfect Character might be attended with the Inconvenience of being envied and hated; and that a benevolent Man should allow a few Faults in himself, to keep his Friends in Countenance.

In Truth I found myself incorrigible with respect to *Order*; and now I am grown old, and my Memory bad, I feel very sensibly the want of it. But on the whole, tho' I never arrived at the Perfection I had been so ambitious of obtaining, but fell far short of it, yet I was by the Endeavour a better and happier Man than I otherwise should have been, if I had not attempted it; as those who aim at perfect Writing by imitating the engraved Copies, tho' they never reach the wish'd for Excellence of those Copies, their Hand is mended by the Endeavour, and is tolerable while it continues fair and legible.

And it may be well my Posterity should be informed, that to this little Artifice, with the Blessing of God, their Ancestor ow'd the constant Felicity of his Life down to his 79th Year in which this is written. What Reverses may attend the Remainder is in the Hand of Providence: But if they arrive the Reflection on past Happiness enjoy'd ought to help his bearing them with more Resignation. To *Temperance* he ascribes his long-continu'd Health, and what is still left to him of a good Constitution. To *Industry* and *Frugality* the early Easiness of his Circumstances, and Acquisition of his Fortune, with all that Knowledge that enabled him to be an useful Citizen, and obtain'd for him some Degree of Reputation among the Learned. To *Sincerity* and *Justice* the Confidence of his Country, and the honourable Employs it conferr'd upon him. And to the joint Influence of the whole Mass of the Virtues, even in the imperfect State he was able to acquire them, all that Evenness of Temper, and that Chearfulness in Conversation that makes his Company still sought for, and agreable even to his younger Acquaintance. I hope therefore that some of my Descendants may follow the Example and reap the Benefit. . . .

My List of Virtues contain'd at first but twelve: But a Quaker Friend having kindly inform'd me that I was generally thought proud; that my Pride show'd itself frequently in Conversation; that I was not content with being in the right when discussing any Point, but was overbearing and rather insolent; of which he convinc'd me by mentioning several Instances; I determined endeavouring to cure myself if I could of this Vice or Folly among the rest, and I added *Humility* to my List, giving an extensive Meaning to the Word. I cannot boast of much Success in acquiring the *Reality* of this Virtue; but I had a good deal with regard to the *Appearance* of it. I made it a Rule to forbear all direct Contradiction to the Sentiments of others, and all positive Assertion of my own. I even forbid myself agreable to the old Laws of our Junto, the Use of every Word or Expression in the Language that imported a fix'd Opinion; such as *certainly*, *undoubtedly*, etc. and I adopted instead of them, *I conceive*, *I apprehend*, or *I imagine* a thing to be so or so, or it so appears to me at present. When another asserted something, that I thought an Error, I deny'd my self the Pleasure of contradicting him abruptly, and of showing immediately some Absurdity in his Proposition; and in answering I began by observing that in certain Cases or Circumstances his Opinion would be right, but that in the present case there *appear'd* or *seem'd* to me some Difference, etc. I soon found the Advantage of this change in my Manners. The Conversations I engag'd in went on more pleasantly. The modest way in which I propos'd my Opinions, procur'd them a readier Reception and less Contradiction; I had less Mortification when I was found to be in the wrong, and I more easily prevail'd with others to give up their Mistakes and join with me when I happen'd to be in the right. And this mode, which I at first put on, with some violence to natural Inclination, became at length so easy and so habitual to me, that perhaps for these Fifty Years past no one has ever heard a dogmatical Expression escape me. And to this Habit (after my Character of Integrity) I think it principally owing, that I had early so much Weight with my Fellow Citizens, when I proposed new Institutions, or Alterations in the old; and so much Influence in public Councils when I became a Member. For I was but a bad Speaker, never eloquent, subject to much Hesitation in my choice of Words, hardly correct in Language, and yet I generally carried my Points.

In reality there is perhaps no one of our natural Passions so hard to subdue as *Pride*. Disguise it, struggle with it, beat it down, stifle it, mortify it as much as one pleases, it is still alive, and will every now and then peep out and show itself. You will see it perhaps often in this History. For even if I could conceive that I had compleatly overcome it, I should probably [be] proud of my Humility.

Ursula K. Le Guin

Born in Berkeley, California, Ursula K. Le Guin (b. 1929) attended Radcliffe College and did graduate work at Columbia University. Residing in Portland, Oregon, since 1958, she has written numerous novels, poetry, children's books, and essays. Le Guin is best known for her works of science fiction and fantasy and has won many awards for her writing, including the Gandalf Grand Master Award. The story included here, "The Ones Who Walk Away from Omelas," was first published in the magazine *New Directions* in 1973 and won the prestigious Hugo Award for best short story the following year.

The Ones Who Walk Away from Omelas

With a clamor of bells that set the swallows soaring, the Festival of Summer came to the city Omelas, bright towered by the sea. The rigging of the boats in harbor sparkled with flags. In the streets between houses with red roofs and painted walls, between old moss-grown gardens and under avenues of trees, past great parks and public buildings, processions moved. Some were decorous: old people in long stiff robes of mauve and gray, grave master workmen, quiet, merry women carrying their babies and chatting as they walked. In other streets the music beat faster, a shimmering of gong and tambourine, and the people went dancing, the procession was a dance. Children dodged in and out, their high calls rising like the swallows' crossing flights over the music and the singing. All the processions wound toward the north side of the city, where on the great water-meadow called the Green Fields boys and girls, naked in the bright air, with mud-stained feet and ankles and long, lithe arms, exercised their restive horses before the race. The horses wore no gear at all but a halter without bit. Their manes were braided with streamers of silver, gold, and green. They flared their nostrils and pranced and boasted to one another; they were vastly excited, the horse being the only animal who has adopted our ceremonies as his own. Far off to the north and west the mountains stood up half encircling Omelas on her bay. The air of morning was so clear that the snow still crowning the Eighteen Peaks burned with white-gold fire across the miles of sunlit air, under the dark blue of the sky. There was just enough wind to make the banners that marked the racecourse snap and flutter now and then. In the silence of the broad green meadows one could hear the music winding through the city streets, farther and nearer and ever approaching, a cheerful faint sweetness of the air that from time to time trembled and gathered together and broke out into the great joyous clanging of the bells.

Joyous! How is one to tell about joy? How describe the citizens of Omelas?

They were not simple folk, you see, though they were happy. But we do not say the words of cheer much any more. All smiles have become archaic. Given a description such as this one tends to make certain assumptions. Given a description such as this one tends to look next for the king, mounted on a splendid stallion and surrounded by his noble knights, or perhaps in a golden litter borne by great-muscled slaves. But there was no king. They did not use swords, or keep slaves. They were not barbarians. I do not know the rules and laws of their society, but I suspect that they were singularly few. As they did without monarchy and slavery, so they also got on without the stock exchange, the advertisement, the secret police, and the bomb. Yet I repeat that these were not simple folk, not dulcet shepherds, noble savages, bland utopians. They were not less complex than us. The trouble is that we have a bad habit, encouraged by pedants and sophisticates, of considering happiness as something rather stupid. Only pain is intellectual, only evil interesting. This is the treason of the artist: a refusal to admit the banality of evil and the terrible boredom of pain. If you can't lick 'em, join 'em. If it hurts, repeat it. But to praise despair is to condemn delight; to embrace violence is to lose hold of everything else. We have almost lost hold; we can no longer describe a happy man, nor make any celebration of joy. How can I tell you about the people of Omelas? They were not naive and happy children—though their children were, in fact, happy. They were mature, intelligent, passionate adults whose lives were not wretched. O miracle! But I wish I could describe it better. I wish I could convince you. Omelas sounds in my words like a city in a fairy tale, long ago and far away, once upon a time. Perhaps it would be best if you imagined it as your own fancy bids, assuming it will rise to the occasion, for certainly I cannot suit you all. For instance, how about technology? I think that there would be no cars or helicopters in and above the streets; this follows from the fact that the people of Omelas are happy people. Happiness is based on a just discrimination of what is necessary, what is neither necessary nor destructive, and what is destructive. In the middle category, however—that of the unnecessary but undestructive, that of comfort, luxury, exuberance, etc.—they could perfectly well have central heating, subway trains, washing machines, and all kinds of marvelous devices not yet invented here, floating light sources, fuelless power, a cure for the common cold. Or they could have none of that: it doesn't matter. As you like it. I am inclined to think that people from towns up and down the coast have been coming in to Omelas during the last days before the festival on very fast little trains and double-decked trams, and that the train station of Omelas is actually the handsomest building in town, though plainer than the magnificent farmers' market. But even granted trams, I fear that Omelas so far strikes some of you as goody-goody. Smiles, bells, parades, horses, bleh. If so, please add an orgy. If an orgy would help, don't hesitate. Let us not, however, have temples from which issue beautiful nude priests and priestesses already half in ecstasy and ready to copulate with any man or woman, lover or stranger, who desires union with the deep godhead of the blood, although that was my first idea. But really it would be better not to have any temples in Omelas—at least, not manned temples. Religion yes, clergy no. Surely the beautiful nudes can just wander about offering themselves like divine soufflés to the hunger of the needy and the rapture of the flesh. Let them join the processions. Let tambourines be struck above the copulations, and the glory of desire be proclaimed upon the gongs, and (a not unimportant point) let the offspring of these delightful rituals be beloved and looked after by all. One thing I know there is none of in Omelas is guilt. But what else should there be? I thought at first there were no drugs, but that is puritanical. For those who like it, the faint insistent sweetness of *drooz* may perfume the ways of the city, *drooz* that first brings a great lightness and brilliance to the mind and limbs, and then after some hours a dreamy languor, and wonderful visions at last of the very arcana and inmost secrets of the universe, as well as exciting the pleasure of sex beyond all belief; and it is not habit-forming. For more modest tastes I think there ought to be beer. What else, what else belongs in the joyous city? The sense of victory, surely, the celebration of courage. But as we did without clergy, let us do without soldiers. The joy built upon successful slaughter is not the right kind of joy; it will not do; it is fearful and it is trivial. A boundless and generous contentment, a magnanimous triumph felt not against some outer enemy but in communion with the finest and fairest in the souls of all men everywhere and the splendor of the world's summer: this is what swells the hearts of the people of Omelas, and the victory they celebrate is that of life. I really don't think many of them need to take *drooz*.

Most of the processions have reached the Green Fields by now. A marvelous smell of cooking goes forth from the red and blue tents of the provisioners. The faces of small children are amiably sticky; in the benign gray beard of a man a couple of crumbs of rich pastry are entangled. The youths and girls have mounted their horses and are beginning to group around the starting line of the course. An old woman, small, fat, and laughing, is passing out flowers from a basket, and tall young men wear her flowers in their shining hair. A child of nine or ten sits at the edge of the crowd, alone, playing on a wooden flute. People pause to listen, and they smile, but they do not speak to him, for he never ceases playing and never sees them, his dark eyes wholly rapt in the sweet thin magic of the tune.

He finishes, and slowly lowers his hands holding the wooden flute.

As if that little private silence were the signal, all at once a trumpet sounds from the pavilion near the starting line: imperious, melancholy, piercing. The horses rear on their slender legs, and some of them neigh in answer. Sober faced, the young riders stroke the horses' necks and soothe them, whispering, "Quiet, quiet, there my beauty, my hope. . . ." They begin to form in rank along the starting line. The crowds along the racecourse are like a field of grass and flowers in the wind. The Festival of Summer has begun.

Do you believe? Do you accept the festival, the city, the joy? No? Then let me describe one more thing.

In a basement under one of the beautiful public buildings of Omelas, or perhaps in the cellar of one of its spacious private homes, there is a room. It has one locked door, and no window. A little light seeps in dustily between cracks in the boards, secondhand from a cobwebbed window somewhere across the cellar. In one corner of the little room a couple of mops, with stiff, clotted, foul-smelling heads, stand near a rusty bucket. The floor is dirt, a little damp to the touch, as cellar dirt usually is. The room is about three paces long and two wide: a mere broom closet or disused tool room. In the room a child is sitting. It could be a boy or a girl. It looks about six, but actually is nearly ten. It is feeble-minded. Perhaps it was born defective, or perhaps it has become imbecile through fear, malnutrition, and neglect. It picks its nose and occasionally fumbles vaguely with its toes or genitals, as it sits hunched in the corner farthest from the bucket and the two mops. It is afraid of the mops. It finds them horrible. It shuts its eyes, but it knows the mops are still standing there; and the door is locked; and nobody will come. The door is always locked; and nobody ever comes, except that sometimes—the child has no understanding of time or interval—sometimes the door rattles terribly and opens, and a person, or several people, are there. One of them may come in and kick the child to make it stand up. The others never come close, but peer in at it with frightened, disgusted eyes. The food bowl and the water jug are hastily filled, the door is locked, the eyes disappear. The people at the door never say anything, but the child, who has not always lived in the tool room, and can remember sunlight and its mother's voice, sometimes speaks. "I will be good," it says. "Please let me out. I will be good!" They never answer. The child used to scream for help at night, and cry a good deal, but now it only makes a kind of whining, "eh-haa, eh-haa," and it speaks less and less often. It is so thin there are no calves to its legs; its belly protrudes; it lives on a half bowl of cornmeal and grease a day. It is naked. Its buttocks and thighs are a mass of festered sores, as it sits in its own excrement continually.

They all know it is there, all the people of Omelas. Some of them have come to see it; others are content merely to know it is there. They all know that it has to be there. Some of them understand why, and some do not, but they all understand that their happiness, the beauty of their city, the tenderness of their friendships, the health of their children, the wisdom of their scholars, the skill of their makers, even the abundance of their harvest and the kindly weathers of their skies, depend wholly on this child's abominable misery.

This is usually explained to children when they are between eight and twelve, whenever they seem capable of understanding; and most of those who come to see the child are young people, though often enough an adult comes, or comes back, to see the child. No matter how well the matter has been explained to them, these young spectators are always shocked and sickened at the sight. They feel disgust, which they had thought themselves superior to. They feel anger, outrage, impotence, despite all the explanations. They would like to do something for the child. But there is nothing they can do. If the child were brought up into the sunlight out of that vile place, if it were cleaned and fed and comforted, that would be a good thing, indeed; but if it were done, in that day and hour all the prosperity and beauty and delight of Omelas would wither and be destroyed. Those are the terms. To exchange all the goodness and grace of every life in Omelas for that single, small improvement: to throw away the happiness of thousands for the chance of the happiness of one; that would be to let guilt within the walls indeed.

The terms are strict and absolute; there may not even be a kind word spoken to the child.

Often the young people go home in tears, or in a tearless rage, when they have seen the child and faced this terrible paradox. They may brood over it for weeks or years. But as time goes on they begin to realize that even if the child could be released, it would not get much good of its freedom: a little vague pleasure of warmth and food, no doubt, but little more. It is too degraded and imbecile to know any real joy. It has been afraid too long ever to be free of fear. Its habits are too uncouth for it to respond to humane treatment. Indeed, after so long it would probably be wretched without walls about it to protect it, and darkness for its eyes, and its own excrement to sit in. Their tears at the bitter injustice dry when they begin to perceive the terrible justice of reality, and to accept it. Yet it is their tears and anger, the trying of their generosity and the acceptance of their helplessness, that are perhaps the true source of the splendor of their lives. Theirs is no vapid, irresponsible happiness. They know that they, like the child, are not free. They know compassion. It is the existence of the child, and their knowledge of its existence, that makes possible the nobility of their architecture, the poignancy of their music, the profundity of their science. It is because of the child that they are so gentle with children. They know that if the wretched one were not there sniveling in the dark, the other one, the flute player, could make no joyful music as the young riders line up in their beauty for the race in the sunlight of the first morning of summer.

Now do you believe in them? Are they not more credible? But there is one more thing to tell, and this is quite incredible.

At times one of the adolescent girls or boys who go to see the child does not go home to weep or rage, does not, in fact, go home at all. Sometimes also a man or woman much older falls silent for a day or two, and then leaves home. These people go out into the street, and walk down the street alone. They keep walking, and walk straight out of the city of Omelas, through the beautiful gates. They keep walking across the farmlands of Omelas. Each one goes alone, youth or girl, man or woman. Night falls; the traveler must pass down village streets, between the houses with yellow-lit windows, and on out into the darkness of the fields. Each alone, they go west or north, toward the mountains. They go on. They leave Omelas, they walk ahead into the darkness, and they do not come back. The place they go toward is a place even less imaginable to most of us than the city of happiness. I cannot describe it at all. It is possible that it does not exist. But they seem to know where they are going, the ones who walk away from Omelas.

Billy Collins

A native of New York City, Billy Collins (b. 1941) is the author of several books of poetry, among them *Pokerface, Video Poems, The Apple That Astonished Paris, Questions About Angels, The Art of Drowning, Picnic, Lightning*, and *Nine Horses*. In 1992, he was chosen by the New York Public Library to serve as "Literary Lion," and from 2001–2003 he served as the U.S. poet laureate. A professor of English at Lehman College of the City University of New York, he has also conducted summer poetry workshops in Ireland at University College, Galway. The following poem, "The History Teacher," appeared in *Sailing Alone Around the Room: New and Selected Poems*, published in 2001.

The History Teacher

Trying to protect his students' innocence
he told them the Ice Age was really just
the Chilly Age, a period of a million years
when everyone had to wear sweaters.

And the Stone Age became the Gravel Age,
named after the long driveways of the time.

The Spanish Inquisition was nothing more
than an outbreak of questions such as
"How far is it from here to Madrid?"
"What do you call the matador's hat?"

The War of the Roses took place in a garden,
and the Enola Gay dropped one tiny atom
on Japan.

The children would leave his classroom
for the playground to torment the weak
and the smart,
mussing up their hair and breaking their glasses,

while he gathered up his notes and walked home
past flower beds and white picket fences,
wondering if they would believe that soldiers
in the Boer War told long, rambling stories
designed to make the enemy nod off.

Abraham Lincoln

Abraham Lincoln (1809–1865) was born in a Kentucky log cabin. The sixteenth president of the United States, Lincoln led the Union to victory in the American Civil War and issued the Emancipation Proclamation that abolished slavery in the United States. Lincoln delivered the following speech at his second inauguration on March 4, 1865, one month before the end of the war and less than six weeks before his death by an assassin's bullet in Ford's Theatre.

Second Inaugural Address

March 4, 1865

At this second appearing to take the oath of the presidential office, there is less occasion for an extended address than there was at the first. Then a statement, somewhat in detail, of a course to be pursued, seemed fitting and proper. Now, at the expiration of four years, during which public declarations have been constantly called forth on every point and phase of the great contest which still absorbs the attention, and engrosses the energies of the nation, little that is new could be presented. The progress of our arms, upon which all else chiefly depends, is as well known to the public as to myself; and it is, I trust, reasonably satisfactory and encouraging to all. With high hope for the future, no prediction in regard to it is ventured.

On the occasion corresponding to this four years ago, all thoughts were anxiously directed to an impending civil war. All dreaded it—all sought to avert it. While the inaugural address was being delivered from this place, devoted altogether to *saving* the Union without war, insurgent agents were in the city seeking to *destroy* it without war—seeking to dissolve the Union, and divide effects, by negotiation. Both parties deprecated war; but one of them would *make* war rather than let the nation survive; and the other would *accept* war rather than let it perish. And the war came.

One-eighth of the whole population were colored slaves, not distributed generally over the Union, but localized in the Southern part of it. These slaves constituted a peculiar and powerful interest. All knew that this interest was, somehow, the cause of the war. To strengthen, perpetuate, and extend this interest was the object for which the insurgents would rend the Union, even by war; while the government claimed no right to do more than to restrict the territorial enlargement of it. Neither party expected for the war, the magnitude, or the duration, which it has already attained. Neither anticipated that the *cause* of the conflict might cease with, or even before, the conflict itself should cease. Each looked for an easier triumph, and a result less fundamental and astounding. Both read the same Bible, and pray to the same God; and each invokes his aid against the other. It may seem strange that any men should dare to ask a just God's assistance in wringing their bread from the sweat of other men's faces; but let us judge not that we be not judged. The prayers of both could not be answered; that of neither has been answered fully. The Almighty has his own purposes. "Woe unto the world because of offenses! for it must needs be that offenses come; but woe to that man by whom the offense cometh!" If we shall suppose that American slavery is one of those offenses which, in the providence of God, must needs come, but which, having continued through his appointed time, he now wills to remove, and that he gives to both North and South, this terrible war, as the woe due to those by whom the offense came, shall we discern therein any departure from those divine attributes which the believers in a Living God always ascribe to him? Fondly do we hope—fervently do we pray—that this mighty scourge of war may speedily pass away. Yet, if God wills that it continue, until all the wealth piled by the bondman's two hundred and fifty years of unrequited toil shall be sunk, and until every drop of blood drawn with the lash, shall be paid by another drawn with the sword, as was said three thousand years ago, so still it must be said, "the judgments of the Lord, are true and righteous altogether."

With malice toward none; with charity for all; with firmness in the right, as God gives us to see the right, let us strive on to finish the work we are in; to bind up the nation's wounds; to care for him who shall have borne the battle, and for his widow, and his orphan—to do all which may achieve and cherish a just, and a lasting peace, among ourselves, and with all nations.

Nathaniel Hawthorne

Nathaniel Hawthorne (1804–1864) was born in Salem, Massachusetts. After trying to establish himself as a writer for several years, Hawthorne saw his first works published in the early 1830s. In 1841, he spent eight months at Brook Farm, a short-lived experiment in utopian communal living in West Roxbury, Massachusetts (which served as inspiration for his novel *The Blithedale Romance*). Near the end of the decade, he attained the post of surveyor in the Salem Custom House. He published his most famous novel, *The Scarlet Letter*, in 1850 and followed it with several other major works. In addition to his literary career, Hawthorne served as American consul at Liverpool and traveled extensively throughout Europe. "The Minister's Black Veil" was first published in 1836 in *The Token*, a Boston gift book, and appeared again shortly thereafter in *Twice-Told Tales*.

The Minister's Black Veil

*A Parable**

The sexton stood in the porch of Milford meetinghouse, pulling lustily at the bell rope. The old people of the village came stooping along the street. Children, with bright faces, tript merrily beside their parents, or mimicked a graver gait, in the conscious dignity of their Sunday clothes. Spruce bachelors looked sidelong at the pretty maidens, and fancied that the Sabbath sunshine made them prettier than on weekdays. When the throng had mostly streamed into the porch, the sexton began to toll the bell, keeping his eye on the Reverend Mr. Hooper's door. The first glimpse of the clergyman's figure was the signal for the bell to cease its summons.

"But what has good Parson Hooper got upon his face?" cried the sexton in astonishment.

All within hearing immediately turned about, and beheld the semblance of Mr. Hooper, pacing slowly his meditative way toward the meetinghouse.

---

*Another clergyman in New England, Mr. Joseph Moody, of York, Maine, who died about eighty years since, made himself remarkable by the same eccentricity that is here related of the Reverend Mr. Hooper. In his case, however, the symbol had a different import. In early life he had accidentally killed a beloved friend; and from that day till the hour of his own death, he hid his face from men.

With one accord they started, expressing more wonder than if some strange minister were coming to dust the cushions of Mr. Hooper's pulpit.

"Are you sure it is our parson?" inquired Goodman Gray of the sexton.

"Of a certainty it is good Mr. Hooper," replied the sexton. "He was to have exchanged pulpits with Parson Shute of Westbury; but Parson Shute sent to excuse himself yesterday, being to preach a funeral sermon."

The cause of so much amazement may appear sufficiently slight. Mr. Hooper, a gentlemanly person of about thirty, though still a bachelor, was dressed with due clerical neatness, as if a careful wife had starched his band, and brushed the weekly dust from his Sunday's garb. There was but one thing remarkable in his appearance. Swathed about his forehead, and hanging down over his face, so low as to be shaken by his breath, Mr. Hooper had on a black veil. On a nearer view, it seemed to consist of two folds of crape, which entirely concealed his features, except the mouth and chin, but probably did not intercept his sight, farther than to give a darkened aspect to all living and inanimate things. With this gloomy shade before him, good Mr. Hooper walked onward, at a slow and quiet pace, stooping somewhat and looking on the ground, as is customary with abstracted men, yet nodding kindly to those of his parishioners who still waited on the meetinghouse steps. But so wonder-struck were they, that his greeting hardly met with a return.

"I can't really feel as if good Mr. Hooper's face was behind that piece of crape," said the sexton.

"I don't like it," muttered an old woman, as she hobbled into the meetinghouse. "He has changed himself into something awful, only by hiding his face."

"Our parson has gone mad!" cried Goodman Gray, following him across the threshold.

A rumor of some unaccountable phenomenon had preceded Mr. Hooper into the meetinghouse, and set all the congregation astir. Few could refrain from twisting their heads toward the door; many stood upright, and turned directly about; while several little boys clambered upon the seats, and came down again with a terrible racket. There was a general bustle, a rustling of the women's gowns and shuffling of the men's feet, greatly at variance with that hushed repose which should attend the entrance of the minister. But Mr. Hooper appeared not to notice the perturbation of his people. He entered with an almost noiseless step, bent his head mildly to the pews on each side, and bowed as he passed his oldest parishioner, a white-haired great-grandsire, who occupied an armchair in the center of the aisle. It was strange to observe, how slowly this venerable man became conscious of something singular in the appearance of his pastor. He seemed not fully to partake of the prevailing wonder, till Mr. Hooper had ascended the stairs, and showed himself in the pulpit, face-to-face with his congregation, except for the black veil. That mysterious emblem was never once withdrawn. It shook with his measured breath as he gave out the psalm; it threw its obscurity between him and the holy page, as he read the Scriptures; and while he prayed, the veil lay heavily on his uplifted countenance. Did he seek to hide it from the dread Being whom he was addressing?

Such was the effect of this simple piece of crape, that more than one woman of delicate nerves was forced to leave the meetinghouse. Yet perhaps the pale-faced congregation was almost as fearful a sight to the minister, as his black veil to them.

Mr. Hooper had the reputation of a good preacher, but not an energetic one: he strove to win his people heavenward, by mild persuasive influences, rather than to drive them thither, by the thunders of the Word. The sermon which he now delivered, was marked by the same characteristics of style and manner, as the general series of his pulpit oratory. But there was something, either in the sentiment of the discourse itself or in the imagination of the auditors, which made it greatly the most powerful effort that they had ever heard from their pastor's lips. It was tinged, rather more darkly than usual, with the gentle gloom of Mr. Hooper's temperament. The subject had reference to secret sin, and those sad mysteries which we hide from our nearest and dearest, and would fain conceal from our own consciousness, even forgetting that the Omniscient can detect them. A subtle power was breathed into his words. Each member of the congregation, the most innocent girl, and the man of hardened breast, felt as if the preacher had crept upon them, behind his awful veil, and discovered their hoarded iniquity of deed or thought. Many spread their clasped hands on their bosoms. There was nothing terrible in what Mr. Hooper said; at least, no violence; and yet, with every tremor of his melancholy voice, the hearers quaked. An unsought pathos came hand in hand with awe. So sensible were the audience of some unwonted attribute in their minister, that they longed for a breath of wind to blow aside the veil, almost believing that a stranger's visage would be discovered, though the form, gesture, and voice were those of Mr. Hooper.

At the close of the services, the people hurried out with indecorous confusion, eager to communicate their pent-up amazement, and conscious of lighter spirits, the moment they lost sight of the black veil. Some gathered in little circles, huddled closely together, with their mouths all whispering in the center; some went homeward alone, wrapt in silent meditation; some talked loudly, and profaned the Sabbath day with ostentatious laughter. A few shook their sagacious heads, intimating that they could penetrate the mystery; while one or two affirmed that there was no mystery at all, but only that Mr. Hooper's eyes were so weakened by the midnight lamp, as to require a shade. After a brief interval, forth came good Mr. Hooper also, in the rear of his flock. Turning his veiled face from one group to another, he paid due reverence to the hoary heads, saluted the middle aged with kind dignity, as their friend and spiritual guide, greeted the young with mingled authority and love, and laid his hands on the little children's heads to bless them. Such was always his custom on the Sabbath day. Strange and bewildered looks repaid him for his courtesy. None, as on former occasions, aspired to the honor of walking by their pastor's side. Old Squire Saunders, doubtless by an accidental lapse of memory, neglected to invite Mr. Hooper to his table, where the good clergyman had been wont to bless the food almost every Sunday since his settlement. He returned, therefore, to the parsonage, and, at the moment of closing the door, was observed to look back upon the people, all of whom had their eyes fixed upon the minister. A sad smile gleamed faintly from beneath the black veil, and flickered about his mouth, glimmering as he disappeared.

"How strange," said a lady, "that a simple black veil, such as any woman might wear on her bonnet, should become such a terrible thing on Mr. Hooper's face!"

"Something must surely be amiss with Mr. Hooper's intellects," observed her husband, the physician of the village. "But the strangest part of the affair is the effect of this vagary, even on a sober-minded man like myself. The black veil, though it covers only our pastor's face, throws its influence over his whole person, and makes him ghostlike from head to foot. Do you not feel it so?"

"Truly do I," replied the lady; "and I would not be alone with him for the world. I wonder he is not afraid to be alone with himself!"

"Men sometimes are so," said her husband.

The afternoon service was attended with similar circumstances. At its conclusion, the bell tolled for the funeral of a young lady. The relatives and friends were assembled in the house, and the more distant acquaintances stood about the door, speaking of the good qualities of the deceased, when their talk was interrupted by the appearance of Mr. Hooper, still covered with his black veil. It was now an appropriate emblem. The clergyman stepped into the room where the corpse was laid, and bent over the coffin, to take a last farewell of his deceased parishioner. As he stooped, the veil hung straight down from his forehead, so that, if her eyelids had not been closed forever, the dead maiden might have seen his face. Could Mr. Hooper be fearful of her glance, that he so hastily caught back the black veil? A person who watched the interview between the dead and the living, scrupled not to affirm, that, at the instant when the clergyman's features were disclosed, the corpse had slightly shuddered, rustling the shroud and muslin cap, though the countenance retained the composure of death. A superstitious old woman was the only witness of this prodigy. From the coffin, Mr. Hooper passed into the chamber of the mourners, and thence to the head of the staircase, to make the funeral prayer. It was a tender and heart-dissolving prayer, full of sorrow, yet so imbued with celestial hopes, that the music of a heavenly harp, swept by the fingers of the dead, seemed faintly to be heard among the accents of the minister. The people trembled, though they but darkly understood him, when he prayed that they, and himself, and all of mortal race, might be ready, as he trusted this young maiden had been, for the dreadful hour that should snatch the veil from their faces. The bearers went heavily forth, and the mourners followed, saddening all the street, with the dead before them, and Mr. Hooper in his black veil behind.

"Why do you look back?" said one in the procession to his partner.

"I had a fancy," replied she, "that the minister and maiden's spirit were walking hand in hand."

"And so had I, at the same moment," said the other.

That night, the handsomest couple in Milford village were to be joined in wedlock. Though reckoned a melancholy man, Mr. Hooper had a placid cheerfulness for such occasions, which often excited a sympathetic smile, where livelier merriment would have been thrown away. There was no quality of his disposition which made him more beloved than this. The company at the wedding awaited his arrival with impatience, trusting that the strange awe, which had gathered over him throughout the day, would now be dispelled. But such was not the result. When Mr. Hooper came, the first thing that their eyes rested on was the same horrible black veil, which had added deeper gloom to the funeral, and could portend nothing but evil to the wedding. Such was its immediate effect on the guests, that a cloud seemed to have rolled duskily from beneath the black crape, and dimmed the light of the candles. The bridal pair stood up before the minister. But the bride's cold fingers quivered in the tremulous hand of the bridegroom, and her deathlike paleness caused a whisper, that the maiden who had been buried a few hours before, was come from her grave to be married. If ever another wedding were so dismal, it was that famous one, where they tolled the wedding knell. After performing the ceremony, Mr. Hooper raised a glass of wine to his lips, wishing happiness to the new-married couple, in a strain of mild pleasantry that ought to have brightened the features of the guests, like a cheerful gleam from the hearth. At that instant, catching a glimpse of his figure in the looking glass, the black veil involved his own spirit in the horror with which it overwhelmed all others. His frame shuddered—his lips grew white—he spilt the untasted wine upon the carpet—and rushed forth into the darkness. For the Earth, too, had on her Black Veil.

The next day, the whole village of Milford talked of little else than Parson Hooper's black veil. That, and the mystery concealed behind it, supplied a topic for discussion between acquaintances meeting in the street, and good women gossiping at their open windows. It was the first item of news that the tavern keeper told to his guests. The children babbled of it on their way to school. One imitative little imp covered his face with an old black handkerchief, thereby so affrighting his playmates that the panic seized himself, and he well nigh lost his wits by his own waggery.

It was remarkable, that, of all the busybodies and impertinent people in the parish, not one ventured to put the plain question to Mr. Hooper, wherefore he did this thing. Hitherto, whenever there appeared the slightest call for such interference, he had never lacked advisers, nor shown himself averse to be guided by their judgment. If he erred at all, it was by so painful a degree of self-distrust, that even the mildest censure would lead him to consider an indifferent action as a crime. Yet, though so well acquainted with this amiable weakness, no individual among his parishioners chose to make the black veil a subject of friendly remonstrance. There was a feeling of dread, neither plainly confessed nor carefully concealed, which caused each to shift the responsibility upon another, till at length it was found expedient to send a deputation of the church, in order to deal with Mr. Hooper about the mystery, before it should grow into a scandal. Never did an embassy so ill discharge its duties. The minister received them with friendly courtesy, but became silent, after they were seated, leaving to his visitors the whole burthen of introducing their important business. The topic, it might be supposed, was obvious enough. There was the black veil, swathed around Mr. Hooper's forehead, and concealing every feature above his placid mouth, on which, at times, they could perceive the glimmering of a melancholy smile. But that piece of crape, to their imagination, seemed to hang down before his heart, the symbol of a fearful secret between him and them. Were the veil but cast aside, they might speak freely of it, but not till then. Thus they sat a considerable time, speechless, confused, and shrinking uneasily from Mr. Hooper's eye, which they felt to be fixed upon them with an invisible glance. Finally, the deputies returned abashed to their constituents, pronouncing the matter too weighty to be handled, except by a council of the churches, if, indeed, it might not require a general synod.

But there was one person in the village unappalled by the awe with which the black veil had impressed all besides herself. When the deputies returned without an explanation, or even venturing to demand one, she, with the calm energy of her character, determined to chase away the strange cloud that appeared to be settling around Mr. Hooper, every moment more darkly than before. As his plighted wife, it should be her privilege to know what the black veil concealed. At the minister's first visit, therefore, she entered upon the subject, with a direct simplicity, which made the task easier both for him and her. After he had seated himself, she fixed her eyes steadfastly upon the veil, but could discern nothing of the dreadful gloom that had so overawed the multitude: it was but a double fold of crape, hanging down from his forehead to his mouth, and slightly stirring with his breath.

"No," said she aloud, and smiling, "there is nothing terrible in this piece of crape, except that it hides a face which I am always glad to look upon. Come, good sir, let the sun shine from behind the cloud. First lay aside your black veil: then tell me why you put it on."

Mr. Hooper's smile glimmered faintly.

"There is an hour to come," said he, "when all of us shall cast aside our veils. Take it not amiss, beloved friend, if I wear this piece of crape till then."

"Your words are a mystery too," returned the young lady. "Take away the veil from them, at least."

"Elizabeth, I will," said he, "so far as my vow may suffer me. Know, then, this veil is a type and a symbol, and I am bound to wear it ever, both in light and darkness, in solitude before the gaze of multitudes, and as with strangers, so with my familiar friends. No mortal eye will see it withdrawn. This dismal shade must separate me from the world: even you, Elizabeth, can never come behind it!"

"What grievous affliction hath befallen you," she earnestly inquired, "that you should thus darken your eyes forever?"

"If it be a sign of mourning," replied Mr. Hooper, "I, perhaps, like most other mortals, have sorrows dark enough to be typified by a black veil."

"But what if the world will not believe that it is the type of an innocent sorrow?" urged Elizabeth. "Beloved and respected as you are, there may be whispers, that you hide your face under the consciousness of secret sin. For the sake of your holy office, do away this scandal!"

The color rose into her cheeks, as she intimated the nature of the rumors that were already abroad in the village. But Mr. Hooper's mildness did not forsake him. He even smiled again—that same sad smile, which always appeared like a faint glimmering of light, proceeding from the obscurity beneath the veil.

"If I hide my face for sorrow, there is cause enough," he merely replied. "And if I cover it for secret sin, what mortal might not do the same?"

And with this gentle, but unconquerable obstinacy, did he resist all her entreaties. At length Elizabeth sat silent. For a few moments she appeared lost in thought, considering, probably, what new methods might be tried, to withdraw her lover from so dark a fantasy, which, if it had no other meaning, was perhaps a symptom of mental disease. Though of a firmer character than his own, the tears rolled down her cheeks. But, in an instant, as it were, a new feeling took the place of sorrow: her eyes were fixed insensibly on the black veil, when, like a sudden twilight in the air, its terrors fell around her. She arose, and stood trembling before him.

"And do you feel it then at last?" said he mournfully.

She made no reply, but covered her eyes with her hand, and turned to leave the room. He rushed forward and caught her arm.

"Have patience with me, Elizabeth!" cried he passionately. "Do not desert me, though this veil must be between us here on earth. Be mine, and hereafter there shall be no veil over my face, no darkness between our souls! It is but a mortal veil—it is not for eternity! Oh! You know not how lonely I am, and how frightened to be alone behind my black veil. Do not leave me in this miserable obscurity forever!"

"Lift the veil but once, and look me in the face," said she.

"Never! It cannot be!" replied Mr. Hooper.

"Then, farewell!" said Elizabeth.

She withdrew her arm from his grasp, and slowly departed, pausing at the door, to give one long, shuddering gaze, that seemed almost to penetrate the mystery of the black veil. But, even amid his grief, Mr. Hooper smiled to think that only a material emblem had separated him from happiness, though the horrors which it shadowed forth must be drawn darkly between the fondest of lovers.

From that time no attempts were made to remove Mr. Hooper's black veil, or, by a direct appeal, to discover the secret which it was supposed to hide. By persons who claimed a superiority to popular prejudice, it was reckoned merely an eccentric whim, such as often mingles with the sober actions of men otherwise rational, and tinges them all with its own semblance of insanity. But with the multitude, good Mr. Hooper was irreparably a bugbear. He could not walk the streets with any peace of mind, so conscious was he that the gentle and timid would turn aside to avoid him, and that others would make it a point of hardihood to throw themselves in his way. The impertinence of the latter class compelled to give up his customary walk, at sunset, to the burial ground, for when he leaned pensively over the gate, there would always be faces behind the gravestones, peeping at his black veil. A fable went the rounds, that the stare of the dead people drove him thence. It grieved him, to the very depth of his kind heart, to observe how the children fled from his approach, breaking up their merriest sports, while his melancholy figure was yet afar off. Their instinctive dread caused him to feel, more strongly than aught else, that a preternatural horror was interwoven with the threads of the black crape. In truth, his own antipathy to the veil was known to be so great, that he never willingly passed before a mirror, nor stooped to drink at a still fountain, lest, in its peaceful bosom, he should be affrighted by himself. This was what gave plausibility to the whispers, that Mr. Hooper's conscience tortured him for some great crime, too horrible to be entirely concealed, or otherwise than so obscurely intimated. Thus, from beneath the black veil, there rolled a cloud into the sunshine, an ambiguity of sin or sorrow, which enveloped the poor minister, so that love or sympathy could never reach him. It was said, that ghost and fiend consorted with him there. With self-shudderings and outward terrors, he walked continually in its shadow, groping darkly within his own soul, or gazing through a medium that saddened the whole world. Even the lawless wind, it was believed, respected his dreadful secret, and never blew aside the veil. But still good Mr. Hooper sadly smiled at the pale visages of the worldly throng as he passed by.

Among all its bad influences, the black veil had the one desirable effect of making its wearer a very efficient clergyman. By the aid of his mysterious emblem—for there was no other apparent cause—he became a man of awful power, over souls that were in agony for sin. His converts always regarded him with a dread peculiar to themselves, affirming, though but figuratively, that, before he brought them to celestial light, they had been with him behind the black veil. Its gloom, indeed, enabled him to sympathize with all dark affections. Dying sinners cried aloud for Mr. Hooper, and would not yield their breath till he appeared; though ever, as he stooped to whisper consolation, they shuddered at the veiled face so near their own. Such were the terrors of the black veil, even when Death had bared his visage! Strangers came long distances to attend service at his church, with the mere idle purpose of gazing at his figure, because it was forbidden them to behold his face. But many were made to quake ere they departed! Once, during Governor Belcher's administration, Mr. Hooper was appointed to preach the election sermon. Covered with his black veil, he stood before the chief magistrate, the council, and the representatives, and wrought so deep an impression, that the legislative measures of that year were characterized by all the gloom and piety of our earliest ancestral sway.

In this manner Mr. Hooper spent a long life, irreproachable in outward act, yet shrouded in dismal suspicions; kind and loving, though unloved, and dimly feared; a man apart from men, shunned in their health and joy, but ever summoned to their aid in mortal anguish. As years wore on, shedding their snows above his sable veil, he acquired a name throughout the New England churches, and they called him Father Hooper. Nearly all his parishioners, who were of mature age when he was settled, had been borne away by many a funeral: he had one congregation in the church, and a more crowded one in the churchyard; and having wrought so late into the evening, and done his work so well, it was now good Father Hooper's turn to rest.

Several persons were visible by the shaded candlelight, in the death chamber of the old clergyman. Natural connections, he had none. But there was the decorously grave, though unmoved physician, seeking only to mitigate the last pangs of the patient whom he could not save. There were the deacons, and other eminently pious members of his church. There, also, was the Reverend Mr. Clark of Westbury, a young and zealous divine, who had ridden in haste to pray by the bedside of the expiring minister. There was the nurse, no hired handmaiden of death, but one whose calm affection had endured thus long, in secrecy, in solitude, amid the chill of age, and would not perish, even at the dying hour. Who, but Elizabeth! And there lay the hoary head of good Father Hooper upon the death pillow, with the black veil still swathed about his brow and reaching down over his face, so that each more difficult gasp of his faint breath caused it to stir. All through life that piece of crape had hung between him and the world; it had separated him from cheerful brother-hood and woman's love, and kept him in that saddest of all prisons, his own heart; and still it lay upon his face, as if to deepen the gloom of his darksome chamber, and shade him from the sunshine of eternity.

For some time previous, his mind had been confused, wavering doubtfully between the past and the present, and hovering forward, as it were, at intervals, into the indistinctness of the world to come. There had been feverish turns, which tossed him from side to side, and wore away what little strength he had. But in his most convulsive struggles, and in the wildest vagaries of his intellect, when no other thought retained its sober influence, he still showed an awful solicitude lest the black veil should slip aside. Even if his bewildered soul could have forgotten, there was a faithful woman at his pillow, who, with averted eyes, would have covered that aged face, which she had last beheld in the comeliness of manhood. At length the death-stricken old man lay quietly in the torpor of mental and bodily exhaustion, with an imperceptible pulse, and breath that grew fainter and fainter, except when a long, deep, and irregular inspiration seemed to prelude the flight of his spirit.

The minister of Westbury approached the bedside.

"Venerable Father Hooper," said he, "the moment of your release is at hand. Are you ready for the lifting of the veil that shuts in time from eternity?"

Father Hooper at first replied merely by a feeble motion of his head; then, apprehensive, perhaps, that his meaning might be doubtful, he exerted himself to speak.

"Yes," said he, in faint accents, "my soul hath a patient weariness until that veil be lifted."

"And is it fitting," resumed the Reverend Mr. Clark, "that a man so given to prayer, of such a blameless example, holy in deed and thought, so far as mortal judgment may pronounce; is it fitting that a father in the church should leave a shadow on his memory, that may seem to blacken a life so pure? I pray you, my venerable brother, let not this thing be! Suffer us to be gladdened by your triumphant aspect, as you go to your reward. Before the veil of eternity be lifted, let me cast this black veil from your face!"

And thus speaking, the Reverend Mr. Clark bent forward to reveal the mystery of so many years. But, exerting a sudden energy that made all the beholders stand aghast, Father Hooper snatched both his hands from be-neath the bedclothes, and pressed them strongly on the black veil, resolute to struggle, if the minister of Westbury would contend with a dying man.

"Never!" cried the veiled clergyman. "On earth, never!"

"Dark old man!" exclaimed the affrighted minister, "with what horrible crime upon your soul are you now passing to the judgment?"

Father Hooper's breath heaved; it rattled in his throat; but, with a mighty effort, grasping forward with his hands, he caught hold of life, and held it back till he should speak. He even raised himself in bed; and there he sat, shivering with the arms of death around him, while the black veil hung down, awful, at that last moment, in the gathered terrors of a lifetime. And yet the faint, sad smile, so often there, now seemed to glimmer from its obscurity, and linger on Father Hooper's lips.

"Why do you tremble at me alone?" cried he, turning his veiled face around the circle of pale spectators. "Tremble also at each other! Have men avoided me, and women shown no pity, and children screamed and fled, only for my black veil? What, but the mystery which it obscurely typifies, has made this piece of crape so awful? When the friend shows his inmost heart to his friend; the lover to his best beloved; when man does not vainly shrink from the eye of his Creator, loathsomely treasuring up the secret of his sin; then deem me a monster, for the symbol beneath which I have lived, and die! I look around me, and, lo! On every visage a Black Veil!"

While his auditors shrank from one another, in mutual affright, Father Hooper fell back upon his pillow, a veiled corpse, with a faint smile lingering on the lips. Still veiled, they laid him in his coffin, and a veiled corpse they bore him to the grave. The grass of many years has sprung up and withered on that grave, the burial stone is moss grown, and good Mr. Hooper's face is dust; but awful is still the thought, that it moldered beneath the Black Veil!

APPENDIXES

APPENDIX A

A BRIEF GUIDE TO READING AND DISCUSSION PROGRAMS FOR SERVICE VOLUNTEERS

M any thousands of people today are making the laudable decision to volunteer or serve. High school students participate in service-learning programs; young adults follow up high school or college with a year of service; older adults sign up to volunteer through their community service center, United Way, or church. Often, service volunteers join organizations that put them to work in high-need areas such as schools, relief agencies, and hospitals—wherever a set of hands can make a difference. Yet few organizations afford their volunteers the opportunity to really reflect on what they are doing, why they are doing it, or the nature of the difference they are making.

One way to help service volunteers reflect more deeply on their activity is to bring them together regularly to read and discuss short texts that raise basic questions about civic activity—texts such as those found in *The Civically Engaged Reader*. We call this practice civic reflection.

As a practice, civic reflection is fairly straightforward. A group of civically engaged people gather around a reading in some hospitable place, preferably with food. A facilitator leads them in a conversation about the reading, asking questions about the text that gradually develop into bigger questions about their own civic ideas and experiences. The result of this simple practice can be wonderfully enriching: it can both challenge and deepen civic engagement, as participants begin to think and talk with peers about the presuppositions and beliefs that underlie their activity.

Readings provide a common and often illuminating object of attention. They also make it easier for participants to engage themselves more deeply and with less personal risk than might be possible in a discussion that depended merely on an exchange of personal stories and testimonials, on one hand, or a lecture format, on the other. Questions about the readings provoke participants to articulate their assumptions and to reflect upon their experience in light of those assumptions. The result, as one participant has observed, is "a resource from which I can draw greater perspective in delivering service."

Here we offer a brief guide to reading and discussion programs for service volunteers, in the form of answers to frequently asked questions. A more extensive guide to civic reflection is available at civicreflection.org, along with numerous descriptions of civic reflection programs.

When and where should discussions take place?

The first thing to consider when planning a civic reflection series is this: logistics matter. Many people are not used to discussing readings in a group, exploring different opinions about complicated ideas, or talking with colleagues about the motives behind their work. The prospect of participating in a civic reflection discussion can therefore make people uncomfortable—so it is important that the conditions surrounding the discussions put people at ease. Schedule discussions at a convenient time of day or night, in an easily accessible and relatively comfortable space. Find a two-hour block on a day when participants already get together. Arrange a room so that people can see each other. Consider starting the discussion after a meal.

Why include food?

The presence of food conveys hospitality—setting the table, as it were. Participants welcome this less formal time together before a serious conversation. It helps people relax and signals a transition from action to reflection.

How frequently will the discussions take place?

In order to sustain energy and make it easier for participants to refer to previous discussions, it helps to schedule sessions every few weeks. Of course, in civic networks that are widely dispersed, this may not be possible.

How many discussions make a series?

It usually takes at least four discussions for participants to become comfortable with one another and the experience. A planned series of five to seven discussions seems to work well, but there is no necessary upper limit to the number of meetings.

Will participants choose to participate, or should they be required to do so?

Many people will not get a clear sense of civic reflection until they try it. On the other hand, coerced participation rarely produces fruitful discussion. You may want to require all the volunteers in your program to participate in the first discussion, after which participation becomes optional. But, for the integrity of the group, those who choose to participate should be expected to attend all remaining sessions.

How many people can participate?

The group can be as small as four and as large as thirty, although the bigger the group, the more likely it is that some people will be reluctant to speak, others will not be able to speak as much as they would like, and still others will not be heard. The ideal size seems to be between eight and fourteen.

Can both volunteers and staff participate?

Civic reflection provides a rare opportunity to build conversation across dividing lines about the purposes of an organization—and to help volunteers and staff come to know each other in a fuller way as persons. Therefore, staff should be included if possible.

Will readings be distributed beforehand?

At the start of a series, it may be helpful to use readings that are no more than two or three pages long—short enough to read aloud together. This enables participants to become familiar with the process and ensures that everyone can participate equally. As a series progresses, participants may be ready—even eager—to read texts in advance.

What kinds of readings work best?

Readings ought to open up rather than close off vigorous discussion. They should be challenging and provocative—and also accessible to any participant willing to read carefully and think patiently. The current hot article or self-help book may be hard to discuss simply because it is current; strong opinions and emotions have been established before the conversation even begins. Likewise, policy papers can be difficult to discuss because the expertise of the author seems to settle things in an authoritative way. The meaning of a story, poem, or passage of philosophy from another time and place is not so easily settled and, as a result, is likely to generate more fruitful discussion. The readings in this anthology provide a good place to start.

What kinds of discussion questions work best?

Questions are the engine of civic reflection. They move discussion forward; they ask participants to consider and reconsider the grounds of their opinions; they even move organizations to reexamine and recommit to their goals. It can be useful to orient every discussion around one or two large and deep questions, but to get at these large questions patiently. This often means paying attention to a specific passage or passages in the text itself.

The best opening questions are those for which the facilitator does not have a ready-made answer or answers; they are genuine and not rhetorical, and they are almost always rooted in a passage of the text that demands interpretation. (One way to think about discussion: when *planning* the discussion, think big; when *beginning* the discussion, ask small and ponder details; as the discussion moves along, move back toward big.)

Appendix B provides a set of discussion questions for each selection in this anthology. Each set of questions moves from the details of the text toward a more general consideration of the topic or ideas that the reading addresses, from questions about what specific passages mean to questions that ponder bigger issues raised by the selection.

Should the facilitator come from outside or within the group?

There are advantages to both. The presence of an external facilitator may make the discussions feel like a special occasion, with whatever additional energy that might bring. And, ideally, an external facilitator will also be a trained facilitator—not necessarily an expert in any particular field, but skilled at leading discussions. The great virtue of internal facilitators is that they are more likely to know the organization, its aims, and the questions rumbling around underneath the shared activities of participants. One solution is to pair an external and an internal facilitator and have them work together.

Why have a facilitator at all?

At the start of a series, participants may be uncomfortable with civic reflection, for all sorts of reasons. They might be intimidated by texts or the names of "great" authors; they might want to believe what they believe without feeling like they have to scrutinize it; they might be shy or unfamiliar with certain words other people seem to know; they might read with difficulty; they might find disagreement threatening; they might not be familiar with the cadence and etiquette of group discussion. For these reasons and many others, discussions work best when one or two people lead them.

What does the facilitator do?

It is true, as the term suggests, that facilitators *facilitate* discussions. They make it easier for people to talk with one another and to share equally in the conversation. But they make it easier so that participants can do something hard: to think and talk about serious questions provoked by complex texts and to identify and explore deep assumptions.

If you are interested in learning more about facilitating civic reflection or other text-based discussions, we encourage you to consult the following two resources. One is the Great Books Foundation, which has been helping groups engage in discussion of texts for more than fifty years. More information about the principles of Shared Inquiry, the Great Books Foundation's text-based, Socratic method of discussion, can be found on pp. xvii–xviii of this book's front matter, following the editors' preface. Another resource is civicreflection.org, a Web site devoted to assisting, evaluating, and improving the practice of reading and discussion, specifically in civic groups.

Finally, what do actual civic reflection series look like?

We conclude this brief guide with an example, a civic reflection series for AmeriCorps service volunteers. Additional program descriptions can be found online at civicreflection.org.

PROGRAM EXAMPLE: JUSTICE TALKING

J ustice Talking is a discussion series administered by the Illinois Humanities Council that gives Chicago-area AmeriCorps volunteers, staff, and alumni an opportunity to reflect on their chosen form of civic engagement.

Justice Talking generates challenging, open discussions about service, justice, and civic engagement. Each session is oriented around one or two brief but provocative readings. Group size is kept below fifteen when possible, and all sessions are led by a trained facilitator. In any given session, a group might look at, say, Jean-Jacques Rousseau's consideration of our obligation to others, or Mary E. Wilkins Freeman's portrait of service gone awry, or Langston Hughes's treatment of the consequences of difference. Whatever the subject, participants are asked to think, speak, and listen carefully. In grappling with these readings and the questions they raise, participants can gain a deeper understanding of their own service and practical ways to improve it.

The set of questions and readings for Justice Talking is dynamic. As groups proceed through the series, they are encouraged to make suggestions, which the organizers endeavor to incorporate. Past questions and readings—some of which are found in The Civically Engaged Reader—have included the following:

What is injustice?

II Samuel, 11–12:15
J. M. Whitfield, "America"

What is justice?

Selections from Plato's Republic
Martin Luther King Jr., "Letter from Birmingham Jail"

What is compassion? What is duty?

Jean-Jacques Rousseau, The Reveries of the Solitary Walker

Gwendolyn Brooks, "The Lovers of the Poor"
William Carlos Williams, "The Use of Force"

What is a right? What does it mean to claim a right?

Henry MacNeal Turner, "I Shall Not Beg for My Rights"
United States Constitution, Amendments 1–10
United Nations Declaration of Universal Human Rights

Why do we try to do (or be) good? How do we do good?

Benjamin Franklin, excerpts from *The Autobiography*
Dave Eggers, "Where Were We"

What others, or what sorts of others, do we care for?

Toni Morrison, "Recitatif"
J. M. Coetzee, *The Lives of Animals*
George Orwell, "Reflections on Gandhi"
Langston Hughes, "Theme for English B"

Why choose to serve?

Martin Luther King Jr., "The Drum Major Instinct"
Mary E. Wilkins Freeman, "Luella Miller"

What should social leadership look like?

Charles Waddell Chesnutt, "The Wife of His Youth"

APPENDIX B

QUESTIONS FOR DISCUSSION

The selections in this anthology are complex and provocative, inviting us to grapple with their meaning. For the civically engaged reader, they offer an additional invitation: to explore the beliefs and assumptions that underlie and motivate civic activity, to understand better what we do and why we do it. Discussion of these selections with others is an excellent way to begin and to deepen the process of exploration. With this in mind, we have provided a set of discussion questions for each of the selections.

In each set, the questions broaden from ones that ask about the text itself to ones that encourage you to draw connections between the reading and your own beliefs, experiences, and civic activities. For each selection you will find more questions than a single discussion can possibly explore. By picking and choosing among these questions, you can create a path through the text—and through your own civic experience—that is interesting and stimulating to you and your discussion partners.

PART I—ASSOCIATING

Aristotle, Selection from *Politics*

Why does Aristotle consider the state or political community to be the highest form of association?

What does Aristotle mean when he says, "man is by nature a political animal"?

Why does Aristotle claim that "he who by nature and not by mere accident is without a state is either a bad man or above humanity"?

According to Aristotle, what is the difference between the bare necessities of life and the good life?

What distinction does Aristotle make between the association of humans and the association of other gregarious animals such as bees?

What do communities and associations make possible for humans? What goods do they serve?

Is justice possible outside the political community?

What associations and communities do you think are most essential to the good life?

Whom do you most need to associate with, and for what purpose?

Constantine Cavafy, "Waiting for the Barbarians"

Why do the people in the poem believe that "the barbarians are due here today"?

What reason do the people have for associating with each other in the forum while they are waiting for the barbarians?

What does waiting for the barbarians enable the people to accomplish that they couldn't do by just carrying on their usual activities?

Are the actions of the people motivated by fear of the barbarians?

When the people finally disperse and head home, why are they "lost in thought"? What might they be thinking?

Is waiting for barbarians one of the reasons people form associations with each other?

Have you ever gathered with others to wait for barbarians? What happened?

Henry MacNeal Turner, "I Shall Not Beg for My Rights"

Why does Turner say, "The great question, sir, is this: am I man?"

What reason does Turner have for emphasizing his own military service?

For Turner, what is the difference between claiming a right and begging for one?

What right is Turner claiming? To whom or what is Turner appealing when he claims it?

What is a right? How are rights different from personal preferences? What are some examples of rights?

Who has the responsibility for deciding which rights exist?

Do rights require protection? Who has the responsibility for protecting them?

Is there any relation between rights and duties? If so, what are some examples of how this relation works?

Abraham Rodriguez Jr., "The Boy Without a Flag"

Why does the boy in this story stop saluting the flag? Why does he start again to salute it?

What reasons for saluting—or not saluting—the flag do the adults in the story give the boy? What other reasons beside those offered would you give the boy?

Why is Miss Colon called "our" Miss Colon?

Why does the father behave as he does, first at home and later when he is called to the school?

Why, at the end of the story, does the boy link his father and the flag?

Do the adults and children in the story connect with one another?

What does this story say about how children develop a civic identity and a sense of belonging to a larger community?

How do children decide what to salute? How do you decide?

Imtiaz Dharker, "They'll Say, 'She Must Be from Another Country'"

Why is the statement "She must be / from another country" an answer to all the situations Dharker's narrator describes?

What does the narrator mean by "country"?

What does the narrator mean when she says the country "where all of us live . . . doesn't look like a country"?

To whom is the narrator referring as "we" in the last stanza?

Why is the narrator finally "happy to say . . . I must be / from another country"?

Franz Kafka, "Fellowship"

Why does the narrator say that he and the other four are "friends"? What is the reason that they continue to associate with one another?

How is the sixth one annoying to the first five? What don't they "want to be six"?

Is there anything that the first five would need to know about the sixth for him to join them?

Why is the narrator skeptical about "long explanations"?

Why does the sixth keep coming back?

Why do you think Kafka titled this piece "Fellowship"?

Where does fellowship originate, and what sustains it?

Jane Addams, "Earliest Impressions"

Why does Addams offer an account of her earliest impressions? How can recalling childhood impressions provide insight into our lives as adults?

Why does Addams emphasize the importance of memorable nightmares and dreams among her earliest impressions?

What does Addams mean by the "moral concerns of life" into which, as she says, her father drew her?

Why did Addams's father discourage Addams from wearing her cloak to church? Do you agree or disagree with him?

What does Addams mean by the "old question eternally suggested by the inequalities of the human lot"? How would you respond to this question?

If you look back on your own childhood, what are some of your own earliest impressions of the "moral concerns of life"?

Does your own life confirm Addams's theory that "our genuine impulses may be connected with our childish experiences"?

Are there connections between your own earliest impressions and your impulse to serve—or not to serve—others?

Alden Nowlan, "He Sits Down on the Floor of a School for the Retarded"

What does the narrator mean when he says that to the audience, the band is "everybody/who has ever appeared on TV"?

Why does the narrator lie to the boy seeking an autograph?

What does the young woman want from the narrator when she puts her head on his shoulder?

Is the narrator correct in saying, "It's what we all want, in the end, / to be held"?

When the narrator and the woman hug, why does he refer to her as "this retarded woman"?

Why does the poem end two hundred thousand years in the past?

Adam Smith, Selection from *The Theory of Moral Sentiments*

According to Smith, what explains the relation between our feelings and the feelings of others?

What does Smith mean when he says that more imaginative people are also more compassionate? Do you think he is correct in thinking this?

Why does Smith claim that awareness of someone else's compassion relieves the person for whom the compassion is felt? Does the compassionate person also feel relief?

Is Smith correct in asserting that an individual's disposition and situation have major influence on his or her capacity to identify with others?

Can we feel compassion for those more fortunate than ourselves?

How important is sympathy in civic activity and in service work more specifically?

Alexis de Tocqueville, Selection from *Democracy in America*

According to Tocqueville, why are Americans "forever forming associations"? Why do Americans associate more than the English or the French?

What link does Tocqueville see between the art of association and the growth of equality?

Why does Tocqueville conclude that the art of association must spread at the same speed as the equality of conditions?

In Tocqueville's opinion, why should government not be allowed to "usurp" the functions of private associations?

According to Tocqueville, how do Americans develop their habit and taste for serving? Do you think he is correct?

Does Tocqueville's assessment of this aspect of American life seem accurate to you?

W. E. B. Du Bois, Selection from *The Souls of Black Folk*

What does Du Bois mean by "these little things that are most elusive to the grasp and yet most essential to any clear conception of the group life taken as a whole"? Why does he think that these things are "peculiarly true of the South"?

Why does Du Bois assert that the destiny of "black freedmen" is "bound up with that of the nation"?

According to Du Bois, why is the "color line" so strong "in the higher walks of life," while it wavers and disappears "at the bottom of the social group"?

What fundamental problem is Du Bois addressing in this selection? According to Du Bois, why does charity "not touch the kernel of the problem"?

What social arrangement does Du Bois have in mind when he calls for a "union of intelligence and sympathy across the color line"?

Does the lack of intellectual and sympathetic unity between people of different races that Du Bois describes still exist today in America?

From your experience, what promotes connections between people of different backgrounds?

Langston Hughes, "Theme for English B"

In what sense will the page that comes out of the teacher's assignment be "true"?

Why does the narrator respond to the assignment by thinking of differences?

What sorts of differences between people matter most to the narrator?

What separates the narrator from his classmates and his teacher? What unifies them?

Would we interpret this poem differently if its author were elderly, or a woman, or a white man?

In order to educate a student, what should a teacher know about him or her? What should a student know about the teacher in order to learn most effectively?

How much of our shared work depends on each of us knowing about the others involved?

What do we most need to know about the people we work with?

Toni Morrison, "Recitatif"

What accounts for the initial connection between Twyla and Roberta? What enables them to connect over time?

Why do Twyla and Roberta continue to ask about each other's mother?

Why does Maggie become much more important as the story moves toward its conclusion?

What do Twyla and Roberta tend to talk about when they run into each other? Are there topics they seem to avoid discussing?

Which characters are white and which are black? What difference would it make if you could tell the difference?

Is this story chiefly about relations between people of different races? What else is it about?

In what ways does the story inspire hope? In what ways does it inspire dismay?

Robert Frost, "Mending Wall"

Do the narrator and the neighbor have similar or different perspectives on the value of the wall?

What is a "good fence"?

Do good fences make good neighbors in this poem?

How can fences both divide and connect people?

Is there something at work in your community that doesn't love a wall? What is it?

Through what kinds of associations do you and your neighbors meet and mend fences?

PART II—SERVING

Mary E. Wilkins Freeman, "Luella Miller"

What is the "wild horror and frenzied fear" that the villagers have inherited from their ancestors?

Why does Lydia Anderson tell the story of Luella Miller?

Why do so many characters in the story serve Luella? What kind of help or service do they offer?

Why does Lydia help Luella? How does her help differ from that offered by other characters in the story?

Why does Lydia tell others about her vision of Luella and the other dead people, even though "she did not expect to be believed"?

What, if anything, should the townspeople have done differently for Luella?

Why does Freeman tell us that at the end of Lydia's life, a neighbor is living with her and helping her out?

Is there anything hopeful about the ending of the story?

What does this story imply about serving others?

Margaret Sutherland, "Dry Dock"

What is the meaning of the story's title?

Why does the narrator decide to be a volunteer? Who is she trying to serve?

Why does the narrator tell us, "I know I've really not come near, not touched," when Michael grips her hand?

How are the lists that make up Michael's book the "facts of life"?

What does the narrator mean when she tells us that her well-meant altruism was "paradoxically, given back to me"?

What is an effective volunteer? Is the narrator effective?

Jan Beatty, "Saving the Crippled Boy"

Why does the narrator in this poem kiss Bob Saunders?

From what does the narrator want "to save him, just to save him"?

What makes the narrator overcome her initial aversion to Bob?

Why does the narrator make a point of telling us that her tenth-grade experience occurred "years before I knew about *mercy fucks*"?

Why does the narrator grow "small and hard" when she tells Bob, "*This is what you can't have*"? Why does this experience lead her to think about her "sick, ailing heart"?

Why do you think the narrator recalls this tenth-grade experience so vividly, many years later? How do you think this experience might afterward have affected her capacity to help others?

Was the narrator's attempt to save Bob a good deed?

Under what circumstances do we find ourselves like the narrator in the poem, growing "small and hard" when we do good deeds? How is it that doing good deeds can sometimes have this effect on us?

Henri Barbusse, "The Eleventh"

Why does the house admit ten vagabonds each month? How does the recollection of the eleventh person, who is not admitted to the house, affect the narrator's ability to serve the others?

Why are there no mirrors in the house?

Why does the narrator finally go to the master and ask for another post? Why does he consider his monthly deed "evil"?

Does the tradition of poor relief practiced by the house do any good?

Have you ever seen your own "eleventh" face-to-face? What did you see?

Who gets shut out when you give and serve?

How do you stay committed to giving and serving—either in a particular organization or as an individual—when you are confronted by difficult choices and your own doubts?

What advice would you give to the narrator of the story?

William James, "The Moral Equivalent of War"

According to James, what benefits does war offer?

What does James mean by the "martial virtues"? Why does James insist on the importance of the martial type of character?

How does James think that the "civic temper" can be inflamed without also inflaming the military temper?

What, in addition to fear, might awaken the "higher ranges of men's spiritual energy"?

What does it mean for something to be "the moral equivalent of war"?

Why does James recommend "conscription of the whole youthful population to form for a certain number of years a part of the army enlisted against nature"?

Would you also make a case for the kind of national service James recommends? If so, would you make the case in James's terms or for other reasons?

Jane Addams, "The Subjective Necessity of Social Settlements"

What does Addams mean by the desire of young people to share "the race life"?

According to Addams, what is the central message of Christianity? How does she think this message can lead to service?

What is the experience, accompanied by a "forlorn feeling," that Addams describes in the second paragraph of her speech? What are the "glimpses" that this experience provides?

What prevents us from acting on the sense of our connection to other human beings that Addams describes?

How does Addams think that the Settlement can "relieve, at the same time, the overaccumulation at one end of society and the destitution at the other"?

Does Addams help you to understand your own motives for service and those of young people today who join youth service programs?

Are there important motives for service that she leaves out of her account?

Martin Luther King Jr., "The Drum Major Instinct"

Why does King think that the desire to be first is a problem? Does he think that there is a solution to this problem?

According to King, what is the relation between the drum major instinct and the race problem?

What does King mean when he says that the drum major instinct is good "if you use it right"?

What is the "new norm of greatness" that King invokes? According to King, how can everybody be great?

For King, what is the relation between death and service?

How does King finally help us understand what we can do to "make of this old world a new world"?

How would you convince others to serve?

The Book of Ruth

Why does Ruth stay with Naomi? Is she admirable for doing so?

How is Ruth, according to the Hebrew meaning of her name, an embodiment of compassion?

What is the reason for Ruth's apparent conversion?

Why does Boaz treat Ruth with such generosity?

Do these people in this story give out of duty or for other reasons? Which of these gifts are obligatory and which are freely given?

Does giving necessarily imply that the receiver should reciprocate? Is reciprocity important to the characters in this story?

How do you decide when you should pay back what has been given to you? When do you expect those to whom you have given to reciprocate?

Walt Whitman, Selection from *Specimen Days*

Why does Whitman call these injured soldiers "specimen cases"? Why is he visiting them in the hospital?

What does Whitman mean when he tells us that the dying boy he visits did not know "the heart of the stranger that hover'd near"?

Why does Whitman make a point to "ventilate the financial question"? Why is this topic a question?

What does Whitman think is the reason that "good women and men" send him money to distribute to strangers? How would you compare the value of their contribution to Whitman's own?

Why does Whitman qualify his statement about the generosity of Americans by saying that they only give "when once sure of their object"?

What are the "magnetic sympathy and unction" that Whitman says are "sovereign still"? Over what are they sovereign?

In his ministering to the soldiers, does Whitman give well?

Gwendolyn Brooks, "The Lovers of the Poor"

What is the purpose of the Ladies Betterment League?

What do the ladies hope to accomplish, and why, in this case, do they seem to fail?

Who is the "citizeness" the ladies encounter? Why does the narrator call her a "citizeness"?

What does the narrator mean by the word "loathe-love"?

Why does Brooks make a point of letting us know about the ladies' life of luxury in the midst of describing their visit to a slum?

How does your own service organization resemble or differ from the Ladies Betterment League?

Adam Davis, "What We Don't Talk About When We Don't Talk About Service"

What distinguishes community service from other forms of service?

Why, according to Davis, do people serve? Do you agree with these explanations? What else might motivate service?

For whom is service good, and in what ways?

Why might service be a difficult subject to discuss?

Where do you see inequality in the world around you? Which instances of inequality are troubling? Which instances seem acceptable or just?

Does service address inequality?

PART III—GIVING

Dave Eggers, "Where Were We"

Why aren't we told the narrator's name?

Why does the narrator want to get rid of the money that came to him "in a windfall kind of way"? Why does he consider getting rid of it a "purging" that "would provide clarity"?

Why do the narrator and Hand combine the ideas of traveling around the world in a week and getting rid of the narrator's money?

Why do so few situations seem "right" to the narrator? What does it mean for a situation to be "right"?

How does Jack's death influence the narrator's actions when he receives the money?

What does Raymond mean when he says, "There is travel and there are babies. . . . Everything else is death"? Why does he suggest that the narrator and Hand stay in Senegal?

Why is the narrator so disturbed, toward the end of the story, when he is called "the big boss"?

What do you think the narrator and Hand should have done differently in giving away the money?

Jean-Jacques Rousseau, Selection from *The Reveries of the Solitary Walker*

When Rousseau finally unraveled what caused him to make the same detour several times on his walk, why couldn't he keep from laughing?

Why does Rousseau give money to the crippled boy? Why does doing so give Rousseau pleasure?

Why is Rousseau disturbed by the boy's familiar attitude in addressing him as Monsieur Rousseau? Why does this lead Rousseau to avoid the boy?

How can the initial pleasure of giving become unpleasant and onerous?

According to Rousseau, how is the contract between benefactor and beneficiary "the holiest of all"?

What does Rousseau mean when he says that the pleasures that "come to us immediately from nature do not rise so high" as those that come from fulfilling our duties?

Having been a benefactor, do we have a responsibility to continue giving to our beneficiary? When is it right to cease giving to a beneficiary?

Maya Angelou, "The Sweetness of Charity"

What does Angelou mean when she says that, "giving liberates the soul"?

Why does Angelou think the fact that we can't influence the speed of time makes it "an imponderably valuable gift"?

According to Angelou, how much should one give?

Why do the donors in Angelou's audience strike her as "ashamed of themselves"?

Is being philanthropic different from being charitable?

How does Angelou think that benefactors can "feel estranged from the objects of their generosity"? Why would estrangement prevent them from taking "little, if any, relish from their acts of charity"?

How does Angelou think we should "change the way we think of charity"?

Why is charity sometimes considered "degrading to accept" and "debasing to give"?

What is charity, and why is it often called sweet? Should we find it sweet?

Pablo Neruda, "The Lamb and the Pinecone"

Why does the boy on the other side of the fence leave the sheep? Why does he disappear after leaving it?

Why does Neruda leave his treasured pinecone for the boy?

What is the widening of the "boundaries of our being" that according to Neruda comes from the affection of those "unknown to us"?

How does the exchange of the sheep and the pinecone bring home to Neruda that "all of humanity is somehow together"?

Why does Neruda call this exchange of gifts "mysterious"?

For something to be a gift, does there have to be an exchange of some kind?

What is the most enduring gift you have received? The best gift you have given?

Andrew Carnegie, *The Gospel of Wealth*, Part I

According to Carnegie, why is there a growing gap in the living conditions of the rich and poor in American society? Why does he seem to welcome this gap?

Why does Carnegie think that individualism is such a good thing for all of us?

Why does Carnegie oppose both the practice of leaving great wealth to one's descendants and the practice of leaving a bequest of money for public purposes?

Who does Carnegie think should be the recipients of philanthropic giving? How does he think philanthropists should decide how much to give?

Do you think that Carnegie's ideas about the problem of the rich and the poor in American society are still valid? How wide can the gap between wealth and poverty become before it is a problem for society?

If you could sit down with Carnegie today as a fellow philanthropist to talk about his advice on giving, would you agree or disagree with him? If you disagreed, what arguments would you use?

Ralph Waldo Emerson, Selection from "Self-Reliance"

What does Emerson mean by a "nonconformist"? Why does he say that a nonconformist "must not be hindered by the name of goodness"?

How could following Emerson's principle that "the only right is what is after my constitution; the only wrong what is against it" allow for the possibility of philanthropic giving?

What does Emerson mean when he advises, "Your goodness must have some edge to it"?

According to Emerson, what is a "wicked dollar"? Why does he think it would take "manhood" to withhold giving it?

What does Emerson mean when he says, "I grudge the dollar, the dime, the cent I give to such men as do not belong to me and to whom I do not belong"? Is it good and right to give only to those persons to whom you belong and who belong to you?

Sogyal Rinpoche, "Compassion: The Wish-Fulfilling Jewel"

Why is Asanga confident that his solitary retreat will result in a vision of Maitreya? What does he hope the vision will give him?

What reason does Asanga have for thinking that his spiritual practice is more valuable and less absurd than the activity of the man trying to make a needle out of an iron bar?

Does Asanga think that the man trying to make a needle and the man trying to move a rock are like himself or completely different?

Why does Asanga encounter the dog only after he decided that his retreat was hopeless and left for good?

What makes Asanga act compassionately toward the dog? Why are we told that he closed his eyes before removing the maggots with his tongue?

Why did Asanga's twelve years of spiritual practice only "slightly" dissolve what was preventing him from seeing Maitreya? Why did compassion entirely remove the "obscurations"?

Why doesn't Asanga understand "the boundless power of compassion" until he performs the test of Maitreya's invisibility in the marketplace? Does Maitreya show compassion for Asanga?

What is given in acting compassionately? Are there different levels of compassion just as there are different levels of giving?

Bertolt Brecht, "A Bed for the Night"

Why does the narrator begin the poem by telling us that what he is going to describe is hearsay? Why is he so specific about the location?

Why does the man in the poem solicit help for the homeless by standing outside in the winter weather? Couldn't he accomplish the same result of providing beds by collecting money somewhere more comfortable to himself?

Why does the narrator make a point of telling us that a bed for the night "won't change the world . . . won't improve relations among men . . . will not shorten the age of exploitation"?

In speaking of the men who have a bed for the night, why does the narrator say that the snow is "meant for them"?

In the middle of the poem, why does the narrator emphasize that the reader is holding a book? Why does he tell the reader not to put down the book, and then proceed to repeat the previous six lines with only slight variations?

What motivates people to try to put themselves into situations similar to those of people they would help?

Elizabeth Lynn and D. Susan Wisely, "Four Traditions of Philanthropy"

What are some of the strengths and weaknesses of the three philanthropic traditions of relief, improvement, and reform?

Are there other traditions of philanthropy and serving not included in the three traditions that are described? If so, what are the strengths and weaknesses of these other traditions?

What do Lynn and Wisely mean by civic engagement? Why do they think this tradition is "an especially important philanthropic response" at the beginning of the twenty-first century?

Is civic engagement a tradition like the others?

Can you identify examples of these traditions in your own giving and serving or that of the organization for which you work? Does one tradition dominate? Is one tradition entirely absent?

How important might it be to participate in any of these traditions as an engaged citizen? How important might it be to participate in all of them?

Moses Maimonides, Selection from the *Mishneh Torah*

What makes the kind of giving first described superior to the other seven? Why is the highest degree of almsgiving the only one that Maimonides supports with a quotation from scripture?

Why does Maimonides think that it is a higher level of giving when both the giver and receiver are unknown to each other than when just one or the other is unknown?

Why does Maimonides call these "degrees" of giving, rather than stages or steps, as we often hear them described?

What reasons does Maimonides give for the order of the degrees? Do you think they are in the proper order?

Is it wrong, or just a lesser good, to give "with a frowning countenance"?

Which of these degrees of charity best describes your giving practices?

Anna Akhmatova, "If All Who Have Begged Help"

What does the narrator want at first from those who have begged her for help?

Why doesn't the narrator say whether she was able to give help to those who begged for it?

What kind of strength does the narrator recognize in the people she describes? What does she mean when she says that "they shared with me their strength"?

What is "even this" that the narrator says she can bear?

Why do we respond or not to someone begging for help?

What do we receive from those who beg for our help?

PART IV—LEADING

Charles Waddell Chesnutt, "The Wife of His Youth"

What is the Blue Vein Society? What are the "correct social standards" that the Blue Vein Society is charged with establishing and maintaining?

What do the Blue Veins mean when they say that their light-colored members "had had better opportunities to qualify themselves for membership" in the organization?

Why does Ryder decide to put on the ball?

Why does Liza Jane believe that Sam Taylor would want her to find him?

What "manner of man" does Ryder see when he looks at the photo of Sam Taylor?

Why does Ryder tell the story of Liza Jane and Sam Taylor to the guests at the ball? Why does he ask the guests to judge whether Liza Jane's husband should acknowledge her?

At the end of the story, why is Liza Jane dressed like an old woman? What does Ryder mean when he introduces her as "the wife of my youth"?

In light of Ryder's quote from *Hamlet*, "To thine own self be true," to which self—Ryder or Taylor—should he be true?

How is Ryder's revelation likely to affect the Blue Vein Society and his "social leadership" of it?

How can we reconcile the competing claims of our origins and aspirations? How can we lead others to move forward without betraying their own origins?

II Samuel, Chapters 11–12

What authority does Uriah appeal to when he refuses to follow David's wish that he should go to his house and wife?

Why does Joab instruct the messenger taking news to David not to mention that Uriah has been killed unless "the king's anger rises" and he questions why the battle was fought close to the city walls?

When Nathan comes to let David know the Lord's displeasure, why does he begin by telling David the story of the two men and the lamb? How is the story related to what happens in chapter 11?

What is "the thing" that the rich man in the story has done that makes David angry?

Who was wronged as a result of David's actions? Is it necessary for those who have been harmed to be aware of what has been done to them in order for us to judge that they were wronged?

How do we judge that a leader has committed wrongs? What different standards of conduct are there for leaders than for other people?

How should a leader be persuaded that he or she has committed wrongs? Who is likely to do this most effectively?

Graham Greene, "The Destructors"

What keeps the Wormsley Common gang together? What is the purpose of the rules that the gang follows?

Why does the leadership of the gang shift from Blackie to T., the newest recruit? How do the gang members know that the leadership has shifted?

When the leadership passes back to Blackie during the destruction of the house, why are we told that T.'s "authority had gone with his ambiguity"?

Why does T. want to destroy Old Misery's house? Why is the house referred to as being "crippled"?

Why do the gang members agree to T.'s plan? How does T.'s ability to give organization to the gang's activities help to secure his leadership?

What does the narrator mean in saying that "destruction after all is a form of creation"? What is the gang creating by destroying Old Misery's house?

In the final stages of the destruction, why did "the question of leadership" no longer concern the gang? Without leadership, what gave direction to their work?

At the end of the story, why does the lorry driver think that the destruction of the house is funny?

Is there any sense in which the boys in this gang are "civically engaged"?

Who should take the lead in judging whether something has outlived its usefulness in the community and must be destroyed? What should be taken into consideration in making such judgments?

Franz Kafka, "The Helmsman"

Why does the narrator ask the stranger and then the crew, "Am I the helmsman"?

Why are we not told the reason that the "tall, dark man" wants control of the helm? Why does the narrator want to prevent him from having control?

What does the narrator expect from the crew when he summons them? Why does he call them both "men" and "comrades"?

Why is the crew both "tired" and "powerful"?

Why does the narrator refer to his rival as a "stranger"? Why is it that the crew "had eyes only for the stranger"?

What is the meaning of the nod that the crew gives to the narrator as they withdraw?

Contrast the ways in which the narrator and the stranger try to establish their leadership of the crew.

Why is there no mention in the story of the ship's captain?

What is the meaning of the narrator's questions at the end of the story?

Toni Cade Bambara, "The Lesson"

Why does Miss Moore "take responsibility for the young ones' education"? Why do the parents of the children make them go along with Miss Moore?

Why does Miss Moore take the children to the toy store?

If Sylvia never talks to Miss Moore, what makes her ask how much a real boat costs? Why doesn't Miss Moore give her an answer to her question?

Why does Sylvia feel "shame" about going into the toy store?

What is Miss Moore trying to teach the children in telling them, "Where we are is who we are"?

What lesson is Miss Moore is trying to teach the children? Do any of the children learn it?

At the end of the story, what does it mean that Sylvia is going "to think this day through"?

How would you describe Miss Moore's style of teaching? Is it the right style for the children in the story?

How can teaching be a kind of leadership? How can a teacher lead students to aspire to better lives without making them ashamed of the lives they are now living?

How can you lead those who seem not to want to be led?

William Carlos Williams, "The Use of Force"

If the parents summoned the doctor to help their daughter, why did they eye him "up and down distrustfully"? What does the doctor mean when he refers to "such cases"?

Why does the doctor tell us in the same breath that he had fallen in love with "the savage brat," while the parents, who are trying to help their daughter, are contemptible to him?

When the doctor tells Mathilda, "You're old enough to understand what I'm saying," what is it that he thinks she should understand?

Who is responsible for escalating the battle between Mathilda and the doctor? Why does the doctor go "beyond reason" in his vehement attempt to get Mathilda to cooperate?

Why aren't the usual reasons for wanting to help a patient and protect others from infection the "operatives" that drive the doctor to use force on Mathilda? What is the "adult shame" that makes him go "on to the end"?

Who should have the authority to determine when is it justifiable to use force against another to protect someone from his or her "own idiocy"? Who should have the authority to justify the use of force as a case of "social necessity"?

How can we reconcile the use of force with the effort to provide help?

Benjamin Franklin, Selection from *The Autobiography of Benjamin Franklin*

If Franklin is trying to "conquer all that either Natural Inclination, Custom, or Company" might lead him into, what is leading him into his project for moral improvement? Why does he call the project "bold and arduous"?

Why didn't Franklin's initial confidence in his sense of right and wrong enable him to carry out his project?

Why does Franklin think that a "Method" will make it possible for him to carry out his project? What does he mean by a "Method"?

Unlike the lists of moral virtues Franklin has come across in his reading, why does he make his own list consist of "a few Names with more Ideas" attached to each virtue? What guides Franklin in his ordering of the virtues?

Why are so many of the virtues that Franklin lists accompanied by guidelines for what he will avoid doing rather than guidelines for what he will do? In the comparison he makes to gardening, why does he emphasize what he will weed out rather than what he will plant and cultivate?

Since the virtue of "Order" is so central to Franklin's method, what does he mean in telling us that this "gave me the most Trouble"?

In concluding that "*a speckled Ax was best*," is Franklin giving up his project? Are there virtues on his list that would support his conclusion that "a benevolent Man should allow a few Faults in himself"?

For Franklin, is there any difference between virtues that improve one's private life and virtues that make one a better citizen?

Why is the virtue of "Humility," which Franklin says gave him "so much Weight with my Fellow Citizens," the only one that involves imitating the behavior of others—Jesus and Socrates?

Does Franklin become the kind of person he originally aspired to be?

What virtues, if any, do you think are missing from Franklin's list? Are there any virtues on the list that you think do not belong?

Ursula K. Le Guin, "The Ones Who Walk Away from Omelas"

What demonstrates that the happiness of the citizens of Omelas is "based on a just discrimination of what is necessary, what is neither necessary nor destructive, and what is destructive"? Why does the narrator invite us to let our imagination elaborate on the middle category but not the other two?

Why does the narrator think that we are not able to believe in and accept the description of "the festival, the city, the joy"? Why does she think that the description of the suffering child will make Omelas more credible to us?

What do the people of Omelas understand that leads them to conclude that the suffering child "has to be there"? What kind of explanation of the child's suffering do they give to their children "whenever they seem capable of understanding"?

Who or what sets the "strict and absolute" terms that "there may not even be a kind word spoken to the child"?

What "terrible paradox" must those who observe the suffering child face? Why do they come to accept the child's confinement as "the terrible justice of reality"?

Why does the narrator think that the "one more thing" she has to tell about those who walk away from Omelas is "quite incredible"? Why does she tell us about them after she has made Omelas credible for us?

Who are the ones who walk away from Omelas? Why does each of them go alone?

Why is the place toward which they walk "even less imaginable to most of us than the city of happiness"?

Have you ever made a decision to walk away from Omelas? What happened?

Do the "goodness and grace" of any society depend on the existence of the suffering child?

Can the terms that determine a society's well-being be so "strict and absolute" that there is no remedy for the injustice that is the basis for its well-being?

Billy Collins, "The History Teacher"

What is the teacher trying to protect his students from? Why does he assume they are "innocent"?

Why does Collins make the teacher's explanations of history comical to us? Would they also be comical to his students?

Are the teacher's explanations of historical events just harmless stories?

Why are we told that when "the children would leave his classroom," they would "torment the weak and the smart"?

Why does Collins depict the teacher gathering up his notes and walking home "past flower beds and white picket fences" while the children are fighting in the playground?

At the end of the poem, why is the teacher wondering whether his students will believe his story about the Boer War?

Is a teacher ever justified in altering or suppressing the truth about what he or she is teaching to students? Are there some positions of authority that require protecting other people from the truth?

Abraham Lincoln, Second Inaugural Address

Why doesn't Lincoln use the occasion of his second inaugural address to offer a "statement, somewhat in detail, of a course to be pursued"?

According to Lincoln, why couldn't the American Civil War be avoided, considering that "All dreaded it—all sought to avert it"? Why does he emphasize that "both parties deprecated war"?

Why does Lincoln point out, "Both read the same Bible, and pray to the same God"? Why doesn't he claim that God is on the side of those who oppose slavery?

Why does Lincoln discuss the meaning of the war in terms of "the providence of God" rather than in terms of the human interests that "all knew" were the cause of the war?

Who is Lincoln addressing when he says, "Let us strive on to finish the work we are in"? Who is it that should finish this work?

Why does Lincoln conclude—rather than begin—his address with his call to Americans to act "with malice toward none; with charity for all"? What does he mean by charity?

What is the "just" and "lasting" peace that Lincoln asks his listeners to do all they can to achieve? Why does he add that this peace is not only "among ourselves" but "with all nations"?

How should a leader speak to divisive factions in order to reunite them?

Should our life together as citizens always be pursued according to the principle "with malice toward none; with charity for all"? Is this principle a safeguard against divisiveness?

Nathaniel Hawthorne, "The Minister's Black Veil"

Why is the minister's first sermon while wearing the black veil so disturbing to his congregation, even though there was "nothing terrible in what Mr. Hooper said"? What "unwonted attribute" in the minister does the congregation sense?

Why does Mr. Hooper leave his mouth uncovered by the veil? Why does the narrator repeatedly remind us of Mr. Hooper's sad smile, "which always appeared like a faint glimmering of light, proceeding from the obscurity beneath the veil"?

When Mr. Hooper glimpses his reflected image at the wedding, why is he affected by the same horror of the black veil that overwhelms everyone else?

Why don't the people of the parish ask Mr. Hopper why he is wearing the veil? What do the members of the delegation sent to inquire mean when they report back to their constituents that the "matter [is] too weighty to be handled, except by a council of the churches, if, indeed, it might not require a general synod"?

What changes the "calm energy" of Elizabeth to terror when she tries to persuade Mr. Hooper to remove the veil?

Why does Mr. Hooper choose to remain lonely and frightened behind his black veil, when he could have the happiness of marriage with Elizabeth?

Since Mr. Hooper says, "I, perhaps, like most other mortals, have sorrows dark enough to be typified by a black veil," why does he alone put on this "material emblem"?

Does the veil symbolize the same thing to Mr. Hooper as it does to others?

How does the black veil make Mr. Hooper "a very efficient clergyman"? Is this the same as being a very good clergyman? Why does he become known as "Father Hooper"?

Why do material emblems affect us so deeply? How should leaders use material emblems to increase their influence? Have you as a leader ever worn a "veil" of some sort?

Did Mr. Hooper become a better or more effective leader on account of the black veil?

ACKNOWLEDGMENTS

All possible care has been taken to trace ownership and secure permission for each selection in this anthology. The Great Books Foundation wishes to thank the following authors, publishers, and representatives for permission to reprint copyrighted material:

Selection from *Politics*, by Aristotle, from THE COMPLETE WORKS OF ARISTOTLE, edited by Jonathan Barnes. Copyright © 1984 by The Jowett Copyright Trustees. Reprinted by permission of Princeton University Press.

Waiting for the Barbarians, by Constantine Cavafy, from C. P. CAVAFY, by Edmund Keeley. Copyright © 1975 by Edmund Keeley and Philip Sherrard. Reprinted by permission of Princeton University Press.

The Boy Without a Flag, from THE BOY WITHOUT A FLAG: TALES OF THE SOUTH BRONX, by Abraham Rodriguez Jr. Copyright © 1999 by Abraham Rodriguez Jr. Reprinted by permission of Milkweed Editions, Minneapolis.

They'll Say, "She Must Be from Another Country," from I SPEAK FOR THE DEVIL, by Imtiaz Dharker. Copyright © 2001 by Imtiaz Dharker. Reprinted by permission of Bloodaxe Books.

Fellowship, by Franz Kafka, translated by Tania and James Stern, from FRANZ KAFKA: THE COMPLETE STORIES, edited by Nahum N. Glatzer. Copyright © 1946, 1947, 1948, 1949, 1954, 1958, 1971 by Schocken Books. Reprinted by permission of Schocken Books, a division of Random House, Inc.

Earliest Impressions, from TWENTY YEARS AT HULL-HOUSE, by Jane Addams. Copyright © 1961 by Henry Steele Commager. Reprinted by permission of Signet, an imprint of Penguin Group (USA) Inc.

He Sits Down on the Floor of a School for the Retarded, from SELECTED POEMS, by Alden Nowlan. Copyright © 1996 by Claudine Nowlan. Reprinted by permission of House of Anansi Press, Toronto.

Selection from THEORY OF MORAL SENTIMENTS, by Adam Smith, edited by Knud Haakonssen. Copyright © 2002 by Cambridge University Press. Reprinted by permission of Cambridge University Press.

Selection from DEMOCRACY IN AMERICA, by Alexis de Tocqueville, edited by J. P. Mayer and Max Lerner, translated by George Lawrence. English translation copyright © 1965 by Harper & Row Publishers, Inc. Reprinted by permission of HarperCollins Publishers.

Selection from THE SOULS OF BLACK FOLK, by W. E. B. Du Bois. Copyright © 1998 by Transaction Publishers. Reprinted by permission of Transaction Publishers.

Acknowledgments

Theme for English B, from THE COLLECTED POEMS OF LANGSTON HUGHES, by Langston Hughes. Copyright © 1994 by the Estate of Langston Hughes. Reprinted by permission of Alfred A. Knopf, a division of Random House, Inc.

Recitatif, by Toni Morrison, from LEAVING HOME, edited by Hazel Rochman and Darlene Z. McCampbell. Copyright © 1983 by Toni Morrison. Reprinted by permission of International Creative Management, Inc.

Luella Miller, from THE WIND IN THE ROSE BUSH AND OTHER STORIES OF THE SUPERNATURAL, by Mary E. Wilkins Freeman. Copyright © 1986 by Academy Chicago Publishers. Reprinted by permission of Academy Chicago Publishers.

Dry Dock, from GETTING THROUGH AND OTHER STORIES, by Margaret Sutherland. Copyright © 1980 by Margaret Sutherland and www.margaretsutherland.com. Reprinted by permission of the author.

Saving the Crippled Boy, from MAD RIVER, by Jan Beatty. Copyright © 1995 by Jan Beatty. Reprinted by permission of the University of Pittsburgh Press.

The Eleventh, from WE OTHERS: STORIES OF FATE, LOVE, AND PITY, by Henri Barbusse, translated by Fitzwater Wray. Copyright © 1918 by E. P. Dutton and Company. Reprinted by permission of Weidenfeld & Nicolson, an imprint of the Orion Publishing Group.

The Moral Equivalent of War, by William James, from THE WRITINGS OF WILLIAM JAMES, edited by John McDermott. Copyright © 1967 by Random House, Inc. Copyright © 1977 by the University of Chicago. Reprinted by permission of Random House, Inc.

The Subjective Necessity for Social Settlements, from TWENTY YEARS AT HULL-HOUSE, by Jane Addams. Copyright © 1961 by Henry Steele Commager. Reprinted by permission of Signet, an imprint of Penguin Group (USA) Inc.

The Drum Major Instinct, by Martin Luther King Jr., from A TESTAMENT OF HOPE: THE ESSENTIAL WRITINGS AND SPEECHES OF MARTIN LUTHER KING JR., edited by James Melvin Washington. Copyright © 1968 by Martin Luther King Jr., renewed 1996 by Coretta Scott King. Reprinted by permission of the Estate of Martin Luther King Jr., c/o Writers House as agent for the proprietor, New York.

The Book of Ruth, from THE NEW REVISED STANDARD VERSION OF THE BIBLE. Copyright © 1989 by the Division of Christian Education of the National Council of the Churches of Christ in the U.S.A. Reprinted by permission. All rights reserved.

The Lovers of the Poor, from SELECTED POEMS, by Gwendolyn Brooks. Copyright © 1999 by Gwendolyn Brooks. Reprinted by permission of Brooks Permissions.

What We Don't Talk About When We Don't Talk About Service, by Adam Davis. Copyright © 2006 by Adam Davis. Reprinted by permission of the author.

Where Were We, excerpt as reprinted in the *New Yorker*, from YOU SHALL KNOW OUR VELOCITY, by Dave Eggers. Copyright © 2002, 2003 by Dave Eggers and McSweeney's Publishing. Reprinted by permission of the author.

Selection from REVERIES OF THE SOLITARY WALKER, by Jean-Jacques Rousseau, translated by Charles E. Butterworth. Copyright © 1992 by Hackett Publishing Company, Inc. Reprinted by permission of Hackett Publishing Company, Inc. All rights reserved.

The Sweetness of Charity, from WOULDN'T TAKE NOTHING FOR MY JOURNEY NOW, by Maya Angelou. Copyright © 1993 by Maya Angelou. Reprinted by permission of Random House, Inc.

The Lamb and the Pinecone, by Pablo Neruda, from NERUDA AND VALLEJO: SELECTED POEMS, edited and translated by Robert Bly. Copyright © 1976 by Robert Bly. Reprinted by permission of Robert Bly.

The Gospel of Wealth, Part I, from THE GOSPEL OF WEALTH AND OTHER TIMELY ESSAYS, by Andrew Carnegie, edited by Edward C. Kirkland. Originally published in the *North American Review* CXLVIII, June 1889, and CXLIX, December 1889. Reprinted by permission of Harvard University Press.

Acknowledgments

Compassion: The Wish-Fulfilling Jewel, from THE TIBETAN BOOK OF LIVING AND DYING, by Sogyal Rinpoche, edited by Patrick Gaffney and Andrew Harvey. Copyright © 1993 by Rigpa Fellowship. Reprinted by permission of HarperCollins Publishers.

A Bed for the Night, by Bertolt Brecht, translated by Georg Rapp, from BERTOLT BRECHT: POEMS, 1913–1956, translated by John Willett and Ralph Manheim. Copyright © 1976, 1979 by Methuen London. Reprinted by permission of Routledge/Taylor & Francis Group LLC and Methuen Publishing, Ltd.

Four Traditions of Philanthropy, by Elizabeth Lynn and D. Susan Wisely, from THE PERFECT GIFT: THE PHILANTHROPIC IMAGINATION IN POETRY AND PROSE. Copyright © 2002 by Elizabeth Lynn and D. Susan Wisely. Reprinted by permission of the authors and Indiana University Press.

Levels of Giving, from MISHNEH TORAH, by Moses Maimonides, edited and annotated by Philip Birnbaum. Copyright © 1944, 1967 by Hebrew Publishing Company. Reprinted by permission of Hebrew Publishing Company.

If All Who Have Begged Help, from ANNA AKHMATOVA: SELECTED POEMS, by Anna Akhmatova, translated by D. M. Thomas. Translation copyright © 1976, 1979, 1985 by D. M. Thomas. Reprinted by permission of D. M. Thomas.

The Wife of His Youth, from THE WIFE OF HIS YOUTH AND OTHER STORIES OF THE COLOR LINE, by Charles Waddell Chesnutt. Copyright © 1968 by the University of Michigan Press. Reprinted by permission of the University of Michigan Press.

II Samuel: Chapters 11–12, from THE NEW REVISED STANDARD VERSION OF THE BIBLE. Copyright © 1989 by the Division of Christian Education of the National Council of the Churches of Christ in the U.S.A. Reprinted by permission. All rights reserved.

The Destructors, from COLLECTED STORIES OF GRAHAM GREENE, by Graham Greene. Copyright © 1955, 1983 by Graham Greene. Reprinted by permission of Viking Penguin, a division of Penguin Group (USA) Inc.

The Helmsman, by Franz Kafka, translated by Tania and James Stern, from FRANZ KAFKA: THE COMPLETE STORIES, edited by Nahum N. Glatzer. Copyright © 1946, 1947, 1948, 1949, 1954, 1958, 1971 by Schocken Books. Reprinted by permission of Schocken Books, a division of Random House, Inc.

The Lesson, from GORILLA, MY LOVE, by Toni Cade Bambara. Copyright © 1972 by Toni Cade Bambara. Reprinted by permission of Random House, Inc.

The Use of Force, by William Carlos Williams, from THE COLLECTED SHORT STORIES OF WILLIAM CARLOS WILLIAMS, edited by Sherwin B. Nuland. Copyright © 1938 by William Carlos Williams. Reprinted by permission of New Directions Publishing Corporation.

Selection from THE AUTOBIOGRAPHY OF BENJAMIN FRANKLIN, by Benjamin Franklin, edited by Leonard W. Labaree, Ralph L. Ketcham, and Helen C. Boatfield. Copyright © 1964 by Yale University Press. Reprinted by permission of Yale University Press.

The Ones Who Walk Away from Omelas, from THE WIND'S TWELVE QUARTERS, by Ursula K. Le Guin, first appeared in *New Dimensions 3*. Copyright © 1973, 2001 by Ursula K. Le Guin. Reprinted by permission of the Virginia Kidd Agency, Inc. and the author.

The History Teacher, from QUESTIONS ABOUT ANGELS, by Billy Collins. Copyright © 1991 by Billy Collins. Reprinted by permission of the University of Pittsburgh Press.

Notes